The Structure of Chaucer's Ambiguity

STUDIES IN ENGLISH MEDIEVAL LANGUAGE AND LITERATURE

Edited by Jacek Fisiak

Advisory Board:
John Anderson (Methoni, Greece), Ulrich Busse (Halle),
Olga Fischer (Amsterdam), Dieter Kastovsky (Vienna),
Marcin Krygier (Poznań), Roger Lass (Cape Town),
Peter Lucas (Cambridge), Donka Minkova (Los Angeles),
Akio Oizumi (Kyoto), Katherine O'Brien O'Keeffe (UC Berkeley, USA),
Matti Rissanen (Helsinki), Hans Sauer (Munich),
Liliana Sikorska (Poznań), Jeremy Smith (Glasgow),
Jerzy Wełna (Warsaw)

Vol. 36

PETER LANG
EDITION

Yoshiyuki Nakao

The Structure
of Chaucer's Ambiguity

Bibliographic Information published by the Deutsche Nationalbibliothek
The Deutsche Nationalbibliothek lists this publication in the Deutsche Nationalbibliografie; detailed bibliographic data is available in the internet at http://dnb.d-nb.de.

This publication was supported
by the Department of English Language
and Culture Education,
Graduate School of Education,
Hiroshima University.

Typesetting by motivex.

Cover Design:
© Olaf Glöckler, Atelier Platen, Friedberg

ISSN 1436-7521
ISBN 978-3-631-62438-8
© Peter Lang GmbH
Internationaler Verlag der Wissenschaften
Frankfurt am Main 2013
All rights reserved.

All parts of this publication are protected by copyright. Any utilisation outside the strict limits of the copyright law, without the permission of the publisher, is forbidden and liable to prosecution. This applies in particular to reproductions, translations, microfilming, and storage and processing in electronic retrieval systems.

www.peterlang.de

For my parents

Contents

Preface 13
Acknowledgements 15
Abbreviations 17

Part I: Our aim and methodology 21
1. Introduction 21
   1.1. The aim of this book 21
   1.2. The statement of the problem 21
       1.2.1. Text interpretation and the role of the reader 21
       1.2.2. The relationship between constituent elements of the text: the question of degrees 21
       1.2.3. A sample: ambiguity as a key concept in representing the totality of the poem's meaning 22
       1.2.4. The reader's inference and the levels at which it works 23
       1.2.5. Linguistic ambiguity: An explanation of its generative process 23
   1.3. The structure of this book 24
2. Previous scholarship 27
   2.1. Methods of language studies and ambiguity 27
   2.2. Chaucer's ambiguity: previous scholarship 30
   2.3. The problem addressed in this book 33
3. Our point of view and method 35
   3.1. The rise of ambiguity 35
       3.1.1. The double prism structure 35
       3.1.2. The first prism (B) 39
       3.1.3. The second prism (D) 41
   3.2. The categories of ambiguity 42
   3.3. Types of ambiguity 43
   3.4. The concept of ambiguity 43
       3.4.1. The definition of ambiguity 43
       3.4.2. Vagueness 44
       3.4.3. The control of ambiguity 44
   3.5. The procedure for examining Chaucer's ambiguity 44

Part II: Ambiguity in textual domains 47

4. Ambiguity in metatext 47
    4.1. Introductory remarks: the double prism structure and metatext 47
    4.2. Linguistic diversity in London and between the scribes 47
    4.3. Production of the manuscripts of Chaucer's texts 48
    4.4. The sixteen manuscripts of *Troilus and Criseyde* 49
    4.5. Modern editions of *Troilus and Criseyde* 50
    4.6. Kinds of readers 50
    4.7. Examination of ambiguity with respect to metatext 52
        4.7.1. Analysis of Tr 2.636 52
        4.7.2. Analysis of Tr 2.1274 53
        4.7.3. Analysis of Tr 3.575-93 55
        4.7.4. Analysis of Tr 5.1240-1 60
    4.8. Final remarks 64

5. Ambiguity in intertextuality 67
    5.1. Introductory remarks: the double prism structure and intertextuality 67
    5.2. Intertextuality in courtly language and the problem of ambiguity:
        a few examples 68
    5.3. Final remarks 73

6. Ambiguity in macro-textual structure 75
    6.1. Introductory remarks: the double prism structure and
        macro-textual structure 75
    6.2. Ambiguity in theme 75
    6.3. Ambiguity in characters 79
        6.3.1. The first-person narrator 79
        6.3.2. Characters 81
    6.4. Ambiguity in plot 84
        6.4.1. Prologues/epilogues and the development of stories 85
        6.4.2. Interactions between situations 87
    6.5. Final remarks 90

7. Ambiguity in reported speech 93
    7.1. Introductory remarks: the double prism structure and reported speech 93
    7.2. Free indirect speech and the problem of ambiguity 94

7.3. Final remarks ... 98
8. Ambiguity in discourse structure ... 101
   8.1. Introductory remarks: the double prism structure and discourse ... 101
   8.2. Ambiguity in cohesion: a focus on reference (1a), substitution (1b), ellipsis (1c) ... 102
   8.3. Ambiguity in cohesion: a focus on causality in conjunction (1d) ... 108
      8.3.1. Causality and degrees of subjectivity ... 108
      8.3.2. Examination: Tr 3.561-947 ... 110
   8.4. Ambiguity in cohesion: a focus on lexical cohesion (1e) ... 117
   8.5. Ambiguity in word order and information structure ... 119
   8.6. Final remarks ... 121

Part III: Ambiguity in interpersonal domains ... 123
9. Ambiguity in speaker's intention ... 123
   9.1. Introductory remarks: the double prism structure and the speaker's intention ... 123
   9.2. Ambiguity in the intention of the characters and the narrator ... 124
   9.3. Integrated examination of [1] Tr 3.554-603 ... 129
   9.4. Integrated examination of [2] Tr 5.1009-50 ... 132
   9.5. Final remarks ... 135
10. Ambiguity in modality ... 137
   10.1. Introductory remarks: the double prism structure and modality ... 137
   10.2. Ambiguity in modal auxiliaries ... 138
      10.2.1. Interaction in external causals: a focus on *moot/moste* ... 138
      10.2.2. Ambiguity due to the interaction between root and epistemic senses of the modals ... 146
   10.3. Ambiguity arising from modal adverbs ... 153
      10.3.1. Introductory remarks ... 153
      10.3.2. The concept of 'epistemicity' ... 153
      10.3.3. The modal adverb *trewely* in Chaucer: previous research ... 154
      10.3.4. Ambiguity caused by the use of *trewely* ... 156
      10.3.5. Examination ... 157
      10.3.6. Final remarks ... 167

10.4. Ambiguity caused by modal lexical verbs 167
    10.4.1. Introductory remarks 167
    10.4.2. Statement of the problem by reference to 'I woot wel' 168
    10.4.3. Ambiguity arising from modal lexical verbs: How it occurs 169
    10.4.4. Description of ambiguity caused by 'I woot wel' 170
10.5. Final remarks 183

Part IV: Ambiguity in linguistic domains 185
11. Ambiguity in syntax 185
    11.1. Introductory remarks: the double prism structure and syntax 185
    11.2. The phrase *as she that* 186
        11.2.1. The meaning of the *as she that*-phrase 186
        11.2.2. The function of the *as she that*-phrase 187
        11.2.3. Ambiguity in the *as she that*-phrase and characterisation
        of Criseyde 189
    11.3. Other examples of syntactic ambiguity 196
    11.4. Final remarks 203
12. Ambiguity in words 205
    12.1. Introductory remarks: the double prism structure and words 205
    12.2. Ambiguity of *slydynge* and related words 206
        12.2.1. Words and context 206
        12.2.2. Criseyde's shifting affections and their expression 207
        12.2.3. Definition of *slide/slydynge* 208
        12.2.4. Words associated psychologically with *slydynge* 212
        12.2.5. Words expressing harsher criticism of Criseyde's inconstancy .. 214
        12.2.6. The semantic field of words denoting change, shifting, etc.:
        a paradigmatic list of vocabulary used to refer to Criseyde's
        inconstancy together with vocabulary not used 215
        12.2.7. Words expressing Criseyde's inconstancy and their
        environments 216
        12.2.8. Final remarks 219
    12.3. Ambiguity in *sely* 220
    12.4. Ambiguity in *weldy* 225

12.5. Ambiguity in *pite* 229
  12.5.1. Pragmatic implications of *pite* 229
  12.5.2. Criseyde's *pite*: internal history of her betrayal 235
  12.5.3. Ambiguity in Criseyde's *pite* 236
  12.5.4. Final remarks 245
12.6. Ambiguity in *frend/shipe* and *gentil/esse* 245
  12.6.1. Introductory remarks 245
  12.6.2. Examination 246
12.7. Final remarks 253
13. Ambiguity in voice 255
  13.1. Introductory remarks: the double prism structure and voice 255
  13.2. Previous scholarship 255
  13.3. Our approach: reconsideration from the viewpoint of the double prism structure 256
  13.4. Examination 256
  13.5. Final remarks 264

Part V: Conclusion 267
14. Concluding remarks 267
  14.1. Summary of this investigation 267
  14.2. The structure of Chaucer's ambiguity 271

Appendix A: Lines referring to Criseyde's shifting affections 275

Appendix B: Words indicative of instability—an overview by works (Tr, Bo, LGW, Henryson) 279

Bibliography 283
Subject index 299
Author index 307

Preface

Semantic studies of Chaucer's language have always been far behind those relating to the phonology, morphology, vocabulary and syntax both in quantity and quality. To establish the semantic range of his words as they appear in their various contexts we need an abundance of philological evidence since we cannot be intuitively sensitive to them. In the course of the narrative as it progresses it is far more difficult to determine the connotations and nuances of a phrase or how its meaning changes with the context. It is no easy task to describe and explain those meanings so objectively that they would be acceptable. Semantics is not the principal object of our study, but of course constructing meaning is an inseparable part of reading a primary text. Everyone experiences this: identifying the central meaning of a phrase among the more peripheral ones, or indeed being unable to decide between them. For instance, what is the meaning of *corages* which nature stimulates in the General Prologue to *The Canterbury Tales* (CT I (A) 11)? Does this word mean 'heart' or 'desire'? This word is not the same with *herte*. What kind of love is *Amor* depicted on the brooch the Prioress has? Is it directed towards a religious love or a secular? This question goes beyond a lexical boundary to a discourse level. The narrator says at the end of *The Nun's Priest's Tale*: 'Taketh the fruyt, and lat the chaf be stille' (CT VII 3443). What part of the narrative does the *fruyt* correspond to? What about *chaf*? The meaning of an expression fluctuates with the development of the story. We are confronted with the problem of how to grasp such fluctuating meanings. There may be two interpretations in one person, or between persons. It might appear that the ambiguity which we will present and describe in this work derives solely from the fact that we are so far removed from Chaucer's time both linguistically and culturally. This may be true to some extent, but we intend to show in the course of this book that similar problems confronted the medieval audience and scribes to those which confound modern readers and editors. We have abundant evidence of this ambiguity in Chaucer's works from beginning to end. The problem of semantic complexity and its inherent ambiguity arise quite naturally from a reading of these works or of any text so far removed from us in time and cultural experience.

In the past literary studies of Chaucer with a semantic emphasis have been of two types—linguistic and interpretative. However, the two types have by and large been kept rigidly apart: linguistic studies have not concerned themselves with interpretation, and studies with the emphasis on interpretation have not presented adequate linguistic description and explanation. Furthermore, interpretation has been undertaken without methodology, while the methodology of the linguistic studies has not been balanced by interpretative content. There have so far been few studies combining linguistic and literary approach. We feel that the problem of ambiguity can only be described and explained in such an integrated way.

Ambiguity is a linguistic phenomenon which presents readers with multiple meanings and induces them to be divided in interpretation. We have attempted to describe the process whereby ambiguity is produced in Chaucerian texts. The speaker observes and cognises a phenomenon and expresses it in words. Through this act the hearer understands the speaker's cognition in one way or another, and then proceeds to an interpretation of it. In the reading process, ambiguity arises when the readers are divided in their interpretation.

In my discussion of these processes I have treated the first observer, i.e. the speaker, as the first prism, and the one achieving understanding through what the speaker says, i.e. the reader, as the second prism. It is through this double prism structure that I have attempted to describe ambiguity. (For details of this structure see Chapter 3.) I have divided expression into the following three domains: textual, interpersonal and linguistic. My description of ambiguity is made according to these domains individually and in combination. I have focused on *Troilus and Criseyde*, which abounds in ambiguity owing to its shifting characteristics and to its rich psychological niceties.

To make clear the universal features of language is regarded as the essence of science. Therefore, linguistic studies which focus on individual features of a particular writer and eliciting the reader's point of view may be regarded as unscientific. But language in general has meanings and for that reason we are apt to err in linguistic communication. Thus ambiguity is a problem we face everyday. A literary writer is likely to prefer a pregnant expression which allows for alternative interpretations. This expression of the writer gives the reader free rein to his or her imagination. I have reached the conclusion that if seeking a single truth is science, then proving objectively that there is not always only one correct answer is also science. In fact, recent discoveries of pragmatics and cognitive science have shed light not so much on the "result" as on the process leading to it, and are uncovering what previous science has disregarded. This study has focused on the parole aspect of language, and attempted to describe and explain ambiguity arising within it. My ideas and findings on ambiguity have developed and emerged gradually during the writing of my papers both orally presented and published in journals. A full list appears in Bibliography.

This book is based on my recent book, *Chaucer no Aimaisei no Kozo* (*The Structure of Chaucer's Ambiguity*) (2004) in Japanese. I am grateful to Shohakusha, the Publisher, for permission to republish it in English. I appreciated the comments of reviewers of my book. I was very happy to have had a number of corrections and suggestions from many readers of it ranging from my framework to detailed arguing points. Some parts of the book have since been published in English with some revisions. I have incorporated them into this English version. Since Chaucer's language is temporally distant from ours, the reader's inference is inevitably necessary to an understanding of it. It may be that I have misunderstood it in parts or read too much or too little into it. I leave that to the judgement of the reader of this book.

Acknowledgements

In writing this work, I have had invaluable help from many people in the form of ideas on ambiguity, suggestions on how to deal with examples, and on the progress of my argument. I am particularly indebted to Professor Kiichiro Nakatani, my mentor when and since I was an undergraduate at Hiroshima University, from whom I learned a lot about English Philology and stylistics with special regard to Shakespeare, Professor Hisashi Takahashi, who taught me the basics of the historical study of English, Dr. Michio Masui, my supervisor when I was a postgraduate at Hiroshima, whose inspiring and insightful lectures on Chaucer and its relevant topics so moved me as to study Chaucer, and Professor Michio Kawai, who gave me an insightful lecture as to how to read English novels. I am most grateful to Professor Norman Davis, who enabled me to study at Oxford and taught me some basics of early middle English verse and prose, and Professor Norman Blake, Professor David Burnley, Professor Brian Donaghey, thanks to whom I was able to develop my idea and methodology on my research topic, ambiguities in Chaucer's language when I was at Sheffield. I cannot thank Dr. Matsuji Tajima enough, who encouraged me to complete my Ph.D thesis about Chaucer's ambiguity and actually was supervisor of the thesis which I submitted to Kyushu University. I appreciate Professors Tomonori Matsushita, P.V.C. Schmidt and David Wallace for reviewing and improving Chapter 4. I am very much obliged to Professor Jacek Fisiak, editor of "English Medieval Literature and Language" Series, who has enabled my book to be published by Peter Lang.

I would like to express my heart-felt thanks to the late Professor David Le Sage for improving the English of my book with penetrating comments and suggestions. I am also grateful to Dr. Takayuki Nishihara, associate professor of Prefectural University of Hiroshima, and Dr. Naoki Hirayama, lecturer of Onomichi University, my former students for a proof reading of my book on the draft stage.

I am also indebted to the editors of journals for permitting me to republish my articles in this book. These articles are slightly edited according to its framework. The following numbers in [xxx] correspond to the Section numbers in the book.

1993.	"The Ambiguity of the Phrase *As She That* in Chaucer's *Troilus and Criseyde*." SIMELL (*Studies in Medieval English Language and Literature*) No. 8, The Japan Society for Medieval English Studies, 69-86. [11.2]
1994.	"The Affectivity of Criseyde's *pite*." POETICA 41, Shubun International, 19-43. [12.5]
1995.	"A Semantic Note on the Middle English Phrase *As He/She That*." NOWELE (*North West European Language Evolution*) 25. Odense University Press, 25-48. [11.2]
1997.	"Social-Linguistic Tension as Evidenced by *Moot/Moste* in Chaucer's *Troilus and Criseyde*." Masahiko Kanno, Masahiko Agari, and G. K. Jember, eds., *Essays on English Literature and Language in Honour of Shun'ichi Noguchi*. Tokyo: Eihosha,17-34. [10.2]
1998.	"Causality in Chaucer's *Troilus and Criseyde*: Semantic Tension between the Pragmatic and the Narrative Domains." Masahiko Kanno, Gregory K. Jember,

and Yoshiyuki Nakao, eds. *A Love of Words: English Philological Studies in Honour of Akira Wada*. Tokyo: Eihosha, 79-102. [8.3]

1999. "Chaucer no Moot/Moste no Imiron: Gaitekiyouin no Mibunkasei" (The Semantics of Chaucer's *Moot/Moste*: The Merge of External Causals). Yukio Oba, et al., eds. *Gengokenkyu no Choryu: Yamamoto Kazuyuki Sensei Gotaikan Ronshu (Current Issues in Linguistic Studies: A Festschrift in Honour of Kazuyuki Yamamoto)*. Tokyo: Kaitakusha, 231-46. [10.2.1]

2002. "Modality and Ambiguity in Chaucer's *trewely*: A Focus on *Troilus and Criseyde*." Yoko Iyeiri and Margaret Connolly, eds. *And gladly wolde he lerne and gladly teche. Essays on Medieval English: Presented to Professor Matsuji Tajima on His Sixtieth Birthday*. Tokyo: Kaibunsha, 73-94. [10.3]

2006. "The Interpretation of *Troilus and Criseyde* 3.587: 'syn I moste on yow triste.'" Michiko Ogura, ed. *Textual and Contextual Studies in Medieval English: Towards the Reunion of Linguistics and Philology*. Studies in English Medieval Language and Literature (Edited by Jacek Fisiak 13). Peter Lang, 51-71. [4.7.3]

2006. "The Structure of Chaucer's Ambiguity with a Focus on *Troilus and Criseyde* 5.1084." *SIMELL* No. 21. The Japan Society for Medieval English Studies, 55-63. [10.4]

2010. "Chaucer's Ambiguity in Discourse: The Case of *Troilus and Criseyde*." In *Kotoba no Fuhen to Henyou* (*Universals and Variation in Language*) *Vol. 5*. Centre for Research on Language and Culture, Institute for the Development of Social Intelligence, Senshu University, 85-97.

2010. "Chaucer's Ambiguity in Voice." Osamu Imahayashi/Yoshiyuki Nakao/Michiko Ogura, eds. *Aspects of the History of English Language and Literature: Selected Papers Read at SHELL 2009, Hiroshima*. Peter Lang, 143-57. [13]

2011. "Chaucer's Language and 'Subjectivisation' and 'Expanding Semantics.'" *SIMELL* No. 25, The Japan Society for Medieval English Studies, 1-41. [12.2]

2011. "Textual Variations in *Troilus and Criseyde* and the Rise of Ambiguity." Tomonori Matsushita, A.V.C. Schmidt and David Wallace, eds. *From Beowulf to Caxton: Studies in Medieval Languages and Literature, Texts and Manuscripts*. Bern: Peter Lang, 111-50. [4]

My thanks also go to my family, Makiko my wife, and my children (Hiroko, Masayuki, Shingo) who listened to me talking with great patience, and enabled me to have time for writing this book. Masayuki edited and typed the initial stage of my book, much of which would not otherwise have been completed. Any remaining errors are of course mine alone.

I would like to dedicate this book to my parents. My father used to say to my mother farming in a field 'If we make one ridge in a field, we have to read a hundred lines of a book.'

Yoshiyuki Nakao

At Mihara, Hiroshima 2012

Abbreviations

Manuscripts and early prints of Chaucer's *Troilus and Criseyde*

A	Additional MS 12044, British Library
Cl	The Campsall MS, Now Pierpont Morgan Library M 817
Cp	Corpus Christi College, Cambridge, MS 61
Dg	MS Digby 181, Bodleian Library
D	University of Durham, Cosin MS V. II. 13
Gg	Cambridge University Library MS Gg.4.27
H1	MS Harley 2280, British Library
H2	MS Harley 3943, British Library
H3	MS Harley 1239, British Library
H4	MS Harley 2392, British Library
H5	MS Harley 4912, British Library
J	St John's College, Cambridge, MS L.1
Ph	Formerly Phillips 8252, Now Huntington Library HM 114
R	MS Rawlinson Poet.163, Bodleian Library
S1	MS Arch. Selden B.24, Bodleian Library
S2	MS Arch. Selden Supra 56, Bodleian Library
Cx	Caxton's edition of TC (c.1483)
Th	Thynne's edition (1532)
W	Wynkyn de Worde's edition (1517)

Chaucer's works (based on Benson 1987)

ABC	An ABC
Adam	Chaucers Wordes Unto Adam, His Owne Scriveyn
Anel	*Anelida and Arcite*
Astr	*A Treatise on the Astrolabe*
Bal Comp	A Balade of Complaint
BD	*The Book of the Duchess*
Buk	Lenvoy de Chaucer a Bukton
Bo	Boece
CkT	The Cook's Tale
ClT	The Clerk's Tale
Compld'Am	Complaint D'Amours
CT	*The Canterbury Tales*
CYT	The Canon's Yeoman's Tale
For	Fortune
Form Age	The Former Age
FranT	The Franklin's Tale
FrT	The Friar's Tale
Gent	Gentilesse
GP	General Prologue
HF	*The House of Fame*
KnT	The Knight's Tale
Lady	A Complaint to his Lady
LGW	*The Legend of Good Women*
MancT	The Manciple's Tale

Mars	The Complaint of Mars
Mel	The Tale of Melibee
MercB	Merciles Beaute
MerT	The Merchant's Tale
MilT	The Miller's Tale
MkT	The Monk's Tale
MLT	The Man of Law's Tale
NPT	The Nun's Priest's Tale
P	Prologue
PardT	The Pardoner's Tale
ParsT	The Parson's Tale
PF	*The Parliament of Fowls*
PhyT	The Physician's Tale
Pity	The Complaint unto Pity
Prov	Proverbs
PrT	The Prioress's Tale
Purse	The Complaint of Chaucer to his Purse
Ret, Retr	Chaucer's Retraction (Retractation)
Rom	*The Romaunt of the Rose*
Ros	To Rosemounde
RvT	The Reeve's Tale
Scog	Lenvoy de Chaucer a Scogan
ShipT	The Shipman's Tale
SHP	Short Poems
SNT	The Second Nun's Tale
SqT	The Squire's Tale
Sted	Lak of Stedfastnesse
SumT	The Summoner's Tale
Thop	Tale of Sir Thopas
Tr	*Troilus and Criseyde*
Truth	Truth
Ven	The Complaint of Venus
WBT	The Wife of Bath's Tale
WomNobl	Womanly Noblesse
WomUnc	Against Women Unconstant

Other works

EETS	Early English Text Society
ES	Extra Series
Fil	*Il Filostrato*
OS	Original Studies

Edited texts of Chaucer

Baugh	Baugh (1963)
Benson	Benson (1987)
Donaldson	Donaldson (1975)
Fisher	Fisher (1989)
Howard	Howard (1976)
Robinson	Robinson (1957)

Root   Root (1952)
Shoaf   Shoaf (1989)
Skeat   Skeat (1898)
Warrington Warrington (1975)
Windeatt   Windeatt (1990)

Dictionaries and other reference works

MED   Middle English Dictionary
OED   The Oxford English Dictionary

Some important recurrent terms

ME   Middle English
OE   Old English
OF   Old French
OHG   Old High Germanic
ON   Old Norse

NRA   Narrative report of action
NRSA Narrative report of speech action
IS   Indirect speech
FIS   Free indirect speech
DS   Direct speech
FDS   Free direct speech

Part I: Our aim and methodology

1. Introduction

1.1. The aim of this book

Ambiguity has long been recognised as a rewarding research area in linguistics and literature. This recognition dates back to the seminal writings of William Empson on this subject. Now that linguistics no longer avoids the problem of meaning, with a great deal of departure from structural linguistics, meaning itself is regarded as indispensable, and ambiguity has come into sharp focus. Much has been achieved in the field of literature since. This study aims to show how ambiguity is likely to occur with special reference to one of Chaucer's works, *Troilus and Criseyde*.

1.2. The statement of the problem

1.2.1. Text interpretation and the role of the reader

Empson's (1930) ideas were based on the view of ambiguity of I. A. Richards. Richards (1936: 135-8) understood that ambiguity results from the interaction between the speaker (writer) and the hearer (reader).[1] This being the case, however clear or alternatively ambiguous the speaker intends his or her speech to be, the meaning is likely to vary from hearer to hearer. Accordingly, the ultimate meaning of an utterance depends on what the hearer reads into it. Since there are no Ur-texts in the case of medieval English writers such as Chaucer, those texts or manuscripts currently accessible to us cannot be called as absolute or fixed, and thus the role played by the reader interpreting such texts becomes all the more crucial.

1.2.2. The relationship between constituent elements of the text: the question of degrees

The meaning of an utterance is usually produced by the relationship between the reader and the text. When faced with a text, the reader infers how the speaker observes and cognises the phenomenon in question, and tries to understand it. If the relationship between the elements involved in the making of a text is absolutely fixed with no alternatives, its meaning is likely to be definitive, with no instance/occurrence of ambiguity. If making the relationship between the above elements becomes a matter of degrees to a reader or between readers, the rise of ambiguity is likely to be inevitable. For in-

---

[1] Richards (1936) says that the semantic content of a sentence is strongly influenced by its contexts and the inferences the reader draws from them. Empson (1930) classifies ambiguity into seven types according to contextual factors. Further Empson (1967) proves that an apparently simple expression (e.g. A is B) can create complex meanings taking various contextual information into account. Regarding the relation between the multi-layered structure of context of 'sign' and the reader's response to it, see Ogden and Richards's 'engram' (1960: 52-3).

stance, we can encounter two types of syntactic relation of an utterance although there may be a difference in the strength of relatedness. Different combinations of words produce different meanings.

Combinations of one element and another make it possible to generate meanings we could not predict from the elements in isolation by itself. And elements cannot necessarily be explicit on the textual surface. On occasion some are implicit. The above syntactic elements are usually on the surface, but the intention of the speaker (command, request, threatening, etc.), or connotations of a word tend to be hidden. As for the speaker's meaning, a more positive participation by the reader in the interpretation of a text is required. In describing ambiguity, we are strongly asked to seek the varieties of meanings condensed in an utterance and examine the extent to which they are functional.

1.2.3. A sample: ambiguity as a key concept in representing the totality of the poem's meaning

Let us take an example. (1) is a monologue by Criseyde, who decides to depart from Troilus because in the Greek camp she was sent to as an exchange-prisoner, she realises that she cannot return to Troy as she promised him.

(1) And *gilteles*, I woot wel, *I yow leve*.
But al shal passe; and thus take I my leve."   Tr 5.1084-5[2]

If we look at *gilteles*, we will see that the reader, inferring the speaker's mental state, relates this word to *I*, Criseyde or *yow*, the assumed listener, Troilus. Or does the reader relate it to both *yow* and *I*? Depending on which character we relate it to we reach a different interpretation. Furthermore, what about the intonation of 'I woot wel'? Does it have a rising or a falling intonation? The rising intonation induces us to take the proposition in question with only a degree of certainty. The falling intonation induces us to take it as objective and certain. What is more, what is the proposition? A manifold combination of such and such an element due to the utterance (1) in conjunction with the reader's different ways of inference is likely to induce different interpretations.

To stop and question the construction of *gilteles* in several ways leads to the ambiguity on different levels so much so that it affects the very theme of the story and the characterisation of Criseyde, in other words, it is regarded as a key concept to the totality of the poem's meaning. Here we are acutely aware of some essential features of Chaucer's language. It is easy in that we can readily access the primary meaning, on the other hand, it is difficult in that if we are sceptical about what sense it can carry, we are sensitive to another interpretation. The meaning of an utterance shifts according to the movement of the story. The problem of ambiguity has gradually becomes clear from this dynamic aspect of the reading with which everyone of us is familiar.

Apart from work done in the fields of semantics and pragmatics, there has been insufficient investigation of meaning from the hearer's as well as the speaker's point

---

2   Quotations of Chaucer and abbreviations of his works are taken from Benson (1987). Italics and underlinings in quotations are mine.

of view. There has been even less examination of Chaucer's ambiguity against the background of these discoveries. It is true that many references have been made to it in previous studies, but there have been few studies of it from theoretical and practical perspectives at the same time. I hope to make good some of the deficiencies of the past and to suggest directions in which future research might go.

1.2.4. The reader's inference and the levels at which it works

When reading a text, the reader's mind is moving on various textual levels. He or she tends to read it with the use of his or her inference, and there resorts to some ways of inference by which to relate the two elements of an utterance. The inference in (1) or the relationship between *I* and *yow* is like this: once one word (*gilteles*) is fixed, which word is it the most strongly related to? Here the inference of contiguity or metonymy is functional. Saying *gilteles*, we suppose who is so, and saying *I* or *yow*, we suppose in what state or what *I* or *yow* are or do. Ambiguity is encouraged to occur according to the activation of contiguity. What does 'Amor vincit omnia' (CT I (A) 162) written on the Prioress's brooch mean? It is uncertain whether *Amor* is intended to be religious since her favor for courtly love is emphasised ('peyned hire to countrefete cheere / Of court' CT I (A) 139-40). The idea of love is applied to two domains, religious and secular, producing two discrete senses. Here the inference of similarity or metaphor is involved.

The above two inferences are a starting point at which the reader tries to capture the speaker's way of cognition through an expression, and explores for the meaning there. These inferences are working on various levels such as the interaction between one text and another, the ideas involved in the theme, the literal meaning and that of the speaker, the syntactic relationship between words, and the sense relations in a word. The interaction of one text and another is due to contiguity, the ideas of the theme are due to similarity, the relation between the literal meaning and that of the speaker is due to contiguity (cause-effect relation), the syntactic relationship is due to contiguity, and the sense relations in a word are due to similarity and/or contiguity. Furthermore, the reader's inference is functional not only according to these classified levels, but across them. An inference on a particular level is only one of the synthetically linked inferences.

1.2.5. Linguistic ambiguity: An explanation of its generative process

Ambiguity is observed not only in language and literature (verbal art), but in paintings, sculpture, thought, culture, etc. Approaches to ambiguity are various according to its nature. We deal with Chaucer's literary language, and need to capture ambiguity arising in it. Literature is made of words as paintings are of colours, sculptures are of trees, bronze, bricks, etc., clothes and hair style are respectively of cloth and hair. As Sapir (1921) says in 'language and literature,' language is the most flexible among those materials constituting art. Whatever materials they may be, they can assert infinite possibilities of interpretations. Paintings and sculpture can extend the relatedness of elements according to who observes them. Abstract ones are a good example of this. But language is distinguished in delivering highly sophisticated information. To understand the multi-layered meanings of linguistic expressions one by one, the reader is required to assume the speaker's point of view and be sensitive to the relatedness between the constituent elements of the text. Chaucer is assumed to be aware not only of the shifting and flexible features of humanity, but also of the true nature of it. But generally speaking, from the reader's point of view, even the true nature of humanity is susceptible to the degrees of relatedness between the textual elements.

As we have seen above, this study aims to show how ambiguity is likely to arise in the text of *Troilus and Criseyde* not only from the writer's point of view, but that of the reader, with a special focus on the relation between the reader and the text.

1.3. The structure of this book

The aim set out in Section 1.1 will be examined according to the plan detailed in (2) below.

(2) Part I: Our aim and methodology
    1. Introduction
    2. Previous scholarship
    3. Our viewpoint and methodology

    Part II: Ambiguity in textual domains
    4. Metatext
    5. Intertextuality
    6. Macro-textual structure
    7. Reported speech
    8. Discourse

    Part III: Ambiguity in interpersonal domains
    9. The speaker's intention
    10. Modality

    Part IV: Ambiguity in linguistic domains
    11. Syntax
    12. Word
    13. Voice

    Part V: Conclusion
    14. Concluding remarks

The book consists of five parts. Part 1 states our aim, reviews its relevant literature, and proposes a framework, i.e. the double prism structure, for describing Chaucer's ambiguity. Parts 2-4 deal with each type of Chaucer's ambiguity according to the framework. They respectively discuss ambiguity in textual domains (Part 2), ambiguity in interpersonal domains (Part 3), ambiguity in linguistic domains (Part 4). Part 5 provides the conclusion of our survey.

Within Part 1, Chapter 1, as shown above, states the aim of this book and the problem of ambiguity. Chapter 2 reviews previous scholarship and achievements as well as suggesting future lines of research. Since ambiguity is essentially related to our way of viewing language, we first trace approaches to language with regard to ambiguity, and then investigate how they can be applied to the description of Chaucer's ambiguity. Chapter 3 describes the angle from which this will be attempted and the methodology to be used. As will be shown in Chapter 3, we propose the 'phenomenon' the writer observes, his way of cognising it ('the first prism'), his 'expression' of it, the reader's way of inference through the expression ('the second prism'), and his or her 'interpretations.' Ambiguity is likely to occur when the reader is divided in interpretation with his or her plural inferences involved in the writer's cognition. On the other hand, when the reader is limited to the speaker's one way of cognition, ambiguity is not likely to occur at least to him or her. We integrate varieties of ambiguities under the category of ambiguity, which enables us not only to describe each type but to run through types in description. In categorising and describing the types of ambiguity, we will use recent discoveries of linguistics, such as intertextuality, cohesion, speech act, metaphor/metonymy, semantic network, etc. It has emerged from my findings that Chaucer used linguistic devices a long time before modern linguistic sciences worked out metalanguages to analyse them.

Parts 2-4 (Chapters 4-13) describe each type of ambiguity according to the category demonstrated in Chapter 3. In Part 2, Chapters 4-8 deal with ambiguity in textual domains: Chapter 4 metatext (scribal/editorial ambiguity), Chapter 5 intertextuality (juxtaposition between one text and another), Chapter 6 macro-textual structure (theme, characterization, plot), Chapter 7 reported speech (free indirect speech), and Chapter 8 discourse (cohesive relation between sentences).

The focus in Chapters 9 and 10, which constitute the whole of Part 3, is on ambiguity in interpersonal domains: Chapter 9 deals with the speaker's intention (illocutionary forces and implications), and Chapter 10 modality (modal auxiliaries, modal adverb, modal lexical verb).

Chapters 11-13 in Part 4 deal with linguistic domains: Chapter 11 syntax (the *as she that* phrase, etc.), and Chapter 12 word (semantic network, polysemy, fuzziness), and Chapter 13 voice (ways of articulation and meanings).

Part 5, Chapter 14, concludes the above discussions.

2. Previous scholarship

2.1. Methods of language studies and ambiguity

We need to have a framework to elucidate the processes whereby Chaucer's ambiguity is likely to arise besides the interpretation of his works. To what extent have previous studies of language contributed to making this framework, and to what extent not? And to what extent have studies in Chaucer's ambiguity applied recently discovered methods to describe it? This chapter aims to clarify these two points.

This section will review approaches to language with respect to ambiguity. Ambiguity is a problem we can never fail to face when using language in communication. Attention has been paid to the mechanisms which give rise to ambiguity since ancient times. However, ambiguity has been dealt with negatively and emphasis has been placed on how to get rid of it for a long time. It is not going too far to say that a positive evaluation of ambiguity has existed only since the 20th century. Recent developments in language studies have transformed our attitudes to ambiguity.

Ancient and medieval rhetoric placed high value on how the speaker could deliver his or her message to the hearer unambiguously, and illustrated with examples the choice of theme for his or her speech, the development of it, linguistic expressions appropriate for persuasive speech, and how to manipulate memory and oral delivery. These constitute the synthetic treatment of communication as a whole, which gives us useful suggestion for the use of language. However, they were primarily concerned with the speaker's persuasion of the hearer, not with the hearer's inference or semantic gradability condensed in a linguistic expression which are main issues for us. Indeed they treated *paronomasia*, and described the speaker's deliberate ambiguity. This device influenced Chaucer in his use of ambiguity, but this is not, as shown later, representative of his use. Further, metaphor and metonymy were treated as instances of difficult colours or with respect to their figurative force. They were not valued as ways of motivating the reader's inference, as shown in Chapter 1.[3]

Medieval allegory is typically shown as a representation of God's plenty: the structure of medieval churches, icons (paintings, sculptures), verbal arts, etc. Verbal arts are concerned with how to condense in language, and express, the pluralistic values of God. St Augustine discussed this in *Doctrina Christiana* (see Chamberlin 2000), Dante intends to show four layers of interpretation in *Nova Vita* (see MacQueen 1970). Multiple interpretations are based on the reader's response to God's pluralistic values. Although writers of these allegories controlled the movement of the reader's point of view, they were able to separate levels of textual meaning into categories such as literal, moral, and biblical. It can be said that they put into structural use two types of inferences, metaphor and metonymy which rhetoricians treated as colours. However, it should be noted that Chaucer is not religiously limited, but by being open to experimental and secular aspects of humanism, he achieves a more flexible type of allegory.

---

3 Chaucer is for example familiar with Vinsauf's rhetoric. In 'difficult colours' he deals with semantic questions with full attention to the semantic extension produced by figures. Cf. Tr 1.1065-71; NunPT VII 3347-52. See Gallo (1971).

As is shown in Chaucer's works, there was a contemporary philosophical discussion 'The wordes moote be cosyn to the dede' (e.g. CT I (A) 742). The realist supported the correspondence between them. On the other hand the nominalist was sceptical about that and asserted an arbitrary relation between them. Descriptions of events are made by humans, therefore the involvement of their view in those descriptions is inevitable. This is a universal problem found in all ages and all parts of the world. It has been discussed throughout history as a philosophical and/or semantic question. Through this dispute medieval people seem to have developed their awareness of ambiguity in language. This reflects a way of understanding language relevant to both the spiritual and the temporal in medieval times, which is thought to have given much inspiration to Chaucer's use of language. He was sensitive not only to the importance of language in its ability to convey the truth, but also to its capacity to clothe a falsehood, as is manifested in his treatment of Fame in HF.

Rhetoric began with oratory, and developed towards poetics in medieval and early modern times. But in the age of modern rationalism (about 1800), its value was reduced to the extent that it became an object of criticism (Lakoff and Johnson (1980)). If the speaker resorts to a number of colours in order to realize a persuasive speech, and repeats doing this one-sidedly, with less concern for the hearer's point of view, the speech is likely to be a means to deception. The change of paradigm as to how to see language, or a new direction to making much of the hearer's response, is observed as late as in the twentieth century. Studies in semantics and new rhetoric by Richards (1936) and Empson (1930) are regarded as a reaction to the past speaker-orientated view of text, or the objectivism demonstrated by American structuralists, that is, the rejection of mentalism. Their recognition that meaning is finally determined by the interaction between the speaker and the hearer and the fact that unlike the old writers on rhetoric they gave due attention to ambiguity are great achievements.

Like Richards and Empson, Yamamoto (1940), taking a stylistic point of view, gave much weight to the hearer's role in the production of the meaning of an utterance.[4] Spitzer (1962) proposed 'philological cycle,' and pointed that we could deepen our understanding of the text by reading it repeatedly relating the part of the text to the whole, and the whole to the part. This has proved helpful in that the various elements making up the text can be seen in their interaction with each other. Toyama (1964) pointed that the preceding contexts are left as an afterimage in the present contexts, while the present contexts are retroactively applied to and influential upon the preceding contexts equally as an afterimage. His concept is that the prominent present contexts and the latent preceding contexts are connected with each other through an afterimage, and make a solid and many-faceted text which he takes to be central to the rise of ambiguity. His note regarding the condition of the occurrence of afterimage merits attention: if the reader reads the text too fast or too slowly, afterimage is not likely to occur. He seems to have applied the idea of 'engram' referred to by Ogden and Rich-

---

4 See Yamamoto (1940: 65-6): The holistic impression the writer experiences by completing sentences does not necessarily correspond with the holistic impression the reader experiences in understanding their meanings. This is because the subjective feelings regarding the semantic structure of the sentences in question are different from each other.

ards (1960: the intrusions of elements from the hearer's past experiences upon his or her understanding of the speaker's utterance) to discourse contexts.

From a poetics point of view, Jakobson (1960) delved into the relation between ways of inference and the rise of ambiguity. He pointed out that the paradigmatic structure of language is based on similarity (contrasts), and the syntagmatic structure of it contiguity. The former conerns the 'code,' and the latter phonotactics, phrase making, collocation, sentence structure, and also the addresser and addressee. According to his view, 'the poetic function projects the principle of equivalence from the axis of selection into the axis of combination' (p.135). He sets up six factors in the build-up of communication (addresser, message, addressee, context, contact, code), and six language functions corresponding to them (emotive, poetic, conative, referential, phatic, metalinguistic). Of the above factors actual communication takes one as a core and the others as subsidiary. As regards poetic function, the message is taken as a core, and the rise of ambiguity is ascribed to it. This ambiguity reflects the projection of 'equivalence from the axis of selection into the axis of combination.' Jakobson determines two ways of inference working at the base of language, and points that they are interactive with each other at various levels of a text. When exploring for and describing the reader's movement of inference, his descriptive framework is of great help.[5] (See the functioning of the first prism and the second prism, and the expression of the double prism structure in Chapter 3.) However, our aim is not to abstract the principles of ambiguity, but to examine why and how ambiguity is realized through the specific context of an individual writer—Chaucer.

Bakhtin (1998) pointed that a polyphony is produced through the cyclic dialogical workings of two elements (writer and reader, reader and text, text and text, form and concept, etc.). This indicates that ways of reading a text are made gradable through the dialogue. This is an important concept in that we grasp the dynamic process of semantic production.

Reacting to the theory of evolution in the nineteenth century or the structuralism in the first half of twentieth century, scepticism and deconstruction came to people's notice (Derrida 1976, Barthes 1977, Culler 1983, etc.). As regards the relationship between the speaker—the text—the hearer, the reader is among others emphasised. Empson is evaluated in this reader-oriented direction. This is why plural texts are produced from one text according to the reader's point of view. The second prism in the double prism structure demonstrated in Chapter 3 is much indebted to this background.

In modern times pragmatics (Leech 1983, Levinson 1983) and discourse analysis (Beaugrande and Dressler 1981, Brown and Yule 1983) make possible a synthetic approach to the speaker's and the reader's points of view. These writers discovered and analysed schemas that determine the speaker's and the hearer's way of thinking, their logical patterns, and their linguistic devices. Grice (1975) proposed the 'cooperative

---

5 Jakobson (1985) points out the relation between the works of romantic and symbolist poets and their use of similarity, and that between novels of realism and their use of contiguity. He ascribes to the operation of contiguity the development of the plot, the relationship of characters and situations, and the correspondence between local and global features in characterisation (the effect of synecdoche). Further he applies the above principles semiotically to pictures, cinema, etc.

principle' between the speaker and the hearer in a conversation, and the maxims to achieve this—Quantity, Quality, Relation, and Manner. He pointed out the implication of an utterance which can be inferred according to whether the maxims are observed or not although textually not made explicit. The second prism's participation in the interpretation of a text is strongly required (see Chapter 3).

Cognitive linguistics is devoted to explaining the polysemy of an utterance with regard to the motivation of semantic relation. This motivation is metaphor and metonymy. According to Lakoff (1987) and Johnson (1985), these are not unique to literary language, but cultivated in everyday language. They make clear how meanings ascribed to the human physical perception are through imagination applied to those ascribed to the human spiritual perception. That they reinterpreted the colours taken up by old rhetoric as those central to human inferential system is very helpful. When meanings are interpreted differently by different readers, it is possible that they are not arbitrary but related to each other through some fixed inference patterns.

Sperber and Wilson (1998) pay attention to ways of inference from a cognitive point of view. They attempt to make clear why and how a message is regarded as relevant in a communicative activity. They analyse metaphor, irony, style, speech act, foreknowledge, implicature, etc. These are useful for drawing attention to the movement of the hearer's point of view and ensuring sensitivity to the senses and nuances involved in an utterance.

Pragmatics and discourse analysis do not aim to elucidate ambiguity, and therefore do not make a systematic treatment of it. But they point out the instability in interpretation between the speaker and the hearer and the psychological background involved in the semantic production, which have become the basis of the double prism structure.

As mentioned above, degrees of awareness to and allowance for ambiguity are changing according to the view of language. With the discoveries of language features in modern times, the change from the speaker's unilateral semantic production to the bilateral one has been made, and concern with the rise of ambiguity is increasingly felt with a clearer sensitivity to the method of describing it.

2.2. Chaucer's ambiguity: previous scholarship

It goes without saying that as our awareness of the value of ambiguity increases so we are paying more attention to that aspect of Chaucer's works. But the modern achievements of linguistics have not yet been applied to this task. We will now present a summary of work in this field so far.

Empson (1930) deals with Chaucer's ambiguity. He takes advantage of semantics and tries to grasp and describe all the patterns of ambiguity. His discussion seems to be based on Richard's (1936) idea of the contextual commitment to semantic production. He classifies it into seven types based on the degrees of disorder. Accordingly those examples ranging from the speaker's intentional ambiguity to his or her unintentional ambiguity expressed in a confused state are dealt with. The variation between the two extremes (order-disorder) are not fixed according to our view, but changeable depending on by which side the reader gives more weight to. It is natural that Empson should make a repeated comment on the fuzziness between types. He searches for values and

2. Previous scholarship

associations ascribed to the referent of a particular expression, and illustrates various devices for semantic production (metaphor, pun, allusion, allegory, syntax, shifting perspectives, tautology, contradictions, etc.). But he has not made a systematic treatment of expression and much less has he described the interaction between them (consideration of the expression in the double prism structure is not enough). He quotes Chaucer's ambiguity from *Troilus and Criseyde* and analyses it as belonging to Type 2. Here he attends to double syntax. It is not certain whether he regards that it is peculiar to Chaucer or takes it merely accidentally. In terms of the contrastiveness of semantic relation, Chaucer uses more varieties of types in accordance with Empson's classification. He does not make any reference to them. Surprised by his insight into ambiguities, we cannot help but feel difficulties in applying his 'types' to ours.

Exegetical studies by Robertson (1962) are part of the allegorical studies shown in Section 2.1. He argues that textual meanings are closely connected with the value systems of Christianity. To identify the religious meaning behind the literal meaning of a text we must look at the interrelation between one text (the Bible) and another text (a literary work). This recognition affects the organization (theme, characterization, plot) and linguistic details. These studies are useful tools in the work of excavating the hidden spiritual meanings of a text, on the other hand if we place too much emphasis on them, we are likely to disregard the interaction between them and the secular and experiential meanings (consideration of the second prism of the double prism structure is not enough).

Taking a lead from Empson and in line with medieval allegorical traditions, Gordon (1970) investigates ambiguities in *Troilus and Criseyde*. She concentrates on Chaucer's active use of Boethius' *De Consolatione Philosophiae* in adapting Boccaccio's *Il Filostrato*. She points out that Chaucer's insertions come to acquire ironical values when compared with the original text of Boethius. The characteristics of the main characters and the narrative development of the story fluctuate between reason and emotion, and are open to ironical interpretation according to the reader's assumptions and moral judgements. Her concept of 'ironical ambiguity' states that an element comes to be contradictory by another hidden element as a criterion. The reader is divided in interpretation according to whether he or she assumes the hidden element. But Gordon does not treat expressions which are a starting point of the reader's interpretation systematically. She is biased in her treatment of them. She is not concerned with and therefore does not describe degrees of the relatedness of linguistic types such as syntax and word (except for *kynde* and *queynte* in Appendix). Accordingly the interaction between elements of superordinate levels (theme, plot, etc.) and subordinate ones is not dealt with systematically (the classification of the expression of the double prism structure into types is not enough).

Brewer (1974) applies Jakobson's (1960) 'metonymic principle' to Chaucer. Pointing out that this principle is applied to various levels of text forming elements, he develops awareness of expressions which are only sketchily dealt with in Gordon (1970). He points out that similarity typical of Romantic poets and Symbolists has been evaluated highly, and by this yardstick Chaucer's poems are measured and as a result underrated owing to their poverty, and that another way of inference, contiguity is not duly evaluated. His awareness that contiguity is applied to various textual levels merits attention. They are as follows: Gothic art of 'juxtaposition' in late medieval times, a literary text and its sources, the narrator and the story he tells, the causal relation between one event and another, furthermore the collocation, lexical network, sense relation in a word in linguistic expressions. He takes Chaucer's use of *sad* in *The Clerk's Tale*, and examines its collocation, its word associations, and its sense relation. Finally he points out that contiguity controls the free associations of a word's meaning, and sets some limits to the way of semantic production. Brewer gives weight to the variety of workings of contiguity, but not to the interaction between contiguity and similarity, therefore the rise of ambiguity due to the message-centered poetic function. Accordingly the variety of the second prism seen in Chapter 3 is not considered enough. We give importance to that fact that contiguity can be made as a matter of degree. Kawasaki (1993: 61) does not treat *Troilus and Criseyde*, but is pertinent enough to our study to pose two extremes "authority" and "experience:" 'generally speaking, "authority" and "experience" tend to merge with each other although opposed to each other, and to reflect Chaucer's humanity the most appropriately, but can they be independent of each other without being transformed?' His reference to the interaction between the extremes above is worth attention in that it is regarded as a vital source of ambiguity. Since this indicates the processes of the speaker's and the reader's cognition of the phenomena in question, it deserves further investigation. On the other hand, since his approach is conducted in literary terms, the classification of the elements forming the text and the interaction between them are not regarded as the object of consideration.

Other studies are not primarily concerned with Chaucer's ambiguity and only partially with it in relation to other topics. There are many studies, most of which are conducted in literary terms or as interpretations of his works. In relation to the writer and his historical background, see Masui (1977), Brewer (1986), Patterson (1987); in relation to his possible sources, see Wetherbee (1984), Windeatt (1979, 1992); in relation to Feminism and gender studies, see Cox (1998); in relation to psychological analyses of his works, see Frank (1972), Spearing (1976); in relation to the characterization of characters, see Donaldson (1970, 1979), Ueno (1972), Pearsall (1986); in relation to the narrative structure of his stories, see Muscatine (1957), Jordan (1985); in relation to stylistic features of his language, see Gaylord (1968-9), Saito (2000). These studies are rich in insight and refer to some types of ambiguity, but their examination of them is segmented and on the whole does not treat them systematically.

There have not been so many studies of Chaucer's linguistic ambiguity as there have in the literary area. As to rhetoric, we have Kökeritz (1954) and Baum (1956, 1958). They limit themselves to examples of *paronomasia*. With regard to lexicological and lexicographical studies, we have Ross (1972). But this is limited to words of literal meanings and sexual implications. In the lexical and semantic area Burnley (1979, 1983) proposes the 'architecture' of Chaucer's language, in other words, a historical/cultural integration of word association, and points out the multiple use of registers to which words are ascribed. Elliott's (1974) treatment of the polysemy of words is in the same vein. However, they deal with ambiguity only partially. In the syntactic field we have Blake (1977) and Roscow (1981), but they do not go into the subject in depth. From a paleographical as well as syntactic point of view, Chickering (1990) is worth consulting. But he treats ambiguity only in relation to scribal variation and variation in the punctuation of modern editors. From a metrical point of view, Masui (1964) points out a chiming effect of rhyming words and its subsequent expansion of the meaning of those words. The expectation of matching words produced by rhyme is interesting, but his examination of ambiguity is limited to rhyming words. These linguistic studies take a fixed methodology to describe Chaucer's ambiguity unlike the literary ones, but on the other are poor at the recognition of the kinds of ambiguity or the examination of the differing interpretations which will be produced by different readers. Jakobson's (1960) treatment of metaphor and metonymy or modern achievements by recent pragmatics and cognitive linguistics have not been applied enough to Chaucer's ambiguity although these findings are indispensable for grasping the plural meanings of an utterance.

The above studies excavate Chaucer's ambiguity, using examples which may allow for the reader to have alternative views and thus be divided in interpretation. However, either they present sufficient interpretation with insufficient methodology, or vice versa. There has been no systematic description and explanation of the process whereby ambiguity is likely to occur, and much remains to be done before it is solved.[6]

2.3. The problem addressed in this book

As shown in Sections 2.1 and 2.2, since ambiguity is closely related to meaning, it has attracted increasing attention as pragmatics and poetics have looked at meaning and made the interaction between the speaker and the hearer. However, there are both strong points and weak points in those studies. Taking these things into account, our research is devoted to showing how Chaucer's ambiguity is likely to arise with particular reference to *Troilus and Criseyde*. This is only possible by integrating methodology and interpretation, which has so far been unattempted.

What point of view and what methodology to adopt in order to solve the question raised in Chapter 2 will be dealt with in Chapter 3.

---

6   Sections 2.1 and 2.2 are based on Nakao (2001a) and Nakao (2004).

3. Our point of view and method

3.1. The rise of ambiguity

3.1.1. The double prism structure

In this section we describe our double prism structure as a means of explaining how and why ambiguity is likely to occur. Empson's (1930) description of ambiguity is dependent on types of contexts, but this cannot easily be applied because these contexts are not easily classified. My description is expression-orientated in that it operates according to the way in which these expressions can be observed and described whether separately or in combination. Each variety of expression, whether a word or phrase, or the text as a whole, constitutes a layer of its own semantic production. In describing ambiguous expressions, I have given 'addresser' and 'addressee' more than 'accessory' importance (cf. Jakobson 1960: 353). This framework is diagrammed in (1).

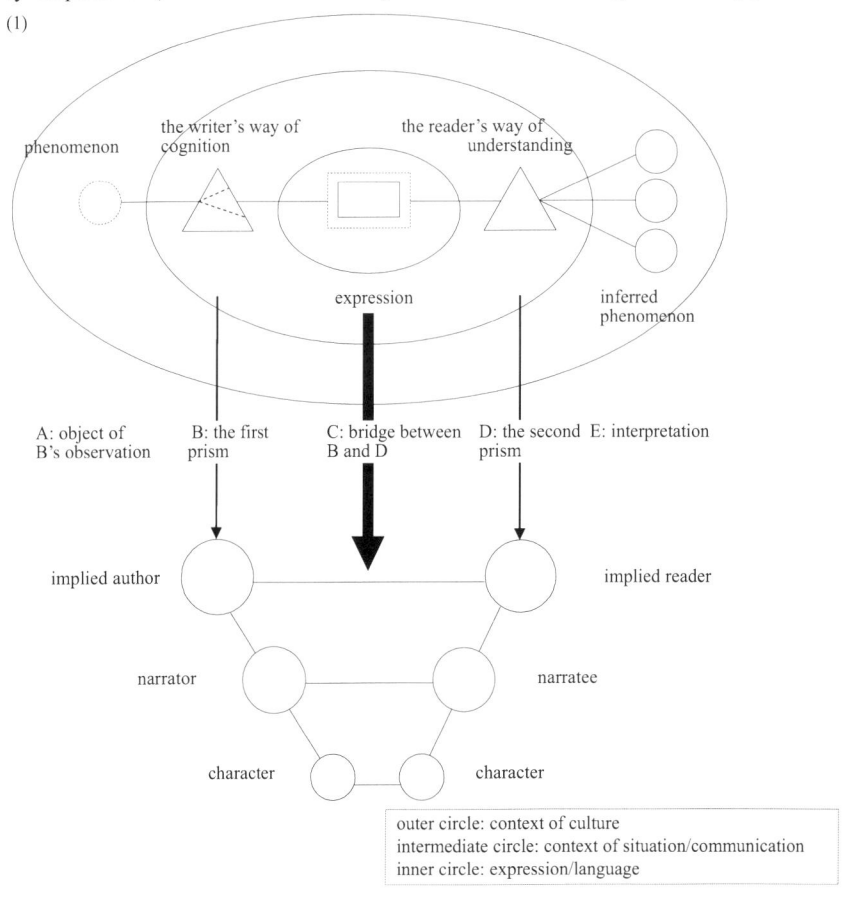

(1)

N.B.: (i) The broken lines indicate that the writer/reader cannot easily determine one stance or value. A phenomenon is susceptible to multivalence when allowing for different views of a single prism or between the two prisms. How the first prism, the writer views the phenomenon is not always textually explicit, but only suggestive, which calls for the reader's inference. An expression can semantically be easily determined, but involved in complex pragmatic contexts, it may be open to varying interpretations. Furthermore the real state of Chaucer's language, only existent through scribes, is open to discussion. On the other hand, why I used solid lines for the reader's stance and his or her interpretation is that the communicative value of the expression is finally assessed by him or her and that to the extent of his or her assessment they can be described, although justification for them may depend on his or her assumption or inference.

(ii) Two broken lines in *B* and three solid lines in *D* indicate that they are not necessarily the same.

(iii) *E* assumes two cases: interpretation divided 'within one reader' and 'between readers.'

A represents a particular phenomenon which the writer, the first prism, observes, *B* represents his or her ways of cognising *A*, *C* represents the expression which the first prism produces to represent *A* or by which the second prism is induced to interpret *A*. *D* represents the reader, the second prism's way of reconstructing *B* through *C*, and finally *E* represents the reader's interpretation. If the second prism is controlled by *C* sufficiently enough to single out the first prism's cognition, and leads to only one reading, ambiguity is likely to be reduced. On the other hand, if the second prism is triggered by *C* to perceive the first prism's wide-ranging cognition, and have, or fluctuate between, two or more readings, ambiguity is likely to be increased. The reason I use 'prism' here is that whether phenomenon or expression, when it passes through the observer's eyes, it does not necessarily produce a straight line, but a refracted line or even a diffused reflection in accordance with their perceptions. On this point Burnely (1983: 222) merits attention: "The meaning of a piece of literature is notoriously Janus-like, since it may be considered to possess the meaning intended by its author as well as a possibly quite different meaning attributed by its reader." Here I am using 'prism' as a metaphor for representing multiple refractions in interpretation, not in a physical-science way.

The factors *A* to *E* are equally important to the rise of Chaucer's ambiguity. Since we have no Ur-texts of Chaucer, there are uncertainties about what phenomenon he observed (*A*), how he cognised it (*B*), and how he expressed it (*C*). Because of these the reader's participation in the production of the text in question, i.e., his or her mode of cognition (*D*) and his or her interpretation (*E*) becomes all the more important.

A to *E* are thus fundamental factors involved in the rise of ambiguity. But the order of their application is not straightforward. Assuming the reader's response *D*, the author may cognise the phenomenon *A* in such a way *B*. Through the expression *C*, the reader may assume the phenomenon *A* and the author's way of cognition of it *B*, and lead to his or her interpretation *E*. We cannot say to what extent Chaucer was conscious of the double prism structure. The first prism may be at one time strongly conscious of it as shown in Chaucer's deliberate use of wordplay (*paronomasia*), and at others only weakly conscious of it as when he is involved in the object of his observation so much so that he cannot censure it. The second prism is encouraged to assume

3. Our point of view and method 37

the author's way of cognition in one way or another, and leads to his or her interpretation. On the other hand, there are chances that he or she cannot state definitely whether the rise of ambiguity is intentional or not. Which type of ambiguity we may encounter, we can position it in the double prism structure, and describe it with supporting evidence. The rise of ambiguity is thus explained by the double prism structure. How and why this double structure is activated is a focal point in later chapters.

We have three more things to make clear regarding the diagram in (1). First let us consider the contexts surrounding the constituent factors A to E of the double prism structure. For the tripartite division of these contexts my most immediate source is Su (1994: 67). Although no mention by him about this, he is based on functionalists' view of the semantic realisation through language. The three circles from the inner, through the intermediate, to the outer are correspondent respectively to the metafunction (ideational, interpersonal, textual), the context of situation (field, participants, mode), and the context of culture. (See Malinowski (Ogden and Richards 1960: 296-336) and Halliday (2004).) The inner circle (C) indicates, according to Su (1994: 67), the 'most immediate context, which includes the surrounding linguistic environment (from phrase and sentence to the entire poem as a linguistic construct), and the subject matter or topic of the text.' The intermediate circle (B/D) indicates the 'immediate context of act of communication, which includes situational factors such as, among others, author-reader relationship, and physical and social milieu' (Su 1994: 67). In our book the 'mode' of language is treated with the same degree of importance as 'field' and 'participants.' This is concerned with how the textual transmission between the addresser and the addressee is made (spoken or written). The outer circle (A) indicates the 'least immediate context, which includes circumstances of authorship, culture and tradition' (Su 1994: 67). The phenomenon in my framework can be traced from the words for it, through the context of situation, further back to the context of culture. The courtly love and the heroine's betrayal of Troilus in *Troilus and Criseyde* are, for instance, adaptations from the longstanding Trojan legend.

Second, in describing Chaucer's ambiguity I have taken into account not only the semantics but pragmatics of his language. Therefore my treatment of it is not based on the 'code model,' but the 'inferential model' of communication according to Sperber and Wilson (1998: 3-38). In this perspective what the first prism (B) intends to say is not directly delivered to the second prism (D), but only indirectly.[7] This inferential

---

7   Ito (1993) proposes the mechanism of literary ambiguity with regard to 'the processes of expression.' There he focuses on the following processes: phenomenon to be observed → the speaker's view of it → the expression. And he takes the stance that as to how to observe the phenomenon, the sender and the receiver do not have the same basic perception. In other words, unlike the ideal speaker-hearer model, the interaction model assumes that the sender and the receiver have the same importance ('Varieties of Ambiguity in Medieval English Romances,' the Ninth Congress of the Japan Society for Medieval English Studies, 1993 at Keio University). The double prism structure I propose here is based on this stance of Ito's. I proposed this model in a paper 'The Structure of Chaucer's Ambiguity with a Focus on Modal Lexical Verbs' I read at the seventy fourth meeting of Japan Literary Society (2002, at Hokusei University), which was published in Nakao (2003). This model is a basic frame to describe Chaucer's ambiguity in Nakao (2004). For further information, see Su's (1994: 67) pragmatic as well as semantic description of poetic discourse (the basic 'Author (A) – Text (T) – Reader (R)' form of written

model seems to suit Chaucerian discourse. His authorial voice is only perceivable through language, but the language is not necessarily his, but scribes'. The two prisms are often found in tension. The reader, the second prism, may challenge the author, the first prism, in that he or she is sensitive to what the first prism may not have been fully conscious about, and even rewrites the expression *C*, as seen in scribes' emendation.

Third, the interaction between the two prisms *B* and *D* is only observable through the triply layered author-reader relationship in *C*, as shown in the second half of the figure in (1): character to character at the bottom, then, narrator (in Chaucer's case the first-person narrator, whether reliable or unreliable) to narratee (the audience assumed to follow the narrator at one stage or another through his or her inference) in the middle, and at the top the implied author (the author assumed to govern the whole text) and the implied reader (the reader assumed to ideally read the text). In reading the text, we are provided with an insight or at least a hint from a character or the narrator to see into the writer's perspective. There do happen uncertainties in the text as to who utters a speech, the narrator or a character (see Chapter 7: Ambiguity in reported speech). Those ambiguities are only perceivable and describable with our assumption of the different points of view. What is important here is to be sensitive to these different points of view and move between them, to progress to the interpretation *E*.[8]

Theoretically there is a difference in perspective between the 'writer' and the 'implied author,' although they can be collapsed. But here in order to make the discussion simple, I basically use 'author' as a blanket term for both except when I need to distinguish between them. The same principle is applied to the 'reader' and the 'implied reader.' The 'reader' includes such readers as medieval audience, scribes, modern editors, critics, the implied reader, and the view-shifting reader 'I,' understood as an integrator of readings.[9] When describing ambiguities, we will specify the kinds of readers.

As an instance of this let us take up Criseyde's shifting heart (Tr 5.1084) as a phenomenon, which has already been dealt with in Section 1.2.3. This phenomenon is a state of mind, and is likely to involve a matter of degree in evaluation. The speaker Criseyde regrets for her immorality and feels duly contrite, but on the other tries to justify it. The author's cognition of this seems to involve the following: the viewpoint of sacred and secular in medieval times, Gothic art of 'juxtaposition' (cf. Brewer 1974: 3), the poet's involvement and detachment, the self-assertion camouflaged by the equivocation of the utterance in the court culture in which the freedom of speech was not guaranteed, etc. The author encapsulates his thoughts and feelings in the surface structure 'And gilteles, I woot wel, I yow leve.' This structure itself is susceptible of multiple meanings (see Chapter 10). The reader is asked to interpret it taking into account various points of view such as Criseyde's and the author's as the basis for it. It is not unnatural that at the final stage of interpretation (*E*) plural readers—the medieval audience living in the culture of sacred and secular, fifteenth-century scribes, editors of

---

communication).
8   See Leech and Short (1981: 269).
9   I use 'the view-shifting reader 'I'' to show a reader who is standing in a vantage-point and can shift his or her view with ease (at one time identify himself or herself with a character and at another with the narrator). See also Section 4.6.

modern printed texts, modern critics—should lead to plural interpretations. To summarize the above discussion, *A* to *E* is represented as in (2).

(2) The double prism structure: Tr 5.1084
    A: Criseyde's shifting heart (a state of mind, tendency to be made a matter of degree)
    B: The author's cognition of *A* (sacred and secular in medieval times, involvement and detachment, deliberate equivocation)
    C: And gilteles, I woot wel, I yow leve. (polysemy)
    D: Assuming *A*, *B* and *C*, the reader directs his or her interpretation
    E: Final interpretation—the rise of ambiguity (plural readers, plural interpretations)

3.1.2. The first prism (*B*)

The late fourteenth century of England was, as Brewer (1974) says, characterised by the Gothic juxtaposition. This mode of thinking is manifested in the interaction between the contemporary 'auctorite' and the 'experience' of individual persons. Chaucer was one of the poets who straddled the two worlds in his works. The two worlds are constructed in various ways: sacred and secular, divine love and human physical love, heaven and hell, abstract and concrete, objectivity and subjectivity, reason and emotion, life and death, 'game' and 'ernest,' meditation and activity, etc.

The deeper Chaucer understands the object of his observation (*A*), and the more sympathetic he is towards it, the more indecisive he is as to how to make a judgement upon it, and as a result he leaves the final judgement to the reader. In medieval times when human rights and the freedom of speech were not very far advanced, to make a self-assertion in a clear-cut way might have led him to losing his life, and thus it would be inevitable that he should refer to a generally admitted message at the surface structure, and at a deeper level hide his intended message (double entendre). An apparently uninformative expression is likely to ask the reader actively to participate in the interpretation of it (*E*). This is how the multi-layered relational structure of it is motivated.

Troilus and Criseyde is a work written from the middle period of Chaucer's writings. It is his longest complete poem. This work was produced when the poet's understanding of humanity was deepened to a great extent. Not only morals to restrict humans socially and as a consequence human ideal attributes, but also individual acts whereby humans depart from morality are highlighted. The courtly love or the theme of this story is embodied in the form of the love between Troilus, a Trojan prince and knight and Criseyde, a widow and courtly lady. In this situation they have difficulty in living up to medieval moral criteria and are induced to show their individual characteristics. The fact that Criseyde accepts Troilus' love and that in the Greek camp she is sent to as an exchange-prisoner she yields to Diomede illustrates this perfectly. Chaucer sheds light on psychological and emotional subtleties to be observed in characters coping with difficult situations. These characters fluctuate between their moral obligations and their true natures. When the first prism's cognition is indecisive or diverse and thus textually remains as a matter of degree or multiple to the reader, ambiguity is likely to be induced. Of course, a similar tendency is seen in Chaucer's other works, but *Troilus and Criseyde* seems to have excelled in this area in that it demonstrates great insight into human psychology and an ability to seek it out and present it in literary form. This poem is abundant in those elements leading to ambiguity.

The interaction between the two extremes is repeated in Chaucer's works. Since in the medieval court freedom of speech was not permitted, it seems that he was forced to express his opinion equivocally. In this situation he wrote *The Book of the Duchess*. This poem focuses on the death of the wife of the Duke of Lancaster, John of Gaunt (the poet's patron), and describes Duke's deep sorrow and search for consolation. The poet deals with this historical event with some equivocation. The story the narrator reads before going into a dream (sorrow and consolation of the wife Alcyone on her husband Seyx's death) and the content of the dream he has (the Black Knight's sorrow and consolation on his wife White's death) are superimposed on each other via contiguity. As regards the content of the dream, the external exploration through the Black Knight's hunting of a hart (hert (=hart) hunting) and the internal exploration through his hunting of the consolation of the heart (hert (=heart) hunting) with much hurt (herte=hurt) from the loss of his dear wife are superimposed on each other metaphorically (external-internal hunting) as well as metonymically (internal spiritual hunting inside external physical hunting). If the heart-hunting and the hart-hunting finish together, the poet seems to have avoided expressing the real social event straightforwardly. He wrote it in such an ambiguous way that the reader could get the message through the exercise of his or her inference.

In *The House of Fame*, Fame, a personified abstraction, appears in a dream to Chaucer. The device of allegory is added to the equivocal way of expression in the court. The heroine Fame is depicted as a dual character formed of *soth* and *fals*. Reputation is something made and open to human subjective judgement. This is a metaphor to show that there is a fine line between truth and falsehood of events. They are likely to be ambiguous in their emphasis. In *The Parliament of Fowles* the narrator sees birds representing various social classes allegorically appear in his dream. Love is a theme of this story. It is dealt with in three ways: religious love (*blisse, commune profit*), courtly love (governed by Venus), physical love (governed by Nature). They are juxtaposed with one another with such an ambiguous effect that if we set high value on one particular love, the other loves are likely to be reduced in value, and that if we regard the situation from a different angle, a different picture of ambiguity emerges.

Ambiguity from Chaucer's earlier period of writings is due to equivocation and allegorical devices within a dream framework. Further developed in conjunction with psychological devices is *Troilus and Criseyde*. This broke away from the dream framework and allegory and illuminated human psychology with much realism. His analysis of human psychology and its subtle descriptions enabled him to achieve psychological ambiguity. There is no greater conspicuous psychological ambiguity than is to be found in *Troilus and Criseyde*.

In *The Canterbury Tales,* there may be a new type of ambiguity in which afterimages produced by running through the tales are positively used. Immediately after *Troilus and Criseyde*, Chaucer wrote *The Legend of Good Women* in which women's goodness is described in contradistinction to Criseyde's betrayal. But the dichotomy of false men and good women is too arbitrary for him. While dealing with positive feminine virtues, he comes gradually to touch upon feminine weaknesses hidden behind those virtues, and the double coherent structure of positive and negative values becomes prominent. In his last work, *The Canterbury Tales*, one teller and another teller, one tale and another tale, one theme and another, and one fragment and another are juxtaposed with degrees of relativism, and there the concept of reversal runs through the collection of the tales. For example as regards the theme of marriage, plural tellers (viewpoints) are set up. In the Prologue to *The Wife of Bath*, the two extreme aspects of marriage—authority and experience—are juxtaposed. The idea of marriage is dynamically treated within a character and between characters across different tales. When the reader feels it uncertain which viewpoint to emphasise, ambiguity is likely to occur. But this method is already used in the realisation of the psychological ambiguity of *Troilus and Criseyde*.

3.1.3. The second prism (*D*)

As shown in Chapter 1, literary language has made the best use of the depth and breadth of ideas being condensed into language. The reader's subject is generally formed plurally since he or she is different in his or her experiential background. What matters is that individual readers assume the author's stance towards the object of his description, and that they establish themselves by which meaning of an expression to emphasise. But readers who modify their reading and seek another reading, and make a dialogue with the text in question are required to be situated in a middle position affording them access to either way of reading. The reader 'I' is, so to speak, a switching device.

Goto (1996: 45) makes an interesting remark on ambiguous sentences and individual readers' perception of them. It is summarised as follows: A context seems to be useful for reducing ambiguous sentences into a single meaning and discovering a single meaning of ambiguous sentences, but not very useful for ascertaining or discovering ambiguous sentences themselves; what is related to the ease of discovering ambiguities seems to be "man" rather than "lexis/structure/construction;" it is found that an individual's "knowledge of the world and all things in nature" or "knowledge of language" is closely related to "the perception of ambiguity." His remark on ambiguity shows how the reader's point of view is involved in the rise of that phenomenon.

There is a big gap in the way of cognition between medieval readers and modern readers. While medieval readers can position a phenomenon between two extreme value systems such as sacred and secular, "game" and "ernest," ideals and realities, and comprehend it in the interaction between them, modern readers tend to understand them analytically. And clearly the consciousness of the sacred is nowadays restricted to a relatively small set of devout people. A synthetic view of two extreme value systems can be said to be a medieval idea itself.

It is not unnatural that readers of different times differing in their value systems, moral judgements, and experiences should make a different response to, or show a different awareness of, the relation between text forming elements. *Troilus and Criseyde* has Criseyde's shifting heart as a 'focal point.' There might have been many ladies in the courtly audience, and there Chaucer the poet took their response into account as one layer of readers, and described Criseyde's betrayal. His assumption of different readers affects his way of cognition of it and his expression of it allows for the subtle response to readers according to their viewpoints.

Each reader may be limited to one view of the relationship between elements, but when many readers are gathered, the text may be flexible enough to permit of multiple interpretations. Or one reader may be encouraged by the 'awareness of ambiguity' demonstrated by Goto (1996) to be undecisive or various about the interpretation and waver between, or read into, the primary interpretation and the secondary one. In this book when referring to 'reader,' as we have already mentioned, we do not use it in a narrow sense as 'a reader of a written book,' but in a broad sense as the 'subject who involves himself or herself in reading of a text,' including, that is, the courtly audience, scribes, modern editors, etc.

3.2. The categories of ambiguity

The expression (*C*) connecting the first and second prisms is subcategorized into three types, which are shown in (3).

(3)
I. Textual domains:
   a. Metatext (scribal/editorial ambiguity)
   b. Intertextuality (multiple texts involved in the making of one text)
   c. Macro-textual structure (theme, characterization, plot)
   d. Reported speech (direct speech, indirect speech, free indirect speech)
   e. Discourse (cohesion, information structure)
II. Interpersonal domains:
   a. The speaker's intention (illocutionary force)   <Interactive>
   b. Modality (e.g. modal lexical verb: *I woot wel* 'I know well')
III. Linguistic domains
   a. Syntax
   b. Word (lexical network, polysemy, fuzziness)
   c. Voice (stress, pause, intonation, etc.)

The domains in which the expression is open to two or three interpretations are divided into three, according to the contexts ranging from the more inclusive to the less. The most inclusive domains are called textual domains, the intermediate interpersonal domains, and the least inclusive linguistic. The three domains are based on Halliday and Hasan's (1976: 29) 'Functional components of the semantic system.' To Category I—Textual domains—are added metatext, intertextuality, and macro-textual structure since we are dealing with a literary text. Textual domains are sufficiently inclusive to cover the reader's critical and metalinguistic treatment of a text he or she is going to read, the mutual expectancy of two or three texts, the macro-structure of a text consisting of elements such as theme, characterization, and plot, speech presentation, and cohesion between sentences. They are respectively metatext (Ia), intertextuality (Ib), macro-textual structure (Ic), reported speech (Id), and discourse structure (Ie). Category II—Interpersonal domains—are concerned with the mental attitudes of characters, and are of two types: the speaker's intention (IIa) and modality (IIb). These are directly related to the rise of psychological ambiguity in *Troilus and Criseyde*. Category III—Linguistic domains—are directly concerned with the construction of proposition, and are of three types: syntax (IIIa), word (IIIb), and voice

(IIIc). We have subcategorized ambiguity into ten types according to kinds of the expression. The need of each type and its definition are shown in each chapter. The above is the framework of the expression through which ambiguity is likely to arise.[10]

3.3. Types of ambiguity

The types of ambiguity in (3) are not independent but interdependent. Therefore the readers move between these types, and should be sensitive to the relation between them. For instance, the type 'I woot wel' (IIb) is related not only to the language to which it is added (IIIa, b), but our evaluation of Criseyde's character (Ic), for detailed analysis of which, see Chapter 10. Ambiguity due to degrees of the validity of the propositional content tends to be functional not only in its domains but also in conjunction.

According to the movement of the reader's inference, let us examine each type of expression in (3) and describe how ambiguity is likely to arise. We will describe how the reader focuses on one of the types in (3), and further on their subtypes, or going beyond that type directs his or her attention to other types, and finally arrives at plural interpretations.

3.4. The concept of ambiguity

3.4.1. The definition of ambiguity

The meaning of ambiguity itself is ambiguous. In this book, as is shown in the double prism structure, we define as ambiguous those cases in which the addressee has two or more ways of interpretation for an expression assuming the addresser's ways of cognition of the phenomenon. The following is the definition of the *OED*.

(4)

†1. Subjectively: Wavering of opinion; hesitation, doubt, uncertainty, as to one's course. *Obs.* c1400–c1590
†2. *concr.* An uncertainty, a dubiety. *Obs.* 1598–1658
3. a. Objectively: Capability of being understood in two or more ways; double or dubious signification, ambiguousness. c1430–
   b. *spec.* in *Literary Criticism* (see quots.)
      1930 W. Empson *Seven Types of Ambiguity* i. 1 An ambiguity, in ordinary speech, means something very pronounced, as a rule witty and deceitful. I propose to use the word in an extended sense, and shall think relevant to my subject any consequence of language, however slight, which adds some nuance to the direct statement of prose. [ed. 3, 1953: I ... shall think relevant to my subject any verbal nuance, however slight, which gives room for alternative reactions to the same piece of language.]
4. *concr.* A word or phrase susceptible of more than one meaning; an equivocal expression. 1591–

---

10 For outlines of the category of ambiguity, see Nakao (2001a).

According to the first prism, the definitions 1 and 2 are relevant, and according to the second prism, 3 and 4 are relevant. Since we give due attention to the reader's point of view and are concerned with literary language, not daily language, we will take the definition 3.b as the most important here. Chaucer the poet never used the word *ambiguity*. He only used *amphibologies* Tr 4.1406 and *ambages* Tr 5.897 in a negative sense. However, he exploited the literary artifice of ambiguity a long time before Empson analysed it.

The phrase 'any verbal nuance' is related to the kinds of meaning, and depends on the extent to which we distinguish meanings of an expression. In our book the kinds and numbers of ambiguity are not based on patterns of combinations of contexts as in Empson's scheme (Section 2.2), but on the kinds of meanings of an expression. This is the category of ambiguity in Section 3.2. In this way we are able to make clear each type and the interaction of one type with another, and to describe them clearly.

3.4.2. Vagueness

Ambiguity here focuses on the semantic fluidity the reader can identify based on an expression (including indirect meaning as found in illocutionary forces). We can specify these meanings. But they are uncertain and vague in that they cannot be determined. On the other hand, vagueness is uncertain and vague in that it is unmotivated and cannot be specified based on an expression. (As regards this difference, see Goto 1996: 61-2.) Let us consider the meaning of 'He must be careful.' It is open to ambiguity when the reader is undecided as to whether he or she ascribes *must* to the ideal of his or her socio-physical world or ascribes it to his or her inferential world (degrees of certainty). On the other hand, whatever his age or hair-colour may be, this is implicit and unspecified in view of the linguistic structure above, and therefore vague.

3.4.3. The control of ambiguity

Ambiguity can be reduced to a single meaning by means of context, linguistic discourse structure, and sounds (in oral communication). With this restriction upon the reader, he or she is encouraged to solve ambiguity according to his or her assumption. This also applies to Chaucer. However, discourse is too elliptical in structure or syntax is too psychologically fluid. Chaucer narrated to the audience, but his sound performance is dependent on the reader's reconstruction. We can glean little or no evidence from the manuscripts of his use of intonation. Punctuation in edited texts is always dependent on the editors' subjective judgements. The commas before and after 'I woot wel' in Section 1.2.3 are those of the editors, not the manuscripts. We will look at the movement of the reader's psychology and examine ambiguity with attention both to its control and promotion.

3.5. The procedure for examining Chaucer's ambiguity

When reading a text, it cannot be easily determined what type of ambiguity the reader first observes, and then what type he or she moves to in the cases in which there occurs an active interaction between types. As is shown in Section 3.3, the type at a higher

3. Our point of view and method

level is grasped by the evidence offered at the lower level, whereas the type at a lower level is affected in interpretation by the type at a higher level. This interaction is pointed out in my treatment of 'I woot wel.' Accordingly, the order of examination is not essential. It is important to pay attention to the interaction between the higher type and the lower type taking place in the reader's reading process. Here we deal with types of ambiguity from the higher type (I) to the lower type (III), and in the cases in which other types are equally involved in the rise of the ambiguity dealt with, make cross-references between them. In what follows, we will concentrate on each type of ambiguity belonging to the categories, I, II, III (Section 3.2), according to the double prism structure, and describe the processes in which it is likely to arise. The category of ambiguity corresponds to the structure of this book as will emerge below. The ambiguity in textual domains (I) is dealt with in Chapters 4 to 8 in Part II. In Chapter 4, we will look at ambiguity occurring in metatext (Ia), in Chapter 5 ambiguity in intertextuality (Ib), in Chapter 6 ambiguity in macro-textual structure (Ic), in Chapter 7 ambiguity in reported speech (Id), and in Chapter 8 ambiguity in discourse structure (Ie). The ambiguity in interpersonal domains is dealt with in Chapters 9 and 10 in Part III. In Chapter 9 we will look at ambiguity occurring in the speaker's intention (illocutionary force) (IIa), and in Chapter 10 ambiguity in modality (IIb). The ambiguity in linguistic domains is dealt with in Chapters 11 to 13 in Part IV. In Chapter 11, we will deal with ambiguity in syntax (IIIa), in Chapter 12 ambiguity in word (IIIb), and in Chapter 13 ambiguity in voice (IIIc).

As mentioned in Section 1.2.1, there are no Ur-texts found as regards medieval works such as those of Chaucer's. Extant manuscripts in our possession do not have the absolute values. This makes the role of the reader, the second prism of the text all the more important. In Chapter 4 we will concentrate on textual variation between manuscripts and modern edited texts, and examine how textual problems are likely to be relevant to the rise of ambiguity.

Part II: Ambiguity in textual domains

4. Ambiguity in metatext

4.1. Introductory remarks: the double prism structure and metatext

As mentioned in Chapter 1, Chaucer's own manuscripts have never been discovered. We therefore have access to his writings only through the extant scribal manuscripts and modern editions. In this study I have used Benson (1987), currently the canonical text for Chaucer studies. Benson's *Troilus and Criseyde* is based on the Cp manuscript, which is regarded as closest to Chaucer's original. However, since this is not Chaucer's original *per se*, the reader needs to regard it with some scepticism, i.e. treat it as a metatext. He or she is required to positively participate in the reconstruction of the original. In this chapter, we pay particular attention to the reader in the double prism structure and investigate into his or her inference and his or her choice of textual elements (choice of words/grammatical structures (e.g. editors' punctuation) / word order, etc.). Ambiguity is likely to arise when the reader cannot concentrate on one interpretation. Here among various readers involved in the evaluation of the text, we have highlighted the scribes engaged in the production of it, who are regarded as the closest to Chaucer's original and modern editors, who are most concerned with textual problems when trying to identify the best text. Although readers of Chaucer's original or of the manuscripts of his texts, they would perhaps have the most challenging attitude to the text, even taking the role of, the first prism (the poet) in that they could influence his texts by rewriting them. Before examining metatextual ambiguity, we will discuss briefly the state of the language in Chaucer's times, the productions of his manuscripts, and the nature of his readers.

4.2. Linguistic diversity in London and between the scribes

The English of the fourteenth and fifteenth centuries in which the manuscripts of *Troilus and Criseyde* were copied was unstable and exposed to a great deal of change on many levels. There was the blurring of the pronunciation of final *-e*, the variation of word forms, syntactic fluidity, the enlargement of vocabulary, semantic diversification due to the coexistence of synonymous words, dialectal mixture, and other factors. Chaucer, as is well known, was aware of this linguistic mutability:

(1) And for ther is so gret diversite
　　In Englissh and in writyng of oure tonge,
　　So prey I God that non myswrite the,
　　Ne the mysmetre for defaute of tonge;
　　And red wherso thow be, or elles songe,
　　That thow be understonde, God I biseche! Tr 5.1793-8

At the end of *Troilus and Criseyde*, Chaucer expresses apprehension that his language will not be copied properly. When copying it in this situation of linguistic diversity, what problems did the scribes of the fourteenth and fifteenth centuries face? How did they respond to the diversities of the English of this time? To what extent were the variations between them due to arbitrary errors such as careless mistakes, dialectal variants, and unnatural syntax? Or from an 'integrated' point of view, are they no mere mistakes but suggestive of ambiguities underlying the text? If there are two cases like these, how can we distinguish between them? Taking into consideration the apparently liberal, not to say slipshod attitude of scribes and editors towards the text, we will attempt to make clear the process whereby ambiguity is likely to arise.

4.3. Production of the manuscripts of Chaucer's texts

In medieval times texts were produced by scribes copying the writer's original.[11] Chaucer's texts remain only as scribal manuscript copies.[12] There are no extant original texts by him. While scribes copied the original faithfully, they rewrote it according to the reader's intention, or made a self-assertion (editing) through their dialectal or literary filtering (Brown 2000: 432). The great dismay experienced by Chaucer when checking manuscripts of his works is revealed in his short poem *Chaucers Wordes unto Adam, his Owne Scriveyn* as in (2).

(2) Adam scriveyn, if ever it thee bifalle
 Boece or Troylus for to wryten newe,
 Under thy long lokkes thou most have the scalle,
 But after my makyng thow wryte more trewe;
 So ofte adaye I mot thy werk renewe,
 It to correcte and eke to rubbe and scrape,
 And al is thorugh thy negligence and rape.

There was little editorial supervision of the manuscript production of Chaucer's secular works and little attention was paid to copyright or proofreading. The case is very different from religious works where the *sententia* of the text was checked by a superintendent. Although *Troilus and Criseyde* and Gower's *Confessio Amantis* are both secular works, the Gower text was, by contrast, copied under the strict control of a supervisor.[13] In Chaucer's case it is absolutely necessary to be free from one edited text and observe it from a multi-textual point of view.

---

11 Michael Benskin & Margaret Laing (1981: 55): ...because a MS. is a copy, and perhaps a copy of a copy ... of a copy, it has been taken to represent not the language of some one scribe or of some one place, but a conglomeration of the individual usages of all those scribes whose copies of the text stand between this present MS. and the original.
12 There is an argument that *Equatorie of the Planets* is Chaucer's holograph. But this has not been substantiated.
13 Derek Pearsall, 'The Gower Tradition' in Minnis (1983: 183): Copy after copy varies in only minute details—in contrast with the texts of Chaucer and Langland, often being copied by the same class of professional scribes. It may be that scribes were influenced by the presence of Latin, which tended to stabilise the English text with which it was associated; it may be too that the shorter verse-lines, with their regularity of metre, were more readily held in mind as scribes copied line by line; but something must be due too to the effect upon them of the sense that they were dealing with a completely finished product. Gower's careful supervision of early production was important here: the poor quality of the majority of *Canterbury Tales* manuscripts shows by contrast the consequences of the absence of such supervision.

4.4. The sixteen manuscripts of *Troilus and Criseyde*

There are two ways of understanding the manuscripts of *Troilus and Criseyde*. One is that variant manuscripts are due to Chaucer's revision. The other is that there is only one original and the variants are due to scribes. Root (1952) is closest to the former, and there he assumes Chaucer's revision in the order of the α, γ and β manuscripts with β as the final one. His understanding of the stemma of *Troilus and Criseyde* is as follows.

(3) The stemma of *Troilus and Criseyde*.[14]

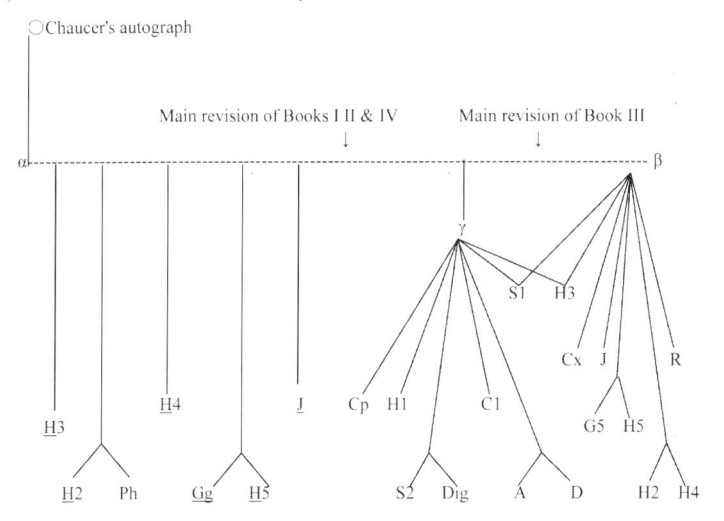

The broken line, α ... β, represents a single MS., Chaucer's own copy of the poem, progressively corrected and revised, until its text, originally α, becomes β. In the case of MSS. of composite character, the α portion of the MS. is represented by underscoring the designation.

Accordingly, Root assumes that the sixteen manuscripts were derived from the three exemplars set up ideally in Chaucer's revision stage. His edited text is based on the intermediate γ (Cp) and the final β (J). On the other hand, Windeatt (1990) is closer to the latter view, possibly a third view in between, and is critical of Root's linear and temporally distinct conception of Chaucer's revision, thinking that Chaucer wrote the text with every possible variation in mind. He assumes that Chaucer's revision, if any, was restricted to a short period, and therefore cannot have been on a scale to warrant being called 'revision.'

From the fact that there is found a mixture of the α, γ and β variants in one manuscript, Windeatt is sceptical of the assertion that Chaucer revised the text at distinctly

---

14   See Root (1916: 272).

different stages. He regards the γ (Cp) as the complete text and makes it the basic text in his edition, and the final β (J) as the scribes' revision. Instead of Root's sequential α/γ/β, he adopts Phetc/Cpetc/Retc respectively on the basis of the unmixed types (Ph/Cp/R) of manuscripts. (For detailed information as to how these manuscript traditions emerge in the mixed-type manuscripts, see Windeatt 1990: 68-75.) The textual transmission of the *Troilus* is so complex that Hanna (1996: 129) is moved to say that 'To cope with this particularly fluid context, I would suggest taking seriously the rhetorical ploys I have built into my argument—that approaches such as game theory may approximate the situation of much vernacular book production more fully than more sober notions.'

4.5. Modern editions of *Troilus and Criseyde*

Another type of readers or modern editors show their way of reading the text in their editions. Scribes produced manuscripts based on their exemplars they had to handle without enough collation of variants. Editors, on the other hand, produce editions by collating variants and attempt to reconstruct the text to accord as closely as possible with Chaucer's original. They provide grammatical punctuation marks in their texts of a type which the scribes by and large did not use. Such punctuation as is used by the scribes is elocutionary in function, rather than grammatical. Modern editors give detailed annotations. Those of scribes, such as they are, are fragmentary marginalia. While the scribes assumed a particular type of reader such as the projected owner of the manuscript, modern editors assume a wide readership. Moreover, it goes without saying that modern editors cannot be as sensitive to the connotations of idiomatic expressions as contemporary scribes.

There is not so much diversity in modern editions as in the manuscripts. For example, Windeatt (1990) uses the γ (Cp) tradition, except when he has serious textual problems, and Barney (1987), the received text we use here, consults Cp, Cl, and J, in that order of preference.[15]

4.6. Kinds of readers

We have so far dealt with scribes and editors, but there were and are other kinds of readers. They are various as shown in (4).

---

15 The manuscripts modern editions are based on are as follows. Pollard et al. (1898): The present text is based on J, and has been corrected throughout from readings of α and β types alone. Skeat (1898): a close collation of Cl and Cp, taking Cl as the foundation, but correcting it by Cp, throughout. Root (1952): In conjunction with Cp, it [J] has been used as a basic authority for the present edition. Baugh (1963): basically that of MS Cp, with occasional readings of the Campsall and the St. John's College. Robinson (1957): Cp. β readings have been consistently rejected in this text, which is based throughout on the γ version. Donaldson (1975): He has adhered to Cp. Warrington (1975): Not mentioned. Howard (1976): Not mentioned. Windeatt (1990): Cp. For the lacking parts of Cp, Cl is used. Nakao's note: the J readings are also recognised. Benson (1987): based on Cp. When Cp is rejected or deficient, this edition prints the readings of Cl or J, in that order. Fisher (1989): Campsall with variants from Cp. Shoaf (1989): based on Baugh.

4. Ambiguity in metatext

(4) The kinds of readers (cf. Section 3.1.3)
   a. The writer: the writer as a reader (the writer sees himself objectively and self-critically)
   b. The audience: the courtly audience who listened to Chaucer's narration directly from the author's mouth
   c. The implied reader: the reader assumed to read the text ideally
   d. Scribes: the bridge between the writer and the medieval readers
   e. The owners of the manuscripts: the wealthy people inside and outside the court
   f. Early editors: Caxton, Wynkyn de Worde, Thynne, etc.
   g. Modern editors
   h. The integrator of readings or the shifting apparatus of reading, 'I'

In producing a text, the writer himself *(a)* may have seen his text with some distance and self-criticism, and modified it. Chaucer's modification is seen in his additions from Boethius' *De Consolatione Philosophiae* in *Troilus and Criseyde*, in the F/G versions of the Prologue to *The Legend of Good Women*, the order of *The Canterbury Tales*, etc. The primary (immediate) audience *(b)* who gave a direct response to Chaucer's narration included the king (Richard II), Queen Anne of Bohemia, the court officials, knights, courtly ladies, and writers (at the end of the *Troilus*, Chaucer dedicates it to the moralist Gower and the philosopher Strode). The secondary audience is much wider, including the middle class, and with the increasing production of manuscripts, perhaps some readers in a narrow sense who were able to read them, not an audience who just listened. This is evident from the following passage from *The House of Fame* (652-60):

(5) For when thy labour doon al ys,
   And hast mad alle thy rekenynges,
   In stede of reste and newe thynges
   Thou goost hom to thy hous anoon,
   And, also domb as any stoon,
   Thou sittest at another book
   Tyl fully daswed ys thy look;
   And lyvest thus as an heremyte,
   Although thyn abstynence ys lyte.   HF 652-60
   Cf. BD 49, PF 15-25, Tr 5.1753, 5.1797, LGW F 30

Further, widening his conception of the readership, Chaucer may have taken into consideration those readers who could interpret the text as he himself did, including future readers *(c)*.

We have next scribes bridging the gap between the writer and the medieval readers who are confined to the fifteenth century *(d)*. They are the central readers here and they are the earliest critics of Chaucer's language and literature. Their rewritings include simple errors, paraphrases (changes that produce more limited and easier interpretations), and acts of creative self-assertion. Their editorial activity was also in accordance with the wishes of the owners of the manuscripts *(e)* as mentioned in Section 4.3.[16]

---

16 M.B. Parkes, Cp Ms. 'History' in Parkes and Salter (1978: 11-2): The earliest identifiable person to have handled the manuscript is John Shirley (c. 1366-1456) of London, the literary entrepreneur, lender of books, and gossipy commentator on Chaucer's minor poems .... Since the manuscript passed through the hands of John Shirley the favourite candidate for the identification of the Anne Nevill referred to in the late-fifteenth-century note on fol. 101v is Anne, the

Then we have early editors from the fifteenth century to the sixteenth century *(f)*. The production of a large number of copies of the text different from that of manuscripts incurred a risk of inaccuracy brought about by economic considerations. The text was rewritten in accordance with the taste of the purchasers who wanted them. (They did not assume universal readers, although perhaps they took into account a few representative readers around them.) And insufficient collation of manuscripts was undertaken. We have then modern editors and critics *(g)*. At this point we will deal with the modern editors' choice of words in conjunction with the variations in manuscripts. And finally, we have the integrator of readings, 'I' *(h)*.

4.7. Examination of ambiguity with respect to metatext

As a phenomenon in the double prism structure, we have focused on the processes whereby Criseyde shifts her affections, or to what extent that shift is positively described or to what extent negatively. How we should evaluate this phenomenon is not clear cut, and the reader is called upon to participate in that interpretation. Criseyde is expected to accept her beloved gradually and with some prudence. A courtly lady must exercise delay in accepting a lover, and she must not herself initiate the process. In medieval times Christian morality and courtly idealism would have forbidden explicit descriptions of physical love. In what follows, let us examine what words/phrases scribes or modern editors choose and what not, and how their interpretations differ.

4.7.1. Analysis of Tr 2.636

(6) So lik a man of armes and a knight
He was to seen, fulfilled of heigh prowesse,
For bothe he hadde a body and a myght
To don that thing, as wel as hardynesse;
And ek to seen hym in his gere hym dresse,
So fressh, so yong, so *weldy* semed he,
It was an heven upon hym for to see.   Tr 2.631-7

In Book 1, Pandarus is told by Troilus about his love for Criseyde, and promises to be a go-between for them. In Book 2, he visits Criseyde at her house, and tells her Troilus's love for her. Immediately after this, Troilus makes a triumphal return to Troy, and goes past her house. In the example below, the emphasis is on the shift in her affections and the effect the sight of him has on her. In seeing him in armour, she descries him as 'So fressh, so yong, so weldy ....' For *weldy* we have lexical variants as below.[17]

(7) weldy]worþi GgH3H5JRCxW

---

daughter of Richard Beauchamp, Earl of Warwick, who was Shirley's chief patron.

17 Materials I have used for the sources of variations between manuscripts: Windeatt (1990), Rossetti (1873), Furnivall (1882), Furnivall & Macaulay (1894-1895), Parkes & Salter (1978), Parkes & Beadle (1979), Beadle & Griffiths (1983), microfilms the libraries containing the *Troilus* manuscripts reproduced.

While the α and γ manuscripts adopt *weldy*, the β manuscripts (Gg, H3, H5, J, R) read *worþy*. Further, the printed editions, Cx based on the β manuscripts and W based on Cx, adopt *worthy* (cf. Thynne: *weldy*). Eleven manuscripts have *weldy*, and five have *worþy*, a ratio of more than 2:1. We must assume that *weldy* was a strange word to scribes and likely to go through their filtering. We think this is why *weldy* is rewritten as *worþy*, signifying a typical attribute of a knight. Among modern editors, only Root adopts *worþy*, and this is because he regards the β manuscripts as representing Chaucer's final revisions—the Ausgabe letzter Hand.

It is clear that *weldy* is a relatively rare word.[18] This occurrence (*OED* s.v. wieldy 'capable of easily 'wielding' one's body or limbs') and *unweldy* (CT, MancP IX (H) 55)[19] are the earliest citations in the *OED*. And while *weldy* appears once in Chaucer, *worþy* appears 184 times in his work (see Benson 1993). It should be noted that *unweldy* is used in the Hengwrt manuscript of *The Canterbury Tales*, the oldest and therefore closest to Chaucer's original (see Blake et al. 1994).

Further, there is an implication in *weldy* not mentioned by the *OED*. In the late fourteenth century the verb *weld* develops a sexual implication based on the original sense of 'wield one's limbs or weapons' (*OED* s.v. *wield*), with regard to which see Hanna's (1971) note on 'welde a womman' and Donaldson's comment (Donaldson 1979: 9). This sexual implication is present in the derived adjective *weldy*. Scribes rewriting the text and editors selecting from among their products give different images to the character of Troilus and that of Criseyde in her observation of him. (See Section 12.4 for the ambiguity from the lexical angle.)

4.7.2. Analysis of Tr 2.1274

(8) God woot if he sat on his hors aright,
Or goodly was biseyn, that ilke day!
God woot wher he was lik a manly knyght!
What sholde I drecche, or telle of his aray?
Criseyde, which that alle thise thynges say,
To telle in short, hire liked al in-fere,
His persoun, his aray, his look, his chere,

His goodly manere, and his gentilesse
So wel that nevere, sith that she was born,
Ne hadde she swych routh of his destresse;
And how so she hath hard ben here-byforn,
To God hope I, she hath now kaught a thorn,[20]

---

18 Examples of rare words being modified: Thop VII 917 *worly*: Ch, El, Hg, Ph1 → *worthy*: Ad1, Bo1, Bo2, Cn, Dd, Ds, En1, En3, Ha3, Ha4, Ii, Ln2, Ma, N1, Ox, Ph2, Py, Se, To. MancP 55 *unweldy*: Hg, El → *vnwelde*: Ha4, La; *vnweld* Ld1, Ra2; *vnweldly*: Ma; vn *weldely*: G1; *vnweli*: Ha3; *vnwery*: Gg; *wery*: En3 (Manly & Rickert 1940 (Vol. 8): 147)

19 *OED* s.v. unwieldy: †1. Of persons, the body, etc.: Lacking strength; weak, impotent; feeble, infirm. 1386-1442. This word is quoted in MancP 55 as the earliest instance. It is found in the Hengwrt manuscript. It is natural to think that Chaucer knew the positive form *weldy*.

20 *OED*: s.v. thorn sb. 2. *fig.* (or in *fig.* context): Anything that causes pain, grief, or trouble; in various metaphors, similes and proverbial expressions, as a thorn in the flesh or side, a constant affliction. c1230-. The example of Tr 3.1104 is quoted.

She shal nat pulle it out this nexte wyke.
God sende *mo* swich thornes on to pike!   Tr 2.1261-74

The context of (8) is this. In Book 2, Pandarus tries to persuade Criseyde to direct her love towards Troilus. On his second visit to her house, he consults Troilus and makes the following plan: Pandarus visits her house and will be in the process of persuading her to accept Troilus's love precisely when Troilus is passing that house on his triumphal return to Troy, and she will naturally be captivated by his manly nature and appearance. The narrator observes this moment and comments upon it.

Mo is worthy of note here. What parts of speech belong with this word determine the reader's interpretation of its meaning: this is what determines the nature of the object of the verb *send*. While ten manuscripts have 'God sende mo swich thornes' as in the above, six manuscripts deviate as can be seen in (9).

(9) mo]*general people*: ʒow AGg; mo folkes R
    specific person: mo...on] hir m...o. DS1CxW; hir... mo H5

Thus some authorities prefer a general interpretation, taking *mo* as 'yow' or 'mo folkes,' while others favour a specific interpretation, restricting the recipient to Criseyde with *mo* as 'more thorns.' The verb *send* is expected to take two objects (recipient and patient). When the recipient is interpreted, however, it is likely to be deleted.

(10) Ther god thi makere yet, er that he dye,
     So sende myght to make in som comedye!   Tr 5.1787-8

     Now Jhesu Crist, that of his myght may sende
     Joye after wo, governe us in his grace,   MLT II (B1) 1160-1

     Sendeth othere wise embassadours;   PardT VI (C) 614

When faced with the potential ambiguities of linguistic expressions, scribes were likely to reduce them if they could do so with as little effort as possible. Applied to *mo*, this suggests that that word was in the original, and that they reduced its ambiguity with their minimum effort. R disregards the metrics of the line.

Mo is used as a noun and an adjective, both of which accord with Chaucer's usage. The *MED* quotes the above example as a noun, but there can only be one interpretation.

(11) *mo* n. 2. a) other persons : *CT* G 485, E 1039, D 663, *Tr* 1.613, *Tr* 2.1274
     mo adj. 2. a) more in number, more numerous *Romaunt* 1834

Editors show also embarrassment and confusion regarding *mo*, and determine its meaning each in their own way, as can be seen in (12).

(12) general people (*mo*=noun): Robinson, Windeatt, Howard, Benson (Barney) 'others';
     Donaldson: me ('men')
     specific person (Criseyde) + 'more thorns' (*mo*= adjective): Benson (Barney), Skeat, Warrington, Shoaf ; Donaldson: me ('me')

Barney is indecisive, taking *mo* as 'more' (adjective) primarily, and as 'people' (noun) secondarily. Robinson and Howard support the reading of 'people in general,' but differing from the scribes, are particular as to whom they refer to. Robinson assumes that

Pandarus is the speaker and in the pangs of love appeals to his beloved indirectly. Howard assumes that Chaucer plays the role of an enthusiastic supporter of love in general, putting forward the idea that it was right for courtly society of the late medieval period to accept love as part of *gentilesse*. At turning points in the story the narrator frequently draws the attention of the audience to this (Tr 1.22-9, Tr 3.1222-5, Tr 3.1324-37, Tr 3.1373-93, Tr 5.1835-41).[21]

In the case of a specific reading of *mo*, editors are obliged to paraphrase it. The normal reading is that Criseyde, who stands hesitantly on the threshold of a love affair, should be given more thorns of love. However, in a wider context where the audience has already been given information in Book 1 about Criseyde's coming betrayal of Troilus, the narrator might have suggested that more thorns should be sent to her.

Donaldson (1975) is bold enough to adopt the reading *me*, not found in any manuscript, unless it is a printing error in his edition. Moreover, since e and o are often difficult to distinguish in the scribal versions, it is possible that through a paleographical reconstruction of these two letters Donaldson has decided to understand *e*.[22] From the viewpoint of the collocation between *send* and its object pronoun, 'God send me ...' is repeated in Chaucer, but 'God send mo ...' is the only attested instance. *Me* is either a reduced form of *men* (not found in the Hengwrt manuscript of *The Canterbury Tales*) or the first-person pronoun. If we take *me* as the first-person pronoun, it is possible that the narrator, keeping some distance from love/lovers, is making a joke.[23]

This is a unique example as regards the ambiguity of *mo*, and as far as the author, the first prism, is concerned, the ambiguity may be purely unintended. However, it induces the reader, the second prism, to adopt many points of view, and read into it several meanings.

4.7.3. Analysis of Tr 3.575-93

(13) Nought list myn auctour fully to declare
 What that she thoughte whan he seyde so,
 That Troilus was out of towne yfare,
 As if he seyde therof soth or no;
 But that, *withowten await*, with hym to go,
 She graunted hym, sith he hire that bisoughte,
 And, as his nece, obeyed as hire oughte.

---

21 Although we adopt the reading of people in general, the referent seems to be different according to the male or female points of view. From the male point of view, we have a reading that they wish women to experience more thorns of love. On the other hand, from the female point of view, we have a reading that they have a critical view of men about their love. This is because in nobles of medieval times marriages based on pure love were scarce.
22 See the manuscript of St John's College (34v, l. 21) for this.
23 The narrator parodies his poverty in the experience of love:
  For I, that God of Loves servantz serve,
  Ne dar to Love, for *myn unliklynesse*,
  Preyen for speed, al sholde I therfore sterve,
  So fer am I from his help in derknesse.   Tr 1.15-8

> But natheles, yet gan she hym biseche,
> Although with hym to gon it was no fere,
> For to ben war of goosissh poeples speche,
> That dremen thynges whiche as nevere were,
> And wel avyse hym whom he broughte there;
> And seyde hym, "Em, syn I *moste* on yow triste,
> Loke al be wel, and do now as yow liste."
>
> He swor hire *yis*, by stokkes and by stones,
> And by the goddes that in hevene dwelle,
> Or elles were hym levere, soule and bones,
> With Pluto kyng as depe ben in helle
> As Tantalus—what sholde I more telle? Tr 3.575-93

The context of (13) is this. In the epic time that elapses between the end of Book 2 and the beginning of Book 3, Troilus and Criseyde have their first meeting and he declares his love. In order to strengthen the relation between Troilus and Criseyde, Pandarus tries to make them meet at his house, comes to her house and invites her to his house for supper. She hesitates to accept the invitation because she apprehends that if Troilus is there, it might bring about a scandal. However, she is strongly persuaded into accepting it.

First let us look at Tr 3.579-80. The word order there is based on the γ (Cp) tradition, and is also that found in the α manuscripts. By contrast, the β manuscripts, H4, J, R, S1, as can be seen in (14), transpose 'withouten await' and 'she graunted.'

(14) But that she graunted with hym forto go
 Withoute awayt syn that he hir bisoughte

Along with the change of word-order, *to* in line Tr 3.579 is changed to *forto*, so as to accommodate the metre, and *that* now appears after *syn*. In this position it may either be interpreted as the pronoun object of *bisoughte* or as part of a compound causal conjunction *syn that*. Cx and W have the same word order as the β manuscripts.

Scribes tend to rewrite the original's poetic syntax into a prosaic and more predictable word order (Windeatt 1979: 136). They memorise and write one line after another line as they are read aloud. Lines of ten syllables are more subject to errors than those of eight, and *Troilus and Criseyde* is composed in ten-syllabled rhyme royal stanzas. But here it should be noted that rewriting by the scribes extends over two lines, and this is deliberate on their part because the rhythm also has to be adjusted over two lines. Among modern editors, only Pollard and Root adopt this word order. Root uses the β manuscripts here as we saw in (7).

The position of the adverbial denoting manner 'withowten await' at the beginning of the line seems to make Criseyde's attitude towards Pandarus's invitation more vivid than the usual order.[24] This being the case, the narrator's claim that she acts only out of the sense of duty proper to a niece produces something of an anticlimax.[25] To accept the situation she is involved in by saying that her decision is inevitable is a pattern of behaviour repeated in the story. In accordance with the ideal of a courtly lady, she

---

[24] For details, see the relation between the word order and the information structure of for instance Tr 2.599 in Section 8.5.
[25] For a similar example, see Tr 3.924.

cannot enter into a potential scandal except under considerable pressure. If we were to remove this adverbial phrase from the beginning of the line and place it in its normal position, the subtleties of Criseyde's character might be reduced, but her honour would be preserved.

As regards the *await* in 'withowten await,' the conversion of a verb to a noun is, according to the *OED*, the earliest in Chaucer. The scribes seem to have been baffled by this word and variation of the phrase is as below (see Windeatt 1990).

(15) that with-owten await] þerwith out H2 Ph; þat with owte more H5
withowten] with H1; Without nayeng Cx.

The bolder rewriting is seen in H1, where the *out* in *withowten* is removed, thus producing the opposite meaning, so that Criseyde's prudence rather than her compliance is emphasised.

Next, let us look at the collocation between *most* and *trist on* (Tr 3.587). In Middle English, the first-person singular of the modal *most* has two basic forms: *must/e* and *most/e*. The Cp text has only the latter (incidentally the same is true of the Hengwrt manuscript of CT). Here it is formally impossible to distinguish between the superlative *most/e* and the auxiliary *most/e*. However, using the context we can distinguish them, perhaps with the sole exception of Tr 3.587, which is the odd man out.[26] As we have seen in the case of *mo*, the scribes attempted a minimal rewriting to obviate ambiguity. Windeatt (1990) notes the variants at 587 as follows:

(16) most] moste CpD; mot GgH4 (mote); must H2H5PhRCxTh

Here six out of sixteen manuscripts clearly take *most/e* as a modal (as do the early printed books Cx and Th). These six are restricted to the α and β manuscripts, while the β (J) and the γ manuscripts (AClH1H3S1S2) are ambiguous.

When we find *most/e* in the J and γ manuscripts, in which sense is it to be understood? When Criseyde leaves everything to Pandarus, does she do so because she 'trusts him most' or because 'she must trust him'? The editors cope with the difficulty as follows:

(17) Windeatt: perhaps "must" rather than the adverb "most," as some scribes thought.[27]
Benson (Barney): 'must' is clearly preferable: Criseyde finds it useful to assert her dependency on her uncle.
Robinson: 'trust most'
Baugh: adverb
Root: I take *triste* to be present indicative, and *most* the superlative; but it is possible that Chaucer wrote *moste* (pret. of *moot*) with infinitive *triste*. See variant readings.
Donaldson: 'must'

---

26 Cf. Ye knowe ek how it is youre owen knyght,
 And that *bi right ye moste upon hym triste*,
 And I al prest to fecche hym whan yow liste." Tr 3.915-7
 Scribal variations: A (most), Cl (moste), Cp (moste), Dg (missing), D (most), Gg (muste), H1 (most), H2 (must), H3 (most), H4 (muste), H5 (must), R (must), S1 (must), S2 (moste). The word *moste* here can be interpreted as a modal.
27 Windeatt (1998: 169): He translates *moste* in 'I moste on yow triste' (iii.587) as 'must' rather than the adverb 'moste,' but notes that 'the construction in the original is–perhaps designedly– ambiguous.'

Skeat: *mot* (following Gg. 4. 27)
Fisher: 'must'
Shoaf: 'most'

The interpretations of the editors are divided into two groups.

(18) modal: Windeatt, Benson (Barney), Donaldson, Skeat, Fisher
adverb: Robinson, Baugh, Root, Shoaf

Incidentally, modern translations are as follows:

(19) Coghill (1971): since I trust you best
Stanley-Wrench (1965): since I now trust most of all in you
Tatlock & MacKaye (1912): since I must trust you
Windeatt (1998): since I must trust you
Karita (1949): ichiban shinraishite imasu yueni [since I trust you most]
Miyata (1979): itto goshinraishite rundesu mono [since I trust you most]

Tatlock and MacKaye and Windeatt support a modal and others the superlative of an adverb. Half the instances of *trist/trust* in CT [Hengwrt] and Tr (33 out of 66) collocate with adverbs (CT *wel*: 28/51; Tr *most*: 5/15). Here in the overwhelming number of cases the word order verb-adverb prevails over adverb-verb. But with regard to the superlative *most/e* with various verbs such as *desireth, honouren, labouren, loue, entendeth, wynne, drede, and greueth*, the orders verb-adverb and adverb-verb compete with each other.[28] The collocation of *triste/trust* with adverbs or degree intensifiers is repeated, but the collocation of *triste/trust* with the modal *mot/most* is restricted to Tr 3.587 (an interpretation) and Tr 3.916 among *The Canterbury Tales* and *Troilus and Criseyde* (it collocates with other modals (*wol/may/shal/wolde*) but very rarely). In terms of Chaucer's usage, the word to collocate with *triste/trust* is predictably an adverb.

In the courtly society of the fourteenth century, trust is an important virtue. When someone does someone good, the latter is often assumed to have an absolute trust in the former, as shown in (20).

(20) "But for the love of God, I yow biseche,
As ye ben he that *I loue moost and triste*,
Lat be to me youre fremde manere speche,
And sey to me, youre nece, what yow liste."   Tr 2.246-9 [29]

Taking into account the usual habit of courtly society, an adverbial reading is more

---

28 The number to the right of the oblique stroke '/' indicates the frequency of verbs and the number to the left indicates the frequency of the collocation between the adverb and the verb.
For the word order of verb + *moost* (adv) in *The Canterbury Tales*, we have consulted Blake, et al. (1994).
verb—*moost*: KnT 2767, WBT 895, WBT 932, WBT 959, SqT 444, ShT 172
moost—verb: KnT 2327, KnT 2409, KnT 2410, WBT 879, WBT 981, WBT 1088, FrT 1395, FranT 604
Troilus and Criseyde
verb—*most*: Tr 1.604, Tr 1.720, Tr 1.1019, Tr 2.247, Tr 2.1368, Tr 2.1410, Tr 4.561, Tr 4.597, Tr 4.1621, Tr 5.592, Tr 5.704, Tr 5.1248
most—verb: Tr 2.1150, Tr 3.587, Tr 3.1265, Tr 5.1063, Tr 5.1757

29 Similar examples are: Tr 2.239-45, 2.411-3, 3.366 (Troilus → Pandarus), *Confessio Amantis* 8.1293, 'trawthe' in *Sir Gawain and the Green Knight* 2348.

natural. If her trust in Pandarus is imposed on her (the modal reading suggests this), the courtly relation between Criseyde and Pandarus will be weakened.

But with regard to the example of Tr 3.587, the trustful relationship between Criseyde and Pandarus alone is not enough. A psychological reading rather than a social one is perhaps more appropriate for Criseyde in this situation. Judging from her question whether Troilus is at Pandarus's house (Tr 3.569), it seems to be her most earnest desire to see Troilus. However, because of the potential scandal, she cannot agree to Pandarus's invitation without some compelling reason to do so. Her obligation to trust Pandarus suggests her avoidance of taking responsibility. This is in accord with 'And, as his nece, obeyed as hire oughte' (Tr 3.581). Criseyde chooses to act thus and so leave responsibility to Pandarus. The modal use here is unnatural, but more appropriate for representing her psychology. (For a fuller discussion of this *most* from a philological point of view, see Nakao 2006a; and cf. Chaucer's repeated use of *and* for Criseyde's choices (Pearsall 1986).)

Next, let us look at the main clause Tr 3.588 following the *syn* clause. The following is an expanded full list of variants from Windeatt (1990).

(21) Cp   Loke al be wel and do now as 3ow liste
            A (well), Cl (lyste), D (alle, wele, you), H3 (whel, doo, you, lust), H5 (all, well, ye), S1 (all, list), S2 (Luke, all, wele, <u>and</u> list)
     Gg   Loke al be wel <u>and</u> do ri3t as 3ow lest   [and: abbreviation expanded]
     H1   Look al be wel do now as 3ow liste
     H2   Loke al be wele y do now as ye lyste
     H4   Looke as be weel for I do as you list
            R (wel, y, yow, liste), Cx (wel, yow, lyste), W (Loke, all, well, lyste), Th (Loke, nowe, lyst)
     J   Loke al be wel for I do þ' yow liste
     Ph   Loke al be wele y do now as 3ow liste

In Middle English idiom, *do*, when collocating with the impersonal construction *as yow liste*, tends to be imperative. In the Hengwrt manuscript, five *do*s out of six collocate with an imperative.[30] The constructions in A, Cl, Cp, D, H3, H5, S1, S2, Gg and H1 are the most predictable. By contrast, *do*s in H2, J, R, H4 and Cx are used as a finite verb. The *y* in the sense of 'I' in the H2 is perhaps due to the confusion of *y* with the virgule (/) or the abbreviation of *and* (&).

Loke and *do* in Cp are imperative, and there Criseyde leaves the responsibility for events to Pandarus. On the other hand, the latter half of the β line is 'for I do ...,' which suggests responsibility for her action. This part of the quoted passage is uttered by Criseyde; and given what we know of Criseyde's moral and ethical make-up, the γ readings would seem to reflect Chaucer's intention most faithfully.

---

30   For the collocation between the imperative form of the verb and 'as yow list,' we refer to Blake et al. (1994).

Now *demeth as yow list*, ye that kan,	KnT I (A) 1355
Dooth as yow list: I am here at youre wille.	WBT III (D) 1016
Right *as yow list gouerneth this matere.*'	ClT V (E) 322
Ye ben oure lord: *dooth* with your owene thyng	
Right *as yow list*. Axeth no reed of me.	ClT V (E) 652-3
Dooth as yow list; haue youre biheste in mynde	FranT V (F) 627

In answer to her request quoted above, Pandarus asserts that he will do it. Scribes rewrite his assertion (Tr 3.589), according to Windeatt (1990), in the following way.

(22) 3es] Cp; this GgH5JRTh; DH2H4Ph *om*; rest 3is.

However, even though we have determined the words from the manuscripts, to what he said 'yes' or 'this' still remains uncertain.[31] Here neither scribes nor editors can manifest their readings; and what 'yes' or 'this' refers to depends on the readers, the second prism. We will examine the question of reference in Chapter 8.

4.7.4. Analysis of Tr 5.1240-1

(23) So on a day he leyde hym doun to slepe,
    And so byfel that yn his slep hym thoughte
    That in a forest faste he welk to wepe
    For love of here that hym these peynes wroughte;
    And up and doun as he the forest soughte,
    He mette he saugh a bor with tuskes grete,
    That slepte ayeyn the bryghte sonnes hete.

    And by this bor, faste in *his* armes folde,
    Lay, *kyssyng* ay, his lady bryght, Criseyde.
    For sorwe of which, whan he it gan byholde,
    And for despit, out of his slep he breyde,
    And loude he cride on Pandarus, and seyde:
    "O Pandarus, now know I crop and roote.
    I n'am but ded; ther nys noon other bote.   Tr 5.1233-46

The above depicts the famous scene where Troilus sees what he judges to be evidence of Criseyde's infidelity in a dream. Here (Tr 5.1240-1) we find an instance of the strong activation of the double prism structure. The subject of the double prism structure 'embracing' itself is social and collaborative, and psychologically even dynamic (shifting from negative attitude to positive or vice versa), bringing about ambiguities on the part of the reader as to who is the trigger of the action and who is the triggered. The fact that the above quotation is the narrator's reconstruction of Troilus's dream makes this problem further confusing. We are asked to infer how the narrator grasps Troilus's dream, and then how Troilus himself feels in that dream. The first prism, the writer himself, seems to be involved in such a complexity that his linguistic control of it is likely to be loosened. If this is right, it would be no wonder that the reader is strongly encouraged to challenge the first prism based on his or her assumptions. Therefore the boundary between the two prisms is made imprecise.

Scribal and editorial variations are pointed out by Chickering (1990). Through the double prism structure, I have reinterpreted them with a focus on their psychological background. Scribes and modern editors are divided in the choice of words, as shown in (24).

---

31   See the note by Windeatt (1990: 281).

4. Ambiguity in metatext

(24) Manuscript variations of Tr 5.1240
his: AClH4; *hir*: DGg (*hyre*) I11R (*hyr*) S1S2Th (*her*); omission H2H3PhCx (CpDgH5 lack this line)
Modern editorial variations of Tr 5.1240
his: Robinson, Barney (Benson), Skeat, Baugh, Warrington, Howard (note. The image is of Criseyde held by and kissing the boar); *hir/her*: Root, Donaldson, Fisher, Pollard

Pronouns may go beyond a sentence boundary to a discourse structure as regards the determination of their reference. They were often a cause of errors for scribes, who copied one line after another line of the original text. It often happens that those pronouns are modified after rereading (later scribes were also involved in their modification). However, the lines above are written by scribes without showing any traces of modification. They chose pronouns with confidence, and were still divided in their choice. *His* refers to the boar, *her* to Criseyde, and the ellipsis of *his/her* suggests no concern with who is more active in the process of 'folding' or perhaps it is intended to suggest reciprocity of their action. Modern editors choose either *his* or *her*. No editors adopt ellipsis of pronouns.[32] They fulfill the metrical demands of the line and then consider the problem of who is more active in the 'folding,' the boar or Criseyde.

The act of 'folding' is characterised by reciprocity, and who initiates it cannot easily be determined. Therefore which is original and which is scribes' revision is hard to determine. This applies to kissing. Scribes did not add grammatical punctuation to the lines. Editors restrict their readings by punctuation in regard to who kisses whom. The punctuation of Tr 5.1241 is seen in (25).

(25) a. Windeatt [his]; Donaldson/Fisher (her)
   Lay kissing ay his lady bright, Criseyde
   b. Baugh (his)
   Lay, kissing ay his lady bright, Criseyde
   c. Robinson/Barney (his); Root/Pollard (her)
   Lay, kissing ay, his lady bright, Criseyde

From a structural point of view, we have a locative inversion here (By this bor ... lay ... Criseyde). Regarding (25a), there is no pause between *Lay* and *kissing*, and if we regard *his lady bright* as an inverted subject, the one initiating a kiss is construed as Criseyde. The comma after *his lady bright* indicates the appositive relation to Criseyde. This reading is syntactically supported. Since *the bor* is governed by the preposi-

---

32 About the pronominal ellipsis of a similar construction, see 'hente/streyne/take/folde, etc. ... in [zero pronoun] armes.' Regarding the scribal variation of the construction, we have consulted Windeatt (1990).

And hym in armes took, and gan hym kisse.	Tr 3.182
armes: hire a. A	
He hire in armes faste to hym hente.	Tr 3.1187
armes faste to hym: hise a.t.h.f. H2 Ph	
This Troilus in armes gan hire streyne,	Tr 3.1205
Gg: þus Troylus in his armys streyne hire gan	
Therwith he gan hire faste in armes take,	Tr 3.1359
in: in his Ph	
Took hire in armes two, and kiste hire ofte,	Tr 4.1219
armes: his a. H2 Ph	

tion *by*, it so cannot conceivably be the subject of the 'kiss' verb. Incidentally, we find a caesura before *his lady bright* in the manuscripts H3 and H4, and the editions Cx and W. This suggests the impossibility of *his lady bright* as an object. Regarding (25b), we have a comma between *Lay* and *kissing ay his lady bright*, and there seems to be some distance between the collocation of *Lay* and the inverted subject *Criseyde*. There may be no difference between (25a) and (25b) about the agent of 'kissing.' Here, however, *kissyng ay his lady bright* is highlighted as a unity. Regarding (25c), since there are commas both before and after *kissing ay*, the separation due to the participial construction is reinforced. The reciprocal action of the boar and Criseyde seems to be brought into relief (see Chickering 1990: 103).[33]

Whether Criseyde is active in 'folding'/'kissing' is classified as below.

(26) a: active in both folding and kissing
　　 b: active in folding, but passive in kissing
　　 c: passive in folding, but active in kissing
　　 d: passive in both folding and kissing

(26a), the reading making Criseyde the most active is adopted by Pollard/Donaldson and (26c), the intermediate reading making her passive in 'folding' but active in 'kissing' is adopted by Robinson/Barney/Skeat/Howard. But (26b), the reading making her active in 'folding' but passive in 'kissing,' is not adopted by any editors. Nor is (26d), the reading making her the most passive. Let us now examine the psychology of the scribes and editors vis-à-vis (26a) and (26c). In the case of (26a), Criseyde is active in the action of physical love, which suggests her conscious infidelity. This is a big departure from the ideal of a courtly lady and to that extent a radical reading. On the other hand, (26c), the intermediate reading seems to correspond to Chaucer's original, *Il Filostrato*, as seen in (27).

(27) E poi appresso gli parve vedere
　　 Sotto a' suoi piè Criseida, alla quale
　　 Col grifo il cor traeva, ed al parere
　　 Di lui, Criseida di così gran male
　　 Non si curava, ma quasi piacere
　　 Prendea di ciò che facea l' animale,
　　 Il che a lui sì forte era in dispetto,
　　 Che questo ruppe il sonno deboletto.　　*Il Filostrato* 7.24.1-8

(And then afterwards it seemed to him that he saw beneath its feet Cressida, whose heart it tore forth with its snout. And as it seemed, little cared Cressida for so great a hurt, but almost did she take pleasure in what the beast was doing. This gave him such a fit of rage that it broke off his uneasy slumber. Translation from Griffin and Myrick, modified. (1978))

If Chaucer has taken his lead from the original, this interpretation is natural.[34] And if Chaucer sees the boar's arm as reflecting that of Diomede (the dream is interpreted in

---

33　A similar example is the degree of relatedness between the participial construction 'Retornyng ...' (Tr 5.1023) and its expected main clause.
34　*MED* boar: 1. a) An uncastrated male swine (either wild or domestic) d) *breme as*–, fierce as a wild boar; *brust as a*–, bristly as a boar, bristling (or showing anger) like a boar; *wod as wild*–, raging like a wild boar. 3. A representation of a boar; *her.* a boar in a coat-of-arms. 4. a) Man likened to a wild boar; esp., King Arthur, Edward III.

this way by Cassandre later), it is natural for the bold and aggressive boar to be the one doing the 'folding.' Further, it is best to reveal Criseyde's 'slydynge' (Tr 5.825) character. In that way, the image of her being controlled by the boar/Diomede, and of her normal instincts being aroused follows, naturally, so that she herself gradually becomes active and kisses him back.

Incidentally a reading whereby the boar is active both in 'folding' and 'kissing' (26d) is one which is most sympathetic to Criseyde in that it is best calculated to preserve her honour as a courtly lady. This would have met with the approval of the sympathetic reader. However, because it is too idealistic, it ignores what she really is. In linguistic terms, the relation between the boar (subject) and 'kissyng ay his lady bright' is very weak.[35] Thus the readers' view of Criseyde determines their choice of pronouns/syntax, and their choice of pronouns/syntax informs their view of Criseyde.[36]

---

35 Modern translations of the quotation in question

Tatlock and MacKaye (1912):
As he roamed up and down through the forest, he dreamed he saw a boar with great tuskes lying asleep in the heat of the bright sun, and by this boar, folding it fast in her arms and continually kissing it, lay his bright Criseyde.

Stanley-Wrench (1965):
And by this boar's side, folded in its arm
Lay kissing it, Criseyde, his lady bright,

Coghill (1971):
And close beside it, with her arms enfolding,
And ever kissing it, he saw Criseyde;

Windeatt (1998):
And beside this boar, tightly clasped in his arms and continually kissing, lay his fair lady, Criseyde.

Karita (1949):
shikamo inoshishino katawarani, sonoudeni shikato dakare, kuchizuke shitsutsu jibunno kagayakashii joseino kuriseidega yokotawatteita. (By the boar, folded in its arms, lay kissing his bright lady Criseyde.)

Miyata (1979):
sobaniha sono inoshishino udeni shikkari dakare nagara, utsukushii aijin kuriseidega yokotawatteite, shikirini seppun shiteirunodesu. (By the boar, folded in its arms, lay his beautiful lover Criseyde, ever kissing.)

36 The double syntax regarding *folde* (pp.) and *kissing* may be an instance due to what Renaissance rhetoric calls amphibology. Amphibology in medieval times is generally regarded as a misuse of language, not an artifice of rhetoric. If we can say that the double syntax is positively used, Chaucer may have used it quite unconventionally in his times. Cf. Willock and Walker (1936: 260), *The Arte of English Poesie by George Puttenham*: 'Amphibologia or the Ambiguous.' Then haue ye one other vicious ſpeach with which we will finiſh this Chapter, and is when we ſpeake or write doubtfully and that the ſence may be taken two wayes, ſuch ambiguous termes they call *Amphibologia*, we call it the *ambiguous*, or figure of ſence incertaine, as if one ſhould ſay *Thomas Taler ſaw William Tyler* dronke, it is indifferent to thinke either th'one or th'other dronke. Thus ſaid a gentlman in our vulgar pretily notwithſtanding becauſe he did it not ignorantly, but for the nonce.

Finally, the scribes and modern editors of the second prism are differentiated in their interpretations, and thus ambiguity becomes inevitable.

4.8. Final remarks

Through the double prism structure, we have focused on a particular phenomenon, Criseyde's fluctuating affections, investigated how the first prism (the author) observed and expressed it, and considered how the scribes and modern editors representing the second prism responded to the expression of the first prism, and described how their rewriting or choice of expressive items led to differences in interpretation or ambiguity. While scribes tried to copy Chaucer's original (or a copy of it) as faithfully as possible, they sometimes made simple mistakes that were hard to admit contextually. However, those parts we have dealt with are more or less generally agreed to be correct, and cannot be said to be incorrect with certainty. The variants found there may be said to be due to differences of opinion on the part of the characters, the narrator, and the author in relation to Criseyde's fluctuating affections.

How far Criseyde was actively responsible is a disputed matter, and this led to scribal variations. Faced with rare words, word order influenced by the poetic medium and the psychological nature of the content, they revised them through a process of filtering. They tended to convert these potentially ambiguous expressions to semantically more general or more limited ones to suit their own viewpoints or those of the manuscripts' owners. However, in getting together the scribal variants, we have found that they are sensitive to the possibility of the ambiguous nature of the original text. Significantly enough, they are involved in the production of the *Troilus* text not only as a reader but as a (re)writer of Chaucer's original.

The scribal variation in manuscripts requires another second prism (the editors) to choose one variant or another in the process of textual reconstruction. They chose one and rejected another, and also showed their way of reading through their punctuation. However, in the totality of reading the text, it was found that scribes and editors were limited in interpretation, where the view-shifting reader, 'I,' was required to participate in it. When the text allows for multiple choices, every variant is and is not Chaucer's. Every variant is and is not a fact. Chaucer can be situated midway between a multiplicity of texts.

Even if we have fixed Chaucer's text, it is still open to another text. In Chapter 5, let us see the interaction between Chaucer's text and another text, that is, the interrela-

---

I ſat by may Lady ſoundly ſleeping,
My miſtreſſe lay by me bitterly weeping.

No man can tell by this, whether the miſtreſſe or the man, ſlept or wept: ...

The word *amphibologies* of Tr 4.1406 is quoted as an earliest instance in *OED* 1 'ambiguous discourse.' I am indebted to the late professor David Burnley, who kindly commented on this construction which 'was criticized in medieval times by lawyers striving after unambiguous wording.' For similar examples, see Chapter 11.

tionship between the intertextuality and ambiguity in Chaucer's *Troilus*. The intertextuality there is closely related to how the author, the first prism, observes phenomena and how he expresses them. (The discussion of Chapter 4 is based on Nakao (2011b).)

5. Ambiguity in intertextuality

5.1. Introductory remarks: the double prism structure and intertextuality

The artistic ability of medieval poets was tested by how much they could adjust conventions to newly created contexts and turn them into innovations or inventions. Chaucer did not translate Boccaccio's *Il Filostrato* faithfully, but modified it with various perspectives including the medieval (see Lewis (1932)). There various sources were employed such as courtly romances, allegory, Christian doctrines, philosophy (e.g. *De Consolatione Philosophiae*), mythology, science (rhetoric, astronomy, medicine, etc.), and folklore (e.g. proverbs). The intertextuality here means that a text is not necessarily produced originally from the beginning to the end, but that it is produced by amplifying, or deleting, or modifying already existent texts, in other words, through the interaction of different texts.[37] This intertextuality was inevitable in Chaucer's times where adaptation was a prevailing method of literary production. If the reader views a text in terms of intertextuality, he or she can be sensitive to both the surface text in question and those underneath which might have affected it. Accordingly, intertextual texts can be said to be existent between the surface text and the reader. In terms of the double prism structure, the reader is asked to discover or assume sources which might have influenced the text, grasp how the author, the first prism, revised them, and bring into focus the hidden layers of meaning behind the text.[38] In *Troilus and Criseyde* we find that intertextuality is operative in many ways such as in the theme, motif, and various ways of expression.

Troilus and Criseyde inherits courtly love principles, and there focuses on the clandestine love between Troilus, a bachelor knight and Criseyde, a widow still in mourning. In terms of the double prism structure, we can assume that when the first prism Chaucer apprehended that the content of the narration and dialogue might offend the social requirements of his times, he was obliged to express it with some equivocation allowing the readers, the second prism, two or three interpretations. One of the methods of equivocation here is intertextuality. The medievalisation of *Il Filostrato* pointed by Lewis (1932) can be reinterpreted in such a way that it is not simply to provide *Troilus and Criseyde* with medieval ways of thinking but to set up one layer of

---

37 Beaugrande and Dressler (1981: 10-11): The seventh standard of textuality is to be called INTERTEXTUALITY and concerns the factors which make the utilization of one text dependent upon knowledge of one or more previously encountered texts. ... Intertextuality is, in a general fashion, responsible for the evolution of TEXT TYPES as classes of texts with typical patterns of characteristics. Within a particular type, reliance on intertextuality may be more or less prominent. In types like parodies, critical reviews, rebuttals, or reports, the text producer must consult the prior text continuity, and text receivers will usually need some familiarity with the latter.... We have now glanced at all seven standards of textuality: cohesion, coherence, intentionality, acceptability, informativity, situationality, and intertextuality.
38 According to Toyama (1964), intertextuality is contributory to the creation of the multi-layered texts of the primary and secondary forces based on the superimposition of the sources on the text being dealt with.

meaning among several others in the text. This is to emphasise the surface moral meaning of the expression based on the authoritative text and conceal the morally problematic emotional meaning behind it. But the expression is not completely authoritative, but susceptible of some transformation (addition, deletion, revision). If the reader observes the text on a higher place through the interaction with another, the validity of the surface text is likely to be open to scepticism and the implication of the deeper text is likely to come to the surface in the form of irony and parody. The ambiguity discussed in this chapter is likely to be produced through the subtle interaction between the surface text and the deeper text.

The language describing a courtly love is endowed with intertextual features from the outset. The religion of love attributed to courtly love favours the language of the religious register. But the content of the expression continues to be concerned with human emotion or desire. The expression here tends to allow for the double semantic structure in accordance with the reader's assumption as to whether the author is oriented toward the sacred/authoritative or the secular/experiential.

This chapter sets out primarily to make clear the viewpoint of intertextuality in its relevance to the question of ambiguity. Our exemplification is restricted to courtly language. Detailed analyses of intertextuality will be dealt with as part of overlapped cases in discussing other types of ambiguity.

5.2. Intertextuality in courtly language and the problem of ambiguity: a few examples

Pandarus hears from Troilus that he is in love with Criseyde. Pandarus comes to her and tells her about his love. He persuades her to accept it. He later works as a bridge between the two. He plans to create an opportunity for them to meet together at his house. This is the context of (1). On the very day that he knows a storm will occur, Criseyde is invited to his house for dinner. She is forced to stay there because of the storm. Troilus, waiting for her at the house, is invited to the bedroom. She at last accepts him although with much hesitation. The quotation below focuses on how her heart softens despite her great anxiety, some time after which they consummate their love.

(1) This accident so *pitous* was to here,
 And ek so like a sooth at prime face,
 And Troilus hire knyght to hir so deere,
 His *prive* comyng, and the *siker place*,
 That though that she did hym as thanne a *grace*,
 Considered alle thynges as they stoode,
 No wonder is, syn she did al for *goode*.　　　Tr 3.918-24

This part is Chaucer's addition to *Il Filostrato*. The narrator considers the courtly lady's stance, and tries to justify her accepting Troilus. (Cf. Chapter 7 in relation to reported speech.) For this justification an intertextual source is used. Gordon (1970) focuses on the parts added by Chaucer at turning points in the story, and notes that the surface text there contributes to the reason while the deeper text there contributes to the emotion, and thus points out the rise of 'ironical ambiguity.' This ambiguity is categorised as ambiguity due to intertextuality. According to Gordon, (1) above is one of the most psychological places in *Troilus and Criseyde*. Here, in conjunction with the category of ambiguity III (syntax, word and voice), let us examine how and why ambiguity due to intertextuality is likely to rise.

Chaucer focuses not on the result of Criseyde's betrayal but on its psychological process or on how and why she is susceptible to it. How she retains the idealistic image of a courtly lady and at the same time accepts Troilus's love is the central issue here. She seems to reconstruct the process of her decision to accept his love in a rational manner on the basis of the concept of the religious allegory of medieval times. In a mundane and physical matter is hidden a divine and spiritual consideration. A religious text or one embodying courtly idealism is introduced to justify her action above. The intertextual structure brings about the subtle tension between the truth of the phenomenon and its expression.

The word *pitous* (*OED* s.v. piteous B. †1. Full of piety; pious, godly, devout c1305-1570; 2. Full of pity c1350-) in (1) is rich in Christian implications, suggesting to the reader, the second prism, the deep love of Christ who is crucified bearing all the sins of the world and for the sake of frail humanity, and the compassion of His Holy Mother Mary.[39] This idea is also typical of courtly idealism, suggesting the process whereby the dream poet goes through the tension between Pite and Daunger, and at length comes to be accepted by Pite in *The Romaunt of the Rose* (*Le Roman de la Rose*). These allegorical characters are introduced in *Troilus and Criseyde* to exhibit her psychological realities in accepting his love. This *pite* is attributed to the *gentil man*, an image contrasted with that of tyrant, which is in accord with courtly idealism. See Burnley (1979). The *prive* (cf. *OED* s.v. privity †1.a. A divine or heavenly mystery a1225-1470) concerns divine mysticism, that is, divine depth or polyvalence in religious terms.[40]. The *grace* (*OED* s.v. grace 11. a. The free and unmerited favour of God as manifested in the salvation of sinners and the bestowings of blessings a1225—) implies divine God's favour or Mary's, and thus is useful to excuse Criseyde's personal favour to Troilus.[41] *Goode* describes a virtuous action derived from grace (cf. I Pars. 450-5, 455-60, 465-70). In terms of her state of mind, her acceptance of Troilus in bed is made possible only through her perceiving it as virtuous.

However, the reader knows about Pandarus's plan, and anticipates what happens next. It is possible that she has come to his house in the expectation that Troilus is there. (In relation to the speaker's intention, see Chapter 9.) The reader's interpretation of the above words only in relation to the authoritative aspect of the surface text is not sufficient. His or her interpretation of them in relation to the empirical aspect of the deeper text, that is, Criseyde's individuality is worth pursuing. The *pite* under discussion leads to the acceptance by the mourning Criseyde of the knight bachelor Troilus

---

39 For religious implications of *pite*, see Section 12.5. For the religious gap between the ideals striven after by characters and their actual behaviour in romances, see Fewster (1987) and Green (1979).

40 Brown (1952: 106):
This World fares as a Fantasy—Whar-to wilne we forte knowe þe poyntes of Godes priuete? 85-6. Cf. MilT I (A) 3164, 3454: Goddes privitee.

41 Cf. ParsT: X (I) 115-20, 250-5, 340-5, 485-90, 810-5, 1005-10.

into her bed. Divine mysticism leads to secrecy due to adultery in courtly love. There are some problems here: whatever immoral actions they do ('His prive comyng, and the siker place'), there are no shames unless known to other people. However "privy and secure" the event, it remains a sin; God sees if no-one else does. The *grace* Criseyde gives to Troilus here is a secular based hidden event. The rhyming echo of *place-grace* contributes to highlighting the sexual implications. (See ambiguity in voice in Chapter 13.) Ross (1972) perceives *grace* as 'grass,' and Smith (1992) understands *syn* as 'sin,' and *good* as 'God' in appreciating paronomasia.[42] We have various kinds of coded meanings here: *grace* stands for 'private parts,' and *sin* stands for 'sin' she did for her goodness in accepting Troilus (in conjunction with syntactic ambiguity), and 'sin' she did for 'God' (interpreted as ironical unless god is Cupid). Incidentally, *syn* is rewritten as *for* in the manuscripts Gg, H2, H5, and Ph, according to Windeatt (1990). These manuscripts hinder the semantic chiming between 'since' and 'sin.'

If we see Criseyde's action (phenomenon) pragmatically, it comes close to the fabliau genre such as the MilT and the MerT. As regards the MilT, Alisoun, the young wife of an old carpenter, has an affair with Nicholas, an Oxford student boarding at his house (*privetee* MilT I (A) 3454, 3493, 3558, 3603, 3623). As regards the MerT, May, the young wife of Januarie, an old knight, has an affair with Damyan, his squire. The linguistic expression in (2) quoted from the MerT is significant in that it is similar to that in (1) above.

(2) This *gentil* May, fulfilled of *pitee*,
Right of hire hand a lettre made she,
In which she graunteth hym hire verray *grace*.
Ther lakketh noght oonly but day and *place*
Wher that she myghte unto his lust suffise,
...
She taketh hym by the hand and harde hym twiste
So *secrely* that no wight of it wiste,   MerT IV (E) 1995-2006

This passage is written in courtly language and attempts at moralisation of May's action of accepting Damyan's desire (*gentil, pitee, grace*), but the real status of the action is sexually oriented ('unto his lust suffise'), and also self-centered ('So secrely that no wight of it wiste').

The expression of (1) is, as far as the surface goes, functional in making Criseyde's action appropriate for an ideal courtly lady based on the text suitable for religious or courtly idealism. On the other hand, the actual scene is close to the fabliau scene as in the MilT and the MerT and suggestive of the realistic feelings of Criseyde behind her reasonable posture. With the religious text as a subsidiary text in between the *Troilus* text and the reader, he or she is encouraged to think of the moralisation of her action. On the other hand, with the fabliau text as a subsidiary text, he or she is encouraged to think of the realism of it. When readers are divided in their interpretation, ambiguity is like to be inevitable.

---

42   For the causality of *syn*, see Section 8.3.

Ambiguity due to the courtly language is seen in the use of the word *love*.[43] The hymn of love dedicated to Venus by the narrator in the prologue of Book 3 is attributed to Troilo who consummated his love with Criseida in *Il Filostrato* (3.74-9). On the other hand, Troilus's hymn of love is replaced by that of the Philosophy in *De Consolatione Philosophiae* (2.m.8) from which Troilo's is derived. *Love* appears both in the narrator's dedication of love to Venus and Troilus's hymn of love, as shown in (3) and (4).

(3) In hevene and helle, in erthe and salte see
Is felt thi myght, if that I wel descerne,
As man, brid, best, fissh, herbe, and grene tree
Thee fele in tymes with vapour eterne.
God *loveth*, and to *love* wol nought werne,
And in this world no lyves creature
Withouten *love* is worth, or may endure.

Ye Joves first to thilke effectes glade,
Thorugh which that thynges lyven alle and be,
Comeveden, and *amorous* him made
On mortal thyng, and as yow list, ay ye   Tr 3.8-18

(4) "*Love*, that of erthe and se hath governaunce,
Love, that his hestes hath in hevene hye,
Love, that with an holsom alliaunce
Halt peples joyned, as hym lest hem gye,
Love, that knetteth lawe of compaignie,
And couples doth in vertu for to dwelle,
Bynd this acord, that I have told and telle.

"That, that the world with feith which that is stable
Diverseth so his stowndes concordynge,
That elementz that ben so discordable
Holden a bond perpetuely durynge,
That Phebus mote his rosy day forth brynge,
And that the mone hath lordshipe over the nyghtes:
Al this doth *Love*, ay heried be his myghtes!—   Tr 3.1744-57

(3) and (4) do not refer explicitly to the pagan deities, Venus and Cupid. They make universal reference to love as in 'God loveth, and to love wol nought werne' and 'Love, ..., Love, ...' The expression 'God loveth' is based on the original '... ti senton ... / E gli uomini e gli dei' (Fil. 3.75.6-7) (... feel thee... and men and gods). 'Withouten love is worth ...' is based on the original 'ne creatura / Senza di te nel mondo vale o dura' (Fil. 3.75.8) (nor hath creature in the world without thee strength or endurance). From an intertextual point of view, Venus as transformed through a Christian perspective may be construed as representing universal divine love which transcends the purely sexual or reproductive love to be found in pagan mythologies.

Troilus's love for Criseyde moves from the microworld (human world) to the macrocosmic world when reaching its ultimate stage in (4). Given a hint about the further development of Troilus's love for Criseyde in (3), and perceiving the elation of

---

43   For detailed discussion of the ambiguity of *love*, see Nakao (2003).

Troilus's love at the ultimate stage in (4), the reader is likely to set up religious or philosophical texts behind the text of *Troilus and Criseyde* as subsidiary texts.

However, the universal love as manifested in (3) is immediately after explained as sexual love 'amorous him made / On mortal thing.' If this latter sexual love is retroactively related to the former universal love, these two are likely to be in conflict with each other. The reader is encouraged to reinterpret the universal love. Here we can perceive a technique of anticlimax as is frequent in the General Prologue to *The Canterbury Tales*, where the narrator praises the characters' attributes and cancels them some time later.[44] (4) reveals Chaucer's further emphasis of cosmic love, the reinforcement of philosophical implications in love in comparison with *Il Filostrato*. But he modifies the order of elements which Love governs in his application of Philosophy's speech in Boethius to that of Troilus. As regards Philosophy, the order is from the macrocosmic perspective to the microcosmic, whereas the order in Troilus's perception is from the microcosmic perspective to the macrocosmic, and again from the microcosmic perspective. The order of elements is shown in (5).

(5) Troilus   Philosophy
     microcosmic Tr 3.1744-50   macrocosmic Bo 2.m.8.1-21 (*Boece*)
     macrocosmic Tr 3.1751-64   microcosmic Bo 2.m.8.21-7 (*Boece*)
     microcosmic Tr 3.1765-71 (Chaucer's addition)

If this order implies the order of Troilus's perception, it will be found that although his vision of love comes close to the macrocosmic level, its emphasis is on his microcosm, reverting the vision of Philosophy. As far as the surface text goes, the reader is encouraged to regard Troilus's concept of love as in a philosophical perspective, but with the Philosophy's vision of love as a subsidiary text in mind, he or she is likely to be sensitive to the emotional status of Troilus's love.[45] Let us see more details of the two texts. Philosophy's 'This love halt togidres peples joyned with an holy boond, and knytteth sacrement of mariages of chaste loves; and love enditeth lawes to trewe felawes' becomes Troilus's 'Love, that with an holsom alliaunce / Halt peples joyned, as hym lest hem gye, / Love, that couples doth in vertu for to dwelle, / Bynd this acord, that I have told and telle.' In Troilus those parts referring clearly to Christian love and/or sacrament of marriage are reduced. Although the concept of his love is extended in a philosophical perspective, this revision is made in accord with the principles of courtly love (e.g. the code of adultery). Philosophy describes the above in the indicative mood (*'love halt ...'*) while Troilus prays for his personal accord in the subjunctive (optative) (*bynd this acord*). Troilus's inclination towards his microcosmic love can only be made clear in relation to Boethius's original.[46]

---

44 See Section 8.4 (the repetition of lexical items and their shifting contexts).
45 Cf. Ueno (1972) brings about the conflict between reason and emotion experienced by the characters in *Troilus and Criseyde*.
46 Gordon (1970) does not observe this from the order of the speaker's recognition. Furthermore, *Troilus and Criseyde* develops according to the framework of tragedy (beginning, development, climax, denouement, conclusion). Compared with the philosophical framework of *De Consolatione Philosophiae* (Boethius in great agony, his development of human awareness, attainment of the philosophical plane), we find that the framework of *Troilus and Criseyde* is completely reversed.

The word *love* has both religious and sexual meanings, while *charite* is restricted to religious love, and *amor(ous)* to sexual love. The polysemy of *love* is comparatively more contributory to the rise of ambiguity than *charite* and *amor(ous)*.[47]

Focusing on some features of courtly language, we have discussed how the second prism readers assume subsidiary texts in conjunction with the text of *Troilus and Criseyde* (such as *Il Filostrato*, religious texts, philosophical texts, and fabliau texts), and can be sensitive to the author, the first prism's revision (addition, deletions, modification, etc.), and are likely to be divided in interpretation as to whether the surface meaning or the deeper meaning is the more relevant.

5.3. Final remarks

Reading *Troilus and Criseyde* in parallel with those texts assumed to have been involved with the production of it, the second prism readers can be acutely aware of the author, the first prism's addition, deletion, modification, etc. There the interaction between the *Troilus* text and others is inevitable. According to which perspective the reader emphasises, the religious authority/courtly idealism or the personally oriented experience, he or she is likely to interpret given passages as for instance of courtly language in a different way. This leads to ambiguity. Courtly language is composed of a subtle balance of heterogeneous texts. Here the double prism structure is triggered a great deal. Intertextuality is frequently in collaboration with other types of ambiguity. We will come back to intertextual texts in later discussion.

In Chapter 6 we will concentrate on the *Troilus* text and describe through the double prism structure ambiguity due to its macro-structure (the theme, characterization, plot of the text in contradistinction to its micro-structure such as word and sentence).

---

47   Similar examples: 'blisse in hevene' (Tr 3.704, Tr 3.1322, Tr 3.1599, Tr 3.1657). Pandarus prepares for Troilus's secret meeting with Criseyde. When he is about to implement it, he tells Troilus to be ready: 'And seyde, "Make the redy right anon, / For thow shal into hevene blisse wende."' (Tr 3.703-4). However, when Troilus ascends to the eighth heaven after his death, he regards worldly joy as total vanity in comparison with heavenly bliss: ... 'and held al vanite / To respect of the pleyn felicite / That is in hevene above ... (Tr 5.1817-9). The same kind of phrase is repeated in medieval lyrics: Brown (1952): 10 An Autumn Song (8, 29); 11 A Song of the Five Joys (60; 131); An Acrostic of the Angelic Salutation (42-43, 119-20). Similarly see ParsT (X (I) 790-5, 805-10, 830-5, 1075-80) and 'blisse' (PF 72, 77), and 'comune profit' (PF 47, 75).

6. Ambiguity in macro-textual structure

6.1. Introductory remarks: the double prism structure and macro-textual structure

The macro-structural elements of the text, theme, characterisation, and plot are most sensitive to the phenomenon, the speaker's point of view, and the expression of the double prism structure. What to do, who does it, and how he or she does it are the central concern here. Ambiguity is reduced when the reader has a fixed grasping, but when he or she has alternative interpretations, ambiguity is the result. *Troilus and Criseyde* seems to have many elements to be attributed to the latter case. There will be no disagreement about the theme of the *Troilus* being love. However, what kind of love is open to question. Whether the attitudes of the narrator and the characters are in tune with the demands of contemporary society is open to question. Moreover, the attitudes of the characters are closely related to their behaviour. When different types of behaviour are juxtaposed, doubt arises in the mind of readers as to which they should emphasise.[48]

6.2. Ambiguity in theme

Troilus and Criseyde is undoubtedly a story of the love between Troilus and Criseyde. The two are often involved in difficulties in achieving and retaining their love. How they cope with those difficulties is the basis of the story. Love is an all-pervading theme of the story, not just a motif.

As Masui (1977) says, Chaucer explores this love from his earliest works to those of his middle period. *The Book of the Duchess* deals with the knight's love for his wife, who died of the plague, his deep sorrow, and the way in which he is condoled by confession. *The House of Fame* is a journey in search of 'love-tydynges' (HF 3.2143). *The Parliament of Fowles* is worthy of attention in that it deals with the multivalence of love and was written immediately before *Troilus and Criseyde*. In this story three types of love are illustrated in rows one by one: first, the absolute love due to Christian God, 'hevene blisse' (PF 72) and 'commune profit' (PF 47); second, the unproductive courtly love induced by the goddess Venus; third and last, the ordinary and productive love brought about by Mother Nature. These types of love are in a state of mutual tension which varies according to the emphasis placed upon them by the individual reader.[49]

Significantly enough, courtly love is situated on an axis between Christian love and natural (sexual) love, and it is subject to the pressures and tensions from either

---

[48] Jakobson (1985: 111) states that poets of Romanticism and Symbolism obey the inference of similarity, whereas the Realists obey contiguity. See Note 5 in Chapter 2. From a stylistic point of view, Barthes (1971: 6) states that style is effective for the explication of a story narrated by a metonymy.

[49] Clemen (1963) examines the value of love in PF and how it is made relative according to which view we regard as primary or secondary.

type. To use a slightly different image, *Troilus and Criseyde*, being a medieval yet also universally human drama, evolves with courtly love as a pivot between the other two types. Depending on the inferences made by the reader, the varieties of love may be seen to be arranged in rows with mutual criticism.

The three loves in *The Parliament of Fowles* are horizontally arranged with an allegorically clearcut boundary, but in *Troilus and Criseyde* they are vertically condensed within a particular character with an implicit boundary. The love between Troilus and Criseyde is dogged by social and moral instability from the outset. The basic elements of the plot have the seeds of tragedy within them: a prince of Troy forming an attachment with a widow still in mourning, herself the daughter of a soothsayer who had foretold the fall of Troy and then defected to the Greek.

Their love is developed, according to the codes of courtly love, and does not end in marriage. This situation is presented as being in defiance of contemporary social morality. Courtly love is intermediate in such a way that it is construed as authoritative compared with human, sexual love, while compared with Christian love it is degraded to merely secular love. However, if we assume that natural love is latent behind courtly love and unavoidable due to human nature, the authoritative aspect of courtly love and Christian love will be regarded as the exaggeration of language ('encresse ... my langage' Tr 3.1335-6). The narrator comments on the validity of the expression with reference to love, as in (1).

(1) And if that ich, at Loves reverence,
    Have any word in eched for the beste,
    Doth therwithal right as youreselven leste.

    For myne wordes, heere and every part,
    I speke hem alle under correccioun
    Of yow that felyng han in loves art,
    And putte it al in youre discrecioun
    To *encresse or maken dymynucioun*
    Of my langage, and that I yow biseche.
    But now to purpos of my rather speche.   Tr 3.1328-37

How to value the expression of love, that is, inflate (*encresse*) or deflate (*maken dymynucioun*), depends on the reader, the second prism. As we have discussed in Chapters 4 and 5, the value of love is likely to shift according to which type of love the reader emphasises.

The love of Troilus and Criseyde begins with Natural love by contrast with *The Parliament of Fowles*, achieves higher status by association with the courtly love aspect and consequently nearly reaches the religious plane in love, but finally ends in an unproductive catastrophe. And after the story is told, judgement is passed on about the love between Troilus and Criseyde in authoritative Christian terms.

Troilus's love begins when he sees Criseyde.[50] His love begins thus in a physical way ('His eye percede, and so depe it wente' Tr 1.272). Immediately before this, the narrator compares the proud Troilus' being hit by the love for her to Bayard's recogni-

---

50 Regarding the function of the characters' sense of sight and the knowledge they acquire through it, see Nakao (2001b).

tion of a horse's law,[51] and relates his love to the binding force of love and 'the lawe of kinde' as seen in (2).

(2) For evere it was, and evere it shal byfalle,
That Love is he that alle thing may *bynde*,
For may no man fordon *the lawe of kynde*.　　Tr 1.236-8

The binding force of love is, as shown in Chapter 5, reveals the Boethian philosophy of love. The 'lawe of kinde' means, according to the *OED*, 'Nature in general, or in the abstract, regarded as the established order or regular course of things (*rerum natura*) Freq. in phr. *law* or *course of kind*. c888....' The *MED* defines it as 'Man's innate or instinctive moral feeling' and quotes the above example.[52] The law of kind shows the power potentialised in human nature, such as physical (generative) power, generous feelings, and moral feelings like faithful love (Section 12.2.4). This phrase refers to the animal feeling of Troilus in relation to Bayard, however in relation to Boethian love, it refers to the bondage of love to be developed later in the story. Courtly love reinterprets sexual love in terms of philosophical/religious love. Therefore, it is situated midway between the two extremes of love.[53]

Natural/sexual love is also shown to affect a courtly lady, Criseyde. Pandarus tells her that Troilus is in love with her, and suggests that she accept him. About this time, she sees that he comes back to Troy triumphantly. Her heart moves quickly, and this is how her love for Troilus starts. The horse he rides on is a 'baye steede' (Tr 2.624), and her visual response to his knightly posture (*seen* Tr 2.632, *seen* Tr 2.635, *semed* Tr 2.636, *see* Tr 2.637, *syghte* Tr 2.702) is repeatedly emphasised. The knightly posture of Troilus coming back to Troy, which she saw for the second time, is depicted in (3).

(3) Criseyde, which that alle thise thynges say,
To telle in short, hire liked in al in-fere,
His persoun, his aray, his look, his chere,

His goodly manere, and his gentilesse,　　Tr 2.1265-8

The passage is entirely indicative of what captured her eyes, perhaps with the exception of *gentilesse*. (Regarding the semantic transformation of *gentilesse* in a visual perspective, see Section 7.2.) Not only the love of Troilus but also that of Criseyde is related to *bayard* (horse) and the sense of sight. This seems to make their future cogni-

---

51　This expression is taken from the colour of a bay horse. *Bay* means 'reddish brown' so most of them are typical of horses. It implies pride (Benson 1987: 1027) with an implication of blindness. In Catholic theology it is regarded as most heinous because all the other six sins flow from it. See Hiscoe (1983: 143).

52　The word *kynde* is frequently used in *Piers the Ploughman*. It is used with a positive value as in *Kynde wyt* 'reason,' while it has a negative value as in *course of kynde* (Passus 3.56) 'impulse.' Cf. Zeeman (1999).

53　In the MerT the young wife May takes advantage of the blindness of her old husband Januarie, and commits adultery with his squire Damyan. At the very moment of her union with him, Januarie is cured of his blindness by Pluto, the god of Underworld. Although May is blamed by him for that action, she manages to excuse herself thanks to Proserpina, wife of Pluto, by saying that 'I was so kynde' (I behaved so kindly as to cure him of his blindness) (MerT IV (E) 2389). May's use of *kynde* has an ethical sense in relation to Januarie. On the other hand, it has the implication of sexual desire in relation to Damyan. For further details, see Section 12.2.4.

tion problematic. It is as if ironically their love, based on physical sight, leads to spiritual blindness. Even when their love is ennobled, and expressed in moral terms, the law of kind is functional as a layer of meaning behind it.[54]

Courtly love is a refinement of love as represented in appearance, behaviour, emotion or psychology, moral, personality, etc. The four codes of courtly love mentioned by Lewis (1936) are well-known: humility, courtesy, adultery, and religion of love. *Troilus and Criseyde* is illustrative of this. The code of humility is manifested in Troilus's attitude as a servant towards Criseyde. The code of courtesy is typically shown in Troilus's and Criseyde's polite behaviour (*gentilesse*). The code of illicit love is demonstrated in the secret love between a prince of Trojan court, Troilus and a widow, Criseyde. The code of the religion of love is seen where sexual love is elated to the religious or philosophical plane.

However, the courtly love presented here is not necessarily that of pure courtly idealism. Many descriptions of it are susceptible to the law of kind (sexual desires). We have already dealt with Troilus's hymn to love (Tr 3.1744-57) in terms of intertextuality. Let us now examine it in a wider context. From his diction, he seems to have attained a philosophical plane of love. However, his love here continues to be physical in nature, following Pandarus's machinations—the supper invitation, and the storm. Thus their love is consummated in secret. Universal religious and philosophical concepts are fragmented by the individuals' minds.

The virtues of courtly love are used as strategies for justifying the characters' actions when these are assumed to be deviant from their required morals. As is detailed in later chapters, virtues such as *pite*, *gentilesse*, and *frendshipe* derive from the circumstances of the individual (self-defence, self-excuse, intention) (see Chapter 12). Diomede is the most obvious case in that while his language is courtly directed towards Criseyde (Tr 5.120-75), his motivation in using it is for his benefit (Tr 5.92-105). His actions have nothing to do with courtly virtues such as humbleness, courtesy, and the religion of love.

Purely Christian love is introduced in the epilogue of Book 5 with a palinodic effect. Troilus ascends to Heaven, the eighth sphere, after his death, and seeing the earth from there, regards worldly happiness as 'al vanite' (Tr 5.1817), and 'The blynde lust, the which that may nat laste' (Tr 5.1824). People are required to love Christ as seen in (4).

(4) And *loveth hym* the which that right for love
    Upon a crois, oure soules for to beye,
    First starf, and roos, and sit in hevene above;   Tr 5.1842-4

---

54 The *Manciple's Tale* is the penultimate of *The Canterbury Tales*. Although it is not well organized in terms of theme, Chaucer at his final creative stage seems to have got together and condensed important ideas which have attracted his attention in this tale. Those ideas are 'nature,' 'gentilesse,' the correspondence between 'word and dede,' the juxtaposition of 'game and ernest,' etc. The lines below illustrate this.
    But God it woot, ther may no man embrace
    As to destreyne a thyng which that *nature*
    Hath natureelly set in a creature.   MancT IX (H) 160-2.

If I am allowed to use the hierarchy of vision, no other visions can be higher than the divine one above. If we look back on the love between Troilus and Criseyde on earth, we will see that that was devoted to unstable things, and therefore cancelled out. In allegorical terms, it represents *cupiditas* or sinful Lust.

Thus the reader is likely to focus on different aspects of love according to which criterion of the first prism he or she assumes. When we make much of natural law, we find that courtly love is open to sexual feelings. By contrast, when we make much of courtly love, natural love is regarded as excessively secular and to be hidden. However, if we regard it in relation to Christian love, it will be found sinful. So far as physical things are the object of the characters' love, they are not worth loving since they vary.[55] The value of love is likely to decline according to the criteria the second prism places on natural love, courtly love and Christian love and thus ambiguity occurs.

Incidentally, if we set up *The Knight's Tale*, a romance of courtly love, at a higher place, and look down as it were from *The Knight's Tale* on to *The Miller's Tale*, a love of fabliau, love in the latter will seem devalued as being a parody of the former. On the other hand, if we follow the opposite procedure, the love in each will seem on a par, since although *The Knight's Tale* is imbued with courtly idealism, the love depicted is superficial. It is love at first sight and eventually leads to the destruction of the friendship between Palamon and Arcite. The intertextuality here will bring about a dual truth (or laughter). The polyvalence of love, observed within one story like *Troilus and Criseyde*, is observed across the two stories in *The Canterbury Tales*.

6.3. Ambiguity in characters

6.3.1. The first-person narrator

Troilus and Criseyde is, as with Chaucer's other works, a narrative of the first-person narrator. The first-person narrator was obligatory since stories were primarily narrated immediately to the audience in Chaucer's times. However, the narrator's subjectivity was not so much conspicuous there as in modern autobiographical novels with a first-person narrator. Most medieval works are anonymous, which suggests that the narrator's point of view is generalised, shared with the audience. Medieval homilies and romances pay more attention to what people ought to do than to what they really are. Therefore, the narrator's omniscient point of view is more prominent there than his personal point of view. However, this is not the case in *Troilus and Criseyde*. Departing from the general tendency in medieval works, it sets up two kinds of narrator: one is the narrator who observes events in the story from an omniscient point of view; the other is the narrator who observes events from the personal point of view of particular

---

55 Chaucer studied laws at the Temple Inn when he was young. It is thought that he had a training to seek for as many observations as possible of a particular case. As for the case of Criseyde's betrayal, he tries to defend her with as much evidence as possible as if he were a defendant for her. Or he makes such a performance. The question of this observation is central to the movements of the first and second prisms. Cf. Howard (1987: 77): Every story, seen as a "case," has a possible intellectual significance apart from its relation to "the facts."

characters. This recalls the narrator's way of narrating the story with an individualistic point of view in *The Canterbury Tales*. The narrator's omniscient view is seen in the description of the facts and historical events in the story (Calkas's betrayal of Troy and his escape from it, the exchange of Criseyde for prisoners, the death of Hector and Troilus in the war, etc.). On the other hand, the narrator's personal point of view is manifested in describing the morally problematic actions in which the characters were involved. Here he comes close to their ways of thinking, shows himself sympathetic to them, and tries to defend them. His vocabulary is semantically widened to the extent that it is socially accepted.

Gordon (1970) points out that ironical ambiguity is caused by the gap between characters' actions and what the narrator's comments on them. However, Chaucer does not seem to look at that gap in an ironical way. At a deeper level, he seems to describe with great sympathy the real state of people's feelings as these transcend social idealism.

The gap described by Gordon (1970) is all the more obvious in the narrator's comments on Criseyde. These places are Chaucer's additions to *Il Filostrato*, and his creative power is the more so obvious. In Boccaccio the narrator takes the stance with which he laments his broken heart, and therefore his sympathetic attitude towards Criseida is controlled. On the other hand, Chaucer stands midway between sympathetic and critical ('I, that God of Loves servantz serve' Tr 1.15).

Criseyde is compelled to pursue socially problematic courses of action. She goes through agonies of conflict in her attempts to compromise. (5) gives an example of this. Pandarus tells her of Troilus's love, and she is forced to accept it. At this time, she sees him coming back to Troy in triumph. She is attracted by his manly appearance (Tr 2.631-7), and says to herself 'Who yaf me drynke?' (Tr 2.651). The passage below is the narrator's comment immediately inserted after her aside.

(5) Now myghte som envious jangle thus:
"This was a sodeyn love; how myghte it be
That she so lightly loved Troilus
Right for the firste syghte, ye, parde?"
Now whoso seith so, mote he nevere ythe!
For *every thing a gynnyng hath it nede*
Er al be wrought, withowten any drede.

For I sey nought that she so sodeynly
Yaf hym hire love, but that *she gan enclyne
To like hym first*, and I have told yow whi;
And after that, his manhod and his pyne
Made love withinne hire for to myne,
For which *by proces and by good servyse*
He gat hire love, and in no sodeyn wyse.

And also *blisful Venus*, wel arrayed,
Sat in hire seventhe hous of hevene tho,
Disposed wel, and with aspectes payed,
To helpe sely Troilus of his woo.
And soth to seyne, she nas not al a foo
To Troilus in his nativitee;
God woot that wel the sonner spedde he.   Tr 2.666-86

Criseyde is expected to test the knightly qualities of Troilus and then to accept his love by degrees. However, she cannot help revealing that she loved him at first sight ('Who yaf me drynke?' Tr 2.651). Moreover her father Calkas is a traitor to Troy and she is now in mourning of her dead husband. In this situation, if she accepts Troilus's love, this will arouse some cynicism in the reader. In the framework of the code of courtly love, this may be acceptable, but from the contemporary moral point of view, it is likely to bring about a scandal. For this reason it is inevitable that she becomes sensitive about maintaining her honour.

The narrator rejects the idea of her falling in love at first sight and emphasises the gradual processes whereby she accepts Troilus's love in accordance with the ideal of a courtly lady. In this way it appears as if he had anticipated and responded to the potential cynicism of the reader, the second prism. The last stanza in the quotation (Tr 2.680-6) makes clear that her acceptance of his love is brought about by the supernatural intervention of Venus. The reader is encouraged to determine whether her love is gradual in accordance with the ideal of a courtly lady or instantaneous. Is he or she persuaded into believing the narrator's evidence of the time-lag involved in her love? Or is he or she likely to treat it as an example of ironical ambiguity, feeling some gap between the narrator's comments and what she actually does? Or is he or she likely to presume a dual structure of her psychology which means that she can only act on the assumption that she is expected to accept Troilus's love gradually although she in fact does so at once? Dependent on these different interpretations, the meaning of this passage is subject to change with the tension between the fiction and reality.

The narrator rejects the cynical assumption (that she loves at first sight) of his reader and defends Criseyde. However, the author, seeing it *in toto* as if it were from above, encourages the reader to look upon the narrator's favourable and defensive opinion relatively. This complex situation brings about ambiguity.

6.3.2. Characters

The characters in *Troilus and Criseyde* are given many chances to make observations and express them in their own words. Dialogues, monologues, and asides are of frequent occurrence and this produces a remarkably dramatic structure. The characterisation is achieved by a psychological analysis typical of modern English novels, not to mention medieval religious or romance features. The main characters, Troilus, Pandarus and Criseyde are free from the allegory or stereotype typical of medieval literature, and are rounded individual human beings.

Generally speaking, Troilus is idealistic, Pandarus is practical, and Criseyde is intermediate between the two. However the distinction is not quite so clear-cut. Behind Troilus's idealistic speech lies his real living personality. Behind Pandarus's realistic strategies lie an insightful depth and philosophical recognition. And Criseyde is often found in a tension between reason and emotion.

The hero Troilus is at first hostile to love, but as soon as he sees Criseyde, daughter of a traitor to Troy and a widow still in mourning, he loves her. Through the sorrow and joy of his love, he is given a chance of spiritual training. According to courtly idealism, he grows spiritually and reaches a religious and philosophical plane. But it should be noted that however profound his thought becomes it is never truly religious or philosophical. His experience of love remains fixed in the world of his imagination. It, on the one hand, depends on Pandarus's strategies for its realisation, and on the other is threatened by the war between Troy and Greece.[56]

In his speech (6) Troilus fuses earthly and heavenly loves immediately before consummating his relationship with Criseyde.

(6) Than seyde he thus: "O *Love*, O *Charite*!
 Thi moder ek, Citheria the swete,
 After thiself next heried be she—
 Venus mene I, the wel-willy planete!—
 And next that, Imeneus, I the grete,
 For nevere man was to yow goddes holde
 As I, which ye han brought fro cares colde.

 "*Benigne Love, thow holy bond* of thynges,
 Whoso wol *grace* and list the nought honouren,
 Lo, his desir wol fle withouten wynges;
 For nodestow of *bownte* hem *socouren*
 That *serven* best and most alwey *labouren*,
 Yet were al lost, that dar I wel seyn, certes,
 But if thi *grace* passed oure desertes.   Tr 3.1254-67

The Cupid prayed to by Troilus is represented by the polysemic word *Love*. Juxtaposed to it is the *Charite* representing Christian love.[57] Then come a prayer to Venus and one to Hymenaeus, the god of marriage. In his imagination the love between Troilus and Criseyde is realised in the form of marriage. Next, the binding force of love is highlighted. The word *Benigne* denoting Christian generosity modifies *Love* (not Cupid), and in the appositive phrase the word *holy* of Christian implication modifies *bond* (suggesting Boethian philosophy of love). The religious implications are further reinforced by religious terms such as *grace*, *bownte*, *socouren*, *serven*, and *labouren*.[58]

---

56 In *Troilus and Criseyde* logic in physical space is extended to that in mental space. In the Troy side sieged with the Greek army, the rules of courtly love are functional. However, when exposed to the Greek side in the unbounded situation, they are threatened by the actual human realism, and subject to destruction. Chaucer seems to have metacognitive awareness of the self-contained feature of courtly love.

57 As mentioned in Section 6.2, *love* has semantically wider scope than *charite* or *amor* (*amorous/li*). In *Troilus and Criseyde*, the meaning of *love* is likely to change, and lead to ambiguity according to which sense the reader, the second prism, gives more weight to among sexual love, courtly love and religious love.

58 Cf. also the terms listed below. Benigne: thurgh the *benigne* grace of hym that is kyng of kynges and preest over alle preestes, that boghte us with the precious blood of his herte (ParsT X (I) 1091); holy: *hooly* ordre is chief of al the tresorie of God and his especial signe and mark of chastitee (ParsT X (I) 893); bownte: Envye comth proprely of malice, therfore it is proprely agayn the *bountee* of the Hooly Goost (ParsT X (I) 485); socour: ... thou me wisse and counsaile / How I may have thi grace and thi *socour* (ABC 155-6); serve: "Crist, Goddes Sone, withouten difference, / Is verray God—this is al oure sentence— / That hath so good a servant hym to *serve* (SecNT VIII (G) 417-9); labouren: Then leseth the synful man the goodnesse of glorie, that oonly is bihight to goode men that *labouren* and werken (ParsT X (I) 251).

Through these words we understand that Troilus perceives his love for Criseyde not as an individual matter but as part of the universal relation with God. How is the reader encouraged to interpret these expressions? Does Troilus grow spiritually into the religious stage of love? By these religious terms, the reader becomes the more sensitive to their moral implications, and therefore likely to question their validity. His attainment of a religious plane of love is only possible in his imaginary world. In summary, we may say that the religious expressions by Troilus are open to layers of interpretation not in spite of their frequency, but because of it.

Criseyde appears as a character who is sensitive regarding her honour from the beginning of the story because she is a daughter of a traitor to Troy, Calkas, and in mourning for her husband. It is natural that she should be frequently concerned with her honour. She tries to justify herself for her actions one step at a time. She hides her true feelings behind a rational exterior. She seems to be moved towards love with Troilus by external pressures, yet she is not averse to it, and perhaps even wishes it.

(7) is part of the monologue in which she expresses hesitation regarding Troilus's love. On the condition that her honour is safeguarded, she tries to cope with the situation.

(7) "What shal I doon? To what fyn lyve I thus?
Shal I nat love, in cas if that me leste?
What, pardieux! I am naught religious.
And though that I myn herte sette at reste
Upon this knyght, that is the worthieste,
And *kepe alwey myn honour and my name*,
By alle right, *it may do me no shame*."   Tr 2.757-63

Her logic in the decision-making process is not based on philosophy, but on practical considerations: she wants his love, but must consider how she will cope and justify herself. Her reasoning is: she is not religious; he is an ideal knight; as far as he safeguards her honour and name, it will do her no shame. 'As far as he safeguards her honour and name …' betrays her apprehension that otherwise her action will lead to a scandal. However, this induces criticism in the reader in that whether it is found out or not, the shame remains the same. Her criteria involved in her moral judgement are not absolute but relative and pragmatic, and determined by her situation. When her honour is interpreted in this context, there arises uncertainty as to whether it is true virtue or belief that she has it.

Criseyde's logic is manifested, as shown in later chapters, at important turning points in the story such as her acceptance of Troilus's love and her decision to forgo it. By using it she conceals her feeling at a deeper level and it helps her to satisfy social and moral requirements at the surface level. It runs through the speeches of Criseyde, which are a conglomerate of her authoritative stance and her experiential realities. This gives rise to an ambiguity in the minds of the readers.

When Pandarus discovers that Troilus is pessimistic about the realisation of his love, his advice to the desperate young man is as appears in (8).

(8) Quod Pandarus, "Than blamestow Fortune
For thow art wroth; ye, now at erst I see.
Woost thow nat wel that *Fortune is comune*
To everi manere wight in som degree?

> And yet thow hast this comfort, lo, parde,
> That, as hire joies moten overgon,
> *So mote hire sorwes passen everechon.* Tr 1.841-7

Pandarus refers to the mutability of Fortune, and assures Troilus that this will act to his benefit: his sorrow will be changed to his joy. This comes to pass, but so in time does the reverse. Of course Pandarus cannot know this, but the ideal reader who views the situation, as it were, from above, sees 'The double sorwe of Troilus to tellen' (Tr 1.1), and that Pandarus's prediction will also be reversed. Pandarus copes flexibly with such and such an urgent need, as a result of which he ceases to be consistent. The proverb Tr 1.946-52 is in similar vein.

In (9) Pandarus tells Troilus that since Criseyde is virtuous, her pity for him is naturally to be expected.

(9) "And also thynk, and therwith glade the,
     That sith thy lady *vertuous* is al,
     So foloweth it that there is some *pitee*
     Amonges alle thise other in general;
     And forthi se that thow, in special,
     Requere naught that is ayeyns hyre name;
     For vertu streccheth naught hymself to shame. Tr 1.897-903

As Gordon (1970) points out, the causal relation between Criseyde's virtue and her *pite* is dependent on shaky assumptions. According to Pandarus, illicit love is justified so long as no-one knows about it. This accords with the code of secrecy surrounding courtly love, but morally must be seen as highly unorthodox.

Pandarus resorts to generalisations in order to get rid of difficulties with which he encounters as the go-between of Troilus and Criseyde. He plays the role of a creator to cover every eventuality. However, he cannot be Philosophy who can solve Boethius's problems. After the exchange of Criseyde for prisoners, his power as a creator is greatly diminished. From the viewpoint of the reader who can see the whole narrative, Pandarus's authority is manipulated by his intention, which is only applied to one particular occasion, by no means generalised to cover everyone at every time. Pandarus's wordings are open to ambiguity according to whether the reader sees them in their restricted contexts or sees them detached from a wider context.

6.4. Ambiguity in plot

Events in *Troilus and Criseyde* are easily linked with one another owing to the activation of contiguity on the part of the reader. As Toyama (1964: 55) says, the event of the previous context remains as *zanzo* in Japanese ('engram' or residue), and superimposed on that of the present context, while the event of the present context, which also functions as *zanzo*, retroactively affects that of the previous context. As far as *zanzo* is functional to the reader, the expression of the event is likely to make a multi-layered semantic structure. On the large scale, we find the interaction between the prologue/epilogue of each Book and its narrative content, and on the small scale, that of one event and another in each Book.

6.4.1. Prologues/epilogues and the development of stories

The prologue/epilogue of each Book is deliberately attached to the main body of the narrative to make explicit the author's view of love. These parts are additions to *Il Filostrato*, except for the prologue of Book 3 where Troilo's hymn to love sung at the high point of his love is moved to the beginning of the Book as prologue. As for the prologue, the reader is given the viewpoint in advance to see the development of the love between Troilus and Criseyde. The epilogue of Book 5 functions as the viewpoint to see the whole story retroactively.

The prologue of Book 1 is predicative of the whole story to be developed, as seen in (10).

(10) The double sorwe of Troilus to tellen,
   That was the kyng Priamus sone of Troye,
   In lovynge, how his aventures fellen
   Fro wo to wele, and after out of joie,
   My purpos is, er that I parte fro ye.   Tr 1.1-5

Reference is made here to vagaries of love experienced by Troilus: 'Fro wo to wele, and after out of joie.' The story does not develop in an ideal way as we see in the development of Boethius who is in dire distress, and yet deepens his awareness of humanity through Philosophy's advice, and attains the state of bliss. Instead Chaucer's tale unfolds in an unstable framework and is tossed about by Fortune. In this vein the reader can easily predict the interactions or the ups and downs of the Books that follow.[59] The narrator shows his stance towards the whole story as in (11).

(11) *For I, that God of Loves servantz serve,*
   Ne dar to Love, for myn unliklynesse,
   Preyen for speed, al sholde I therfore sterve,
   So fer am I from his help in derknesse.   Tr 1.15-8

The narrator does not take a position as a participant in love, but an indirect stance as 'I, that God of Loves servantz serve.' By contrast, *Il Filostrato* takes a 'biographical stance' by which he dedicates the book to his lover from whom he had separated (see Windeatt 1990: 85). Chaucer's narrator can observe and describe the love of Troilus and Criseyde. Immediately after he asks the courtly audience to be sympathetic to Troilus who encounters and seeks to overcome the difficulties of love (*pyte* Tr 1.23, *compassioun* Tr 1.50). These values are essential courtly virtues. Here we are given hints of the narrator's sympathetic view.

In the prologue of Book 2 where the love between Troilus and Criseyde begins to move, the narrator describes the emergence of their love symbolically (Tr 2.1-7), and notes that the actions of love and the words and deeds of love vary from country to country, and cannot be evaluated by the same criteria.

---

59   The structure of *Troilus and Criseyde*, divided as it is into five books, is: introduction (beginning of Troilus's love-sickness), development (dawning of his discovery of love-sickness), consummation of love (achievement of his love with Criseyde), denouement (his movement from his joy to his sorrow), and conclusion (his broken heart and tragic death). Cf. The contrast presented by the three stages of the plot in Dante's *Divinia Comedia* (hell → purgatory → heaven) and that in Chaucer's *House of Fame* (desert → the house of Fame → the house of Rumour).

(12) For every wight which that to Rome went
    Halt nat o path, or alwey o manere;
    Ek in som lond were al the game shent,
    If that they ferde in love as men don here,
    As thus, in opyn doyng or in chere,
    In visityng in forme, or seyde hire sawes;
    Forthi men seyn, "*Ecch contree hath his lawes.*"   Tr 2.36-42

The scene of Troilus's love is ancient Troy of about 1200 BC. But Chaucer relocates it in medieval London. In this setting we have the three types of love of the Christian middle ages referred to above (Section 6.2). The narrator seems to ask the reader not to try too hard to separate the three types.

As we have seen in Chapter 5, the prologue of Book 3 introduces the possibility that the love between Troilus and Criseyde will develop along religious lines. But immediately after Venus leads Jove her father to 'amorous him made / On mortal thyng' (Tr 3.17-8), and Troilus is on the way to sexual love. It is possible that the earthly love here is retroactive enough to refer to the cosmic love above with the working of *zanzo* or 'engram.' The reader is shown layers of interpretation in which he or she may decide which type of love to emphasise.

Let us think of Books 1 to 3 where the love of Troilus and Criseyde develops and reaches its climax as an ascending scene, and Books 4 to 5 where the love declines and meets catastrophe as a descending scene. In terms of the latter, the fluctuation of love is implicitly represented in relation to the wheel of Fortune. The realistic aspect of love in contradistinction to its ideal state is represented. In the prologue of Book 4, the mutability of Fortune is shown as in (13).

(13) But *al to litel*, weylaway the whyle,
    Lasteth swich joie, ythonked be Fortune,
    That semeth trewest whan she wol bygyle
    And kan to fooles so hire song entune
    That she hem hent and blent, traitour comune!
    And whan a wight is from hire whiel ythrowe,
    Than laugheth she, and maketh hym the mowe.   Tr 4.1-7

The narrator proclaims that earthly love is swayed by unstable Fortune and is ephemeral by contrast with heavenly love. The love of Troilus and Criseyde is predicted in this way. Her later fluctuating affections are described in parallel with the wheel of Fortune (cf. 'slydynge of corage' Tr 5.825). In the prologue of Book 5, the narrator states that she is sent to the Greek camp in exchange for prisoners, and that her love with Troilus comes to destruction. Here it is also emphasised that her being sent out of Troy accords with the wheel of Fortune.

(14) *Aprochen gan the fatal destyne*
    That Joves hath in disposicioun,
    And to yow, angry Parcas, sustren thre,
    Committeth to don execucioun;
    For which *Criseyde moste out of the town*,
    And Troilus shal dwellen forth in pyne
    Til Lachesis his thred no lenger twyne.   Tr 5.1-7

The actions of Fortune superimposed on the effects of a real human character, i.e. Criseyde's unstable personality, produces a see-saw rhythm of 'Fortune' or 'character.' This may be seen to demonstrate the narrator's sympathetic view of her.[60] In the epilogue or palinode to Book 5, Troilus ascends to the eighth sphere after his death, looks down at the earth, and criticises human beings enjoying earthly love. This is an evaluation of the story as a whole. From a celestial perspective, earthly love described in the story is set at nought, as we saw in Section 6.2.

6.4.2. Interactions between situations

The author uses the double prism structure to express the past and future actions of the characters. Through this the reader, the second prism is offered dual points of view with which to interpret the story both prospectively (via the prologue) and retrospectively (via the epilogue).

In (15) Troilus is expatiating in ecstatic anticipation on his love for Criseyde at Pandarus's house. Elated of his experience of love, he ascribes it to cosmic domains, escaping from his real world and praying to the gods, thanking them for his love. In between Troilus's asides and religious statements (Tr 3.712-35), we find the insertion of Pandarus's pragmatic utterances which lead to the physical union of Troilus and Criseyde in bed.

(15) Quod Pandarus, "Ne drede the nevere a deel,
 For it shal be right as thow wolt desire;
 So thryve I, this nyght shal I make it weel,
 Or *casten al the gruwel in the fire*."
 "Yet, blisful Venus, this nyght thow me enspire,"
 Quod Troilus, "As wys as I the serve,
 And evere bet and bet shal, til I sterve.

 "And if ich hadde, O *Venus* ful of myrthe,
 Aspectes badde of Mars or of Saturne,
 Or thow combust or let were in my birthe,
 Thy fader prey al thilke harm disturne
 Of grace, and that I glad ayein may turne,
 For love of hym thow lovedest in the shawe—
 I meene Adoun, that with the boor was slawe.

 "O *Jove* ek, for the love of faire Europe,
 The which in forme of bole awey thow fette,
 Now help! O *Mars*, thow with thi blody cope,
 For love of Cipris, thow me nought ne lette!
 O *Phebus*, thynk whan Dane hireselven shette
 Under the bark, and laurer wax for drede;
 Yet for hire love, O help now at this nede!

---

60 In Henryson's *The Testament of Cresseid*, there is likely to be ambiguity as to whether Cresseid's betrayal is due to Fortune (78, 84, 89, 121, 385, 412, 454, 469, 470) or to her character (549-54, 558-60, 568-74).

> "*Mercurie*, for the love of Hierse eke,
> For which Pallas was with Aglawros wroth,
> Now help! And ek *Diane*, I the biseke
> That this viage be nought to the looth!
> O *fatal sustren* which, er any cloth
> Me shapen was, my destine me sponne,
> So helpeth to this werk that is bygonne!"
>
> Quod Pandarus, "Thow wrecched mouses herte,
> Artow agast so that she wol the bite?
> Wy! *Don this furred cloke upon thy sherte*,
> *And folwe me*, for I wol have the wite.
> But bid, and lat me gon biforn a lite."
> And with that word *he gan undon a trappe*,
> And *Troilus he brought in by the lappe*.   Tr 3.708-42

In (16) Pandarus interrupts Criseyde in proclaiming to Troilus her *trouthe* as a courtly lady (Tr 3.988-1050, Tr 3.1053-4). Pandarus tells her to stop speaking, and finally casts Troilus in bed, and begins to tear off his clothes.

> (16) "O nece, pes, or we be lost!" quod he,
>   "Beth naught agast!" But certeyn, at the laste,
> For this or that, *he into bed hym caste*,
> And seyde, "O thef, is this a mannes herte?"
> And *of he rente al to his bare sherte*,   Tr 3.1095-9

Muscatine (1957) calls it 'structural ambiguity' when the words and deeds of the characters are juxtaposed, and they can be seen to represent opposing values. Contiguity is functional between two actions progressively and regressively with a consequent occurrence of ambiguity. Troilus's devotion to mythological gods (Venus—Jove—Mars—Phebus—Mercurie—Diane—fatal sustren) makes a cohesion between stanza and stanza and line and line through the association/linking of their respective powers. This encourages the reader to be sceptical of Pandarus's pragmatism, while his pragmatism encourages the reader to be sceptical of Troilus's inactivity and escapism from his real world. To criticise Troilus's inertia from Pandarus's pragmatic view seems to have more impact on the reader than the other way round in that Troilus's 'authority' is subverted by Pandarus's 'experience.' Here Troilus's human weakness can be seen to undermine his religious stance.

(17) appears to stop the development of the plot, but suggests how the characters develop by reference to their prior and subsequent actions. Immediately before Criseyde yields to Diomede, the narrator summarises the characteristics of the three main characters involved in this action.

> (17) This Diomede, as bokes us declare,
>   Was in his nedes prest and corageous,
> *With sterne vois and myghty lymes square,*
> *Hardy, testif, strong, and chivalrous*
> *Of dedes*, lik his fader Tideus.
> And som men seyn he was of tonge large;
> And heir he was of Calydoigne and Arge.

6. Ambiguity in macro-textual structure

> Criseyde *mene was of hire stature*;
> *Therto of shap, of face, and ek of cheere,*
> Ther myghte ben no fairer creature.
> And ofte tymes this was hire manere:
> To gon ytressed with hire heres clere
> Doun by hire coler at hire bak byhynde,
> Which with a thred of gold she wolde bynde;
>
> And, *save hire browes joyneden yfeere*,
> Ther nas no lak, in aught I kan espien.
> But for to speken of hire eyen cleere,
> Lo, trewely, they writen that hire syen
> That Paradis stood formed in hire yën.
> And *with hire riche beaute evere more*
> *Strof love in hire ay*, which of hem was more.
>
> She *sobre was, ek symple, and wys* withal,
> The *best ynorisshed* ek that myghte be,
> And *goodly of hire speche* in general,
> *Charitable, estatlich, lusty, fre*;
> *Ne nevere mo ne lakked hire pite*;
> *Tendre-herted, slydynge of corage*;
> But trewely, I kan nat telle hire age.
>
> And Troilus wel woxen was in highte,
> And *complet formed by proporcioun*
> So wel that kynde it nought amenden myghte;
> *Yong, fressh, strong, and hardy as lyoun*;
> *Trewe as stiel in ech condicioun*;
> Oon of the beste entecched creature
> That is or shal whil that the world may dure.
>
> And certeynly in storye it is yfounde
> That Troilus was nevere unto no wight,
> As in his tyme, in no degree secounde
> In durryng don that longeth to a knyght.
> Al myghte a geant passen hym of myght,
> *His herte ay with the first and with the beste*
> *Stood paregal*, to durre don that hym leste.   Tr 5.799-840

In *Il Filostrato* the narrator has no digression corresponding to the above, but he says simply that Criseida yields to Diomede (*Il Filostrato* 6.8.608). But in Chaucer's version Criseyde begins to act in Tr 5.841, after the above quotation. This digression prevents the reader from inferring contiguity (Diomede's wooing → Criseyde's acceptance of it). This provides an interval before the onset of her infidelity. It activates another inferential system, "similarity." Before she yields to Diomede, she has a spatial distance to repel him. This spatial distance is metaphorically a temporal distance before she gives in. It is also a metaphor of a psychological gap between them. This space is semantically extended through metaphor. Here there seems to be a great sympathy for Criseyde on the part of the poet who does not want to say unequivocally or immediately that Criseyde cheated on her lover. Chaucer's insertion of this digression is not merely a diversion from the plot, but is an integral part of it, and endowed with multiple implications.

Let us look at the contents of this breathing space and in particular at the relationship between the stanzas. The first stanza refers to Diomede, the next three to Criseyde, and the final two to Troilus. As Schaar (1967) points out, she is, as it were, in a tug-of-love between them. This order is metaphorical, and by which side she is more attracted in the coming scenes seems to have an effect of "metonymical" tension.

The characters are portrayed in the form of *effictio* and *notatio*. These two types of descriptions are juxtaposed. The external implies the internal, and the internal implies the external. This is in accord with the schematic pattern of the medieval way of characterisation.[61] In terms of inferential method, the inclusive relation between the external and the internal is due to "metonymy," and the physical-spiritual semantic relation is due to "metaphor." Diomede's wild voice, and hardy and strong limbs are suggestive of his ferocious temperament, Criseyde's medium statue and fair features of her sincerity and her deep pity and love (there is an opinion that her close eyebrows show that she is unstable in her affections),[62] Troilus's proportional form of his fidelity and his features of an ideal knight. The characterisation of these three characters suggests further development of the story based on the "metonymical" relationships (cause-effect): Diomede's tenacious pursuit of Criseyde and her sincere attitude towards him which does not involve obvious rejection and her subsequent shift of affections, Troilus's unchangeable love for her, and his subsequent tragic death. Criseyde in the tension between Diomede and Troilus is the most prominent. She is torn between Troilus (spiritual existence) and Diomede (physical existence) in the Greek camp. Does she accept Diomede physically while loving Troilus spiritually? Or on deeper level, is she more attracted to the physically present Diomede than to the physically absent but spiritually present Troilus? The attraction referred to derives from Chaucer's creative use of contiguity. For a detailed analysis of Criseyde's state of psychology, see Chapters 9 to 13.

The interaction between event and event is realised in the expression of the double prism structure, that is the prologue/epilogue and the story, and scene and scene. Due to the interaction here, structural ambiguity and "metonymical" as well as "metaphorical" ambiguity are likely to be produced.

6.5. Final remarks

The macro-structural elements of the story such as the theme, the characterisation, and the plot highlight the phenomenon, the first prism, and the expression of the double prism structure. The theme is love, but its polyvalence is brought to the fore. In *Troilus and Criseyde* the polyvalence of love is not horizontally dealt with as in *The Parliament of Fowles*, but vertically condensed in the characters. Here more delicate ambiguity is likely to be produced. On the surface level rational or religious love is visibly described, and real feelings are concealed on the deeper level. These two are combined. Finally, the physical love of Troilus and Criseyde is cancelled by Christian absolute love. We find that the narrator has not only an omniscient view but also a lim-

---

61 More typically this is manifested in the physiological features of, for instance, madam Blanche (Whyte) in *The Book of Duchess* and the Wife of Bath in the General Prologue to *The Canterbury Tales*.
62 Regarding the interpretation of 'slydygne of corage,' see Section 12.2.

6. Ambiguity in macro-textual structure

ited view like an additional character. The love between Troilus and Criseyde unfolds in accordance with a code of adultery based on courtly love, which is problematic from a social-moral point of view. The narrator and characters are required to be cautious in the justification of the processes whereby they accept, and develop, the love they are involved with. Their speeches are likely to bring to the reader a dual nature composed both of reason and emotion. Their actions are represented in the development of the plot interactively with contrastive effect. Through the macro-structual elements (theme, charactersation, plot) of this poem, the reader is offered a complex view of each of them, and this is likely to lead to a multiple and ambiguous interpretation.

In Chapter 7, we will deal with the presentation form of the narrative text, another macro-structural element of the work. Here are reflected the narrator's and characters' points of view. We will focus on a medieval equivalent of free indirect speech found in modern English novels where there is an uncertainty as to whether the narrator or a particular character is speaking at any one time.

7. Ambiguity in reported speech

7.1. Introductory remarks: the double prism structure and reported speech

In *Troilus and Criseyde* Chaucer's understanding of the human condition is profound, his psychological analysis of the characters is subtle, and thus his presentation of them is highly successful. This characterisation makes it possible to distinguish between the narrative sections and the sections consisting of the dialogue between characters endowed as they are with their individual points of view, in short: presentation form. Presentation form is closely related to the speaker's point of view and his or her way of expressing it in terms of the double prism structure. As an expression of the characters' responses (psychology, words and actions), *Troilus and Criseyde* contains the narrator's summary of the characters' words and thoughts, their indirect speech and their direct speech (dialogue/monologue) in a way close to that found in modern psychological novels. However, the boundary between the narrator's control and the characters' assertion from their own points of view is not necessarily clear-cut. The characters' points of view are included in the narrative parts, and the narrator's control is perceived in the characters' speeches. It is a matter of degree whether a given passage presents the narrator's or the characters' view.[63] In this chapter we examine the processes by which this matter of degree induces the reader's inference, and as a result brings about ambiguous interpretation.[64]

---

63   The narrative parts at the beginning of *The Merchant's Tale* seems to reflect Januarie's expectation of marriage. The narrative descriptions in *Sir Gawain and the Green Knight* seem to reflect the internal view of Gawain in a severe and dangerous expedition to complete his challenged objective.

64   Leech and Short (1981: 318-36) classifies forms of speech presentation into the following types according to the degrees of the narrator's control:

Cline of 'interference' in report (Leech and Short (1981: 324))

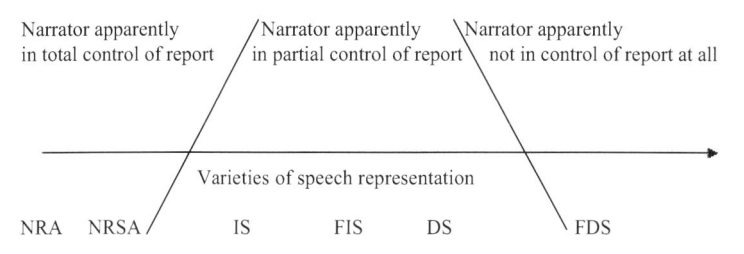

Narrator apparently   Narrator apparently   Narrator apparently
in total control of report   in partial control of report   not in control of report at all

Varieties of speech representation

NRA   NRSA   IS   FIS   DS   FDS

NRA (Narrative report of action), NRSA (Narrative report of speech action), IS (Indirect speech), FIS (Free indirect speech), DS (Direct speech), and FDS (Free direct speech). Here when we refer to 'free indirect speech,' we use it in a somewhat looser way. We include NRSA in FIS since it reflects a character's view although its wording is strongly controlled by the

In Chapter 6, we have pointed out two roles of the narrator, that is, his objective role in describing facts, and his subjective role in demonstrating sympathy with characters' feelings and evaluating them. If his subjective role is increasingly felt, it is likely to be unclear whether the narrator's viewpoint or that of the characters predominates, and this brings about an effect of free indirect speech. This possibility has already been pointed out by Pearsall (1986) as the problem of how to represent Criseyde's way of thinking. The same is true of Fludernik (1993: 194), where characters' real status as against their ideal status is brought into relief in the character portrayal of the General Prologue to *The Canterbury Tales*.[65]

Direct speech in Chaucer is of course not distinguished in the manuscripts unlike in modern editions. This is quite natural in that most of the medieval transmission was conducted orally. It is an interesting question how Chaucer's direct speeches were performed and whether the narrator imitated the speakers' tones of voice. Direct speeches in modern editions are generally distinguished because they are intended to be read. Our examination of speech presentations is based on Benson (1987). Monologues or asides indicative of characters' thoughts are quoted with double inverted commas. In these parts the first person pronoun 'I' is used. Since I regard them as direct speech, I exclude them from consideration here. Free indirect speech, a kind of indirect speech, is presented by the third person pronoun 'he/she,' and cannot be recognised by punctuation. The reader is required to be sensitive to the characters' ways of thinking and their ways of expressions (word choice, syntactic structure) found in the passages he or she is dealing with.

7.2. Free indirect speech and the problem of ambiguity

In cases where the real state of the characters is assumed to deviate from the ideal state they live up to, the narrator does not describe them straightforwardly, but makes them equivocal by the use of expressions of wide application. Free indirect speech is effective in thus presenting characters' point of view. This is manifested in the narrator's description of difficulties with which Criseyde ought to cope as to how she can develop her love of Troilus or her reprehensible action in the contemporary social-moral terms. Let us look at some examples.

Criseyde is told of the love of Troilus by Pandarus, and urged to accept it. Her reaction to the return of Troilus to Troy in triumph is presented not in direct speech but in the narrator's indirect speech. As shown in (1), it is a merger of his objective observation and her subjective emotion. We have already touched upon this example in (5) in Chapter 4. We will now reinterpret it here in terms of free indirect speech.

(1) So lik a man of armes and a knyght
 He was to seen, fulfilled of heigh prowesse,
 For bothe he hadde a body and a myght

---

 narrator. For a rhetorical device of sounds—*acclamatio*—I am indebted to Professor Masahiko Agari, formerly of Kumamoto University.
65 Cf. the Monk's opposing conception of the contemporary view of labour in the General Prologue to *The Canterbury Tales* (I (A) 184-8).

> To don that thing, as wel as hardynesse;
> And ek to seen hym in his gere hym dresse,
> *So fresssh, so yong, so weldy semed he,*
> *It was an heven upon hym for to see.* Tr 2.631-7

This is a description of the third person 'he' controlled by the narrator. If we assume that the narrator's description of Troilus's knightly features is made objectively, it is the same whoever may see them. (The semantic subject of the infinitives (*To seen* Tr 2.632, Tr 2.635, Tr 2.637) is suppressed in the surface syntax.) However, if we look at various subjective expressions, that is, the repetition of an intensive *so*, a deictic *that*, the chain of evaluative adjectives, *fresshe, yong, weldy*, a modal lexical verb, *semed*, and a hyperbole indicative of great joy, 'It was an heven ...,' Criseyde's (one of the spectators) own way of perception will be more dominant. Here the description is closer to free indirect speech where Criseyde sees, feels, and utters. If the narrator avoids direct speech, it is because he intends an equivocal mode of expression in that the description includes the physical love between the bachelor prince Troilus and the widow Criseyde. The reading of it in a generalised sense and at the same time from Criseyde's personal view makes the meanings and implications of details of expression divided and thus give rise to ambiguity. The referential meaning of *that* is discussed as part of cohesion in Chapter 8, and the implications of *weldy* are treated in Chapter 12 with regard to lexical ambiguity.[66]

In medieval Christian theology the love of Troilus and Criseyde was regarded as lechery, one of the deadly sins (see ParsT). This was the knowledge shared between the writer and the audience. Chaucer seems to have been fully aware of this sin. However, Chaucer did not wish to be constrained by this narrow attitude to human behaviour. He was not a preacher. He was cognisant of the moral rules people ought to abide by, but he also had a deep insight into human frailty and recognised that they did not always live up to these ideals. In Chaucer's times human rights and freedom of speech were very little safeguarded compared with modern times. Free indirect speech displays Chaucer's compromise between his realistic recognition of Criseyde's true nature and his understanding of what a courtly lady ought to be, which he goes into at length.

The quotations (2), (3) and (4) are the narrator's descriptions of the knightly features on his triumphant return to Troy. These are perhaps what attracted Criseyde's gaze. The problem is to what extent Chaucer controls (or edits) her way of thinking there. As regards the order of the elements of Troilus's attributes as listed, it reflects the order of her perception as seen in free indirect speech although coming close to what Leech and Short (1981) calls NRSA (Narrative Report of Speech Action), that is, the narrator's summarised comment of what she said to herself.[67]

---

66 Regarding the dualistic interpretation of *body* and *that thing*, see Section 8.2. The words *fressh* and *yong* can be used with sexual implications as shown in the Wife of Bath's statement 'Housbondes meeke, *yonge, and fressh abedde* (WBP III (D)1259). As for the polysemy of *weldy*, see Section 12.4. Furthermore, regarding the line 'It was an *heven* upon hym for to see' it is uncertain whether it is a mere narrative tag to express the narrator's admiration (SqT V (F) 558, Tr 2.826, Tr 3.1742, etc.) or functions sexually with a connotation that 'it will bring about Criseyde's ecstasy to see him.'

67 Cf. The word order of an utterance in terms of information structure in Section 8.5.

(2) And with that thought, for pure ashamed, she
 Gan in hire hed to pulle, and that as faste,
 Whil he and alle the peple forby paste,

 And gan to caste and rollen up and down
 Withinne hire thought *his excellent prowesse,*
 And his estat, and also his renown,
 His wit, his shap, and ek his gentilesse; Tr 2.656-62

(3) Now was hire herte warm, now was it cold;
 And what she thoughte somewhat shal I write,
 As to myn auctour listeth for t'endite.

 She thoughte wel that *Troilus persone*
 She knew by syghte, and ek his gentilesse, Tr 2.698-702

(4) God woot wher he was lik a manly knyght!
 What sholde I drecche, or telle of his aray?
 Criseyde, which that alle thise thynges say,
 To telle in short, hire liked al in-fere,
 His persoun, his aray, his look, his chere,

 His goodly manere, and his gentilesse,
 So wel that nevere, sith that she was born,
 Ne hadde she swych routh of his destresse; Tr 2.1263-70

(2), (3) and (4) are devoted to describing Troilus's appearance, and finally introduces *gentilesse*. Gaylord (1964: 26) and Gordon (1970: 84) think that since *gentilesse* is located finally after a succession of items referring to his appearance, it is interpreted as 'manners,' and 'social deportment.' If the order of listing items here reflect Criseyde's ways of cognition, it will be his appearance that moves her heart and attracts her to him (in (2) her attention is drawn also to his strength and reputation as a soldier). This indicates the operation of the 'lawe of kinde' or human emotion due to the stimulation of the sense of sight which we saw in Section 6.2. This is in contrast to the reason she afterwards confesses to Troilus, i.e. that she had a sympathy for him owing to his 'grete trouthe and servise' (Tr 3.992) and 'moral vertu' (Tr 4.1672).

(5) was discussed in (1) of Chapter 5 from the viewpoint of intertextuality. Let us reexamine it from the viewpoint of free indirect speech. Criseyde is forced to stay at Pandarus's house after supper because of the storm. Troilus is guided into her bedroom. She is embarrassed by his sudden appearance. But sympathetic with his sorrow caused by his love, she is attracted to him. Checking to see that they will not be discovered, she is inclined to accept his love in accordance with the ideal of a courtly lady.

(5) This accident *so pitous* was to here,
 And ek *so like a sooth* at prime face,
 And Troilus hire knyght to hir *so deere,*
 His prive comyng, and the siker place,
 That *though that she did hym as thanne a grace,*
 Considered alle thynges as they stoode,
 No wonder is, syn she did al for goode. Tr 3.918-24

The narrator understands her psychology, sympathises with her, and comes close to her viewpoint. The narrator's viewpoint and that of Criseyde become merged with each other. The narrative in (5) comes close to free indirect speech. The reader is likely to be undecided as to whether he emphasizes the narrator's objective judgement, or Criseyde's. The words, *pitous*, *prive*, *grace*, and *goode* are related not only to religious or courtly idealism, as shown in Chapter 5, but to Criseyde's real feelings concealed behind it. If one is sympathetic to Criseyde, these words are likely to be associated with the former, but observing her with some scepticism, they are likely to be associated with the latter. This example is likely to deepen ambiguity in conjunction with intertextuality (see Chapter 5), and with the lexical ambiguity shown in Chapter 12.[68]

This is the context of (6). It is determined at the Trojan Parliament in Book 4 that Criseyde should be sent to the Greek camp in an exchange of prisoners. Troilus and Criseyde suffer greatly as a result. As a countermeasure, she proposes that she should go to the Greek camp first, and then return to Troy within ten days. She persuades him that she is faithful to him. The quotation below is a sympathetic comment made by the narrator assuming that the audience will be critical of Criseyde's decision. They are told at the beginning of the story that Criseyde will be unfaithful to Troilus.

(6) And treweliche, as writen wel I fynde
That *al this thyng was seyd of good entente,*
And that hire herte trewe was and kynde
Towardes hym, and spak right as she mente,
And that she starf for wo neigh whan she wente,
And was in purpos evere to be trewe:
Thus writen they that of hire werkes knewe.   Tr 4.1415-21

The narrator emphasises the point repeatedly that Criseyde was sincere when she vowed her truth. The narrator's logic of explanation of her truth seems to imitate hers as Pearsall (1986) points out. This is similar to her decision-making in that she accumulates evidence for it in accord with social demands (see repetition of *and*), and justifies herself for it. With the narrator's point of view, the evidence here will be increasingly objective. On the other hand, with Criseyde's point of view it will be susceptive to her subjectivity suggesting that she desires it to be so rather than objectively so. Thus the narrator's point of view and Criseyde's are subtly interactive to each other, which brings about an effect of ambiguity ascribable to free indirect speech.[69]

When Criseyde is escorted to the Greek camp by Diomede, the Greek knight, she is advanced in love by him. (7) is a response she politely made to him.

(7) But natheles she thonketh Diomede
Of al his travaile and his goode cheere,
And that hym list his frendshipe hire to bede;
And she accepteth it in good manere,
And *wol do fayn that is hym lief and dere,*
And tristen hym she wolde, and wel she myghte,
As seyde she; and from hire hors sh'alighte.   Tr 5.183-9

---

68   Regarding the analysis of this example in terms of causality, see Section 8.3.2.
69   The ambiguity brought about the modal force of *treweliche* is treated in Section 10.3.4.

There seems to be a transition in speech presentation from what Leech and Short (1981) calls NRA (Narrative Report of Action) or NRSA to a near direct speech. The lines of Tr 5.187-8 are suggestive of her tone of voice. As regards the line of Tr 5.188, since 'as seyde she' is parenthetical, the content of her speech itself comes to the more notice. This seems to be intermediate between ID (Indirect Speech) and FIS (Free Indirect Speech). Criseyde thanks Diomede for his kindness, further building up the human relationship between them. (The repetition of *and* suggests that she accumulates evidence to accept Diomede.) There seems to be uncertainty in her response here as to whether it is construed as within her politeness shown to Diomede or more positively as her expectation to make further relation with him (see ambiguity in the speaker's intention in Chapter 9). This is why the speech presentation is made indirect with alternative tones of voice.

In (8) considering Diomede's words, his social status, the dangerous situation of Troy, and her loneliness in the Greek camp, Criseyde comes to decide to stay at Greece.

(8) And Signifer his candels sheweth brighte
 Whan that Criseyde unto hire bedde wente
 Inwith hire fadres faire brighte tente,

 Retornyng in hire soule ay up and down
 The wordes of this sodeyn Diomede,
 His grete estat, and perel of the town,
 And that she was allone and hadde nede
 Of frendes help; and thus bygan to brede
 The cause whi, the sothe for to telle,
 That she took fully purpos for to dwelle.   Tr 5.1020-9

Criseyde promises to Troilus to come back to Troy within ten days, but on the very tenth day she begins to decide to stay at Greece. The narrator makes a summary of her psychological state (NRSA). This seems to belong to the narrative part of the story fully controlled by the narrator. The participial construction beginning with 'Retornyng ...' seems to reflect Criseyde's way of thinking. Pearsall (1986) notes the half-independence of the construction of its main clause (see ambiguity in syntax in Chapter 11), and ascribes it to her psychology to avoid sinful decision. The narrative accumulation of evidence for her to stay at Greece is reflective of her logic of self-justification for it. The reader, the second prism, is here encouraged to become sensitive to Criseyde's way of thinking behind the narrator's indirectly veiled description.

7.3. Final remarks

In terms of the double prism structure, ambiguity due to free indirect speech is summarised as below. As regards acceptance of Troilus's love or Diomede's (the phenomenon of the double prism structure), Criseyde is forced to be against the courtly idealism or social demands of Chaucer's times. The author is sympathetic with her situation, observes her decision-making with some equivocation (the involvement of the first prism in it), and describes it in free indirect speech (the expression). Since her point of view is covertly represented in the expression, ambiguity is likely to occur as regards whether the reader, the second prism, takes it as reflecting the narrator's perspective or hers.

In Chapter 8 let us examine the discourse or linguistic devices of intersentential relation, located intermediately between the macro-structure and the micro-structure of the text. In terms of the double prism structure, we will describe the speaker's observation of events, his or her expression of them, and the reader's participation in the interpretation.

8. Ambiguity in discourse structure

8.1. Introductory remarks: the double prism structure and discourse

The conversations and other dialogue items in *Troilus and Criseyde* progress smoothly and convincingly. The interconnections of sentences and the cohesive structure of the discourse ensure this feature of the poem.

However, it should be noted that this cohesive device leads not only to rational and smooth progress, but also to psychological effect. Psychological development in conversation and its subsequent ambiguity are explained under the double prism structure. If the actions the characters are required to perform are assumed to be against their honour, they proceed taking their conversation for granted. Thus the discourse appears self-explanatory in the mouths of the participants, but presents problems to the reader, the second prism. In this way a double interpretation arises from a fiction, that is, the interplay between the participants in a conversation, and the interplay between those participants and the audience. The reader is the more actively encouraged to take part in the interpretation of the discourse as the more abbreviated it is, the less informative.[70] What relation to make between one sentence and another is a matter of interpretation.

Halliday and Hasan (1976) divides intersentential linking elements into two kinds, structural kind (information structure) and unstructural (cohesion). To borrow Jakobson's (1960) words, these discourse elements are the workings of contiguity on the syntagmatic level of the text.

Cohesion is classified by Halliday and Hasan (1976) as in (1).

(1) a. reference
    b. substitution
    c. ellipsis
    d. conjunction
    e. lexical cohesion

(1a) is the referential relationship between pronouns or demonstratives and their antecedents, (1b) is the substituted *one*s and their antecedents, (1c) is ellipsis of words or phrases, (1d) is the relationship using conjunctions, and (1e) is the maintenance of concepts by lexical repetition or variation. Halliday and Hasan (1976: 327) points out that (1) is observed not only in the discourse of conversation but also in that of other forms, especially that of narrative (including verse narrative). All these discourse devices are found in *Troilus and Criseyde*.

---

70 Cf. Grice's (1975) conversational implicature dealt with in Chapter 9. The excessively economised speech goes against the maxim of quantity, one of the maxims to establish conversation. Here the reader, the second prism, is presented with the less information than required to understand the conversation he or she is involved in. However, he or she is encouraged to infer its meaning activating the cooperative principle between the speaker and the hearer.

In terms of information structure, Halliday and Hasan (1976) deals with theme and rheme, or the arrangement of given information and new information. Further, Ohe (1984) pays attention to the process whereby the speaker observes a phenomenon, or how the order of cognition is reflected in the word order. *Troilus and Criseyde* is written in verse and its words are arranged in accordance with the metre and rhyme (rhyme royal) (see Masui (1964)). It is difficult to make a distinction as to whether this arrangement is made to deliver natural informational meaning or fully controlled by metrics. As Brewer (1977: 111) says 'Chaucer's poetic power is only rarely distilled in a word or a phrase; it is to be sought in the paragraph and even larger units,' it is not unnatural that Chaucer should be sensitive to the movement of the psychology of his characters or their images, and reflect them in the order of words.

In this chapter we examine cohesion and the order of words under the double prism structure, and make clear why and how it will give rise to ambiguity

8.2. Ambiguity in cohesion: a focus on reference (1a), substitution (1b), ellipsis (1c)

(2) below is the beginning of the conversation between Pandarus and Criseyde when he is introducing to her the idea of Troilus as a lover.

(2) "For, nece, by the goddesse Mynerve,
  And Jupiter, that maketh the thondre rynge,
  And by the blisful Venus that I serve,
  Ye ben the womman in this world lyvynge—
  Withouten paramours, to my wyttynge—
  That I best love, and lothest am to greve;
  And *that* ye weten wel youreself, I leve."   Tr 2.232-8

That (Tr 2.238) is an anaphoric reference by use of demonstrative. It appears that the speaker Pandarus and the hearer Criseyde have understood the reference of *that* as given information. It is moved to the initial position to emphasise the cohesion with the preceding context. Commonsensically this is so. However, the reference of *that* is uncertain despite his oath by way of emphasis. As will be shown in our discussion of syntax (Chapter 12) and voice (Chapter 13), the immediately preceding sentence 'Ye ben the womman in this world lyvynge— / Withouten paramours, to my wyttynge— / That I best love, and lothest am to greve' (Tr 2.235-7) is open to various interpretations. How we interpret Pandarus's intention—the reliability of the relationship between Pandarus and Criseyde or the presence of her lover—affects our understanding of 'Withouten paramours.' In other words, whether we should relate it to the words 'I best love ... greve' immediately following these two lines, or to 'lyvynge' immediately preceding it presents us two different interpretations. Those who recognise the problematics of the phenomenon might perceive that the conversation proceeds in a secure way because of its wider application.

(3) "And here I make a protestacioun
  That in this proces *if ye depper go*,
  That certeynly, for no salvacioun
  Of yow, though that ye sterven bothe two,

8. Ambiguity in discourse structure 103

Though al the world on o day be my fo,
Ne shal I nevere of hym han *other* routhe."
"*I graunte wel*," quod Pandare, "by my trowthe.

"But may I truste wel to yow," quod he,
"That of this thyng that ye han hight me here,
Ye wole it holden trewely unto me?"
"*Ye, doutelees*," quod she, "myn uncle deere."
"Ne that I shal han cause in this matere,"
Quod he, "to pleyne, or ofter yow to preche?"
"*Why, no, parde*; what nedeth moore speche?" Tr 2.484-97

In our daily discourse we take a great deal for granted in the way of recognitions, presuppositions or ellipses. (3) is a specimen of this. The comparative 'if ye depper go' (Tr 2.485) and *other* (Tr 2.489) have the potential criteria 'than ....'[71] Formulae indicative of positive response, 'I graunte wel,' (Tr 2.490) and 'Ye, douteles,' (Tr 2.494) and a formula indicative of negative response 'no, parde,' (Tr 2.497) are uttered on the assumption of preceding statements or questions.[72] The conversation between Criseyde and Pandarus goes easily. But if we try to reconstruct the unspoken parts, this is not as simple as it appears. The criterion assumed for the comparison of Tr 2.485 is made clear if we relate it to 'Swych love of frendes' (Tr 2.379) prevailing through the town according to Pandarus, but the 'Swych' again requires a criterion for making clear its reference. The criterion for the comparison of Tr 2.489 is also made imprecise since the *routhe* itself is made a matter of degree.[73] In reply of this, Pandarus agrees by saying 'I graunte wel' (Tr 2.490), but his agreement remains unclear because the criterion for the above comparison is also unclear. Criseyde replies in the affirmative to Pandarus's question whether she can keep her promise of this (Tr 2.492-3), but the content of her agreement is still not certain. Finally, we have Criseyde's negative response of 'Why, no' (Tr 2.497) to Pandarus's question whether he has any cause to complain or ask her further about 'this matere' (Tr 2.995), but there remains uncertainty about what exactly is shared between Criseyde and Pandarus as regards the above question and answer. The characters, Criseyde and Pandarus, seem to take for granted their route to the action in question. But from the viewpoint of the reader, the second prism, the certification of the assumption in question remains unfulfilled, and with the final solution left to him or her, ambiguity is likely to arise.

Criseyde's curiosity is aroused by what Pandarus says, and she asks him how he comes to know of Troilus's love, whether anyone else knows about this except them, and whether he himself knows much about love. They gradually relax. Then Pandarus engages in some wordplay (double entendre), as seen in (4).

(4) "And right good thrift, I prey to God, have ye,
That han swich oon ykaught withouten net!
And be ye wis as ye be fair to see,
Wel in the ryng than is the ruby set.

---

71 See 'comparative reference' in Halliday and Hasan (1976: 76).
72 See 'ellipsis in question-answer and other rejoinder sequences' in Halliday and Hasan (1976: 206).
73 See the implication of *pite* in Section 12.5.

Ther were nevere two so wel ymet,
Whan ye ben his al hool as he is youre;
Ther myghty God graunte us see *that houre*!"

"Nay, *therof* spak I nought, ha, ha!" quod she;
"As helpe me God, ye shenden every deel!"
"O, mercy, dere nece," anon quod he,
"*What so I spak*, I mente naught but wel,
By Mars, the god that helmed is of steel!
Now beth naught wroth, my blood, my nece dere."
"Now wel," quod she, "foryeven be *it* here!"   Tr 2.582-95

There is a sexual implication in 'Wel in the ryng than is the ruby set' (Tr 2.585) and 'Ye ben his al hool as he is youre' (Tr 2.587) where, as Gordon (1970) and Ross (1972) point out, the word *hool* seems to carry the senses of 'wholly' and 'hole.' Pandarus's longing to see *That houre* (Tr 2.588) with a demonstrative, Criseyde's response using *therof* (Tr 2.589) with a pronoun, his use of a free relative 'What so I spak' (Tr 2.592), a near equivalent of substitution, and finally, her use of the pronoun *it* (Tr 2.595)—these proforms are assumed to refer to the same thing. But the referent is not specified on the text surface (exophoric).[74] Pandarus and Criseyde are aware of the potential scandal of the action and take it for granted as something to be thought about when the time comes.

After Pandarus goes home, she devotes herself to meditation. The crowd begin to shout with joy at Troilus's triumphant return to Troy. As we can see from (5), she is taken with the sight of the brave, young, and vigorous Troilus.[75]

(5) So lik a man of armes and a knyght
    He was to seen, fulfilled of heigh prowesse,
    For bothe he hadde a body and a myght
    To don *that thing*, as wel as hardynesse;
    And ek to seen hym in his gere hym dresse,
    So fressh, so yong, so weldy semed he,
    It was an heven upon hym for to see.   Tr 2.631-7

As regards '... he hadde a body and a might / To don that thing' (Tr 2.633-4)[76], what do the demonstrative *that* and a general word for substitution *thing* refer back to? Assuming that Troilus's military prowess is focused here, we can interpret *that* as a case of anaphora of endophoric reference.[77] On the other hand, assuming that Criseyde is strongly attracted by his body and her desire for it is the focus of the sentence, then

---

74 According to Halliday and Hasan (1976), the antecedents of proforms are divided into 'endophoric' (the antecedents being located inside the text) and 'exophoric' (the antecedents being located outside the text). The proform here belongs to the latter type. Further, the former endophoric type is divided into 'anaphoric' (the antecedents precede the proforms) and 'cataphoric' (the antecedents follow the proforms).

75 This example was dealt with in relation to the metatext in Chapter 4 and to the speech presentation in Chapter 7.

76 See 'nominal substitution' in Halliday and Hasan (1976: 91). Cf. Halliday and Hasan (1976: 278): lexical cohesion–'general words.'

77 *OED* s.v. thing: 4. That which is done or to be done; a doing, act deed, transaction. c1000-.

that is a case of exophoric reference and implies a sexual content.[78] As for the latter interpretation, *thing* is used elsewhere by Chaucer as a euphemism of that implication.[79] How the reader assumes Criseyde's psychological state will cause the rise of ambiguity.

In (6) we have a record of the conversation of Pandarus and Criseyde after he has persuaded her to come to dinner.

(6) Soone after this, she to hym gan to rowne,
And axed hym if Troilus were there.
He swor hire *nay*, for he was out of towne,
And seyde, "Nece, I pose that he were;
Yow thurste nevere han the more fere;
For rather than men myghte hym ther aspie,
Me were levere a thousand fold to dye." Tr 3.568-74

She asks him in a whisper if Troilus is there, but he immediately denies this, and says that Troilus is out of town. However, he adds "Suppose that he were there, you would have nothing to fear. I would rather die than men might find him there" (Tr 3.571-4). This addition will be further dealt with in Chapter 9 as a question of speech act or implication. She ought to decline the invitation owing to her honour as a courtly lady. His negative reply seems to be due to his consideration of this. How she understands his response and how she comes to accept his invitation are shown in (7).

(7) Nought list myn auctour fully to declare
What that she thoughte whan he seyde *so*,
That Troilus was out of towne yfare,
As if he seyde *therof* soth or no;
But that, withowten await, with hym to go,
She graunted hym, sith he hire that bisoughte,
And, as his nece, obeyed as hire oughte.

But natheles, yet gan she hym biseche,
Although with hym to gon it was no fere,
For to ben war of goosissh poeples speche,
That dremen *thygnes* whiche as nevere were,
And wel avyse hym whom he broughte there;
And seyde hym, "Em, syn I moste on yow triste,
Loke al be wel, and do now as yow liste."

He swor hire *yis*, by stokkes and by stones,
And by the goddes that in hevene dwelle, Tr 3.575-90

The antecedents of the pronominal adverb *so* in 'whan he seyde so,' (Tr 3.576) and the pronoun *therof* in 'he seyde therof' (Tr 3.578) are easily disambiguated, which clearly refer to 'That Troilus was out of towne yfare' (Tr 3.577). But there are plenty of hidden implications in 'What that she thoughte' (Tr 3.578) expressed in a free relative.

---

78 As shown in free indirect speech in Chapter 7, it is probable that this quotation contains Criseyde's point of view.
79 *OED* s.v. thing: 11.c. *euphem.* Privy member, private parts. c1386 WBP III 121-; Cf. 7.c. Used indefinitely to denote something which the speaker is not able or does not choose to particularize, or which is incapable of being precisely described. 1602-. The sexual implication of this word is pointed out by Donaldson (1970) and Ross (1972).

They are made uninformative since as the narrator says they are what 'myn auctour' (Tr 3.575) (the author of the original) would not like to make clear. The narrator stops the development of the plot and emphasises the uncertainty of her reaction. However, his emphasis of this might be functional in an anticlimactic way from the viewpoint of the reader, the second prism, who is outside the text and can see through it. (For further details, see Chapter 9.)

She draws Pandarus's attention to people's public gossip, saying that people dream *thynges* that would never exist (Tr 3.585). The word *thynges* is interpreted as a general/inclusive word, but on the other hand, it is also suggestive of a scandalous action, as is shown in (4). The same is true of *thyng* (Tr 3.763). Finally, she leaves everything to Pandarus and asks him to do as he likes, since she trusts him (Tr 3.587-8). His reply is *yis* (Tr 3.589). Spearing (1976: 15) comments: 'A powerful way of swearing 'yes'— but 'yes' what? It is not clear whether P [Pandarus] is swearing yes, he will 'loke al be wel' (and again, it is unclear what that would mean), or yes, he will do as he pleases.' What does Pandarus respond to?; supposing that he responds to the immediately preceding request by Criseyde, what does *al* (Tr 3.588) refer to?[80] and what is the object of *do* (Tr 3.588)?[81]; these questions cannot be answered. The referential relation using proforms is tacitly understood by Criseyde and Pandarus. From the above mentioned implication, it appears that Criseyde preserves her honour with a generalised statement and at a deeper level requests Pandarus to further her relationship with Troilus. Pandarus seems to be sensitive to this special situation, and responds accordingly. Of course, this is just one implication, and may be cancelled by the reader, if he chooses a different interpretation as a solution to the ambiguity.

What (Tr 3.844), 'al ... that' (Tr 3.845), *this* (Tr 3.846), and 'doth right so' (Tr 3.847) in (8) and *herof* (Tr 3.939) in (9) are more or less in the same vein. The referential meanings of these proformal expressions cannot be determined as can those of *al* (Tr 3.588) and *so* (Tr 3.576) in (7).

(8) "Ye woot, ye, nece myn," quod he, "*what is*.
I hope *al* shal be wel *that is amys*,
For ye may quenche al *this*, if that yow leste—
And *doth right so*, for I holde it the beste."   Tr 3.844-7

(9) "Than, em," quod she, "doth *herof* as yow list.
But er he com, I wil up first arise,   Tr 3.939-40

While Criseyde is in the Greek camp, she stays with her father and is visited for the second time by Diomede. Their meeting is described in (10).

(10) Criseyde, at shorte wordes for to telle,
Welcomed hym and *down hym* by hire *sette*—
And he was ethe ynough to maken dwelle!   Tr 5.848-50

Roscow (1981) analyses the rise of ambiguity due to ellipsis here in the following way. Assuming that the subject of *sette* (Tr 5.849) is Diomede, which is deleted after *and* (Tr 5.849), we can interpret that he is forward enough to take a seat without being

---

80   See 'nominal ellipsis' in Halliday and Hasan (1976: 147).
81   See 'modal ellipsis' in Halliday and Hasan (1976: 199).

asked (*him* (Tr 5.849) is here functional as reflexive). On the other hand, if the subject of *sette* is Criseyde, we can interpret the clause as meaning that she asks him to sit down.[82] If we interpret it thus, she appears more welcoming of Diomede than one might expect. Her action, however, may be the politeness of a hostess.[83]

Criseyde does not reject him out of hand. As can be seen from (11), she promises that "when you have won the town, I will do what I have not done" (Tr 5.990-3). But since it is clear that Troy is inferior in arms to Greece, her promise is not an empty one. It is, for example, more realistic than that made by Dorigen to Aurelius in *The Franklin's Tale*, i.e. that she will accept his love when the treacherous rocks in the sea are no more.

(11) "Myn herte is now in tribulacioun,
And ye in armes bisy day by day.
Heraftter, whan ye wonnen han the town,
Peraventure so it happen may
That whan I se that nevere yit I say
Than *wol I werke that I nevere wroughte*!
This word to yow ynough suffisen oughte.

To-morwe ek wol I speken with yow fayn,
So that ye touchen naught of *this matere*.
And whan yow list, ye may come here ayayn;
And er ye gon, *thus muche* I sey yow here: Tr 5.988-98

The content of a free relative *that* in 'wol I werke that I nevere wroughte' (Tr 5.993) is exophorically functional, and can only be determined by reference to the intention of the speaker, Criseyde, and the understanding of the hearer, Diomede. The reference of *This word* (Tr 5.994) is parallel to this. And so is the proform *thus muche* (Tr 5.998). (Cf. *this matere* Tr 5.996.) Naturally Diomede will choose to interpret these demonstratives so as to keep his hopes alive. Criseyde safeguards her honour as far as she can, and at the same time goes out of her way to encourage his expectations.

(12) is the well-known dream scene involving Criseyde and the boar.

(12) So on a day he leyde hym doun to slepe,
And so byfel that yn his slep hym thoughte
That in a forest faste he welk to wepe
For love of here that hym these peynes wroughte;
And up and doun as he the forest soughte,
He mette he saugh a bor with tuskes grete,
That slepte ayeyn the bryghte sonnes hete.

And by this bor, faste in *his* armes folde,
Lay, kyssyng ay, *his* lady bryght, Criseyde.
For sorwe of which, whan he it gan byholde,
And for despit, out of his slep he breyde,   Tr 5.1233-43

---

82 See the discussion of syntactic ambiguity in Chapter 11.
83 In terms of the speaker's intention in Chapter 9, it is uncertain whether the expression shows Criseyde's positive involvement with Diomede or is merely a politeness marker.

We have already discussed this quotation from a different point of view in Chapter 4 (see (22)). Here we consider the reference of the pronoun *his* in 'his lady bryght' (Tr 5.1241). We have already observed the wide variation in scribal and editorial choice as regards *his* (Tr 5.1240), but there are no variants of *his* in the line in question here. It could not be *her*. However, is the referent of *his* in this line so clear? Both the scribes and the editors do not appear doubtful as to its content, so that the reader, the second prism, is forced to interpret it. The word can have one of two references. It may be the boar in the preceding line (this boar will later be explained as a symbol of Diomede by Cassandra the soothsayer). Troilus sees Criseyde already possessed by the boar, in other words, have accepted his love. The other possibility is that *his* refers to Troilus, who is having the dream. By this interpretation she is still "his own," and he expects their love relationship to continue. In this one small word – *his* – we can see how rich in connotations Chaucer's language is.

(1a, b, c) are used to strengthen the cohesion within a discourse, however in *Troilus and Criseyde* for the phenomena which are problematic in moral terms, they are used in a taken-for-granted way by the characters and their interlocutors. This taken-for-granted conversation stimulates the reader's inference (based on contiguity), and when his or her way of reconstructing it is assumed in various ways, ambiguity is likely to arise. (For details of the referential ambiguity in *Troilus and Criseyde*, see Nakao (2010a).)

8.3. Ambiguity in cohesion: a focus on causality in conjunction (1d)

8.3.1. Causality and degrees of subjectivity

Halliday and Hasan (1976: 321) point out that there are two kinds of conjunctive relations—'external' and 'internal.' Causal relation is an example of them. 'External' means that it functions in an ideational world, and 'internal' means that it functions in an interpersonal world.[84] The former deals with an objective or logical causal relation, and the latter deals with a subjective causal relation reflective of his or her opinion.[85]

---

[84] Halliday and Hasan (1976: 29): an utterance is a conglomeration of three semantic systems, that is, 'ideational,' 'interpersonal,' and 'textual' systems. The 'ideational' semantic system is concerned with the logical relation of a proposition, the 'interpersonal' one with the attitudes between the speaker and the hearer, and the 'textual' one with the cohesion and the information structure at the intersentential level. This is the category we used for establishing the category of ambiguity in Section 3.2.

[85] Sweetser (1990) developed her pragmatic stance, and divided Halliday and Hasan's 'internal' further into 'epistemic' and 'speech act.' For example, she distinguishes the following meanings of *since* as below.
 a. *Since* John wasn't there, we decided to leave a note for him.
 (His absence caused our decision in the real world.) This *since* is called a 'content conjunction.'
 b. *Since* John isn't here, he has (evidently) gone home.
 (The *knowledge* of his absence causes my *conclusion* that he has gone home.) This *since* is called an 'epistemic conjunction.'
 c. *Since* we're on the subject, when was George Washington born?

Since a causal relation arises from the speaker's or hearer's way of inference,[86] it is difficult to make clear whether the actual causal relation is external/objective or internal/subjective.

Troilus and Criseyde, though basically an adaptation of a love romance, abounds in those parts descriptive of the characters'/narrator's inferences and reasoning designed to persuade the interlocutors into performing the action in question, or to motivate such decisions in the minds of the performers themselves, etc. In particular, where the actions of the characters in the story are ethically dubious, they are asked to justify themselves with appropriate reasons before performing such actions. In that respect, this work comes close to being an expository writing like *Melibee* and *The Parson's Tale* in *The Canterbury Tales*. Therefore it is no wonder that we should find a large number of causal expressions in the story. Interestingly enough, we are encouraged more often than not to test the validity of the causality.

We have to remember, of course, that all the causality actually belongs to Chaucer's imagination rather than to any real people inhabiting a real world, and that maybe it is asking too much to reconstruct the perfect non-contradictory clarity in everything. What is interesting here is whether we can identify his use of particular strategies of suggestion. Contradictory causality may be one of them. Since the validity of the causality is basically dependent on the audience's/reader's inference, and the criteria for it are only sporadically hinted at or implied, I think it makes estimation highly problematical. There are at least three kinds of people who make judgements: the author who sees through the story, the unreliable narrator in particular or fictional characters, and the reader, the second prism, who is involved with the first two judgements. Causal relation is likely to vary from external to internal according to how the reader assumes the viewpoint of the narrator or character. Theoretically a cause leads to a result, but from a human recognition point of view, we usually recognize the resulted action first and then infer the cause for it. It is no wonder that this should cause ambiguity.

With regard to the external use of causals, a variety of conjunctions denoting causality are illustrated with examples. Kerkhof (1982) discusses Chaucer's causals, such as *sin, as, for, because*, etc.[87] But he makes little or no reference to the internal use of

---

(I *ask* you because we're on the subject—the fact that we're on the subject, for example, enables my *act* of asking the question.) This *since* is called 'speech act conjunction.'

Here, we have regarded the b, c above as belonging to the internal category of Halliday and Hasan (1976).

86 Regarding the causal relation between the two elements (cause—result), the inference of contiguity is activated. Whether the causality is classified as 'external' or 'internal' depends on whether the cause-result contiguous relation is strong (directly related) or weak (indirectly related).

87 *OED* s.v. causality 2. the operation or relation of cause and effect; 'the law of mind which makes it necessary to recognise power adequate to account for every occurrence.'

Mitchell's (1985) treatment of causality: The word 'cause' is used here in a narrow grammatical sense, embracing both 'that which produces an effect; that which gives rise to any action, phenomenon, or condition' (*OED*, s.v. cause I.1) and 'a fact, condition of matters, or consideration, moving a person to action; ground of action; reason for action, motive' (*OED*, s.v. cause I.3). Cause in this sense is, of course, most frequently expressed in what formal grammarians classify as clauses of cause. As I use this term, it covers any clause which states

them. From a lexicographical point of view, the *OED/MED* are the same, and pay little attention to their attitudinal implications vis-à-vis their pragmatic contexts. Since the internal use of causals is due to the speaker's way of cognition and intention, it derives its function from the pragmatics involved. In this respect the findings of Pearsall (1986: 17) and Smith (1992: 277) are worth noting.[88] They delve into the psychological state of the narrator or characters with reference to the effects of subversion in relation to causals. However, Pearsall (1986) focuses on Criseyde's logic of choice through the repetition of *and*, and Smith focuses on the punning effect of *syn* (since + sin) with an ancillary treatment of causals. Causals in *Troilus and Criseyde* are still worth reexamination.

8.3.2. Examination: Tr 3.561-947

Our particular attention is drawn to one of the focal points in the story where Criseyde is encouraged by Pandarus to give her heart to Troilus. Here, the causality is exploited by the narrator as well as by the characters with their subtle psychological states. Pandarus promises to bring Troilus and Criseyde together at his house (Tr 3.193-200). From a cause-effect point of view, the narrator explains how she is invited to it as shown in (13) and (14). (For this quotation, see the analysis of (12) in Chapter 4 and that of the speaker's intention in Chapter 9.)

(13) At which she lough, and gan hire faste excuse,
　　　And seyde, "It reyneth; lo, how sholde I gon?"
　　　"Lat be," quod he, "ne stant nought thus to muse.
　　　This moot be don! Ye shal be ther anon."
　　　So at the laste herof they fille aton,　　　　　　　Tr 3.561-5

　　　Nought list myn auctour fully to declare
　　　What that she thoughte whan he seyde so,
　　　That Troilus was out of towne yfare,
　　　As if he seyde therof soth or no;
　　　But that, withowten await, with hym to go,
　　　She graunted hym, *sith* he hire that bisoughte,
　　　And, as his nece, obeyed as hire oughte.　　　　Tr 3.575-81

---

　　　the cause or reason for a consequence, the grounds for an assertion, or the definition of a remark made in the clause with which it is associated.
　　　Kerkhof's (1982: 470-1) treatment of causality: Clauses of cause and reason are mostly introduced by: as (a), bycause (b), for (c) and syn (d); here again that is often added. (Kerkhof's underlines). Here the pragmatic view is disregarded.
　　　Mustanoja (1960), Visser (1969), and Roscow (1981) have not dealt with this causal construction.

88　Pearsall (1986: 17):
　　　I normally confine myself to talking about Chaucer's irony ... though *but* and *for* may have many hidden subtleties, *and* is pretty straightforward.
　　　Smith (1992: 277):
　　　In *Troilus and Criseyde* ... the explicative function of *syn* is often subverted by hyperbole, paradox, and irony. We can rarely trust wholly the narrative persona, who presents himself as varyingly engaged, detached, bemused, troubled, and through it all concerned to understand and defend—or correct—the perplexities inhering in the text of his "auctour."

8. Ambiguity in discourse structure

(14) But natheles, yet gan she hym biseche,
  Although with hym to gon it was no fere,
  For to ben war of goosissh poeples speche,
  That dremen thynges whiche as nevere were,
  And wel avyse hym whom he broughte there;
  And seyde hym, "Em, *syn* I moste on yow triste,
  Loke al be wel, and do now as yow liste."

  He swor hire yis, by stokkes and by stones,   Tr 3.582-9

To which function do we ascribe *sith* (Tr 3.580) and *syn* (Tr 3.587): external or internal?[89] The former conjunction is open to alternative interpretations as regards external or internal in relation to the main clause 'She graunted hym ...' (Tr 3.580). The latter is in conjunction with the imperative construction 'Loke al be wel ...' (Tr 3.588), and therefore regarded as united with a potential 'I ask/command.' Here it functions as internal.

Pandarus's invitation of Criseyde to supper at his house implies a moral question particularly with regard to Troilus's potential presence there. The narrator, perhaps with this implication in mind, is very cautious in treating her acceptance, which is intended to exclude any free choice on her part, with regard to which see first Pandarus's use of modals denoting necessity/obligation (Tr 3.564) and second the *sith*-clause (Tr 3.580). If the causality is taken as external, the reader's involvement in the judgement about the validity of the action above will be excluded.

However, hints are given about Criseyde's inclination to favour acceptance (Tr 3.568-9, Tr 3.575-8, Tr 3.579: the fronted position of 'withowten await' seems to indicate that she is already well-disposed to the idea). Provided that she is ignorant of Troilus's presence, external causality is fully proved. If she guesses that he is there and immorality will ensue, or if she more positively desires it, and in its full realisation accepts the invitation, then the external causality, coloured by the narrator's subjectivity, is open to scepticism. His viewpoint seems to merge with Criseyde's because of his sympathy for her. She, a courtly lady, facing a potential immoral action, is circumspect about the honour she is expected to safeguard and is only allowed to be made minimally responsible for it by the social pressure imposed on her. In this causal we find the narrator's internal recognition reflected.

The causal *syn* in (14) is functional as internal. Although she may be motivated by her inner desire concerning the acceptance, she intends to make everything due to her

---

89   Causal conjunctions dealt with in this section: the *OED*'s definitions.
  OED s.v. sith [reduced from OE *siþþan* (subsequent to, or since the time that)] 2. seeing that; =*Since* conj. 4. Now *arch.* or *poet*. Very common from c1520-c1670, being freq. used to express cause, while *since* was restricted to time.
  OED s.v. sin [contracted form of *sithen*] 2. Seeing or considering that. 1300-1818 †b. So *sin that. Obs.* c1375-1474
  OED s.v. for: for that (reduced forms of Old English *for þæm* (dative of *that*) *þe* †1. because 1200-1872 *Obs.* or *rare*. 2. Introducing the ground or reason for something previously said: Seeing that, since. L. *nam* or *enim*, Fr *car*, Ger *denn*. c1150-1883
  OED s.v. because: B. conj. 1. For the reason that; inasmuch as, since. c 1305-. 1386 Chaucer Frankl. Prol.8

uncle, or to evade the responsibility for the potential immoral act by appeal to the social pressure upon her—her obligation to trust in him.

When she is forced to stay at Pandarus's house, the narrator brings into focus the *causez* (Tr 3.620) for her stay, which is attributed to the divine will, as shown in (15).

(15) But O Fortune, executrice of wierdes,
O influences of thise hevenes hye!
Soth is, that under God ye ben oure hierdes,
Though to us bestes ben *the causez* wrie.
This mene I now: *for* she gan homward hye,
But execut was al bisyde hire leve
The goddes wil, *for which* she moste bleve.   Tr 3.617-23

The conjunction *for* (Tr 3.621) and the preposition *for* (Tr 3.623) are employed to emphasise the point that her stay overnight at Pandarus's house is by no means in accord with her volition but divinely ordained. This is assumed to be so according to the narrator who tries to safeguard her honour. However, since the rain was part of Pandarus's plan, or more significantly, she perhaps came to his house with the expectation that she was to meet Troilus, the reader is encouraged to be sceptical of the causality here.[90] In this causality there is a merger of the objective 'reasoning' and the subjective 'feelings.'

Criseyde's decision is expressed as seen in (16).

(16) "I wol," quod she, "myn uncle lief and deere;
Syn that yow list, it skile is to be so.   Tr 3.645-6

In the view of Criseyde, 'it is reasonable to do so, since it is favorable to him.' The causality stemming from the uncle-niece familial relationship, however, is only apparently plausible. This causality is assumed to imply Criseyde's individually directed emotion, that is an evasion of her responsibility for the potential scandal, as shown in (13) or (15).

In (17), Pandarus stresses her ability to remedy what is *amys* (Tr 3.845) and the point that this is the best thing for her to do.

(17) I hope al shal be wel that is amys,
For ye may quenche al this, if that yow leste—
And doth right so, *for* I holde it the beste."   Tr 3.845-7

And yet it is regarded as 'the best' (Tr 3.847) according to Pandarus's view ('I holde') (Tr 3.847). (18) is the justification by Pandarus urged upon Criseyde for her instant acceptance of Troilus.

(18) "So shal I do to-morwe, ywys," quod she,
"And God toforn, so that it shal suffise."
"To-morwe? Allas, that were a fair!" quod he;
"Nay, nay, it may nat stonden in this wise,
For, nece myn, thus writen clerkes wise,

---

90   The conjunction *for* collocates frequently with the epistemic phrases: *hardely* (Tr 2.304), *certes* (Tr 3.1478), *douteles* (Tr 4.430), *trewely* (Tr 5.410); 'by my trouthe' (Tr 1.906), 'withouten any drede' (Tr 3.418); 'God woot' (Tr 2.995), 'wel I woot' (Tr 3.337), 'certeyn is' (Tr 4.569), 'trusteth wel that' (Tr 4.1667); *wol* (Tr 1.573), *shal* (Tr 4.1279).

8. Ambiguity in discourse structure

That peril is with drecchyng in ydrawe;
Nay, swiche abodes ben nought worth an hawe.

"Nece, *alle thyng hath tyme*, I dar avowe;
For whan a chaumbre afire is or an halle,
Wel more nede is, it sodeynly rescowe
Than to dispute and axe amonges alle
How this candel in the strawe is falle.
A, benedicite! For al among that fare
The harm is don, and fare-wel feldefare!"   Tr 3.848-61

(19) emphasises the point that Troilus's coming to her is unknown to everyone and therefore not a sin.

(19) That dar I seyn, *now ther is but we two*.
But wel I woot that ye wol nat do so;
Ye ben to wys to doon so gret folie,
To putte his lif al nyght in jupertie."   Tr 3.865-8

"Now loke thanne, if ye that ben his love
Shul putte his lif al night in jupertie
For thyng of nought, now by that God above,
Naught oonly this delay comth of folie,
But of malice, if that I shal naught lie.
What! Platly, and ye suffre hym in destresse,
Ye neyther *bounte* don ne *gentilesse*."   Tr 3.876-82

"Now have I told what peril he is inne,
And *his comynge unwist is to every wight*;
Ne, parde, *harm* may ther be non, ne *synne*:
I wol myself be with yow al this nyght.
Ye knowe ek how it is youre owen knyght,
And that bi right ye moste upon hym triste,
And I al prest to fecche hym whan yow liste."   Tr 3.911-7

The internal causal *for* (Tr 3.852, Tr 3.856) expressing the reason for the speaker's statement is available for the introduction of a more material example of the abstract proposition,[91] as is typically shown in the line 'alle thyng hath tyme' (Tr 3.855). Proverbs and examples are commonly introduced by *for* in this way. In conjunction with

---

91   This causal pattern is frequently used in medieval expository texts as shown below.
    Stanley (1960), *The Owl and the Nightingale*:
    For Aluered seide of olde quide—
    An ȝut hit nis of horte islide,
    'Wone þe bale is alre hecst
    þonne is þe bote is alre necst;'   685-8

    Wherfore we axen leyser and espace to have deliberacion in this cas to deme. / *For* the commune proverbe seith thus: 'He that soone deemeth, soone shal repente.' Mel VII 1029-30

    Whoso thanne wolde wel understande thise peynes and bithynke hym weel that he hath deserved thilke peynes for his synnes, certes, he sholde have moore talent to siken and to wepe than for to syngen and to pleye./ *For*, as that seith Salomon, "Whoso that hadde the science to knowe the peynes that been establissed and ordeyned for synne, he wolde make sorwe." ParsT X (I) 228-9

the generalisation/moralisation involved in the causality, Pandarus's frequent evocation of courtly and religious ideals are worth noting: see his use of *wys* (Tr 3.867), *bounte* (Tr 3.882), *gentilesse* (Tr 3.882); *harm* (Tr 3.913), *synne* (Tr 3.913). However, the juxtaposition of these virtues adduced in favour of her acceptance of Troilus without delay and his practical comments about the secrecy 'now ther is but we two' (Tr 3.865), and 'his comynge unwist is to every wight' (Tr 3.912) seem to hint that Pandarus regards the (immoral) liaison of Criseyde and Troilus as virtuous so long as it is not known by others. This would imply criticism from a moral point of view. The above proverbs are used as an escape from the difficult alternative of confronting the truth. Or, seen more from a psychological than amoral perspective, the causality here may be assumed to arise from his due consideration to Criseyde, a courtly lady, whose honour is vulnerable to criticism.

Our primary concern in (20) is with Tr 3.918-24, which is most probably the narrator's reconstruction of Criseyde's introspection as to how and why she can accept Troilus. This quotation has already been discussed in (1) of Chapter 5, and (5) of Chapter 7. Let us reexamine it from the viewpoint of causality.

(20) This accident *so* pitous was to here,
　　And ek *so* like a sooth at prime face,
　　And Troilus hire knyght to hir *so* deere,
　　His prive comyng, and the siker place,
　　That though that she did hym as thanne a grace,
　　Considered alle thynges as they stoode,
　　No wonder is, *syn* she did al for goode.

　　Criseyde answerde, "As wisly God at reste
　　My soule brynge, as me is for hym wo!
　　And em, iwis, *fayn wolde I don the beste*,
　　If that ich hadde grace to do so;
　　But whether that ye dwelle or for hym go,
　　I am, til God me bettre mynde sende,
　　At dulcarnoun, right at my wittes ende."　　　Tr 3.918-31

In order to reinforce the justification for her acceptance of Troilus, a sin in the eyes of the Church and the potential source of scandal from a social point of view, he lists a series of contextual factors (*pitous, sooth, hir knyght, prive, siker*) through the repeated causality 'so ... that' (Tr 3.918, 919, 920, 922) and the *syn*-clause (*syn ... for goode*) (Tr 3.924) appended finally with some effect of end-focus in the stanza. The above factors are concerned with courtly and/or religious idealism. *Pitous* is central to the courtly ideal *gentilesse* and carries some religious overtone of the Virgin Mary's pity; *grace* is endowed with divine connotation; *prive* is associated with God's private mysteries, etc. In this way we are encouraged to endorse the validity of the causality above.

The view of the narrator, who is sympathetic to Criseyde, is likely to be merged with hers, and thus it is uncertain whether the above narrative is through the narrator's inference about the state of her psychology or reflects it more directly (see FIS in Chapter 7). With regard to the view in clause Tr 3.922-4, 'No wonder is' in the present tense is worth noting. Functional as a narrative tag for an interplay between the narrator and the audience,[92] it seems to refer to the contemporary reaction to such a circumstance. That is, supposing all that goes previously, it is not a cause for wonder to Chaucer's audience that Criseyde might have bestowed her favours on Troilus. The following causality in 'syn ...' whose dominant sense is probably internal is perhaps tacked on as an after-thought, since he is being so clear-cut in asserting 'No wonder is.' It seems to shift more towards a narrator's opinion than free indirect speech. Incidentally, in some instances of FIS in Chaucer, the (historical) present tense can be used owing to the habitual or generalised character of the propositional contents in question. If this is applied here, it seems that the causality in Tr 3.912-4 is also subject to Criseyde's view.

The application of the moral terms to the immoral act referred to above is not completely successful as a camouflage, but acts rather as a stimulant to scepticism for the Christian audience. A Pandarian virtue 'His prive coming, and the siker place' (Tr 3.921) and the juxtaposition of a spiritual *grace* (Tr 3.922) and a physical (secret) *place* (Tr 3.921) emphatically in a rhyming position are suggestive of this critical interpretation.[93] The narrator seems to be saying that the causality arises from Criseyde's habit or character, which requires her always to act for the best in the given situation, with a fuzzy implication of relativism (borne out in the next stanza, 'fayn wolde I don the beste' (Tr 3.327)). Therefore, in view of the dominant subjectivity, the causality here is open to question. Criseyde, though bound by the courtly idealism she has to live up to, has succeeded paradoxically in being pressed by external ethical pressures into accepting Troilus into her bed.

In (21) Criseyde intends to justify her action by leaving the choice wholly to Pandarus.

(21) "Than, em," quod she, "doth herof as yow list.
But er he com, I wil up first arise,
And for the love of God, *syn* al my trist
Is on yow two, and ye ben bothe wise,
So werketh now in so discret a wise
That I honour may have, and he plesaunce:
For I am here al in youre governaunce."

"That is wel seyd," quod he, "my nece deere.
Ther good thrift on that wise gentil herte!   Tr 3.939-47

The first causality (*syn* Tr 3.941) is functional internally, since it is followed by the imperative; the second one (*for* Tr 3.945) is perhaps of a similar nature, an addition to the first, as indicated by the editorial colon. Based on the morally pressed causality (*trist, wise, discret, honour and governaunce* ('rule'/'manner')), she places herself under the total control of Pandarus. Since the ambiguous narrative context seen in (20) is still latent on the part of the reader, the validity of these causals are made problematic and therefore open to ambiguity.

When Criseyde accepts Troilus into her bed, she explains to him why she is inclined to take pity on him as in (22).

---

92   GP I (A) 641, CIT IV (E) 337, LGW F 525, etc.
93   As for the rhyming pair of 'grace-place,' see the MerT IV (E) 1997-8 in Section 5.2.

(22) "Lo, herte myn, as wolde the excellence
 Of love, ayeins the which that no man may—
 Ne oughte ek—goodly make resistence,
 And ek *bycause* I felte wel and say
 Youre grete trouthe and servise every day,
 And *that* youre herte al myn was, soth to seyne,
 This drof me for to rewe upon youre peyne. Tr 3.988-94

In the view of Criseyde, the causality introduced by *bycause* (Tr 3.991), which can probably be ascribed to the category "external causal," is solid. Troilus is persuaded to believe it. It is endorsed by her courtly and religious virtues (*trouthe, servise* Tr 3.992),'youre herte al myn was'—absolute commitment). However, the reader can assume that it is controlled by her intention, and so it is regarded as due to her capability for shifting affections according to the varying situation.[94] Taking together the hints about her instant love for Troilus seen in Chapter 6 and about the subjectivity of her causality (Tr 3.580-1, Tr 3.588-9, Tr 3.918-24), we are likely to assume that she here states how she ought to behave as an ideal courtly lady rather than how she actually feels. Here occurs once again a causality with ambiguous overtones of both the objective 'reasoning' and the subjective 'feelings.'

The causalities are introduced by the narrator as well as the characters in *Troilus and Criseyde* on some crucial occasions where they are asked to perform potentially immoral actions, and yet are acutely sensitive to the idealism which they have to live up to. They intend to make clear why and how they justify themselves in performing those actions.

As regards the cause and effect relation, the result is, according to the speaker's cognition, recognised before the cause in most cases rather than the other way round. This also applies to our case: Criseyde's inconstancy is derived from the inherited plot, but why she behaved as she did depends on the writer's inference or (re-)interpretation.

Among the external and internal of causal conjunctions, external ones have been much discussed (Kerkhof (1982), Mitchell (1985), *OED/MED*, etc.), but internal ones

---

94 Just before she is sent to the Greek camp, Criseyde gives her explanation as to why she felt sorry for Troilus ('had on yow routhe') and accepted him as her lover.
 "*For* trusteth wel that youre estat roial,
 Ne veyn delit, nor only worthinesse
 Of yow in werre or torney marcial,
 Ne pompe, array, nobleye, or ek richesse
 Ne *made* me to rewe on youre destresse,
 But moral vertu, grounded upon trouthe—
 That was *the cause* I first hadde on yow routhe!

 "Eke gentil herte and manhod that ye hadde,
 And that ye hadde, as me thoughte, in despit
 Every thyng that sounded into badde,
 As rudenesse and poeplissh appetit,
 And that youre resoun bridlede youre delit,
 This *made*, aboven every creature,
 That I was youre, and shal while I may dure. Tr 4.1667-80

have not been given due attention, although occurring as often or perhaps oftener. Internal causality involves the speaker's epistemology and intention. Criseyde's inconstancy is justified by repeated and reinforced social pressures (ranging from religious virtues through the courtly idealism/human common sense to a more subjective order as illustrated by Pandarus). However, this does not exhaust the question. In the view of the audience/reader who is capable of accessing a much wider context than the protagonists in the story, the speaker's intended causality is made problematic and subjectivised with some implication of criticism. The audience/reader is encouraged to be sensitive to and uncover the subjective filter 'I think'/'I intend to say/mean,' which is made in most cases textually implicit and assumed even unconsciously on the part of the speaker. The filter can be part of condensed meanings in the simple causality as formed by *syn* and *for*.

The semantic tension in causality between external and internal is most probably due to the conflict in Chaucer between the two opposing attitudes (sympathetic/critical) towards the ideal courtly lady who is asked to perform the immoral acts. From the discussion above, it may safely be concluded that Chaucer uses ambiguity or contradiction—implying an imaginary switching on and off of 'I think'/'I intend to say/mean'—in causality as a measure of the moral status of his characters, and that it is central to our view of the narrator and the characters such as Criseyde and to the poem's meaning as a whole. (For details of the subjective use of causality, see Nakao (1998).)

8.4. Ambiguity in cohesion: a focus on lexical cohesion (1e)

In the oral transmission of middle English literature lexical repetition and variation are indispensable and perhaps the easiest way to maintain the key concepts in the memory of the audience.[95] Needless to say, Chaucer exploits this method. However, what concept a word condenses does not remain the same, since a word is repeated in shifting or even reversed contexts. In semantic terms words are likely to be affected by their variable contexts, and in this state maintain the cohesion within the discourse. Provided that a word's preceding contexts are maintained and overlap with the word's present context by the reader, they are likely to be interactive with each other with deep implications. (Refer to the concept *zanzo* or 'engram' in Toyama (1964).) Let us see a few examples as to how *zanzo* is effective in producing ambiguity of repeated words.

First, let us look at the *zanzo* effect regarding those words expressing the secular and the sacred. The distance of these repeated words is variously extended from a comparatively small distance to an extreme (the beginning of the story to the last). As regards the intertexture of the *Troilus* in Chapter 5, we have pointed out that 'God loveth ....' (Tr 3.12-4) is paraphrased into *amorous* (Tr 3.17), as a result of which universal love and earthly (sexual) love are interactive with and critical of each other. We have pointed out in Chapter 6 that the idea of love is repeated from the 'lawe of kynde'

---

[95] Halliday and Hasan (1976: 279) subdivides the means of lexical reiteration into the following four types: 'the same word, a synonym or near-synonym, a surperordinate, a general word.'

(Tr 1.228) (the beginning of the story) through courtly love (Book III) to Christian love (the ending of the story), and that these various types of love are interactive with and critical of each other.

The phrase expressing the consummation of Troilus and Criseyde's love, 'blisse in hevene' is repeated in the text. From an intertextual point of view, this is appropriate for a religious text whose subject is heavenly love. It is applied to the physical liaison between Troilus and Criseyde via the religion of love ascribed to courtly love (Tr 3.704, Tr 3.1202-4, Tr 3.1599-60, Tr 3.1658-9). On the other hand, it is used in the original sense at the ending of the story (Tr 5.1818-9). Keeping this original sense as *zanzo* and reinterpreting those previous phrases retroactively, the tension between the sacred and the secular is likely to be increasingly felt.[96]

Troilus laughs at lovers in Book 1 (*smyle* Tr 1.194, Tr 1.329), and that corresponds to his laughter after his death when he ascends to the eighth sphere (*lough* Tr 5.1821), and gains an insight into earthly blindness. The former is a blind terrestrial laughter; the latter is the cosmic laughter of one released from the shackles of earthly existence. The interaction between *smyle* and *lough* in this instance is unique since it bridges over the beginning and the end of the story.

Second, let us look at the interaction between human nature and Fortune which transcends it. In *Boece*, *slydynge* is used as an epithet of Fortune ('slydynge Fortune' Bo1.m.5.34). This word is applied to the event in which Troy and Troilus slides through Criseyde's heart (*slide* Tr 5.769), and to her unstable state of mind ('slydynge of corage' Tr 5.825). Taking into account the intertextual repetition here, with the mutable nature of Fortune as *zanzo*, the *slydynge* (Tr 5.825) is likely to be ambiguous as to whether it is directly derived from her character or instigated by Fortune. (For further information on *slydynge*, see Section 12.2.)

Third, the referent of *pite* and its synonymous words are ironically interactive with each other in that Criseyde shows pity to Troilus and accepts his love (*routhe* Tr 4.1673), while in the Greek camp, she shows pity to Diomede and accepts his love (*routhe* Tr 5.1000). Her pity is applicable to both Troilus and Diomede. It is functional in a double edged way. (For details see Section 12.5.)

Fourth, proverbs are used in mutually opposing contexts. In (23) Pandarus encourages Troilus, who is desperate for his love, with favourable proverbs.

(23) "For thilke grownd that bereth the *wedes wikke*
Bereth ek thise *holsom herbes*, as ful ofte
Next the *foule netle*, rough and thikke,
The *rose* waxeth swoote and smothe and softe;
And next the *valeye* is the *hil* o-lofte;
And next the *derke nyght* the *glade morwe*;
And also *joie* is next the fyn of *sorwe*. Tr 1.946-52

Pandarus expands proverbial wisdom by repeating the idea of two contrastive things being close to each other. He uses various oxymoronic metaphors such as 'wholesome herbs near weeds,' 'the rose near the foul nettle,' 'hills near valleys,' 'glad morning

---

96 The repetition of 'blisse in hevene' (Tr 3.704, etc.) is referred to in Note 47 in Chapter 5 in terms of intertextuality.

near dark night,' and 'joy near the end of sorrow.' He focuses on the positive aspect of love in order to encourage Troilus towards it. (This proverb is quoted in Whiting (1967). 'Joy after wo, and wo after gladness (varied) Chaucer CT I (A) 2841, Usk 82.180, CT II (B) 421-4, Lydgate Troy I 157, 471-2, Temple 17.397, etc.) However, the juxtaposition of two contrastive values has an implication that even though the positive value is highlighted for the present, the negative value will be highlighted if the situation shifts in the opposite direction. The audience is informed at the beginning of the story about Troilus's fortune 'Fro wo to wele, and after out of joie (Tr 1.4). From a holistic point of view, the love between Troilus and Criseyde ascends from Books 1 to 3, while it descends from Books 4 to 5. Pandarus's intended proverb applies to the earlier part where the positive value is functional, but significantly suggests the latter part where the negative value is functional. The reader, the second prism, is made to perceive ambiguity in his use of proverbs which dwell on the idea of vicissitude.

Pandarus uses 'Fortune is comune' (Tr 1.843) positively at one time and at another 'hire yiftes ben comune' (Tr 4.392) negatively in order to cheer up Troilus in a predicament. The same is true of his use of 'everything has time.' By this expression he encourages Troilus to move slowly and with caution ('for every thing hath tyme' Tr 2.989) and Criseyde to make haste ('alle thyng hath tyme' Tr 3.855). Pandarus is sensitive to shifting occasions and copes with them adroitly. However, his flexible nature results in his advice being subversive.

Finally, chiming effects due to the repetition of rhyming pairs to which reference has already been made by Masui (1964) can be included here. The rhyme pair *Troiejoie* has a chiming effect if these are seen as a lexical unit, and is repeated across the contrastive contexts with an effect of discourse chiming. When the love between Troilus and Criseyde develops in an ascending way, the effect of the chiming is positively valued (Tr 2.643-4, Tr 2.881-2), but when their love is descending, the chiming is likely to produce an ironical semantic tension if it is superimposed with the former positive chiming as *zanzo* (Tr 5.729-31, Tr 5.1546-7). (See ambiguity of voice in Chapter 13.)

The repetition or the variation of a word contributes to the cohesion within the discourse, but when it is conducted in shifting contexts, the effect of cohesion is not straightforward but tends to produce a subtle semantic interaction between the linked words and as a result to lead to ambiguity. The degrees of the operation of *zanzo* as regards the repeated words are not monolithic but perhaps variable according to the strength of the reader, the second prism's concern or his or her ability to remember observed items.

8.5. Ambiguity in word order and information structure

Chaucer is assumed to have written his texts with attention not only to the individual word or sentence unit, but to the discourse unit. The order of sentence elements is controlled by the metrical scheme of rhyme royal in *Troilus and Criseyde*. However, since this text was produced for communication with the audience, understanding it is subject to the aspects of information structure as well as metrical considerations. Through the arrangement of sentence elements, the reader is naturally encouraged to perceive the narrator's or characters' intended meaning.[97]

Pandarus gives Criseyde a letter from Troilus. She appears to read it with her polite self-control, but the word order of (24) suggests that she is deeply moved. The positionings before the verb of 'no lenger' and 'streght into hire closet' are worth attention.

(24) Criseyde aros, *no lenger* she ne stente,
But *streght into hire closet* wente *anon*,
And set hire doun as stylle as any ston,
And every word gan up and down to wynde
That he had seyd, as it com hire to mynde,   Tr 2.598-602

The adverb *streght* collocates with the rhyme word *anon*, which endorses this immediacy. She concentrates on reading the letter. Looking down at Troilus returning to Troy in triumph, she murmurs 'Who yaf me drynke?' (2.651), and blushes at the thought. She thinks about his knightly attributes one by one. As we saw in our discussion of FIS in Chapter 7, this list begins with and is mostly devoted to his appearance. Part of it deals with *gentilesse* and this is the quality which the list ends. (See Tr 2.1266-8: 'To telle in short, hire liked al in-fere, / His persoun, his aray, his look, his chere, / His goodly manere, and his gentilesse.')

Bringing forward the prepositional phrase is also seen in 'And streght into hire chamber gan she gon' (Tr 2.1173) and 'And into a closet, for t'avise hire better, / She wente allone,….' (Tr 2.1215-6). This shows her to be impatient to read Troilus's letter alone.

In (25) where she has received Pandarus's invitation, Criseyde's thoughts are not made explicit, but the reversed word (Tr 3.579), seems to suggest that she would expect to see Troilus there.

(25) Nought list myn auctour fully to declare
What that she thoughte whan he seyde so,
That Troilus was out of towne yfare,
As if he seyde therof soth or no;
But that, *withowten await*, with hym to go,
She graunted hym, sith he hire that bisoughte,
And, as his nece, obeyed as hire oughte.   Tr 3.575-81

As we have seen in the discussion on metatext in Chapter 4, the location of the prepositional phrase 'withowten await' seems to indicate a more urgent response than the normal word order. The α and γ manuscripts have the reverse word order. Only the β manuscripts (H4, J, and S1) have the usual word order.

We have examined some examples where the word order seems to reflect the characters' state of mind. In particular, we have seen that what comes first to their mind is indicated by the word order which brings certain sentence items forward. Of

---

97   Leech (1981) and Ohe (1984) regard the arrangement of sentence elements not as a purely formalistic conglomeration of words, but as an operation for establishing communication between speaker and hearer in order for the speaker to get the hearer to understand his or her intention by means of his or her language expression.

course, this interpretation is not watertight. Even if the characters' perceptive processes are reflected in the word order, we have to take note of what they intend to say in the process of evaluation. Furthermore, despite the word order, those characters may recognise the phenomena not sequentially but simultaneously. Or that order may be due to metrical demands. Here how the reader, the second prism, recognises the word order, which is given by the observer of the phenomena, induces the rise of ambiguity.

8.6. Final remarks

In this chapter we have described under the double prism structure how the cohesion and information structure of discourse are likely to produce ambiguity. Facing with the problematic phenomena from a social-moral point of view, the participants in the discourse are likely to describe them pronominally (pronouns, substitution, ellipsis) in a taken-for-granted way. This description encourages the reader to specify the referents through his or her inference. When those inferred referents vary from each other, ambiguity is likely to occur. How they can justify themselves for morally reprehensible actions determines whether the reader takes their causality as objective or subjective. Lexical repetition and variation go through their changeable contexts. With an effect of *zanzo* or 'engram,' they tend to produce a multi-layered semantic structure. Finally, the word order of sentence elements seems to reflect the perceptive processes of characters. In that way the reader gains insights into human emotions. However, such assumptions are open to interpretation, which gives rise to further ambiguity.

In Part II of Chapters 4 through 8, we have examined through the double prism structure how ambiguity is likely to arise in the textual domains of *Troilus and Criseyde*. In Chapter 4 we argued that the reader's participation is essential to understanding Chaucer's texts for which there is no Ur-text. We have paid attention to variant readings in the double prism structure, especially readings of the scribes and modern editors. Among variant readings we have chosen and examined those parts which seem to reflect not only errors but also the ambiguous state of Chaucer's language. In the discussion of intertexturality in Chapter 5, we have dealt with the interaction between one text and another in conjunction with the medieval mode of adaptation, and found that this gives rise to ambiguity. In Chapter 6, in relation to the structure of *Troilus and Criseyde*, we have pointed out that the macro-structure of the text (the theme, the characterisation, and the plot) highlights respectively the phenomena, the first prism, and the expression of the double prism structure, and that each has a relative and multiple aspect for promoting ambiguity. In our discussion of speech presentation in Chapter 7, we have focused on the narrator's descriptions of Criseyde's unstable nature, and there we have found that there are uncertainties as to whether they are the narrator's objective statements or the character's subjective ones. We have also pointed out that Chaucer was sensitive to the machinery of FIS. In Chapter 8 we have focused on discourse features including taken-for-granted cohesive devices as an expression of morally reprehensible actions, the effect of *zanzo* or 'engram' due to the lexical repetition and variation of discourse, and the implication of the perceptive processes in the word order of sentence elements. In each chapter the expressions are open to various meanings on the part of the reader, the second prism, and ambiguity is inevitable.

We have observed ambiguity in the text itself, the interaction between texts, macro-structure of the text, speech presentation, and discourse structure. Next, in Part III, we will deal with ambiguities in the interpersonal domains—ambiguities due to the intention or attitude the speaker takes towards the contents of the proposition. We will deal with the speaker's intention in Chapter 9, and his or her mental attitude (modality) in Chapter 10.

Part III: Ambiguity in interpersonal domains

9. Ambiguity in speaker's intention

9.1. Introductory remarks: the double prism structure and the speaker's intention

The speaker's intention is not necessarily the literal meaning understood by the reader, the second prism, directly based on the structure of the expression, but the meaning inferentially created based on his or her assumption of the speaker's intention. As shown in Chapter 3, in Chaucer's times, awareness of preserving human right and freedom of speech was scarcely developed compared with modern times, and therefore it was necessary to employ expressions capable of multiple interpretation when conveying content which might invite social criticism. In this chapter we focus on these deliberately polysemantic expressions, and examine ambiguity involving the reader's inference.[98]

According to Austin (1962)[99] and Searle (1969)[100], an utterance has a locutionary force immediately based on linguistic structures and an illocutionary force urging the listener to perform an action based on the locutionary force. The illocutionary force is of two types: direct and indirect. The former uses performative verbs and shows the speaker's intended action on the linguistic surface. The latter implies his or her intended action behind the linguistic surface. The latter is more often than not made problematic in semantic terms, and thus relevant to ambiguity. Linguistic structures and illocutionary forces do not have one-to-one correspondence, but variable correspondence according to situations.

An indirect speech act is related to the 'conversational implicature' by Grice (1975). This stipulates the conditional factors for realising communication. As a su-

---

[98] From a communicative point of view taking into account the speaker's intention and the hearer's response, a sentence is said to form the three layers: the propositional, the attitudinal, and the performative layers. The speaker describes an event or state he or she experiences in the world (proposition), adds to this proposition his or her judgement or evaluation (attitude), and then conveys it with his or her intention projected on the hearer (performative function). These three layers are by no means independent of, but interrelated and cooperative with, one another. The performative layer is dealt with in the present chapter, the attitudinal layer in Chapter 10, and the propositional layer in Chapters 11-13. For further information on the three layered structure of a sentence, see Halliday and Hasan (1976), Ando (1986), Sweetser (1990), and Sawada (1995).

[99] Austin (1962) divides performative act into three components: locutionary force, illocutionary force, and perlocutionary force or psychological effects due to illocutionary force on the hearer (surprise, sorrow, etc.). Here, we have focused on the first and second forces.

[100] To achieve a speech act, the speaker and the hearer have to satisfy a set of conditions. Searle (1969) proposes 'felicitous conditions': a. Propositional content, b. Preparation, c. Sincerity, d. Essence. In his book (pp. 66-7) he illustrates the working of the four conditions with the examples 'Request,' 'Assert,' 'Question,' 'Thank,' 'Advise,' 'Warn,' 'Greet,' and 'Congratulate.' Levinson (1983) also shows some useful insights into the matter.

perordinate condition, the cooperative principle is functional between the addresser and the addressee (the addresser tries to help the addressee to understand his or her message; the addressee tries to understand it). As subordinate conditions, four maxims are set up. The first three maxims, the maxims of quantity, quality, and relevance are related to the contents of the utterance, and the last maxim—that of manner—is related to the way of expression. The maxim of quantity is a requirement not to say too much or too little. The maxim of quality is not to tell lies or not to say things with little evidence. The maxim of relevance is to say things coherently. The maxim of manner is not to say things ambiguously/with obscurity but to say things in an orderly fashion. An indirect speech act includes the implicature of the utterance which apparently violates one or more of the above maxims, but arises with the cooperative principle as a superordinate condition. In other words, even if the utterance is left uninformative, and the expression is lacking in clarity, the listener supplies the lacking parts with his or her inference or activating his or her contiguity (for instance a cause-effect relation). In what follows we examine Chaucer's examples based on Austin/Searle or Grice. We first demonstrate that this problem of implicature is observable in every main character, and second examine two integrated discourses in terms of implicature.

9.2. Ambiguity in the intention of the characters and the narrator

Pandarus sympathises with Troilus in deep sorrow, and tells him not to conceal the cause of it from him.

(1) "I wol parten with the al thi peyne,
     If it be so I do the no comfort,
     As it is frendes right, soth for to seyne,
     To entreparten wo as glad desport.
     I have, and shal, for trewe or fals report,
     In wrong and right iloved the al my lyve:
     Hid nat thi wo fro me, but telle it blyve."   Tr 1.589-95

Pandarus emphasises his friendship with Troilus by expressing 'for trewe or fals report, / In wrong and right iloved the.' If he gave more weight to their friendship than to the right and wrong of the matter concerned, it would be construed as literal.[101] Or he might have indicated the strength of their friendship by resorting to the rhetorical effect of hyperbole.[102] Whichever he chooses, he seems to have no scepticism of it. Nor has Troilus. He goes so far as to request him to maintain it (Tr 1.596-602). However, the expression 'for trewe or fals report, / In wrong and right iloved the' can imply criticism in moral terms with the rise of ironical implications.

(2) also shows Pandarus's determination to co-operate with Troilus in the realisation of his love.

---

101 In *Amis and Amiloun* (1.1453), Amiloun helps Amis with more weight on friendship than on justice.
102 Hyperbole is a very common rhetorical figure in the literature of all ages. The reader's judgement is required to determine whether or not irony is intended. Cf. Blake (1977, Chapter 8): 'Parody.'

(2) Ne, by my trouthe, *I kepe nat restreyne*
The fro thi love, theigh that it were Eleyne
That is thi brother wif, if ich it wiste:
Be what she be, and love hire as the liste!   Tr 1.676-9

Does this expression carry the literal meaning: whether or not your love is devoted to Helen, your brother's wife, love her as you please? Or does he intend to show his sincere attitude with an implication that he will make every effort to help Troilus realise his love? The former highlights the immorality of his statement, and the latter reduces it since it merely intends a rhetorical exaggeration. This judgement is left to the second prism readers.

Pandarus's suggestion 'even if your love were for my sister, she should be yours by my will' (Tr 1.860-1) is more or less in the same vein. See (3) below.

(3) For whoso list have helyng of his leche,
To hym byhoveth first unwre his wownde.
To Cerberus yn helle ay be I bounde,
Were it for my suster, al thy sorwe,
By my wil she sholde al be thyn to-morwe.   Tr 1.857-61

The narrator comments on Pandarus's remarks above in such a way that 'Thise wordes seyde he for the nones alle' (Tr 1.561), and 'Thise wordes seyde he for the nones alle' (Tr 4.428), urging the audience to interpret them not literally but as an exaggeration for the particular occasion. However, this sympathetic comment encourages them to question the validity of Pandarus's remarks.

Diomede visits Criseyde on the tenth day when she has promised she will return to Troy, and tries passionately to win her heart. On the one hand, she loves Troy and Troilus, and on the other, she praises the Greeks' achievements. She is thus torn between them. At last she replies to Diomede's wooing as shown in (4).

(4) "Myn herte is now in tribulacioun,
And ye in armes bisy day by day.
Herafter, whan ye wonnen han the town,
Peraventure so it happen may
That whan I se that nevere yit I say
Than wol I werke that I nevere wroughte!
This word to yow ynough suffisen oughte.

"To-morwe ek wol I speken with yow fayn,
So that ye touchen naught of this matere.
And whan yow list, ye may come here ayayn;
And er ye gon, thus muche I sey yow here:
As help me Pallas with hire heres clere,
If that I sholde of any Grek han routhe,
It sholde be youreselven, by my trouthe!

"*I say nat therfore that I wol yow love,*
N'y say nat nay; but in conclusioun,
I mene wel, by God that sit above!"
And therwithal she caste hire eyen down,
And gan to sike, and seyde, "O Troie town,
Yet bidde I God in quiete and in reste
I may yow sen, or do myn herte breste."   Tr 5.988-1008

She promises 'That whan I se that nevere yit I say / Than wol I werke that I nevere wroughte!' (Tr 5.992-3) or 'If that I sholde of any Grek han routhe, / It sholde be youreselven, by my trouthe!' (Tr 5.1000-1). According to Grice (1975), these promises violate the maxim of manner (do not say ambiguously) and the following are especially worth noticing: the insertion of a modal adverb *Peraventure* (see the discussion on ambiguity in modal adverbs in Section 10.3), deliberate equivocation of clear reference (the use of a free relative *that* Tr 5.992-3), the use of the subjunctive (repetition of *sholde* Tr 5.1000-1), the denial that she loves Diomede, and the denial of the denial (Tr 5.1002-3), and the retention of an intermediate position with 'I mene wel' (5.1004) as a result. Her expressions are Janus-like. She can choose any direction to suit the occasion. She cannot easily yield to Diomede since she is a courtly lady or loves Troilus, and on the other hand, she has to defend herself by taking into consideration the objective circumstances. Her psychological dilemma is discernible in her mode of expression. However, Diomede expands his inference from her speech by activating the cooperative principle, and reads it in such a way that she pretends to misunderstand what he says because of her social status, but that on a deeper level she is positive towards his advancing in love upon her. The interpretation of what Diomede reads into her speech comes from the reader, the second prism, who can observe him holistically.

Troilus thanks Pandarus for working as a go-between of himself and Criseyde, and ascribes his action not to 'bauderye' (Tr 3.397) but to 'gentilesse, / Compassioun, and felawship, and trist' (Tr 3.402-3), and states that there is 'diversite requered / Bytwixen thynges like' (Tr 3.405-6). As his thanks for this, he says that he will offer him whichever of his sisters Pandarus chooses, 'Polixene,' 'Cassandre,' or 'Eleyne' (Tr 3.409-10). Gordon (1970) comments that critics who regard Troilus as 'a pure and noble lover' disregard this remark as a mere 'hyperbole,' but that what Pandarus has actually done is indeed *bauderye* (Tr 3.397) and that Troilus has touched upon the truth unknowingly. As is seen in Pandarus's examples (2) and (3), ambiguity is likely to arise because of the violation of Grice's (1975) maxims of quality and relevance. The author hidden behind Troilus seems to tell a lie assuming that it would be disclosed by a critical reader. Incidentally, the narrator says that Troilus and Pandarus are satisfied with this state of affairs (Tr 3.421).

Criseyde watches Troilus's triumphal return to Troy, and falls in love more or less at first sight ('Who yaf me drynke?' Tr 2.651). The narrator inserts (5) as if he wished to negate the possibility of her 'sodeyn love.' This is an addition to the original passage in *Il Filostrato*.

(5) Now myghte som envious jangle thus:
"This was a sodeyn love; how myght it be
That she so lightly loved Troilus
Right for the firste syghte, ye, parde?"
Now whoso seith so, mote he nevere ythe!
For every thing a gynnyng hath it nede
Er al be wrought, withowten any drede.

For I sey nought that she so sodeynly
Yaf hym hire love, but that *she gan enclyne
To like hym first*, and I have told yow whi;

9. Ambiguity in speaker's intention 127

And after that, his manhod and his pyne
Made love withinne hire for to myne,
For which *by proces* and by good servyse
He gat hire love, and in no sodeyn wyse.

And also blisful Venus, wel arrayed,
Sat in hire seventhe hous of hevene tho,
Disposed wel, and with aspectes payed,
To helpe sely Troilus of his woo.
And soth to seyne, she nas not al a foo
To Troilus in his nativitee;
God woot that wel the sonner spedde he.   Tr 2.666-86

The meaning of 'Who yaf me drynke?' (Tr 2.651)—i.e. whether it means the early stages of love or instant love—is crucial to the interpretation of this insertion. If the former is the case, it satisfies Searle's (1969) sincerity condition. But if the latter is the case, this part is against all Grice's (1974) maxims of quantity, quality, relevance, and manner. The violation of the maxim of quantity is seen in the excessive expansion of the gradability involved in her accepting Troilus's love. From the intertextual point of view, an addition to *Il Filostrato* is the expansion of quantity. As a factor of her acceptance of Troilus's love, the narrator even introduces the heavenly position of Venus at Troilus's birth. The violation of the maxim of quality is to say things unsupported by evidence. The violation of relevance is to say things not easily predicted or lacking in coherence in the flow of discourse. The violation of the maxim of manner (to speak in an orderly fashion) is seen in a series of expressions indicating the time scale of events: the generalised remark that every event needs to have a beginning before it is completed (Tr 2.671-2), the expression indicating intermediate stage of her love created by the aspect of the verb (the possibility of *gan* showing an inchoative aspect rather than working as a mere metrical filler), the meaning of a verb (*enclyne, like*) (Tr 2.674-5), and the expression by means of conjunction or prepositional phrases ('And after that' 2.676, 'by proces' Tr 2.678).

There can be no time lag before she loves Troilus if her love is caused instantly. If there is a gap between the expression and the phenomenon and yet the cooperative principle is activated, the following inference is possible. The narrator is assumed to have tried a sympathetic justification of Criseyde's action in order to safeguard her honour as a courtly lady or in accord with what she intends to be rather than what she really is. Donaldson's (1970) remark that Chaucer smiles at the narrator's 'rhetorical failure' seems to show the narrator's dual roles or perhaps the poet's double consciousness—he is involved with and at the same time detached from Criseyde—which asserts that her love is not instant but which may lead to an anticlimactic response on the part of the reader, the second prism.

Before the story descends to the exchange of Criseyde for the prisoners and her betrayal of Troilus in the Greek camp, the narrator shows his holistic stance towards it, as shown in (6). This is a departure from *Il Filostrato*.

(6) *For how Criseyde Troilus forsook—*
 Or at the leeste, how that she was unkynde—
 Moot hennesforth ben matere of my book,

As writen folk thorugh which it is in mynde.
Allas, that they sholde evere cause fynde
To speke hire harm! And if they on hire lye,
Iwis, hemself sholde han the vilanye.   Tr 4.15-21

The clause 'Or at the leeste, how that she was unkynde' (Tr 4.16), a paraphrase of the immediately preceding 'how Criseyde Troilus forsook' (Tr 4.15), is made problematic in interpretation. According to Masui (1977), the narrator is sympathetic towards Criseyde, and rephrases *forsook* in a word showing less his devaluation.[103] He thinks that the modal auxiliary *Moot* is the evidence of his sympathy for her. On the other hand, Donaldson (1970) stresses the narrator's critical stance, regarding it as anticlimax that he makes clear the fact of her betrayal first and tones it down later. According to Grice (1975), the latter is an implication due to the violation of the maxim of manner (speaking in an orderly fashion) and its subsequent activation of the cooperative principle on the part of the reader. If either sympathy or criticism is intended, there would have been no need for the paraphrase above. Only one of them is enough. This discrepancy is not to be solved, but—it is assumed—to be deliberately maintained in its ambiguity by the author, the first prism.

Criseyde, who is sent to the Greek camp in exchange for prisoners, is faced with an unexpected amorous approach by the Greek knight Diomede. Her response to it is given in (7).

(7) But natheles she thonketh Diomede
Of al his travaile and his goode cheere,
And that hym list his frendshipe hire to bede;
And she accepteth it in good manere,
And wol do fayn that is hym lief and dere,
And tristen hym she wolde, and wel she myghte,
As seyde she; and from hire hors sh'alighte.   Tr 5.183-9

The expression of her thanks to Diomede's offer is simply functional as a politeness marker of a courtly lady (an assertion), or (especially Tr 5.186-9) suggestive of other illocutionary forces such as an offer and a suggestion, in other words, her being more positively ready to accept his love. Although she does not intend the 'offer,' it will give him room for an alternative illocutionary force like 'offer' if it is regarded by Diomede as too much for her simple expression of politeness (violation of the maxim of quantity).

Diomede visits Criseyde who is living with her father. He asks her if she thinks the Greek customs strange, and why her father does not marry her to an eligible knight. This is seen in (8).

(8) Fro that demaunde he so descendeth down
To axen hire if that hire straunge thoughte
The Grekis gise and werkes that they wroughte;

And whi hire fader tarieth so longe
To wedden hire unto som worthy wight.
Criseyde, that was in hire peynes stronge

---

103   Concerning *unkynde*, see Section 12.2.4.

9. Ambiguity in speaker's intention

> For love of Troilus, hire owen knyght,
> As ferforth as she konnyng hadde or myght
> Answerde hym tho; but as of his entente,
> *It semed nat she wiste what he mente.*   Tr 5.859-68

These questions ('axen hire if ...' Tr 5.860) not only seek information, but are part of his advances to her and are intended to elicit a response about it. But the narrator seems to be sensitive to what the reader's inference may be, and says that it did not seem that she knew about his intention (Tr 5.868). This narrator's additional note may be regarded as against the maxim of quantity, and if this is right, it leads to an implication that the reality is the other way round. Even if she notices Diomede's intention, she cannot accept it, nor can she mention her lover Troilus. (Her love for Troilus is made problematic from a social-moral point of view. This is controlled by 'secrecy,' one of the codes of courtly love.) The narrator deliberately obfuscates the situation regarding her awareness of Diomede's intention by saying 'It semed nat ....' (Tr 5.868).[104] This encourages the reader more positively to participate in its interpretation.

Diomede piles up evidence presaging the fall of Troy and makes strong advances towards her. The narrator describes his facial expression, tone of voice, and gesture as shown in (9).

(9) *And with that word he gan to waxen red,*
And in his speche a litel wight he quok,
And caste asyde a litel wight his hed,
And stynte a while; and afterward he wok,
And sobreliche on hire he threw his lok,
And seyde, "I am, al be it yow no joie,
As gentil man as any wight in Troie.   Tr 5.925-31

It is not certain whether the narrator's description indicates that Diomede is embarrassed with Criseyde because he is attracted to her despite his strategy to capture her or whether he deliberately pretends to be so in attempt to gain her sympathy with him. This depends on the fulfillment or the violation of the maxim of quality. The former shows that Diomede has a human side on him despite his calculating nature, whereas the latter shows that he is purely cold and cunning.[105]

When characters or the narrator express socially reprehensible actions (highlighting the phenomena of the double prism structure), they are required to express them so as to be widely applied (literal meaning and speaker's meaning). In order to interpret such expressions the reader is encouraged to assume the intention of the observers of the phenomena. The interpretation is likely to vary as regards whether those expressions are literal or imply illocutionary forces, which leads to the rise of ambiguity.

9.3. Integrated examination of [1] Tr 3.554-603

(10)-(15) are part of the scene where Pandarus invites Criseyde to supper at his house. This supper meeting is an excuse to create a situation leading to the physical union

---

104 See modal lexical verbs in Section 10.4.
105 Shifts in the personality traits of characters arise from ambiguity in characterisation as we have shown in Section 6.3. See also the analysis of voice in Chapter 13.

between Troilus and Criseyde. Let us reexamine those examples from the speech act point of view. Pandarus's invitation virtually brooks no refusal, as shown in (10). He predicts that she will be forced to stay at his house because of the storm. He tells Troilus to come to his house and await his opportunity.

(10) Whan he was com, he gan anon to pleye
 As he was wont, and of hymself to jape;
 And finaly he swor and gan hire seye,
 By this and that, *she sholde hym nought escape,*
 Ne lenger don hym after hire to cape;
 But *certeynly she moste, by hire leve,*
 Come soupen in his hous with hym at eve.

 At which she lough, and gan hire faste excuse,
 And seyde, "It reyneth; lo, how sholde I gon?"
 "Lat be," quod he, "ne stant nought thus to muse.
 This moot be don! Ye shal be ther anon."
 So at the laste herof they fille aton,
 Or elles, softe he swor hire in hire ere,
 He nolde nevere comen ther she were.   Tr 3.554-67

Pandarus compels Criseyde to come to his house (Tr 3.557, Tr 3.559-60, Tr 3.564), obviates the possibility of her refusal, and removes all the subsequent responsibility from her. She yields to his insistent request, but asks him in a whisper if Troilus is there (i.e. at his house), as seen in (11).

(11) Soone after this, *she to hym gan to rowne,*
 And axed hym if Troilus were there.
 He swor hire *nay*, for he was out of towne,
 And seyde, *"Nece, I pose that he were;*
 Yow thurste nevere han the more fere;
 For rather than men myghte hym ther aspie,
 Me were levere a thousand fold to dye."   Tr 3.568-74

Is her use of *sotto voce* (Tr 3.568) merely coincidental or to imply her expectations regarding Troilus, or indirectly to ask Pandarus to prepare for them to meet?[106] Pandarus answers 'no' to her question. She would have no choice but to decline his invitation if she knew that Troilus was there. His negative answer seems to anticipate this (she can accept only if the answer is in the negative). However, Pandarus immediately adds 'you would not need to be afraid. I would rather die a hundred times than let men spy on him' (Tr 3.572-4). Pandarus's additional note is against the maxim of quantity or that of relevance (immediately after answering in the negative, he suggests the opposite answer to it). If the cooperative principle is activated on the part of Criseyde, something more than his *nay* (Tr 3.570) or that Troilus might be at Pandarus's house

---

106 Criseyde's questions to Pandarus about Troilus's presence at the supper (illocutionary force: request) is analysed as below, if we apply Searle's (1969) felicitous conditions to them.
 a. Propositional content: a future action
 b. Preparation: Criseyde would like Troilus to be at the meeting. If she does not say about this, Pandarus might not notice it. Since this request implies a scandal, she cannot say it explicitly.
 c. Sincerity: she thinks it sincerely.
 d. Essence: she expresses her feeling of request by interrogation.

9. Ambiguity in speaker's intention

will be implied. This indirect meaning of Pandarus's words seems to correspond to her indirect request. Incidentally Pandarus has already made a promise that Troilus and Criseyde will meet at his house (Tr 3.193-6).

How she responds to and accepts Pandarus's implication above is described in (12).

(12) *Nought list myn auctour fully to declare*
What that she thoughte when he seyde so,
That Troilus was out of towne yfare,
As if he seyde therof soth or no;
But that, withowten await, with hym to go,
She graunted hym, sith he hire that bisoughte,
And, as his nece, obeyed as hire oughte.   Tr 3.575-81

According to the narrator, 'myn auctour' (Tr 3.575) does not want to make clear what she thought when she heard that Troilus was out of town. This is against the maxim of quantity (suppressed information). In terms of intertexture, Boccaccio does not address this matter. In this respect this is against the maxim of quality (do not tell lies). Here if the cooperative principle is activated, the implication is likely to arise that although she notices Troilus's presence at Pandarus's house, the narrator equivocates at this point because it is against her honour. However, this is due to the reader's inference. There arises an inferential ambiguity here.

Criseyde reminds Pandarus that there will be other guests at the supper, and warns him that some of them may gossip at a later stage, as seen in (13).

(13) But natheles, yet gan she hym biseche,
Although with hym to gon it was no fere,
For to ben war of goosissh poeples speche,
That dremen thynges whiche as nevere were,
And wel avyse hym whom he broughte there;
And seyde hym, "Em, syn I moste on yow triste,
Loke al be wel, and do now as yow liste."   Tr 3.582-8

To be conscious of being under the scrutiny of others is a mark of Criseyde's politeness as a courtly lady or against the maxim of quantity (too much information). If the latter is the case, the cooperative principle is likely to be operative with Pandarus, with an implication that she is confirming his scrupulous care on the assumption that Troilus is there.

In this implied exchange between Criseyde and Pandarus, she leaves everything to him, and he responds to her as in (14).

(14) He swor hire *yis*, by stokkes and by stones,   Tr 3.589

As is argued about the ellipsis in Chapter 8, this is against the maxim of quantity (to what he said 'yes' is not mentioned: left uninformative), or against the maxim of manner (what is elliptical cannot be referentially determined). Pandarus seems to have coped with Criseyde's implication (Tr 3.587-8) by violating these two maxims.

The narrator confirms that Criseyde is innocent of all the knowledge that Troilus is staying at Pandarus's house, as is seen in (15).

(15) But who was glad now, who, as trowe ye,
    But Troilus, that stood and myght it se
    Thorughout a litel wyndow in a stewe,
    Ther he bishet syn mydnyght was in mewe,

    Unwist of every wight but of Pandare?   Tr 3.599-603

If Criseyde is aware of Pandarus's suggestion (Tr 3.570-4), or she remembers his promise that he will get Criseyde and Troilus together at his house, it is unavoidable that the narrator's comment above is against the maxim of quality. The implication is that if he does not mention her innocence in this matter, she, a courtly lady, will not join in the supper party. Pandarus and Criseyde act as the speaker and the hearer respectively and vice versa in these dialogues which concern morally problematic actions, and so illustrate the phenomenon of the double prism structure. And the narrator makes an interplay with the reader over the above implication.[107]

9.4. Integrated examination of [2] Tr 5.1009-50

We focus on Tr 5.1009-50. This part occurs at one of the structurally most significant junctures in the story, that is, at the very moment when Criseyde shifts her emotions towards Diomede. In the Greek camp Diomede visits Criseyde on the tenth day, exactly the day when she has promised Troilus to be back in Troy. Diomede unexpectedly advances to her with an earnest proclamation of a knightly service. She experiences a conflict between her love for Troy and her admiration of the Greeks. But Diomede 'al fresshly newe ayeyn / Gan pressen on' and prayed her mercy (Tr 5.1009-11):

(16) But in effect, and shortly for to seye,
    This Diomede al fresshly newe ayeyn
    Gan pressen on, and faste hire mercy preye;
    And after this, the sothe for to seyn,
    Hire glove he took, of which he was ful feyn;
    And finaly, whan it was woxen eve
    And al was wel, he roos and tok his leve.   Tr 5.1009-15

First let us ask what meaning is intended in 'Hire glove he took.' The statement itself, apparently restricted to a mere surface event, is capable of a metaphorical evaluation, for which see Donaldson (1970). This evaluation is perhaps due to the reader's background assumption of gift-presenting. According to the decorum of a courtly lady, it may naturally be assumed that her 'heart' should accompany her 'gift' (cf. *ryng* Tr 3.885). Otherwise she will be a 'wench' as is exemplified in May in *The Merchant's Tale*. Some—perhaps sceptical readers of Criseyde—are likely to draw their inference

---

107 In *The Book of the Duchess,* Chaucer, a character as well as the narrator makes a speech violating the maxim of relevance (the expression of the double prism structure). The Black Knight is encouraged to fill in the gaps in the speech, make it coherent, and extend it. He is given consolation by giving vent to his suppressed feelings. Cf. Austin: (1962) 'perlocutionary force.' Chaucer behaves here as if he were a psychiatrist. The Black Knight responds quite innocently to Chaucer's violation of the maxim of relevance. However, the reader, the second prism, seeing through the whole context is encouraged to activate the cooperative principle, and is sensitive to the role the apparently ignorant narrator is given, or his deep consideration for the knight.

from that assumption, with the implication that he took her 'heart' in conjunction with her *glove* (her *glove* being perhaps an instance of metonymy because her heart is included in her glove). This interpretation shows that her subsequent hesitation suggests the reasons she later concocts in her defence. However, others may assert that Diomede's strong pressure forced her to give up her glove (with her heart still devoted to Troilus). If this is right, the implied criticism above is cancelled.

On the tenth night (in astrological terms), she comes back to her father's tent, turning over Diomede's words, as in (17).

(17) And Signifer his candels sheweth brighte
　　　Whan that Criseyde unto hire bedde wente
　　　Inwith hire fadres faire brighte tente,

　　　Retornyng in hire soule ay up and down
　　　The wordes of this sodeyn Diomede,
　　　His grete estat, and perel of the town,
　　　And that she was allone and hadde nede
　　　Of frendes help; and thus bygan to brede
　　　The cause whi, the sothe for to telle,
　　　That she took fully purpos for to dwelle.　　　Tr 5.1020-9

Probing the motives for her inclination to stay in the Greek camp ('Retornyng...') (Tr 5.1023), the narrator seems to slip imperceptibly into her mind, and to merge his point of view with hers. This speech presentation may be classified as 'NRSA' (Narrative Report of Speech Action).[108] If this is right, the truth condition of this speech is open to question. One solution is: this is a genuine beginning of her decision to stay in the Greek camp. The other is: this is a self-deceptive beginning, possibly a mere justification for her earlier decision, which may be evidenced in Tr 5.990-3, Tr 5.1000-4, and Tr 5.1013. She remains a courtly lady in her intentions although not in her actions.

For a near counterpart of this questionable shifting, see how she turns her affections towards Troilus in 'Who yaf me drynke?' (Tr 2.651—a suggestion of instant love)—the narrator's apologetic comment on her love (Tr 2.679—'in no sodeyn wyse')—her self-debate about love—Antigone's song for encouraging love—Criseyde's dream of a symbolic eagle (Tr 2.931—'And forth he fleigh, with herte left for herte')—her decision to accept Troilus's love. Is this a genuine hesitation decided consciously by Criseyde, the courtly lady, or as an act of self-justification? Criseyde and the narrator co-operate in the development of this equivocal logic.

Diomede comes back to Criseyde on the morning of the eleventh day, and assuages the main part of all her pain:

(18) The morwen com, and gostly for to speke,
　　　This Diomede is come unto Criseyde;
　　　And shortly, lest that ye my tale breke,
　　　So wel he for hymselven spak and seyde
　　　That *alle hire sikes soore adown he leyde;*
　　　And finaly, the sothe for to seyne,
　　　He refte hire of the grete of al hire peyne.　　　Tr 5.1030-6

108　See the discussion from the viewpoint of free indirect speech in Chapter 7. Leech and Short (1981: 337) gives useful information about the variation of speech presentation.

The ordering of the two actions—'he subdued all her bitter sighs' and 'he relieved her of the main part of all her pain'—with a temporal/causal conjunction 'And finaly' can be normal or abnormal according to the reader's assumption. The former assumption is that the 'subduing sighs' is only part of the action for 'removing pain.' The latter is that 'subduing sighs' and 'removing pain' are effectively concurrent with no or little significant difference. Donaldson (1970: 80) takes this latter view. This view, taken in Gricean terms, is regarded as the narrator's repeated violation of the maxims—quality: do not say what you believe to be false; relevance: say something coherently; manner: be orderly. The implication (through the cooperative principle) is: an apparent stage-by-stage development of Criseyde's emotional shift is doubtful, possibly stemming from the narrator's psychological and imaginative creation. However, the above concurrence is only a matter of likelihood; this can occur, but not always. It may be that 'subduing sighs' is just one (not the total) aspect of 'removing pain.' If so, the former does not entail the latter. And thus they are to be taken as happening at different times: Diomede's consolation of Criseyde's pain was first applied to externally, and then to its essence internally.

All she has done for Diomede seems to the narrator still short of a complete surrender. The *grete* (Tr 5.1036), according to the *MED* (8. (1)) means 'the major part, important part,' and therefore, before Diomede wins her, there is more to do, as seen in (19). But how much?

(19) *And after this* the storie telleth us
That she hym yaf *the faire baye stede*
The which he ones wan of Troilus;
And ek *a broche*—and that was litel need—
That Troilus was, she yaf this Diomede.
And ek, the bet from sorwe hym to releve,
She made hym were *a pencel of hire sleve*.

I fynde ek in stories elleswhere,
Whan thorugh the body hurt was Diomede
Of Troilus, *tho wep she many a teere*
Whan that she saugh his wyde wowndes blede,
And that *she took, to kepen hym, good hede*;
And for to helen hym of his sorwes smerte,
Men seyn—I not—that *she yaf hym hire herte*.   Tr 5.1037-50

The period of time covered by 'after this' remains unclear in the text. The reader can shorten or expand its referential period, according to his or her assumption. Incidentally, 271 lines before this, while Criseyde determines to return to Troy—'For which, withouten any wordes mo, / To Troie I wole, as for conclusioun!' (Tr 5.764-5), the narrator states 'But God it wot, er fully monthes two, / She was ful fer fro that entencioun!' (Tr 5.766-7). The one-by-one illustration by the narrator of her gifts to Diomede, in Donaldson's terms, 'roughly in ascending order of importance'—the 'faire baye steede' (Tr 5.1038), Troilus's 'brooch' (Tr 5.1040), 'a pencel of hire sleve' (Tr 5.1043), her tears for Diomede's wound (Tr 5.1046), her care in curing it (Tr 5.1048), and finally 'hire herte' (Tr 5.1050)—is quite problematical with its psychologically double-sided effect. (See the discussion from the viewpoint of information structure and word order in Chapter 8.) On the one hand, the reader is prompted to read in a time lag for each of the gifts, and to deduce that after an immeasurably long time she decided to give him the greatest gift 'hire herte.' On the other hand, he or she can question this time lag, assuming that the series of her gifts with the repeated 'and' is not temporally partitioned by 'months and years' but rather by 'days' or even by 'hours.' Moreover, he or she can suspect that the apparently last gift 'hire herte' is a mere surface representation of what is implied in the above gifts, and what is more significant, in 'Hire glove' that he took (Tr 5.1013) as early as on the tenth day.

Regarding the progress in the shift in Criseyde's affections, a significant phenomenon of the double prism structure, the author, the first prism—a manipulator of two narrators—manages to hold two semantic worlds of time in balance. One narrator, so sympathetic towards Criseyde, encourages the reader to stress what is 'stated' in the utterance, and thus to create a gradual time-consuming development of her change in affections. The other narrator, keeping some distance from Criseyde, induces the reader to question the statements, with an implication that she had already undergone this development at a quite earlier stage (perhaps the tenth day when Diomde 'tok her glove') despite his prolonging the progress of the shift. Thus these two worlds of time are juxtaposed ironically. This temporal ambiguity, by extension, involves the interpretation of the well known crux of Criseyde's character—'slydinge of corage' (Tr 5.825)—and also the thematic question in the story—to what category her love may belong: a sensual love; a rational love as should be attributed to an ideal courtly heroine (see Chapter 6).

Thirty lines later, the narrator attracts our attention directly to the problem of time.

(20) But trewely, *how longe it was bytwene*
That she forsok hym for this Diomede
Ther is non auctour telleth it, I wene.
Take every man now to his bokes heede,
He shal no terme fynden, out of drede.
For though that he bigan to wowe hire soone,
Er he hire wan, yet was ther more to doone.   Tr 5.1086-92

As is suggested in Tr 3.1334-6, it is left to the reader to 'encresse' ('yet was ther more to done' Tr 5.1092) or 'maken dymynucioun / Of' (Tr 3.1335-6) the time,' as may be thought fit.

9.5. Final remarks

We have examined ambiguity arising from the way the reader interprets the speaker's intention under the double prism structure. The character and the narrator hide the morally problematic action (phenomenon) behind words of wide semantic and pragmatic application. Some readers may be satisfied with the meaning with the linguistic surface but others may be encouraged to look into the illocutionary forces or implications developing from it. The interpretation is subject to ambiguity according to the reader.

We have illustrated the speaker's intention with examples according to characters in this chapter. We have also made two integrated analyses of the passages including immoral phenomena of the day. It is understood that ambiguity is brought about through the interaction between the speaker's intention and the reader's interpretation of it.

Ambiguity due to interpersonal domains is observed not only in illocutionary forces of the expression but also in the speaker's attitude towards the propositional contents. In Chapter 10 we will deal with ambiguity caused by modality.

10. Ambiguity in modality

10.1. Introductory remarks: the double prism structure and modality

In *Troilus and Criseyde* Chaucer developed his insight into human understanding and particularly into human psychology. Kittredge (1915) calls this work as a 'psychological novel,' and indeed the focus is frequently upon the characters' states of mind, and their judgement and evaluation of the predicaments they find themselves in. When their basic human instincts are in conflict with conventional social morality, we are presented with a description of how they justify their actions and achieve their ends. In such times of instability we are also shown how they inject a degree of certainty into their lives. This verbal justification and the inferences the characters draw about the certainties they have created are central to modality. In this way modal expressions play an important role in the story. This chapter examines the abundance of ambiguity flowing from them.

The speaker can concentrate his or her undivided state of mind on the propositional content (phenomenon) in modal expressions. That the proposition is not presented as a fact but as a matter of degree induces the reader, the second prism, to think about alternative interpretations. When the readers vary in their interpretations of the psychology behind the speaker's proposition, ambiguity is likely to arise.

Modality is represented by the following devices.

(1) a. modal auxiliaries
    may/myghte, wil/wolde, shal/sholde, moot/moste, owe/ought, etc.

   b. modal adverbs and adverbials
      certain, certainly, certes, in certein, dredeles, douteles, iwis, paraventure, paraunter, sikerly, sothe, sothly, forsothe, for sothe, trewely, etc.

   c. modal lexical verbs and verb phrases with adjectives or nouns
      I gesse, I leve, I suppose, I trow, I understand, I undertake, trust (imperative) me, I wene, I woot, God woot, it is certein, I am certein, certein is that, that is douteles, soth is that, the soth is this, etc.

   d. subjunctive
      Kerkhof (1982: 42-51): The subjunctive is used in adverbial clauses of place, time, condition (and supposition), result, purpose, concession and comparison. E.g. 'If she *be* fayr, thow woost thyself, I gesse' (Tr 1.882). In most cases it denotes uncertainty, supposition, possibility, probability, desirability and the like, but occasionally, notably in clauses of time and concession mere facts may be indicated.

   e. intonation
      In Chaucer's day the transmission of epic literature was by way of oral recitation. Intonation would undoubtedly have played a vital role in showing the orator's attitude towards the realisation of the proposition or the degrees of certainty involved in it. (See ambiguity of voice in Chapter 13.)

This chapter focuses on (1a-c).

10.2. Ambiguity in modal auxiliaries

We describe the state of human psychology conveyed by modal auxiliaries focusing on the following two points inducing the reader's judgement. One is the external causals behind the speaker's use of modal auxiliaries. Modal auxiliaries are generally used with the speaker's assumption of evidence or what we call here as 'external causals' which motivate the realisation of the proposition. The other is the polysemy of modal auxiliaries caused by the semantic interaction between their root sense and their epistemic sense.

10.2.1. Interaction in external causals: a focus on *moot/moste*

10.2.1.1. Semantic development of *moot/moste* and external causals

Chaucer's *moot/moste* originally meant 'possess land distributed by God,' and described the action and the state of the subject in the sentence. But the unity of the *moot/moste* and its compliment (the infinitive which it governed) increased with time, and the auxiliary came to express the speaker's judgement towards the content of the main verb, i.e. to have a modal function. In the late middle English in which Chaucer wrote, the modal was in the transitional period from lexical verb to auxiliary, a process which was fully completed in early modern English.

The semantic origins of this word and its equivalents in related languages are obscure. It has no cognates in North Germanic; in Gothic the word *gamotan* is used to translate Greek χωρέω 'contain, have room for,' which might, with a little imagination, be seen to contain the seeds of a meaning akin to permission. (Cf. Mark 2.2, John 8.37 and II Cor 7.2.) Certainly, by the time the West Germanic languages (including OE) are attested, that is the meaning attaching to the word. The jump from permission to obligation is more difficult to explain. First this can easily be imagined if the verb was frequently used in the jussive subjunctive: i.e. the meaning 'may he do such and such' borders on 'let him' and then 'make him' and so on. Second, as the *OED* (s.v. mote, v.1) says, 'it may have arisen from the use in negative contexts, where the two senses ('may not', 'must not') are nearly coincident.' Third, the semantic transition can be explained from a cognitive linguistic point of view. If the action in question is regarded by the hearer with a positive value, it will be interpreted as permission, whereas if it is hard to achieve and regarded as negative, it tends to be interpreted as obligation. The sense of obligation can be observed even in the late OE period and becomes firmly established as the principal meaning in ME.[109] Obligation is now seen to stem from religious or quasi-religious obligation (imposed by God or Fate) later to legal and social obligation and gradually to self-imposed necessity.

In time the sense of obligation now conveyed by *moot/moste* could also be applied to the speaker's imaginative world and so produce expressions of virtual certainty. The

---

[109] For the reason why the obligatory sense of *moot* is developed, see Nakano (1993). The example of this sense is observed in late OE, for which see Ono (1969).

metonymic principle (the cause-effect relation) seems to have played an important role in this semantic extension. The metaphorical principle is also applied in that the obligation sense is extended from the socio-physical world to the spiritual world.[110] In what follows we refer to the obligation/permission meaning as the root sense and the virtual certain meaning as the epistemic sense.[111] Since the epistemic sense of *moot/moste* developed through the sense of obligation, its development was late in comparison with *shal/sholde*. As preceding studies show (*OED*, *MED*, Visser (1969: 1810-1) and Traugott (1989: 42)), the fourteenth century was the initial stage of its emergence. The inclusion of this ambiguous sense gave rise to widely applied readings on the part of readers, and naturally caused ambiguity. We now examine the semantic development of *moot/moste* in terms of external causals.

10.2.1.2. Interactions between external causals

As we have seen in Section 10.2.1.1, those meanings of *moot/moste* to be established in the early ModE emerged in Chaucer's time and were preserved thereafter. However, within this lexical unit the different senses were not evenly distributed as to frequency of occurrence. The permission sense was in decline, and the epistemic sense was just emerging, while the obligation was dominant. In this section we limit ourselves to the external causals involved in the speaker's use of the obligation sense.

Historical studies of modals have so far been devoted to explaining the latent senses, and dealt mainly with syntactic elements collocating with modals, with regard to which see Visser (1969), Ono (1969), and Goossens (1987). By contrast, elements relating to the subject producing the structure rather than the structure itself have been given little attention although they are semantically indispensable. External causals are among those elements. Ando (1976), Traugott (1989), and Nakano (1993) are in the forefront of research. Hardly has any attention been paid to external causals in Chacuer's modals. As Traugot (1989) says, we can predict in principle that the movement from objective to subjective is unidirected. On the other hand, it is not so simple to assess the degree of objectivity or subjectivity of external causals using actual examples. When the objective and the subjective factors involved in the speaker's use of *moot/moste* operate in separate directions, the meaning is easily delineated. Chaucer's external causals are, however, often in a state of tension between the objective and the subjective, and give rise to various shades of meaning and thus ambiguity owing to the combinations involved.

10.2.1.3. Semantics of modal auxiliaries: positioning of external causals

Modal auxiliaries are related to the speaker's mental attitude towards the proposition, and provided with semantic properties in conjunction with the following three condi-

---

110 Sweetser (1990) ascribes this semantic change to similarity. With the concept of 'necessity' as a common core, she thinks that its application was expanded from the socio-physical world to the mental world. For the principle of metaphor and metonymy to lead to polysemy, see Yamanashi (1995: 19-88).
111 We use the terms of 'root sense' and 'epistemic sense,' according to Coates (1983) and Sweetser (1990).

tions.[112] They are factors belonging to the proposition, those of higher clauses containing modal clauses, and those belonging to pragmatic factors including the interpersonal relation between the speaker and the hearer and the communicative situation in which they are.

(2) a. Conditions of the content of the proposition
    (i)   person of the subject (1st/2nd/3rd person, animate, inanimate)
    (ii)   lexical features of the subject
    (iii) aspect of the verb (dynamic, stative)
    (iv) tense of the verb (past, present, future)
    (v)   polarity of the verb (positive, negative)
    (vi) voice of the verb (active, passive)
    (vii) lexical features of the verb
    (viii) adjunct of the verb (adverbial phrases denoting time or place)

  b. Conditions of higher clauses (types of clauses including modal auxiliaries or harmonics collocating with them)
    (i)   within independent sentences (types of sentences: declarative, interrogative, optative)
    (ii)   within main clauses in conjunction with subordinate clauses (kinds of subordinate clauses: adverbial, adjectival, nominal)
    (iii) within subordinate clauses (kinds of subordinate clauses: adverbial, adjectival, nominal)
    (iv) types (idiomatic expressions, etc.)
    (v)   harmonics

  c. Pragmatic conditions
    (i)   the speaker/hearer's viewpoint (who sees?)
    (ii)   the social relation between the speaker and the hearer (degrees of authority)
    (iii) external causals (evidence on which the speaker bases his utterance when using modals)
    (iv) genre (romance, fabliau, sermon, philosophy, etc.)

External causals are indicative of evidence on which the speaker bases his or her utterance when using modals. They are one of the pragmatic conditions in (2c). Modals are generally used for certain reasons as shown in (3).

(3) But I *moot* been in prisoun <u>thurgh Saturne</u>,
    And eek <u>thurgh Juno</u>, jalous and eek wood,   KnT I (A) 1328-9

The knights Palamon and Arcite have been captured and imprisoned. Arcite is permitted to go out of the prison through the mediation of his friend. Palamon remains in prison. He complains of his misfortune in (3). The speaker Palamon shows his attitude towards the propositional content 'I am in prison.' In his opinion the causal leading to the proposition is the gods' (Saturn's and Juno's) determination. External causals are related to the speaker's motives for the use of modals, and provide the basic outlines of their meaning.

In the case of obligation towards the proposition, external causals are clearer than those inducing volition or ability in that they are externally based rather than internally or naturally. They are extralinguistically functional, reflecting varieties of compulsion

---

112   See Nakao (2002a).

in the speaker's physical-social world. *Moot/moste* are stronger in restrictive force than *shal/sholde* or *owe/oughte (to)*. External causals are sometimes textually explicit, and at others implicit since they are taken for granted. In the former case modals are used in conjunction with phrases or clauses denoting reasons (reasons following 'as/by/thrugh/for'; reasons followed by 'and than/therefore/or ellis'; reasons with 'the Apostle seith,' 'by the sentence of Plato,' etc.). Some examples are given in (4).

(4) a. He that is usaunt to this synne of glotonye, he ne may no synne withstonde.
  He *moot* been in servage of alle vices, <u>for</u> it is the develes hoord ther he hideth hym and resteth. ParsT X (I) 821

  b. And if myn housbonde eek it myghte espye,
  I nere but lost; and therfore I yow preye,
  Lene me this somme, <u>or ellis</u> *moot* I deye.   ShipT VII 184-6

  c. This olde man gan looke in his visage,
  And seyde thus: "For I ne kan nat fynde
  A man, though that I walked into Ynde,
  Neither in citee ne in no village,
  That wolde chaunge his youthe for myn age;
  <u>And therfore</u> *moot* I han myn age stille,
  As longe tyme as it is Goddes wille.   PardT VI (C) 720-6

  d. Eek <u>Plato seith</u>, whoso kan hym rede,
  The wordes *moote* be cosyn to the dede.   GP I (A) 741-2

On the other hand, the latter implicit case is to be inferred by the reader taking into account the extended discourse context or even the extralinguistic context. Here the broad semantic scope of *moot/moste* is most exploited.

External causals are related to the epistemology of the medieval society in which Chaucer lived. Generally speaking, the less the speaker's involvement in the obligation is, the more objective these causals are, and the greater, the more subjective. In that medieval society external causals gradually become more subjective and more multifarious. God and social obligations are added and finally individual self-imposed obligations. The reason why we do not say 'substituted' but 'added' is that they tended to be coexistent in medieval times. They are roughly divided into the following categories from the objective to the subjective.

(5) a. laws of natural phenomena
  b. reason
    (i)   God or saints
    (ii) philosophers (Plato, Aristotle, etc.)
    (iii) Fortune
  c. everyday characteristics of humans/animals/abstract entities (joy, sorrow, love, sickness, secrecy, etc.)
  d. people's social roles or moral status (king, knight, judge, courtly persons, husband, wife, etc.)
  e. regulations for specific groups (parliamentary decisions, rules of games like a tournament, etc.)
  f. promises among individual relationships

In Chaucer (5b, c, d and e) are frequently used. Divine obligations gradually shift to human ones. Or original divine obligations lie behind human ones.[113]

Incidentally, about half of the examples of Chaucer's *moste* are in the indicative not the subjunctive. It seems to correspond nearly to ModE 'have to' for its connotation of objective obligation. This reinforces the impression that the ME word had that sense too.[114]

The above inseparability between external causals expands as personal freedom increases. Whatever times people live in, they are never without a desire to express their individuality. The difference between one age and another is not that one possesses total freedom while another possesses none. It is a matter of degree. In some periods individuality has been permitted or even encouraged, while in others—e.g. Chaucer's day—it was suppressed along with freedom of speech and other things that we regard today as "human rights." For that reason some strategy or filter was needed for the expression of one's individuality, e.g. the allegories or proverbial wisdom typical of medieval literature. This is true of the external causals expressed by *moot/moste*. They may be objective and reflect real obligation imposed from without, or they may be only apparently so in that the speaker presents them as such by attempting to suppress his own feelings/intentions. In this way the subjective and objective overlap. This can be seen when Chaucer, the first prism, observing the phenomenon of the double prism structure, explores unvarnished humanity. This induces the reader, the second prism, to make his or her own interpretation as to subjectivity or objectivity. This is a bridge phenomenon for the future individual implications of *moot/moste*. Incidentally what Coates (1983: 38) calls the most subjective type, 'performative stereotype' (You are obliged to do X because I say so) cannot be found except in the case of a person of an appropriate social status (a judge's autocratic verdict: SumT III (D) 2037 and 2038).

10.2.1.4. Amibiguity in external causals in *Troilus and Criseyde*

When the characters in *Troilus and Criseyde* are put in a predicament and required to express their individualism, they are sensitive to offending against the social ideal, and hesitate to show their true feelings. At the surface level they assume an objective posture, but on the deeper level (pragmatically) make their self-assertion. Here the overlapping status of external causals is adroitly made use of. The second prism is given some latitude of interpretation. Here are some examples. Pandarus's dinner invitation to Criseyde would be most probably seen by the medieval audience as reprehensible. At this point *moot/moste* is employed to underline the extent to which Criseyde's hand

---

113 Leech and Coates' (1980: 82) classification of external causals regarding 'cannot' is of great use although it is based on current English. For Chaucer's use of external causals regarding *moot/moste*, see Nakao (1999). When modals are open to dual interpretations, Coates (1983-78-9) distinguishes 'merger' (both A and B) where since the two senses are related strongly to each other, it does not matter which one is understood, and 'ambiguity' (either A or B) where though one of the two is regarded as solely relevant, it cannot be proved.

114 Of course, the ModE *must* can be used to refer to objective causals (a natural phenomenon or the divine will in the Bible), but it is assumed to do so through the speaker's subjective agreement with them. See Nakao (1996) and Nakao (2002a).

was forced in the matter and so to mitigate her guilt as far as possible, as can be seen from (6) below.

(6) Whan he was com, he gan anon to pleye
     As he was wont, and of hymself to jape;
     And finaly he swor and gan hire seye,
     By this and that, she sholde hym nought escape,
     Ne lenger don hym after hire to cape;
     But certeynly she *moste,* by hire leve,
     Come soupen in his hous with hym at eve.

     At which she lough, and gan hire faste excuse,
     And seyde, "It reyneth; lo, how sholde I gon?"
     "Lat be," quod he, "ne stant nought thus to muse.
     This *moot* be don! Ye shal be ther anon."
     So at the laste herof they fille aton,
     Or elles, softe he swor hire in hire ere,
     He nolde nevere comen ther she were.   Tr 3.554-67

If the real intention became apparent, Pandarus knows well that she would have no choice but to decline the invitation, since it would violate the 'honour'/'chastitee,' attributed to the courtly lady as a cardinal virtue. Thus he is careful to conceal the real reason for his invitation. One of the ways in which he secures her acceptance is by the use of the external causals of *moot/moste.*

From the context we can infer that those causals are threefold: the familial relationship of uncle and niece (5d), the constraints of courtly existence (5e) and the dispensation of Fortune (5b.iii). As her uncle, and also as her guardian (her father being a traitor and in exile), he gains a degree of authority, and therefore can exert the more pressure on her to accept the invitation. This invitation is overtly regarded as socially natural. The fact that she is encouraged to accept it as a niece is explicit in 'And, as his nece, obeyed as hire oughte' (Tr 3.581). In their conversations he addresses her repeatedly as *nece* (Tr 3.571, Tr 3.631, Tr 3.649, Tr 3.659, etc.); Criseyde calls him *unlce* in Tr 3.645; and the narrator underlines their relationship in 'he streght o morwe unto his nece wente – ' (Tr 3.552) and 'Pandarus, hire em' (Tr 3.680). According to the ideal behaviour required of a courtly lady, Criseyde is expected to have a balanced sense of *daunger* and *pite*. In the courtly circle, her excessive distrust of Pandarus and her sheer rejection of the invitation would be regarded as extreme, impolite and to all appearances unjustified. Lastly, Pandarus seems to have stressed that her acceptance of the invitation has the inevitability of an event ordained by Fortune, with regard to which see the juxtaposition of 'sholde ... nought' (Tr 3.557) and *moste* (Tr 3.559) [indirect speech] and also of 'moot' (Tr 3.564) and *shal* (Tr 3.564): 'Ye shal be ther anon' [direct speech]. If the readers are concerned with the external causals behind Pandarus's use of *moot/moste,* they tend to be aware that Pandarus has exploited multiple social forces inherent in *moot/moste* to achieve added objectivity.

From their vantage point, however, the audience is informed that everything about this invitation is contrived by Pandarus as an individual, with a view to the fulfilment of Troilus's desire, and that it does not stem directly from the social demands which society places upon Criseyde, nor is in accordance with the law of Fortune. Thus the careful readers are likely to say that so far as the linguistic meaning of *moot/moste* is concerned, it is intended to function objectively, but that pragmatically, or as seen by Pandarus and perhaps by Criseyde, it is intended to depersonalize (objectify) the otherwise personal invitation. They are encouraged to be sensitive to individually directed implications of the above external causals. (As shown in Chapter 9, Criseyde seems to have understood that Troilus is at Pandarus's house through the illocutionary forces of his speech. See Tr 3.568-78.)

Criseyde, probing the invitation and attempting to confirm that it does not put her honour in jeopardy, leaves everything to Pandarus.

(7) But natheles, yet gan she hym bisech,
 Although with him to gon it was no fere,
 For to ben war goosissh poeples speche,
 That dremen thynges whiche as nevere were,
 And wel avyse hym whom he broughte there;
 And seyde hym, "Em, syn I *moste* on yow triste,
 Loke al be wel, and do now as yow liste."   Tr 3.582-8

Criseyde is dependent on Pandarus as to how to accept the above invitation, since she feels obliged to have trust in him. In the courtly circle, when she asks someone to do something for her, it is expected that she should trust them. This idea occurs not only in Tr 2.239-45, Tr 2.411-3, Tr 3.366, but also in *Confessio Amantis* viii 1293 and in *Sir Gawain and the Green Knight* 2348 ('trawthe'). However, if we can assume that she intuitively understands that Troilus is there and that in spite of or more probably because of this she has decided to go there, her apparent resort to social/objective considerations seems disingenuous. Internally, she seems to leave it to him whether she chooses the action above, and thus to avoid responsibility for it. With the guarantee of this social acceptance, she seems capable of moving one step towards the potential scandal mentioned above.

When she tries to leave Pandarus's house, she encounters the heavy rain and is thus forced to stay there, as seen in (8). (See Section 8.3.)

(8) But O Fortune, executrice of wierdes,
 O influences of thise hevenes hye!
 Soth is, that under God ye ben oure hierdes,
 Though to us bestes ben the causez wrie.
 This mene I now: for she gan homward hye,
 But execut was al bisyde hire leve
 The goddes wil, for which she *moste* bleve.   Tr 3.617-23

The heavy rain is of course a natural phenomenon. The narrator elaborates on the objective external causals forcing her stay there such as *Fortune* (Tr 3.617), 'influences of thise hevenes hye' (Tr 3.618), and 'the godes wil' (Tr 3.623). Her personal involvement in it is completely excluded.

Looking at the wider context, however, we cannot help but question the validity of this alleged objectivity. We know that Pandarus invites her to the supper at his house deliberately on the very day when he knows it is going to rain heavily. He plays the role of 'God' since he was a creator/contriver of the supper and the subsequent physical liaison between Troilus and Criseyde. Troilus acts in accordance with his plan. More significantly, as has already been suggested, Criseyde may have guessed that he would be there (Tr 3.568-78). If so, we may safely say that all three of them are the active participants in this set of events. Further, the unnatural juxtaposition of an emotional *O* (interjection) (Tr 3.617, Tr 3.618) and an analytical conjunction *but* (Tr 3.622) and a half-humorous insertion of 'This mene I now' (a possible means of mitigating the hyperbole here) (Tr 3.621) suggest that the objective causals are functional as a linguistic veil for safeguarding her honour and promoting her stay there. The superficial reader constituting the second prism will be persuaded into believing the narrator's objective causals, while the careful reader will not fail to observe Pandarus's plays upon human psychology in a mastery way. (For details of the subjectivisation of *moste*, see Nakao (1997).)

Troilus stays at Pandarus's house according to the plan. Pandarus tells Criseyde that Troilus has come to him in a state of great distress because she has cast amorous glances at Horaste. Pandarus comes to Criseyde and tells her, as seen in (9), that she must trust and accept him since no one will see them and no sin will occur.

(9) "Now have I told what peril he is inne,
    And his comynge unwist is to every wight;
    Ne, parde, harm may ther be non, ne synne:
    I wol myself be with yow al this nyght.
    Ye knowe ek how it is youre owen knyght,
    And that bi right ye *moste* upon hym triste,
    And I al prest to fecche hym whan yow liste."   Tr 3.911-7

Besides the 'uncle-niece' relation mentioned above, Pandarus also exploits the social (courtly) relation between Troilus and Criseyde (Tr 3.915): an ideal knight and a courtly lady. This social force is perhaps suggested in the inserted phrase 'bi righte' collocated and semantically linked with *moste*. Since he is noble and reliable (*gentilesse* Tr 2.702, Tr 2.1268, 'Trewe as stiel' Tr 5.831), she is expected to be *gentil* (Tr 3.882) and *pitous* (Tr 3.918) to him and to be capable of trusting him (cf. 'Hire love of frendshipe' Tr 2.962). Her trust of Troilus here is thus posed as a social obligation, and thus much external pressure is exerted on her to accept him. In view of this she can only assent and move one stage nearer to the inevitable intimacy. However, the open-minded observer can only be sceptical of Pandarus's integrity. Note in particular lines 'And his comynge unwist to every wight; / Ne, parde, harm may ther be non, ne synne' (Tr 3.911-2). 'His comynge' must attract opprobrium. In theological terms, it is a sin whether discovered or not. In the view of Pandarus, it is not regarded as a *synne* if *unwist* to everyone. *Moste* here is in the same vein. The linguistic sense of *moste* is objective (socially based), and yet pragmatically it is likely to be subjectivized in that he and Criseyde seem at a deeper level to have taken advantage of its objective force for their depersonalization of the socially problematic deed. Here is also seen an interaction between the objective and the subjective sides of *moot/moste*.

We have examined one of the semantic aspects of *moot/moste*, i.e. the pragmatic aspect of external causals as these determine its semantic properties. These causals generally function according to the idealism of the medieval society: divine laws, social laws, common sense, etc. In Chaucer it should be noted that the objective use of *moot/moste* is still current. We have seen that Pandarus/Criseyde/narrator can rely on this point in justifying the dangerous action of the hero and heroine. Linguistically these external causals function in a normal objective way, and pragmatically, through Pandarus/Criseyde/narrator (commentator), are endowed with subjective implications. It is left to the reader, the second prism,, to decide how he or she understands them and this produces ambiguity.

10.2.2. Ambiguity due to the interaction between root and epistemic senses of the modals

10.2.2.1. Semantic condensation in modal auxiliaries

English modals were originally full verbs and described the actions and states of their subjects. As their meanings were modified, they began naturally to collocate with infinitives. As they began more positively to express the user's mental involvement, so the link with the infinitive became more inevitable. Gradually the original meanings began to be lost and they developed the basic auxiliary senses, first the root senses (senses of obligation, will, ability, etc.), then the epistemic senses (senses denoting degrees of certainty). Attested English down to late ME evinces a transition from the former to the latter.

The English practice of combining the root and epistemic senses in one modal form is in contrast to the Japanese case in which these two senses are represented in different forms such as 'shinakereba naranai' (the root sense of *must*) and 'nichigai nai' (the epistemic sense of *must*). Sweetser (1990: 49) notes 'The ambiguity of modal expressions between "root" (or deontic) and "epistemic" senses.' Determining the central meaning of modals involves taking their whole contexts into account. However, determining the modal implications is largely dependent on the reader's inference since in Chaucer's English the development from the root sense to the epistemic sense is in a transitional stage.

The circumstances in which the hero and heroine find themselves and the mental attitudes into which speaker and reader are forced create a situation of great complexity and potential ambiguity as we shall see below.

In the following dialogue Criseyde promises that her sojourn in the Greek camp as a hostage will be but brief. But should we interpret *shal* in the second line as expressing determination or certainty?

(10) For, dredeles, withinne a wowke or two
 I *shal* ben here; and that it may be so   Tr 4.1278-9

In (11) below we see that Troilus is sceptical about the likelihood of Criseyde's return. The word *may* in line Tr 5.1191 could denote her ability to do so or Troilus's conjecture about the likelihood.

(11) She [i.e. Criseyde] seyde, 'I shal ben here, if that I may,
 Er that the moone, O deere herte swete,
 The Leoun passe, out of this Ariete.'

 "For which she *may* yet holde al hire byheste."   Tr 5.1188-91

Previous studies of modals (Fridén 1948, Visser 1969, Ono 1969, Kerkhof 1982, *OED*, *MED*) have attempted to determine their meanings in an analytical way. The reason why the speaker uses a modal is that he or she has something hard to analyse for the proposition in question. A modal is a simple way of expressing complex feelings on the part of the speaker. By observing closely the variety of meanings encapsulated in one modal, we can better understand how it works from the point of view of the speaker and hearer. This section examines the various senses of modals and how they are likely to overlap with each other through metonymical/metaphorical association and then to give rise to ambiguity.

10.2.2.2. Root sense and epistemic sense: *moot/moste, may/myghte, shal/sholde* and *wol/wolde*

We limit ourselves to the root and epistemic senses of the four modals, *moot/moste, may/myghte, shal/sholde,* and *wol/wolde*. Prior to discussion of ambiguity caused by these senses, we make clear the semantic development of each modal. We have already discussed the history of *moot* in Section 10.2.1.1. At this point we present a similar treatment of the other three modals listed.

May originally meant '... am/is/are physically strong.' In conjunction with the infinitive it developed the sense of physical ability. Intellectual ability was originally expressed by *can*. But *may* was gradually applied also to intellectual ability. In this way the meaning of *may* became generalised. From this wide sense of ability developed those of '... can do ... situationally' and 'can do socially.' The external causal here is a situation rather than personal ability, out of which meanings involving permission arose. Further, the sense 'ability' led to an epistemic sense 'possibly' based on a metonymical association that if he (the subject) can do ..., it is likely that he does ....'[115] All these senses are observed in Chaucer's English. Since the objective senses of the modal derived from the etymology remained in use there, the root and epistemic senses overlapped easily, as shown in Section 10.2.1.1.[116]

Shal is originally associated with the notion of debt and fault. Cognate nouns and adjectives with these senses in modern Germanic languages alongside the modal auxiliaries with meanings of futurity and obligation (German *Schuld, schuldig, sollen*; Danish *skyld, skulle*) make this quite clear. In English the sense of obligation deriving from external causals such as Fortune/God/legal and moral duty was an inevitable development. Following this comes personal sense of obligation and—in the case of second and third person use—promise or threat. Then come such senses as habituality, prediction, and epistemicity based on the sense of obligation. Furthermore, it developed the future tense meaning (the future tense determining the speaker's determination or the simple future). In Chaucer *shal* developed the future tense compared with *wol,* but its future meaning was not so clear as it is in modern English.

The original meaning of *wol* is 'want.' In combination with the infinitive it developed the sense of intention. Because of the notion of persistence and inclination the

---

[115] The weakly subjective necessity/possibility and the strongly subjective necessity/possibility correspond to what Leech (1971: 75-7) calls 'theoretical necessity/possibility' and 'factual necessity/possibility.' From a historical point of view, Traugott (1989) points out that the epistemic sense of modals was weakly subjective in ME.

[116] See Bybee (1993: 192-4) for this.

idea of futurity developed, and in time also an epistemic sense: if he wants to ... it is possible that he does .... Because the achievement of one's desire is inevitably in the future, it is not difficult to see how this modal came to be a means of expressing the future tense. Unlike *shal* which expresses determination, it indicated a spontaneous feeling and tended to be used with the first person subject and preferably in colloquial contexts.[117] *Wol* tended to function in pure future with the case of the second/third person subject, while *shal* tended to function with the speaker's will/inclination (command, promise, threat, etc.).[118]

As we have seen above, the root sense of the modals developed from their original verbal meaning and the speaker oriented epistemic sense were undivided, and there the overlapping state was made problematic.

10.2.2.3. Ambiguity arising from the interaction between root sense and epistemic sense: from three points of view

The modals were sensitive to three conditional factors as listed in (2a, b, c) and this widened their semantic scope. These are: the condition of the proposition, the condition of the higher clause including the modals, and the pragmatic conditions. Types 'a' and 'b' in (2) have to do with propositional content and kinds of clauses containing modals. These have been a common subject of research in the past, but insufficient attention has been paid to 'c,' the pragmatic area. Further to grasp the totality of the meaning, it is vital to take into account not only the intention of the fictional narrator, but the response of the reader, the second prism, who can question or oppose it. Let us now consider ambiguity arising from the interaction between the root and epistemic senses of *moot, may, shal,* and *wol*.

10.2.2.4. Examination

The following lines are from the letter Troilus sends to Criseyde while she is in the Greek camp questioning the fact that she has overstayed the self-imposed length of her sojourn there. He would like to complain about her continued absence, but says that he dare not because 'I ... like all that you like' (Tr 5.1352-3).

(12) "But for as muche as me *moot* nedes like
    Al that yow liste, I dar nat pleyne moore,
    But humblely, with sorwful sikes sike,
    Yow write ich myn unresty sorwes soore,
    Fro day to day desiryng evere moore
    To knowen fully, if youre wille it weere,
    How ye han ferd and don whil ye be theere;   Tr 5.1352-8 [119]

Like is an impersonal verb with a stative aspect feature (see aspect of the predicate verb of the propositional condition, (2a.iii)). Since the 'self-controllability' of this verb, or the degree to which the agent is able to manipulate his or her action con-

---

117 I am indebted to Fridén (1948: 163) about this.
118 The semantic development of *shall* and *will* is investigated in Masui (1954: 1-55).
119 According to Windeatt (1990), there are scribal variants with regard to Tr 4.1279 *shal*: *wyl* H3, Tr 5.1352 *moot*: *must* DGgH2H4R, and Tr 5.993 *wol*: *shal* H2H3S1.

cerned, is weak, the *moot* collocating with it is naturally construed as having an epistemic sense. *Nedes* (Tr 5.1352) functions as harmonics, which is used to supplement the epistemic sense in its emerging period in which *moot* itself is not adequate to show its epistemic concept (see harmonics of the conditions of the higher clause within which the modals are used, (2b.v)). However, taking into full account the state of Troilus's psychology, the real status of the modal seems to be more complex (see the viewpoint of the speaker/hearer of the pragmatic conditions, (2c.i)). Is the epistemic sense of *moot* objective or subjective? Troilus tends to regard individual events as occurring deterministically. In view of this personality of his, the reader, the second prism, is likely to support the objective sense. However, assuming that he is involved in a specific situation (possibility of her returning to Troy) and then sceptic about his favorite feeling for her, he is likely to choose the subjective sense. This subjective interpretation is abnormal in view of the emergent stage of the epistemic sense of *moot*.

If the reader emphasises the deterministic evidence behind Troilus's epistemology, he can interpret the modal sense in such a way that 'he is obliged to like her' (a stative verb shifts to a transitional aspect verb when converted to a dynamic verb) by external forces—Fortune, God, the code of courtly love. Even though he is unhappy about her not fullfiling her promise, he endeavours himself to behave as an ideal courtly knight, a faithful servant of his beloved.[120]

In this way the reader, the second prism, is likely to perceive subltly ranging meanings in *moot,* and thus the rise of ambiguity rather than limiting himself or herself to one particular sense of it. This ambiguity is due to the polysmey of *moot.*[121]

Pandarus plans to help Troilus to have a date with Criseyde at his house. He invites her to the supper at his house on the very day when he predicts it will storm. She is forced to stay there after supper because of the strom. Pandarus tells her that he will take Troilus to her without anyone's notice of him. *May* in (13) is used to justify it.

---

[120] Japanese makes a formal lexical distinction between the root and epistemic senses of *must* in English. Karita (1949), understanding the deontic sense, translates this as 'manzokuseneba naranu' (I must be satisfied or content), whereas Miyata (1979) prefers the epistemic sense and translates this as 'nozomashii hazu' (will inevitably be desirable).

[121] Cf. But syn thus synfully ye me begile,
My body *mote* ye se withinne a while,
Ryght in the haven of Athenes fletynge,
Withoute sepulture and buryinge,   LGW 2550-3

This is quoted from *The Legend of Good Women* written immediately after *Troilus and Criseyde.* This is the context. Queen Phyllis helps the knight Demophone to get out of prison. She loves him instantly. She promises to marry him. But he forsakes her, going back to Athenes, his native city. She regrets her gullibility, and writes to him criticising his betrayal. The above quotation is the final part of her letter, and there she tells him he will soon see her corpse floating in the harbour. If we understand that Queen Phyllis accuses him for his betrayal, a sinful action, by means of the *syn*-clause, with the authority appropriate to a Queen, we are likely to take the meaning of *mote* in the root sense. On the other hand, if we understand that the *syn*-clause indicates not as much her social accusation for his betrayal as her determination to kill herself due to her mortification of being betrayed, the obligatory sense of *mote* is likely to be weakened, and instead its epistemic sense is likely to arise.

(13) "Now have I told what peril he is inne,
    And his comynge unwist is to every wight;
    Ne, parde, harm *may* ther be non, ne synne:
    I wol myself be with yow al this nyght.
    Ye knowe ek how it is youre owen knyght,
    And that bi right ye moste upon hym triste,   Tr 3.911-6

Since the subject of the sentence having the modal *may* is the existential *ther* (Tr 3.913), by which the agent implied in the modal is suppressed (see (2a.i) above 'the person of the subject of the propositional conditions'), and the *parde* (Tr 3.913) denoting the speaker's certainty is functional as 'harmonics' or a phrase to reinforce the modal's epistemic force, *may* is likely to be interpreted as epistemic. The degree of subjectivity can be certified by examining the viewpoint of the speaker/hearer and the social relation between them (see (2c.ii) 'the social relation between the speaker and the hearer of the pragmatic conditions'). Since the result of her entertaining Troilus in her room could involve sin and scandal, Pandarus needs to calm her fears by asserting that 'there need be no harm or sin. Pandarus here seems to be making two different points (a) that there can be no harm/scandal because no other human being knows about it; (b) that there can be no sin, because nothing sexual will happen seeing that he himself will be there as a chaperon. Only on this understanding can she accede to his request. The objective epistemic sense is easily metonymically related to the inherent root sense. However, from a Christian point of view, the recognition will be made problematic that accepting Troilus will be no sin as far as people do not notice it (Tr 3.912-3). The reader, the second prism, is asked to reinterpret Pandarus's inference in such a way that there will be no sin according to his view.

When Criseyde does not return from the Greek camp to Troy as promised, Troilus thinks he has miscaluculated the date. *May* is used by Troilus in (14) when he is driven by great anxiety.

(14) But natheles, he gladed in this:
    He thought he misacounted hadde his day,
    And seyde, "I understonde have al amys.
    For thilke nyght I last Criseyde say,
    She seyde, 'I shal ben here, if that I may,
    Er that the moone, O deere herte swete,
    The Leoun passe, out of this Ariete.'

    "For which she *may* yet holde al hire byheste."   Tr 5.1184-91

The verb *holde* seems to have both a dynamic and stative aspect. *May* could therefore have either its deontic or its epistemic sense. Combination of *yet* with this verb allows it to have both senses (see (2a.viii) 'adjunct in the predicate verb of the propositional conditions'). The mental state of Troilus and the social relation between him and Criseyde are, as we have seen in (12), dependent on the inference of the reader. What does Troilus infer from Criseyde's promise that she will 'return to Troy before the moon leaves Aries and passes through Leo' (a case of external causals; see (2c.iii) above). He says either that it is still possible for her to keep her promise, or that given her ability she would choose to do so. It is up to the reader, the second prism, to decide which sense to give more weight to. In this way ambiguity is the result.

10. Ambiguity in modality

The use of *shal* in the following lines seems unproblematical on the face of it. It conveys determination, as it would do in modern English. Criseyde is sent to the Greek camp by the exchange of her for the prisoners. She promises to Troilus to return to Troy within a week or two, as shown in (15).

(15) "Now, that I shal wel bryngen it aboute
To come ayeyn, soone after that I go,
Therof am I no manere thyng in doute;
For, dredeles, withinne a wowke or two
I *shal* ben here; and that it may be so
By alle right and in a wordes fewe,
I shal yow wel an heep of weyes shewe.   Tr 4.1275-81

The first person subject of the sentence and the modal *shal* lead to the speaker's determination. On the other hand, 'Therof ... in doute' (Tr 4.1277) and *dredeles* (Tr 4.1278) might seem to imply the very seeds of the doubt in the speaker's mind that she is seeking to banish. Thus determination and an epistemic sense are found in one and the same modal. Further, the reader, sceptical of her optimism/good intensions, may say that she is simply using *shal* to express what she knows are the obligations on her—alongside her detemination.[122] Several meanings can be found in *shal*, and this leads to ambiguity for the reader. *Shal* in the line below is in the same vein.

(16) And er that trewe is doon, I *shal* ben heere;   Tr 4.1314

On their way to the Greek camp, Diomede offers Criseyde his friendship and service. We are probably meant to uderstand that she does not hear the bit about love because she does not react accordingly. Certainly, Chaucer says (Tr 5.178) that she only heard the odd word of his speech. She nevertheless thanks him.

(17) But natheles she thonketh Diomede
Of al his travaile and his goode cheere,
And that hym list his frendshipe hire to bede;
And she accepteth it in good manere,
And wol do fayn that is hym lief and dere,
And tristen hym she *wolde*, and wel she myghte,
As seyde she; and from hire hors sh'alighte.   Tr 5.183-9

The description of her response proceeds gradually from simple report (*accepteth*, etc.) (Tr 5.186) to a kind of indirect speech ('as seide she') (Tr 5.189). The word *wolde* here is not fully part of direct speech, which does not begin until she meets her father. If this were direct speech, she would of course have said *I wol* (and also *I may*, Tr 5.188). Chaucer's choice of indirect speech, which obliges him to use the third person, mitigates any foreboding of future infidelity we might be tempted to see here.[123]

---

122 While Karita (1949) translates this part as 'kitto kokoe modotte mairimasuwa' (I shall surely come back) with an emphasis on the epistemic sense, Miyata (1979) translates it into 'kochirani modotte kimasuwa' (I am determined to come back here) with an emphasis on the root sense.

123 See Karita's (1949) translation 'mata karewo shinjirukotoni shiyou, kitto soushitai' (And I will trust him, surely I would like to do so) and Miyata's (1979) 'anatawo goshinnrai itashimasho, jubun goshinrai dekiruto zonjimasu' (And I will trust him, I can trust him). Their translations read as close to direct speech where the modals are interpreted in the root sense of volition and ability. Cf. Criseyde's vacillating attitude towards Diomede is also seen in the use of the adverb

We have an example of *wol* in Criseyde's speech, where she yields at last to Diomede's advances in love on the Greek camp.

(18) "Myn herte is now in tribulacioun,
 And ye in armes bisy day by day.
 Herafter, whan ye wonnen han the town,
 Peraventure so it happen may
 That whan I se that nevere yit I say
 Than *wol* I werke that I nevere wroughte!
 This word to yow ynough suffisen oughte. Tr 5.988-94

Wol seems to be open to two interpretations. The obvious one is that it expresses volition. The fact that it bears the metrical stress reinforces this. On the other hand, the strength of will implied here is weakened when we consider the complicated clause structure surrounding it. First comes the temporal clause (Tr 5.990) where *whan* (Tr 5.990) can almost equate to 'if and when' in modern colloquial English. Then the words 'Peraventure so it happen may' (Tr 5.991) further weaken the force of any subsequent expression of intent. In this main clause is embedded another complex clause which is composed of the temporal clause 'whan I se …' (Tr 5.992) and the clause containing *wol*. This syntactic complexity encourages the reader to make an epistemic interpretation.

This semantic tension between the two senses mirrors that of Criseyde herself. She is torn between her sense of her self-defensiveness having accepted Diomede's love and thereby gone up in his estimation, and her feelings of guilt from having betrayed Troilus. The former leads us to take volition as the implied sense, and the latter produces an epistemic interpretation. In this dialogue the sense of her volition is favorable for Diomede, and can be taken by him.

Wol in (19) is in the same vein. After betraying Troilus, she decides to be true to Diomede in her monologue. If one takes *algate* (Tr 5.1071) to mean 'always', *wol* expresses volition, whereas it has an epistemic sense if one translates the adverb as 'at any rate.'

(19) To Diomede algate I *wol* be trewe. Tr 5.1071

The modals are unique in that they can express in condensed form the conflicting thoughts of the characters. The reader, the second prism, must decide which aspect to give more weight to. The scope for ambiguity is obvious.[124]

10.2.3. Final remarks

We have focused on the overlapping state of the external causals of *moot/moste*, and the interaction between the root and the epistemic senses, and described in each case how ambiguity is likely to arise through the double prism structure. The love between

---

fayn (Tr 5.187). The *OED* s.v. fain (adj) 2 has: Const. to with *inf.* Glad under the circumstances; glad or content to take a certain course in default of opportunity for anything better, or as the lesser of two evils. c1330-1882

124 For a similar example, see CT FrT III (D) 1514: cynical ambiguity due to the devil's language—volition or prediction.

Troilus and Criseyde and its fulfillment presented to the characters a social and moral dilemma, and the justification of their sinful and potentially scandalous actions. They exploit the word *moot* to imply irresistible obligations upon them. But depending on the second prism, these external causals may be seen as objective or subjective. Sometimes an additional factor is intervened (e.g. Diomede's seduction of Criseyde), and here equivocation occurs. Then the boundaries between root and epistemic senses of the modals become blurred, so that the reader introduces ambiguity at his or her own level.

10.3. Ambiguity arising from modal adverbs

10.3.1. Introductory remarks

History is etymologically related to *story* in meaning the 'narrative of past events, account, tale, story' (*OED* s.v. history ad L *historia*), the synonymous *tale* can also mean 'falsehood' (*OED* s.v. tale 5. c1250-), and so can the Japanese equivalent of *tale*: *katari*. The relationship of cause and effect behind events in the story is apt to be clouded because it is seen through the eyes of the narrator and the characters. Chaucer makes full use of speaker-involvement, especially at important points in the narrative.

The psychological conflicts in which the characters are placed are seen through the eyes of the narrator and characters. The narrator sometimes abandons his role as an omniscient overseer of events, and appears to become personally involved in them (see Chapter 6 above where we discussed the narrator's sympathetic handling of Criseyde's inconstancy). Thus it is often difficult for us to form a clear judgement on important issues such as Criseyde's *untrouthe* (Tr 5.1098). Nothing is black and white any longer, and the reader, the second prism, must perhaps compromise his or her own notions of right and wrong. When 'truth' becomes relative, there are various ways in which this can be realised linguistically. We listed them in Section 10.1. In Section 10.2 we looked at the role of modal auxiliaries. This section concentrates on a modal adverb *trewely*. This word occurs repeatedly in the story, particularly at significant junctures. Typically it is found in connection with references to Criseyde's *untrouthe*, encouraging the reader to make mental links between the two cognate words and their semantic contents. We examine this term through the double prism structure and show how it is concerned with degrees of truth and thus with ambiguity in our author.

10.3.2. The concept of 'epistemicity'

As a working definition of epistemicity we take that of Palmer (1979: 50-1). This concept deals with the speaker's judgement of the certainty of the event, or to borrow his word, the 'proposition.' In theory there may be two types of judgement—objective and subjective—, but as Warner (1993: 14) says, judgement is very rarely purely objective because the person doing the judging is the speaker himself.[125]

What assists the speaker to gain access to the source of information may be called 'evidential.' This can be of various kinds—hearsay, written material and so on. If a person repeats what he hears as it is without adding his judgement of it, this source

---

125 Cf. Lyons (1977: 797-809)

will be regarded as evidential. On the other hand, if the evidential is tempered by subjective judgement/opinion, then it becomes epistemic. In *Troilus and Criseyde* and everywhere in medieval epic literature, we repeatedly find a variety of expressions appealing to the source such as 'the author tells us ...,'[126] which is occasionally of the author's invention as discussed below in Chaucer.

The concept of epistemic is similar to what Quirk et al. (1985) calls 'style disjunct' (expressions denoting manner of utterance) and 'content disjunct' (expressions denoting degrees of certainties of the proposition). In pragmatic terms it is similar to what Lakoff (1973) calls 'hedges' (self-defensive expressions to evade the inquiry about the truth of the proposition from the opponent). It has a common background to what Leech (1983) calls 'politeness' (the speaker makes the truth of the proposition a matter of degree, and leaves room for alternative interpretation on the part of the interlocutor). Further, it is similar in effect to swearing or asserveration such as 'by God' or 'by my trouthe.'

10.3.3. The modal adverb *trewely* in Chaucer: previous research

The *OED* defines *trewely* as follows:

(20) OED s.v. truly OE *treowliche*
- 1. a.   Faithfully, loyally, constantly, with steadfast allegiance. *arch.* 1000-1852
- †2.   Honestly, honourably, uprightly. *Obs.* 1362-1558
- 3.   In accordance with the fact; truthfully; correctly (in reference to a statement). 1303-1875
- 4. a.   In accordance with a rule or standard; exactly, accurately, precisely, correctly. 1375-1875
- 5. a.   Genuinely, really, actually, in fact, in reality; sincerely, unfeignedly. c.1380-1874
-     b.   Used to emphasize a statement (sometimes as a mere expletive): Indeed, forsooth, verily. c1205 - 1869

Cf. OED s.v. truth OE *treowþe*
- 1.†b.   By my truth, as an asseveration. *Obs.* 13.-1605
- 9. a.   True statement or account; that which is in accordance with the fact: chiefly in phr. *to say, speak,* or *tell the truth*, to speak truly, to report the matter as it really is. 1362-
- 14. a.   Phrases *in truth, of a truth,* †*of truth,* †*for a truth*: in fact, as a fact; truly, verily, really, indeed: mostly used to strengthen or emphasize a statement. 14..

While the *OED* definitions 1a, 2, 3, 4a and 5a are used as adverbs of manner, 5b is used epistemically to show the speaker's attitude towards the propositional content. 3 includes examples of *trewely* occurring with verbs of saying (*bid, speak, tell, swear*), and 5a includes an example of *trewely* occurring with a verb of thinking (*believe*). Here we find borderline cases similar to epistemic expressions like 'trewely to tell' (*Ywaine & Gawaine*, 329). The *OED* 5b only mentions the function of *trewely* as an emphatic adverb, 'sometimes as a mere expletive.' It does not refer to the modal aspect of this word nor distinguish between the modal sense and the speech act sense. As far as epistemic meaning is concerned, there is substantially no difference between the

---

126   As for the semantic development from 'evidential' to 'epistemic,' Brinton (1996: 231-5, 243-4) is useful.

OED and the *MED*, with regard to which see *MED* s.v. treuli: '8. Actually, in fact; really, indeed; genuinely, sincerely; also as intensifier or in parenthetical expressions with reduced semantic content; also in stock simile.'

Kerkhof (1982: 404-5) lists 'Adverbs of Modality,' but does not describe them in semantic or pragmatic terms. He does not include *trewely* there.

From the semantic and pragmatic point of view, Brinton's (1996: 230-1) description is valuable. She examines the historical development of 'first person epistemic parentheticals' from the point of view of grammaticalisation and subjectification (see Section 10.4). Her comments on the relation between these parentheticals and the contents to which these are attached are very useful: 'they are most often appended to utterances expressing personal opinion, evaluation, or interpretation' (p. 218). But she sketches modal adverbs very briefly stressing the same function with the first person epistemic parentheticals. Her sketch does not include *trewely*. Traugott's (1989: 46-7) discussion of adverbs like *apparently/evidently* in relation to the rise of epistemic meaning is also of interest. But like Brinton she does not deal with *trewely*, too. Their discussions are primarily about grammaticalisation, and therefore ambiguity is not really their concern.

Many scholars have concentrated on these expressions from a stylistic or literary critical point of view, but mainly in relation to narrative devices typical of orally transmitted literature. Bennett (1947: 85) describes them as follows:

(21) This is not to deny, however, as has been admitted above, that Chaucer made use of rhyme-tags and padding material. All medieval writers drew upon a large rag-bag full of tags, alliterative and stock phrases to save themselves trouble, to give their listeners time to absorb some fact or interesting detail, or to drive home the importance of a statement.

Malone (1951) focuses on the effects of those tags in the GP to *The Canterbury Tales* as ascribable to a secret conversation between the narrator and the audience. In relation to the interaction between the narrator and the audience, Mehl (1974) points out that those expressions are functional in encouraging the audience to participate in the interpretation of the narrative text. From a metrical point of view, Masui (1964: 237-45) deals with them in connection with Chaucer's rhyming technique. He says 'This word (i.e. *trewely*) is sometimes used to emphasise a statement, sometimes as a mere expletive, the latter being often the case with Chaucer' (p. 239). These studies have contributed to the study of narrative devices in ME oral transmission, but are little concerned with finding a modal angle by which ambiguity is likely to occur.

Donaldson (1970: 74) and Elliott (1974: 115) have directed their attention to *trewely*. Donaldson (1970) emphasises the anti-climactic effect of this word in *Troilus and Criseyde* comparing it with ModE *surely*, and Elliott (1974) looks at its effect of 'ironical twist' in Books 4 and 5. Elliott does not distinguish between *trewely* as an adverb of manner and as an epistemic adverb. Both writers confine the effect of *trewely* to the counterfactual although *trewely* can function as an objective epistemic.

To experience the full potential of Chaucer's *trewely*, we need to investigate how the first prism speaker observes the phenomenon (proposition), and expresses it, and how the second prism reader interprets it, from the point of view of modality and ambiguity.

10.3.4. Ambiguity caused by the use of *trewely*

To borrow the terminology of Sweetser (1990), the senses of *trewely* discussed in Section 10.3.3 range over the three different domains listed below.

(22) a. Proposition
 b. Propositional attitude
 c. Speech act

Trewely (22a) works as an adverb of manner within the scope of the predication, whether the modified word is a verb, adjective or adverb (the *OED* s.v. truly 1a, 2, 3, 4a, 5a). (22b) works as a disjunct or modal adverb, indicating that the truth of the proposition is not self-evident, but open to the speaker's/listener's judgement (the *OED* s.v. truly: part of 3 collocating with verbs of saying, part of 5a collocating with verbs of thought, 5b). (22c) is functional with a performative force with the implications of the speaker's politeness/familiarity/attention-calling and, when the most formalised, comes to be restricted to a local context, working as a mere tag or filler with some tautology in the narrative communication. In historical terms, the sense of *trewely* is developed from (22a) to (22c), and all three senses are found in Chaucer.

Chaucerian scholarship treated above in Section 10.3.3 has tended to ignore (22b) and place emphasis almost exclusively on things such as pause-making, attention-calling, addresses to the audience, irony—all features of (22c). The hitherto neglected aspects categorised under (22b) are our central conern here. Mere intensification, tagging or irony do not exhaust the use of this word.

We consider why *trewely* is used at all. If the speaker and the hearer agree with the proposition, there is no need for using it. *Trewely* is a marker for remedying the discrepancy between them as regards the understanding of the proposition concerned. Here the speaker draws the hearer's attention to its truth by saying *trewely*. Its modal nature can be classified into two types, according to Oh (2000: 252-3): one functions in a local scope and the other in a global scope. The former 'locally intensifies the meaning of the clause in which it occurs,' which might correspond to the *OED* 5b in (20), and the latter is more pragmatic, 'the function of contradicting prior expectations.' Chaucer's modalising use of *trewely* and its consequent ambiguity is central to this global function. Cf. the following.

(23) a. for *trewely*, all tho that conseilleden yow to maken sodeyn werre ne been nat youre
 freendes.   CT Mel VII 1363   [Prudence to Melibee]

 b. And *trewely*, as to my juggement,   [Clerk to the company]
 Me thynketh it a thyng impertinent,   it=tale by Petrach
 Save that he wole conveyen his mateere;   ClP IV (E) 53-5

 c. This Chauntecleer, whan he gan hym espye,
 He wolde han fled, but that the fox anon
 Seyde, "Gentil sire, allas, wher wol ye gon?
 Be ye affrayed of me that am youre freend?
 Now, certes, I were worse than a feend,
 If I to yow wolde harm or vileynye!
 I am nat come youre conseil for t'espye,
 But *trewely*, the cause of my comynge   [fox to Chaunticleer]

```
                    Was oonly for to herkne how that ye synge.
                    For trewely, ye have as myrie a stevene
                    As any aungel hath that is in hevene.                NPT VII (B2) 3282-92

        d.  I wol yow teche pleynly the manere
            How I kan werken in philosophie.
            Taketh good heede; ye shul wel seen at ye
            That I wol doon a maistrie er I go."
                    "Ye," quod the preest, "ye, sire, and wol ye so?
            Marie, therof I pray yow hertely."
                    "At youre comaundement, sire, trewely,"       [canon to the priest]
            Quod the chanoun, "and ellis God forbeede!"
                    Loo, how this theef koude his service beede!  CYT VIII (G) 1057-65
```

Of course, the degrees of epistemicity derived from *trewely* are sensitive to the kinds of content to which it is applied or more globally/pragmatically to the personlity of the speaker or to the interaction between personality and content. The content in (23a) is assertive (the verb is indicative *been*), and the speaker is Prudence persuading Melibee to abstain from war. *Trewely* emphasises the truth of the statement and is thus regarded as 'local scope.' (If we assume *trewely* expresses the wife's politeness to her husband in expressing her opinion, the function of *trewely* shifts to (22c).) *Trewely* in (23b) introduces an epistemic parenthetical 'as to my juggement,' and underlines the main clause 'me thynketh it a thyng impertinent,' all of which express the speaker's evaluation, i.e. that the geographical descriptions presented by the Clerk's source are irrelevant except for the purpose of introduction. The speakers of (23c, d) are characterised as hypocrites in the tales, and their use of *trewely* is intended to deceive Chanticleer/the priest. These uses may be characterised as of 'global scope' since they are open to the reader's contradiction.

(22c) includes examples of *trewely* used as a narrative tag or line filler in the sense described by Bennett. They are also often found in the rhyming position and so it cannot be doubted that they function as padding and perform a prosodic function. However, less than half the instances of *trewely* occur at the end of a line (see (24) below). The use of *trewely* for rhyming purpose does not tell the whole story.

Since *trewely* has the senses of (22a-c), the reader is encouraged to infer the most appropriate one. This section is devoted to the modal implication of (22b).

10.3.5. Examination

In Chaucer nearly all the examples of *trewely* are found with the epistemic sense (22b). Of the 128 examples of epistemic use 96 occur alone; 6 occur with verbs of saying, and 9 with verbs of thinking (all these verbs are in the first person singular present tense). There are 17 instances where *trewely* is clearly an adverb of manner. Details of the frequency of this word in its various semantic roles is given in (24). Distinguishing between categories (22b) and (22c) is very important, but can only be done by qualitative analysis.

(24) The frequency of *trewely* in Chaucer according to semantic categories

function of *trewely*	CT	BD	HF	Anel	PF	Bo	Tr	LGW	SHP	Astr	Rom	Total
adverb of manner	6/0	0	2/2	0	0	0	5/1	2/1	1/0	1/0	0	17/4
with verb of saying	4/2	0	1/1	0	0	0	0	0	1/0	0	0	6/3
with verb of thinking	3/0	4/2	0	0	0	0	2/1	0	0	0	0	9/3
epistemic adv.	33/10	18/7	2/2	0	0	0	33/12	6/2	2/0	0	2/2	96/35
Total	46/12	22/9	5/5	0	0	0	40/14	8/3	4/0	1/0	2/2	128/45

N.B.: The number to the left of the slash indicates the total items, and to the right the frequency of the item in a rhyming position. 'With verb of saying' means *trewely* occurring with verb of saying.

(25) The frequency of *trewely* in Langland, Gower, and romances analysed according to semantic categories

function of *trewely*	Langland	Gower	Amis	Launfal	Squire	Wedding	Total
adverb of manner	7/7	6/0	1/0	1/0	0	0	15/7
with verb of saying	3/3	1/1	1/0	0	0	0	5/4
with verb of thinking	1/1	4/3	0	0	0	0	5/4
epistemic adv.	4/4	3/2	0	0	0	2/2	9/8
Total	15/15 [alliteration]	14/6	2/0	1/0	0	2/2	34/23

N.B.: Langland=Piers Plowman, Gower=Confessio Amantis, Amis=Amis and Amiloun, Launfal=Sir Launfal, Squire=The Squire of Low Degree, Wedding=The Wedding of Sir Gawain and Dame Ragnell.

Trewely appears in *Troilus and Criseyde* almost as frequently as in *The Canterbury Tales* which is about twice the length. In the four contemporary romances investigated (see (25)), only two epistemic instances were found. Although *Troilus and Criseyde* has great linguistic affinity with romance works at that time, the frequent use of *trewely* therein seems to display a deviation from them. This story focuses on the processes of Criseyde's betrayal. The degrees of truthfulness involved in it is made problematic in the story, and as a result, explanations or justifications sometimes produce the flavour of expository style as seen in a sermon.

10. Ambiguity in modality

Who uses *trewely* to whom and when (which Book) can be seen in (26). It should be noted that *trewely* is found where Chaucer departs from his original, Boccaccio's *Il Filostrato*, with the exception of Tr 4 687 and Tr 5.483. Most instances are concentrated in Books 4 and 5, where we see Criseyde's development from the time of the decision that she should go to the Greek camp to the beginning of her adventure with Diomede. *Trewely* is increasingly used as the relationship between Troilus and Criseyde progressively deteriorates. The kinds of statements descriptive of her *trouthe/untrouthe* are significantly introduced by *trewely*. Pragmatically, who uses *trewely* to whom also has an important effect on the degrees of modalisation. If we compare near equivalents of *trewely* such as 'by my trouthe'/'have my trouthe' or 'soth to seyne,' we find that their use is not closely connected by the development of the story, and that 'by my trouthe'/'have my trouthe' are restricted to the dialogues between characters. These asseverations involved are lighter in tone and more accidental than *trewely*.

(26) The frequency of *trewely* according to Book and who uses it to whom in *Troilus and Criseyde*

who uses *trewely* to whom	Book 1	Book 2	Book 3	Book 4	Book 5	Total
T→C			1489	1450		2
T→P					483	1
T: M				1055 1063	1704 1720	4
C→T				1288	1623	2
C→P		164 241 1161	835	939		5
C→D					987	1
C: M					1075 1082	2
P→T	985				380 410 494	4
P→C		541				1
Calkas→Greek				116		1
Women→C				687		1
D→C					146	1
N	346	628		1415	19 816 826 1051 1086	8
Total	2	5	2	8	16	33

N.B.: T= Troilus, C=Criseyde, P=Pandarus, D=Diomede, N=narrator, M=monologue. *The numbers show line references.*

160   Part III: Ambiguity in interpersonal domains

We now examine passages where *trewely* contributes to the degrees of certainty of the proposition. They are concentrated in Books 4 and 5 in remarks by the narrator concerning the doubtful nature of Criseyde's *trouthe* as a courtly lady. He is completely on her side and seeks, as always, to assert her integrity. His use of *trewely* in these places is insistently repeated suggesting that he expects scepticism on the part of the reader and is seeking to forestall it.

Let us look first at the passage where Criseyde is explaining to Troilus the ruse whereby she will deceive her father in the Greek camp and so fulfil her promise of a speedy return. If her plan goes wrong, she says, she will kill herself (Tr 4.1412-4). The narrator immediately prefaces his comment on her speech with the modal *treweliche*, and in the succeeding six lines twice refers to Criseyde's *trewe* which he may by this time reasonably expect his readership seriously to doubt—a typical example of global scope in that he assumes the reader's contradiction (Tr 4.1415- 21).

(27) And but I make hym soone to converte
And don my red withinne a day or tweye,
I wol to yow oblige me to deye."

And *treweliche*, as writen wel I fynde
That al this thyng was seyd of good entente,
And that hire herte trewe was and kynde
Towardes hym, and spak right as she mente,
And that she starf for wo neigh whan she wente,
And was in purpos evere to be trewe:
Thus writen they that of hire werkes knewe.   Tr 4.1412-21

Treweliche is introduced not by the adversative *but* nor by the causal *for*, but the coordinate and unobtrusive *and*. We are encouraged to understand the following speech as a matter of course. *Treweliche* is placed at the beginning of the stanza at an important turning point in the story as well as in the initial position of the sentence with a topicalised implication under which the statement is to be understood. The statement, consisting of evaluative adjectives, describes Criseyde's moral status and involves the speaker's judgement. This is typical of *trewely* in (22b). If it is admitted to all people as self-evident, we would have a bare statement of 'al this thing was seyd of good entente' (Tr 4.1413), with no need of an attitudinal marker. Incidentally, no scribal variants are found for *treweliche* according to Windeatt (1990). Viewing *treweliche* through the double prism structure, we need to ask the following five questions.

(28) a. What is the statement to which *treweliche* is attached?
 b. Assuming that the narrator's statement is fixed, how much the audience, the second prism, believe it?
 c. What is the scope of the modal force of *treweliche* in relation to the repetition of the statements through the coordinate conjunction *and*?
 d. Why is the reconfirmation of the evidential 'Thus written they that of hire werkes knewe' (Tr 4.1421) necessary?
 e. Is there any effect of *paronomasia* perceivable in the co-occurrence of *treweliche* and *trewe*?

Regarding (28a), *treweliche* is semantically applied to the statement in the *that*-clause, since the contents are evaluative (*good, trewe, kynde*, etc.). After *treweliche*, it should be noted that an evidential or source of information, 'as written wel I fynde' (Tr 4.1412) is inserted to substantiate his opinion. However, in relation to the complement marker *that*, *treweliche* is taken grammatically as attached to 'I fynde ....' If this is right, the modality is overtly attached to the quotation of the narrator, and only indirectly to the validity of her *trouthe* since it is located in the embedded clause.

Thus when the proposition is framed both by an epistemic *treweliche* and an evidential, the relation between *treweliche* and the proposition it modifies becomes looser, since two propositions are involved. The uncertainties between the second prism readers are reflected in their modern English translations of this part as in (29).

(29) Tatlock and Mackaye (1912): And truly, as I find it written, all this was said with sincerity and good intent, and her heart was true and loving towards him ...

Stanley-Wrench (1965): And truly, as I find it written, too, / All this was said to him with good intent, / And I believe her heart was kind and true ...

Coghill (1971): And truly, it is written, as I find, / That all she said was said with good intent, / And that ...

Windeatt (1998): And truly, I find it written that all of this was said with good intentions, that ...

In Windeatt (1998) and Coghill (1971) quotative forms are construed grammatically as superordinate clauses, but in Stanley-Wrench (1965) and Tatlock-Mackaye (1912) they are treated parenthetically, where *treweliche* is more directly related to the statements.

With regard to (28b), the validity of the adjectives (*good, trewe, kynde*) are generally dependent on the criteria the speaker/listener set up in his or her mind. One of the criteria here is the question of time involved in Criseyde's change in the object of her affections. If the audience limits attention to this particular occasion on which she is dealing with the matter of her dispatch to the Greek camp, they may take her intentions as sincere and devoid of deception. On the other hand, taking a longer view of her promises, and assuming that they will not be kept, the audience is likely to be sceptical of her sincerity. The global scope imiplication of *trewliche* is obvious here. Donaldson (1970) points to the effect of anticlimax it produces. Paradoxically, her excessive sensitivity and pliancy in the face of the various situations she encounters can be said to imply future instability. Depending on the assumptions of the audience, the impression of subjectivity made by this statement is seen to vary.

Let us consider the use of *treweliche* as part of the act of quoting itself. As we have seen, this portion of the story does not occur in *Il Filostrato*: it is Chaucer's own addition. Comparing *Troilus and Criseyde* and the original, we must make our individual judegments about the information which is alleged to be the source of the narrative. In ME poetry the narrator's references to the authorities are conventionally used to strengthen the validity of the statements he conveys to the audience, but psychologically they imply that the statements in question are not necessarily self-evident, and therefore need some evidential support for their justification, with regard to which see Fukaya and Tanaka (1996: 265-70). Chaucer is no exception. When he makes a metacomment on the sources of the proposition concerned, this tends to be paradoxically his original, but when he is reticent about the authorities, the proposition in question is likely to be based on the authorities. Therefore, with Chaucer, references to the authorities and their subsequent validity are occasionally open to the second prism's judgement. As can be seen with Fame in HF, the sources of information themselves can be biased. We are reminded of the message 'of fals and soth compouned.'[127]

With regard to (28c), the scope of modality is made problematic. Because of the repeated assertions of her integrity, each of which is prefaced by *and*, the force of modality is acoustically weakened, and as a result the credibility of those statements is gradually strengthened. This is, as Pearsall (1986) says, reflective of Criseyde's processes of reasoning—she accumulatively lists reasons for her justification, gradually comes to see them as objective, and then reaches her conclusion. The narrator seems to be sympathetic with Criseyde, so much so that he slides into her way of thinking. Of course, if we bear in mind the repeated use of the word *that* which stresses that this is second-hand information, then the weakening of the modality disappears. Here we have an ambiguity due to the scope of modality.

With regard to (28d), Chaucer's reconfirmation of his appeal to his sources in Tr 4.1421 was probably felt by him to be necessary because of the gradual weakening of the force of *treweliche* and of a similar appeal in Tr 4.1415. But as mentioned before, it is uncertain whether the reader, the second prism, is persuaded into believing it or being more cautious.

With regard to (28e), it should be noted that *treweliche* (Tr 4.1415), at this important turning point in the story, occurs in a passage where Criseyde's *trewe* (Tr 4.1417, Tr 4.1420) is at issue. To the obvious semantic link between the two words is now added the acoustic effect arising from their close juxtaposition. This is what Leech (1969) calls a 'chiming effect.' The phenomenon also appears in medieval rhetoric as *paronomasia*. Here with an earlier meaning of (22a) ('faithfully') superimposed on a later epistemic meaning (22b) ('surely'), *treweliche* enriches its implications. This is an example of ambiguity arising from the polysemy of this word. In this context *treweliche* could not, for obvious reasons, be replaced by *certes* or *iwis*.

There are similar instances of *trewely* by the narrator. In (30) Criseyde is escorted by Diomede to the Greek camp.

(30) Ful redy was at prime Diomede
    Criseyde unto the Grekis oost to lede,
    For sorwe of which she felt hire herte blede,
    As she that nyste what was best to rede.
    And *trewely*, as men in bokes rede,
    Men wiste nevere womman han the care,
    Ne was so loth out of a town to fare.   Tr 5.15-21

The narrator sheds light on Criseyde's sorrow, which is in *Il Filostrato* Troilus's (see Windeatt 1990: 447). *Trewely* is attached to people's recognition of 'men wiste' (Tr 5.20) and the content of their recognition is 'nevere woman han the care,' / Ne was so loth out of a town to fare' (Tr 5.20-1). Whether *trewely* relates to the assertion 'nevere

---

127 Both sothe sawes and lesinges (HF 676), And of fals and soth compouned (HF 1029), A lesyng and a sad soth sawe (HF 2089), Thus saugh I fals and soth compouned / Togeder fle for oo tydynge (HF 2108-9).

10. Ambiguity in modality

womman ...' or to the narrator's statement that this was known remains uncertain. 'As men in bokes rede' (Tr 5.19) is an evidential, the same kind as we saw in (27). The nararator reinforces his observation of Criseyde departing from Troilus with *sorrow*. This part is in fact Chaucer's addition. Further, the immediately preceding line 'As she that nyste what was best to rede' is, as will be discussed in Chapter 11, open to a dual interpretation ('since she nyste what was best to rede'; 'like one who nyste what was best to rede'). Immediately after Diomede's matutinal visit to Criseyde's bedchamber—with the inevitable result—the narrator inserts the following lines.

(31) I fynde ek in stories elleswhere,
 Whan thorugh the body hurt was Diomede
 Of Troilus, tho wep she many a teere
 Whan that she saugh his wyde wowundes blede,
 And that she took, to kepen hym, good hede;
 And for to helen hym of his sorwes smerte,
 Men seyn – I not – that she yaf hym hire herte.

 But *trewely*, the stories telleth us,
 Ther made nevere womman moore wo
 Than she, whan that she falsed Troilus.
 She seyde, "Allas, for now is clene ago
 My name of trouthe in love, for everemo!
 For I have falsed oon the gentileste
 That evere was, and oon the worthieste! Tr 5.1044-57

The narrator does not go straight into her shedding of tears for Diomede hurt by Troilus, and into her healing him of his sharp sorrows (this action itself is virtuous unless we regard it is shown to Diomede, not Troilus), but inserts an evidential clause 'I fynde ek in stories elleswhere' (Tr 5.1044) as supporting evidence. When about to say that she also gave Diomede her heart, he inserts first an evidential 'Men seyn' and then a disclaimer—'I not'—thus distancing himself from the sources. But then in the followng line (Tr 5.1051) he adduces them again as the customary evidence of his veracity. However, his metacomments on the propositions themselves are reflective of their not being self-evident, i.e. whether we are to assume Criseyde's *pite* or *slydynge* nature is at work here. So he makes her devotion to Diomede imprecise at this point.

The narrator's logic underlying this ambiguity is that her virtue (her acute sensitivities to those around her) is the source of her vice (to put it euphemistically, her moral flexibility). She is, one might say, the perfect example of the old-fashioned English phrase, 'a girl no better than she ought to be.' This is a contradiction in her nature, and Chaucer makes full use of the ambiguity characteristic of his diction to mask the aspects of it which he evidently finds uncomfortable.

Having thus briefly—in one half line—introduced the subject of Criseyde's emotional as well as physical infidelity, the narrator clearly feels the need to use the adverstative *But* to preface the excuse that he makes for her over two lines and her personal, remorseful lament over 32 lines. Incidentally there is a contradiction—therefore a source of ambiguity—between lines Tr 5.1050 (people say she gave him her heart, but I do not know) and Tr 5.1071 (I will be true to Diomede in every way/at any rate), a promise which her contemporaries and those people down the centuries whom she alludes to as denigrating her ought to find bitterly ironic to say the least.

But here again *trewely* is added with the evidential 'the stories telleth us' (Tr 5.1051) before going into the content of her sorrow. It should be noted that her devotion to Diomede and her great sorrow at betraying are both attributed to the sources by Chaucer. The precise syntactic relationship between *trewely* and 'The stories telleth us' (Tr 5.1051) and 'Ther made ...' (Tr 5.1052) is complex and unclear; nor does it really matter since the result is ambiguous over the sincerity of her sorrow, and that may be what Chaucer aimed at for the second prism (reader or audience). (At his point, does he call upon the basic tenet of Christianity that the sinner must be forgiven no matter how many times he sins, provided he is genuinely sorry?)

In her remorseful and self-justificatory monologue Criseyde uses the word *trewely* twice. The third stanza of the passage quoted below, immediately succeeding this monologue, presents the narrator's defence of her by reference to the fact that no one knows how long it took her to succumb to the blandishments of Diomede and this is introduced by the adversative *But*. This is an addition of Chaucer's.

(32) "But, Troilus, syn I no bettre may,
And syn that thus departen ye and I,
Yet prey I God, so yeve yow right good day,
As for the gentileste, *trewely*,
That evere I say, to serven feythfully,
And best kan ay his lady honour kepe."
And with that word she brast anon to wepe.

"And certes yow ne haten shal I nevere;
And frendes love, that shal ye han of me,
And my good word, al sholde I lyven evere.
And *trewely* I wolde sory be
For to seen yow in adversitee;
And gilteles, I woot wel, I yow leve.
But al shal passe; and thus take I my leve."

But *trewely*, how longe it was bytwene
That she forsok hym for this Diomede,
Ther is non auctour telleth it, I wene.
Take every man now to his bokes heede,
He shal no terme fynden, out of drede.
For though that he bigan to wowe hire soone,
Er he hire wan, yet was ther more to doone.   Tr 5.1072-92

Criseyde acknowledges her betrayal of Troilus and yet hopes that Troilus will serve her and maintain her honour. Does *trewely* there (Tr 5.1075) function as an adverb of manner (22a) and mean that she wishes for it sincerely? Or does she attach it as a modal adverb designed to tone down her privately expressed wish, assuming that Troilus, who cannot in any case hear it, would be sceptical of her sincerity and reject it out of hand? Then again, does it emphasise the word *gentileste*? Or is it merely a politeness marker, a tag, or a rhyming device?

The narrator inserts a sympathetic comment on her decision but as shown in (31), introduces *trewely* with an adversative *But* (Tr 5.1086) assuming the disagreement of the audience. The content to which *trewely* is attached refers to the time to be taken for

10. Ambiguity in modality

her forsaking Troilus for Diomede although in an interrogative way 'How long it was ...' (Tr 5.1086). This is presented to the audience as if to get rid of their scepticism arising from her sudden change of partners. This temporal implication becomes obvious in the line 'Er he hire wan, yet was ther more to doone' (Tr 5.1092). As we have seen before, there is an appeal to the sources: 'Ther is non auctour telleth it' (Tr 5.1088). So much unfavorable evidence for her honour is accumulated that he is less and less assured of it. When referring to Criseyde's virtues, the narrator strengthens them by quoting the authorities, but when referring to her vices, he is non-committal, saying 'I do not know' or 'there are no authorities.' *Trewely* is given another content 'Ther is non ...' (Tr 5.1088) to be related to. Syntactically this seems to be more natural. Further, this is modalised by 'I wene,' (Tr 5.1088) and the same thing is repeated in 'He shal no termes fynden, out of drede' (Tr 5.1090). However, the precise relationships between all these assertions and expressions of suppositions are unclear. In spite of his denying the authorities, the first prism author must know that his direct source *Il Filostrato* says that her betrayal takes place very quickly as shown in Fil.6.8.6-8. Chaucer sidesteps the issue by saying that the sources are not clear, but that it must have been a while.[128] It is ambiguous whether the reader is meant to believe the narrator's justification of her behaviour or to take it with a pinch of salt. This temporal ambiguity stemming from her psychology was dealt with in Section 9.4.

We have so far observed the narrator's use of *trewely*. We now examine the use of this word by the characters. Troilus's use of epistemic *trewely* is in 'a local scope' (see Oh 2000), and can be regarded as honest in that few or no discrepancies are found between what he says and what actually happens. His absolute commitment to Criseyde as her servant/knight ('the which thing, trewely, / Me levere were than thise worldes tweyne' Tr 3.1489-90) is, for instance, confirmed superlatively, and this is actually well attested by his later services. For similar examples, see Tr 4.1450, Tr 5.1704, Tr 5.1720. Two instances (Tr 4.1055, Tr 4.1063) are used in his debates between free will and predestination based on Boethius. Significantly enough, no epistemic instances of *trewely* are found in *Boece* although a variety of epistemic expressions such as *certain, certes, forsothe, without doute, nedes, I trow*, etc. are used.

Criseyde's use of *trewely* is more complex than that of Troilus in that her words and her actions do not necessarily correspond, which might be considered as belonging to 'a global scope' (Oh 2000). Her promises and vows are likely to shift not in spite of but because of her sensitivity and general pliancy to the situations she faces. For instance, her proposal to go first to the Greek camp and then come back to Troy is taken as hopeful by Troilus.

(33) And for the love of God, foryeve it me
　　If I speke aught ayeyns youre hertes reste;
　　For *trewely*, I speke it for the beste.　　　　　Tr 4.1286-8

Her decisions are relative, since her superlative 'for the beste' (Tr 4.1288) is applied only to this occasion. This decision is soon altered by her father and the situations she

---

128　Cf. Tr 5.766-70: after Criseyde went to the Greek camp, she forgot Troy and Troilus within two months. On the other hand, Boccaccio says that Diomede drove out Troilo and Troie from Criseida's heart 'E 'n breve spazio' (*Il Filostrato* 6.8.6). See (9) in Chapter 12.

encounters in the Greek camp. For similar examples, see Tr 2.241, Tr 2.1161, Tr 4.939, Tr 5.987, and Tr 5.1623. Pandarus's use of *trewely* is more or less the same as Criseyde's. His use is strategically directed for the purposes he has on particular occasions. He, for instance, resorts to the belief/feelings attributed to other people for persuasion, as shown in (34).

(34) For *trewelich*, of o thing trust to me:
If thow thus ligge a day, or two, or thre,
The folk wol seyn that thow for cowardice
The feynest sik and that thow darst nat rise!"   Tr 5.410-3

He thus induces Troilus to go out although the above belief is neither certified nor substantiated later. For similar examples, see Tr 1.985, Tr 5.380, and Tr 5.494.

Diomede's use of *trewely* is open to question since we are told that he intends to use all means at his disposal to win her round (Tr 5.92-105, Tr 5.771-98). He says the same things as Troilus and his intensions are the same, but are not honourable, as seen in the fox in the NPT (VII (B2) 3289-92) or the canon in the CYT (VIII (G) 1063-5).

(35) For *trewely*, ther kan no wyght yow serve,
That half so loth youre wratthe wold disserve.   Tr 5.146-7

Incidentally, the narrator's use of *treweliche* in relation to Diomede's words ('For *treweliche* he swor hire, as a knyght, / That ther nas thyng with which he myghte hire plese, / That he nolde don his peyne and al his might / To don it, for to don hire herte an ese;' (Tr 5.113-6)) is worthy of note. It is taken to be collocated with the verb of utterance *swor* (22a), but introduced by the coordinating conjunction *For* and placed sentence-initially, conditionally motivated to be taken as an epistemic adverb with implied irony (22b). (As regards the collocation between *trewely* and a conjunction and its position in the sentence, see Nakao (2002b)).

Langland and Gower do not use *trewely* as frequently as Chaucer, as shown in (24). Their use of it is mainly to strengthen their statements, as the *OED* says in 5b, and straightforward like the use by Troilus, which might be classified as 'a local scope.' Typical examples of each poet are *The Vision of Piers Plowman* 7.180 and *Confessio Amantis* 5.2536.

One of the Early Modern English equivalents of *trewely* is *sure*. Shakespeare's use of this in *Julius Caesar* merits attention. At Caesar's funeral Antony is making a speech with repeated reference to Brutus's evaluation of Caesar, not forgetting to comment on Brutus's character, 'Brutus is an honourable man' (*Julius Caesar*, Act III, Sc. II, 101).

(36) ... The noble Brutus
Hath told you Cæsar was ambitious ...
(For Brutus is an honourable man, ...)
But Brutus says he was ambitious,
And Brutus is an honourable man ...
Yet Brutus says he was ambitious,
And Brutus is an honourable man. ...
Yet Brutus says he was ambitious,
And *sure* he is an honourable man.   *Julius Caesar*, Act III, Sc. II 79-101

Antony's third comment on his character is given an epistemic parenthetical, *sure*, which is calculated to suggest that Brutus is anything but honourable. *Sure* occurs only once here, but follows immediately on Brutus's assessment of Caesar; and thus Brutus's character and his judgement are called into question. This is an example of a modal adverb in a global scope.[129]

10.3.6. Final remarks

We have focused on the modal function of *trewely* in *Troilus and Criseyde* and described through the double prism structure how it is likely to induce ambiguity. The frequency of *trewely* is conspicuous particularly in Books 4 and 5 which build up to and describe Criseyde's betrayal. The narrator makes clear his belief in her sincerity, but at the same time, suggests to his readers an opposite or at best variable view. *Trewely* there functions on a global scope. Sometimes *trewely* is used in conjunction with an appeal to the sources. Sometimes it is not certain whether it relates to the text of the narration or to Chaucer's evidence for it. Expressions such as 'as is written in books' are used repeatedly. But those contents uttered can be found to be additions by Chaucer to his original. The authenticity of the sources themselves are open to scepticism as is manifested in HF.

Troilus's use of *trewely* is on a local scope with little discrepancy between what he says and what he does. Criseyde's use, on the other hand, is apt to shift because her decisions or promises are overtaken by events and thus abandoned because she adapts to the situation of the moment. Pandarus's use is made strategically in order to persuade Troilus to act in one way or another. Diomede's use is superficially like that of Troilus, but the sincerity of his words must be doubted because he is motivated by lust not love.

Ambiguity arising from the function of *trewely* can extend over the three domains of (22a, b, c) but on most occasions it is between the two sides of (22b)—true or false. We have seen that *trewely* is used to comment on the truth as to how characters are really *trewe*. It is of great significance that this word is used in the uncertain boundary between the truth and the falsehood as regards the morality of the characters.

10.4. Ambiguity caused by modal lexical verbs

10.4.1. Introductory remarks

The modal lexical verbs such as *I gesse, I leve,* and *I woot* have so far received attention as to their interpersonal function, particularly their illocutionary forces (the narrator's drawing attention to the audience, the speaker's use of politeness markers, the effect of phatic communion, metrical adjustment, etc.). See Bennett (21) in Section 10.3.3. In this respect, Brinton (1996) is worthy of note in that she pays due attention to their modal forces. She lists the modal lexical verbs in *Troilus and Criseyde* with notes on kinds of discourse (characters' speech, the narrator's description) and the propositions those verbs are attached to. However, her principal interest is in the pro-

---

129 Cf. Jakobson (1960: 375).

cesses of the grammaticalisation of these verbs, and she deals little with ambiguity arising from their modal function. Here we deal with the modal lexical verbs under the double prism structure and examine how they are likely to induce ambiguity.

The modal lexical verbs are, as is the case with the modal adverbs, distinguished into the following three stages in Chaucer's English.

(37) a. Proposition
   b. Propositional attitude
   c. Speech act

The original meaning of (37a) (e.g. *guess* as a full verb denoting 'consider') was developed to (37b) (e.g. *guess* as a modal lexical verb where the speaker's attitudinal meaning toward the proposition was developed), and finally to (37c) (e.g. *guess* where the performative (illocutionary) forces were developed). Ambiguity arising from modal lexical verbs is likely to be induced between (37a, b, c). This section deals with ambiguity due to the modal implication of (37b). We focus on 'I woot' (Tr 5.1084) and describe the processes whereby it is likely to induce ambiguity.

10.4.2. Statement of the problem by reference to 'I woot wel' (Tr 5.1084)

As an illustration of this problem consider the following lines.

(38) And trewely I wolde sory be
   For to seen yow in adversitee;
   And gilteles, *I woot wel*, I yow leve.
   But al shal passe; and thus take I my leve."   Tr 5.1082-5

We have already looked at this quotation in (1) in Chapter 1 and much more recently in (32) in Section 10. These words occur in her monologue of remorse after she has been unfaithful to Troilus with Diomede. This is also her last monologue in the poem, unless her letter can be considered. She regrets her betrayal of Troilus, but gradually recovers herself, and finally decides to depart from him.

How will the second prism readers understand 'And gilteles, I woot wel, I yow leve' (Tr 5.1084)? From a modern reader's point of view, how to articulate the sentence seems to vary from reader to reader. One way is to make a small pause after 'gilteles,' and articulate 'I woot wel' with a quiet voice or with a slight rising intonation, as is typical of a parenthetical epistemic phrase. Another way is to make a big pause after 'gilteles,' and articulate 'I woot wel' with a loud voice or with a falling intonation. In these ways, meanings of the above sentence are conveyed differently. Rough translations of 'And gilteles, I woot wel, I yow leve' are given in (39).

(39) a. And guiltless, I think, I depart from you.
   b. And guiltless, I know well that I depart from you.

Why is 'I woot wel' necessary? What kind of the mental state or attitude of Criseyde does the modal phrase show towards the proposition in question? What does the proposition 'gilteles ... I yow leve' mean? When the sentence is interpreted in more than two ways regarding 'I woot wel,' ambiguity is induced. How this ambiguity is likely to arise according to the double prism structure is outlined in (40).

(40) *A*: Phenomenon: Criseyde's inconstancy (she is unstable)
 B: The first prism's observation – the speaker Criseyde in between the sacred and the secular, the author's sympathy with and detachment from the phenomenon, his equivocation
 C: Expression: And gilteles, I woot wel, I yow leve.
 D: The second prism's viewpoint: the reader assumes the speaker's/author's way of observation and directs his or her way of interpretation accordingly.
 E: The reader's interpretation: When several interpretations are produced by one or more readers, ambiguity is likely to be the result.

10.4.3. Ambiguity arising from modal lexical verbs: How it occurs

According to the reader's inferential process of the double prism structure, the following five questions are worth asking. We deal with them one by one in order to make clear how and why the above 'I woot wel' can cause ambiguity.

(41) Subtypes of ambiguity in 'I woot wel'
 [1] How much semantic is the modal phrase, 'I woot wel'?
   a. semantically directed
   b. metrically directed
 [2] (If [1a] is chosen) what degrees of grammaticalisation are there?
   a. full verb use (know)
   b. modal use (degrees of certainty)
   c. performative use (politeness marker, attention-calling, etc.)
 [3] (If [2b] is chosen) the following questions are worth asking regarding the phrase's modalising function.
   a. What type of modal lexical verb is 'I woot wel'? (a comparative view)
     i. objective
     ii. subjective
   b. How evaluative is the proposition to which the modal is attached?
   c. Whether the proposition is modalised through modal auxiliary/adverb?
   (Cf. Coates 1983, 'harmonics,' collocating phrases to reinforce the modal force such as 'may'/'perhaps' in the proposition collocating with 'I think')
 [4] (If the proposition is evaluative) what kinds of criteria does the speaker apply?
   a. local scope: The speaker emphasises the truth of the proposition (the agreement between the speaker and the hearer is assumed)
   b. global scope: The speaker expects that the hearer will contradict him or her (the disagreement between the speaker and the hearer is assumed)
 [5] (Besides degrees of certainty of the proposition) whether the proposition *per se* is taken as polysemous?
   a. the word *leve*
   b. the syntax regarding *gilteles*

First, the reader is encouraged to check whether the modal lexical phrase is used semantically or as a mere metrical filler ([1]). If he or she regards it as being used semantically, he secondly goes on to check whether the phrase still retains the full verb use, or is used as a modal, or develops more pragmatically to a performative such as attention-calling or politeness marker ([2]). Thirdly, if he or she decides that the meaning is modal, what type of modal lexical verb is *I woot wel*? How different is it from, say, *God woot* or *I gesse*, in terms of subjectivity ([3a])? How evaluative is the proposition of the double prism structure, that is, Criseyde's *untrouthe* ([3b])? Is there any possibility of harmonics ([3c])? Fourthly, provided the proposition is subject to evaluation, it involves the speaker's judgment. The criteria are divided into two: local scope and global scope, as seen in Section 10.3.4 ([4]). By which scope will Criseyde's *untrouthe* be understood? Fifthly and finally, the proposition to which the modal phrase is attached deserves further attention, since it is susceptible to different interpretations at once lexically and syntactically. What does the word *leve* mean? 'Depart from' or 'think'? Who is *gilteles*? Troilus or Criseyde? To which proposition is the modal meaning attached ([5])? The reader activates his or her inference to reconstruct Criseyde's way of understanding her *untrouthe*, and produce his or her interpretation of the double prism structure. When the interpretation varies according to the points of view of the second prism, ambiguity is likely to arise.

These subtypes referred to are in accordance with the reader's inferential processes of how to understand the modal function of 'I woot wel.' They include the order of the reader's inferences, the cause-effect relation between the types, and the development from the surface understanding to the deep understanding. I do not mean that five types are concurrently functional with five interpretations. The reader limits his or her attention to one or another type, or combines several types, to urge some semantic direction. Alternatively he or she may have difficulty in applying any of the subtypes listed in the examples.

10.4.4. Description of ambiguity caused by 'I woot wel'

10.4.4.1. [1] How much semantic is the modal phrase, 'I woot wel'?
  a. semantically directed
  b. metrically directed

'I woot wel' is used to meet the metrical conditions, as seen in (42).

(42) Metrical patterns of 'I woot (wel, etc.)'   (S=strong, W=weak)

a. "In every thyng, I woot, ther lith mesure;	Tr 2.715	W	S		
I woot my fader wys and redy is,	Tr 5.964	I	woot		
I woot she meneth riden pryvely.	Tr 5.1150				
b. I have no cause, I woot wel, for to sore	Tr 1.670	W	S	W	
And gilteles, I woot wel, I yow leve.	Tr 5.1084	I	woot	wel	
c. But wel I woot, the mene of it no vice is,	Tr 1.689	S	W	S	
But wel I woot, a broche, gold and asure,	Tr 3.1370	wel	I	woot	
For wel I woot it wol my bane be,	Tr 4.907				
d. Now woot I wel, ther is no peril inne."	Tr 2.875	S	W	S	
Than woot I wel that she nyl naught sojorne.	Tr 5.598	woot	I	wel	
e. And wel woot I thow mayst do me no reste;	Tr 1.600				
"Ek wel woot I my kynges sone is he,	Tr 2.708	S	W	S	
For wel woot I myself, so God me spede—	Tr 2.744	wel	woot	I	
But wel woot I thow art now in drede,	Tr 2.1504				
f. "I woot wel that it fareth thus be me	Tr 1.652	W	S	W	S
"I woot wel that thow wiser art than I	Tr 2.1002	I	woot	wel	that
Cf.		S	W	S	W
But wel I woot that ye wol nat do so;	Tr 3.866	wel	I	woot	that
g. For aught I woot, for nothyng ellis is	Tr 4.1269	W	S	W	S
"For aught I woot, byfor noon, sikirly,	Tr 5.1122	for	aught	I	woot

10. Ambiguity in modality 171

Variations of 'I woot wel' accord with the requirement of the iambic patterns. But they tend not to be located in a rhyming position.[130] 'I woot wel' in (38) accords with the weak-strong-weak rhythmic pattern. If the reader opines that the modal phrase is used only for metrical purposes or at most for phatic communion, he or she will not be sensitive to ambiguity. However, if he or she admits that it fulfils the metrical requirement and functions semantically, ambiguity is likely to arise as to which meaning is primary, and which is subsidiary.

10.4.4.2. [2] (If [1a] is chosen) what degrees of grammaticalisation are there?
    a. full verb use (know)
    b. modal use (degrees of certainty)
    c. performative use (politeness marker, attention-calling, etc.)

If we assume 'I woot wel' has a modal function, then we need to examine the degrees of grammaticalisation. When a given word combination is grammaticalised or strengthens its unity, it tends to develop a semantic transfer and gain more subjective meanings. In the findings below we present the results of our investigation of Chaucer's use of *woot* (*witen*), *gesse* and *leve* according to the degrees to which they have been grammaticalised. They are examined from the following points of view, as shown in (43).

(43) a. Full verb use:
With a noun phrase as object e.g. '... woot the man/thing,' etc.; the verb with a third person subject; past tense use, non-finite use, subjunctive use.
Modal use:
With a noun clause such as 'I woot/God woot' with *that* (complementizer) *or* zero-*that*/interrogative ...; 'I woot that/it (pronoun)' as a reconfirmation of the preceding proposition)
  b. Position of the modal lexical phrase
    sentence-initial (si)
    sentence-medial (sm)
    sentence-final (sf)[131]
  c. The use or non-use of *that* after a modal lexical verb
  d. The modal phrase after the coordinate conjunctions *and, but, for*; those conjunctions promoting the speaker's inference
  e. The use of a modal auxiliary or adverb within the proposition (harmonics)
  f. The modal phrase in a rhyming position (suggesting the narrative tag)
  g. Kinds of speaker (narrator, character: degrees of speaker's involvement)[132]

Our findings on these three verbs are presented in the following tables.

---

130 The rhyming of the modal phrases 'I woot wel' / 'God woot' and other words is observed in *Troilus and Criseyde* only in such ways as: 'wel woot I' (Tr 4.1017) where 'I' is a rhyme word and 'God woot how' (Tr 1.334) where 'how' is a rhyme word.
131 Brinton (1996: 260) regards the positional variation of a modal lexical verb in a sentence from a functional point of view. The modal phrase in the initial position has a 'thematised' function, that in the medial position an 'interpolated' function, and that in the final position an 'adjoined' function.
132 Regarding the subjectification of modal lexical verbs, see Traugott (1989) and Brinton (1996: 229-35).

(44) gesse

	CT	BD	HF	PF	Anel	Bo	Tr	LGW	SHP	Rom A	Astr
a. gesse (root)	3	0	2	1	0	2	7	1	1	1	1
b.& c. gesse (mod.)	28	1	0	3	0	1	9	5	2	2	0
I gesse: si-0that	0	0	0	0	0	0	0	0	0	0	0
si-that	3	0	0	0	0	0	0	0	0	0	0
si-wh	0	0	0	0	0	0	0	0	0	0	0
sm-0that	0	0	0	2	0	0	2	1	0	0	0
sf-0that	5	0	0	0	0	0	4	2	1	0	0
as I g. si-0that	1	0	0	0	0	0	0	0	0	0	0
sm-0that	10	0	0	0	0	1	1	1	1	2	0
sf-0that	9	0	0	1	0	0	2	1	0	0	0
d. conjunction											
and	3	0	0	1	0	0	3	0	0	1	0
but	2	1	0	0	0	0	1	1	0	0	0
for	3	0	0	1	0	0	2	2	1	1	0
e. modality in proposition											
indicative	20	1	0	3	0	1	9	4	2	2	0
wol	1	0	0	0	0	0	0	0	0	0	0
wolde	1	0	0	0	0	0	0	0	0	0	0
shal	3	0	0	0	0	0	0	1	0	0	0
sholde	0	0	0	0	0	0	0	0	0	0	0
may	1	0	0	0	0	0	0	0	0	0	0
myghte	0	0	0	0	0	0	0	0	0	0	0
moot	0	0	0	0	0	0	0	0	0	0	0
moste	0	0	0	0	0	0	0	0	0	0	0
can	0	0	0	0	0	0	0	0	0	0	0
coude	2	0	0	0	0	0	0	0	0	0	0
owe	0	0	0	0	0	0	0	0	0	0	0
oghte	0	0	0	0	0	0	0	0	0	0	0
f. rhyme											
rhyme word	25	1	0	3	0	0	9	5	2	2	0
non-rhyme word	3	0	0	0	0	1	0	0	0	0	0

10. Ambiguity in modality   173

g. speakers											
narrator	17	1	0	2	0	0	2	2	2	2	0
character	11	0	0	1	0	1	7	3	0	0	0

N.B.:   *root=full verb use, mod.=modal, si=sentence-initial, sm=sentence-medial, sf=sentence-final, -0that (zero that), g.=gesse, wh=wh-interrogative.*

(45) leve

	CT	BD	HF	PF	Anel	Bo	Tr	LGW	SHP	Rom A	Astr
a. leve (root)	5	3	2	1	0	1	10	4	0	0	0
b.& c.leve (modal)	3	1	1	0	0	0	4	1	1	0	0
I leve: si-0that	0	0	0	0	0	0	0	0	0	0	0
si-that	0	0	0	0	0	0	0	0	0	0	0
si-wh	0	0	0	0	0	0	0	0	0	0	0
sm-0that	1	0	0	2	0	0	2	0	0	0	0
sf-0that	0	0	0	0	0	0	1	0	0	0	0
as I leve: si-0that	0	0	1	0	0	0	0	0	0	0	0
sm-0that	0	0	0	0	0	0	0	1	0	2	0
sf-0that	0	0	0	0	0	0	1	0	0	0	0
leve me [imp]: si	0	0	0	0	0	0	0	0	1	0	0
sm	0	0	0	0	0	0	0	0	0	0	0
sf	2	0	0	0	0	0	0	0	0	0	0
leve hit [imp]: si	0	0	0	0	0	0	0	0	0	0	0
sm	0	1	1	1	1	0	0	0	0	0	0
sf	0	0	0	0	0	0	0	0	0	0	0
d. conjunction											
and	0	1	1	0	0	0	0	0	0	0	0
but	0	0	0	0	0	0	1	0	1	0	0
for	1	0	0	0	0	0	0	1	0	0	0
e. modality in proposition											
indicative	2	1	0	0	0	0	2	0	1	0	0
wol	0	0	0	0	0	0	0	0	0	0	0
wolde	0	0	0	0	0	1	0	0	0	0	0
shal	0	0	0	0	0	0	0	0	0	0	0
sholde	0	0	1	0	0	0	1	0	0	0	0
may	0	0	0	0	0	0	1	0	0	0	0
myghte	0	0	0	0	0	0	0	0	0	0	0

174   Part III: Ambiguity in interpersonal domains

moot	0	0	0	0	0	0	0	0	0	0	0
moste	1	0	0	0	0	0	0	0	0	0	0
can	0	0	0	0	0	0	0	0	0	0	0
coude	0	0	0	0	0	0	0	0	0	0	0
owe	0	0	0	0	0	0	0	0	0	0	0
oghte	0	0	0	0	0	0	0	0	0	0	0
f. rhyme											
rhyme word	2	1	1	0	0	0	4	1	0	0	0
non-rhyme word	1	0	0	0	0	0	0	0	1	0	0
g. speakers											
narrator	0	0	0	0	0	0	0	0	1	0	0
character	3	1	1	0	0	0	4	1	0	0	0

N.B.:   *[Imp] indicates 'used in an imperative sentence.'*

(46) woot (witen) (restricted to *Troilus and Criseyde*)

a. witen (root)	136
b.& c. wit (modal)	78
I woot: si-0that	18
si-that	8
si-wh	1
sm-0that	5
sm-wh	0
sf-0that	1
as I w.: si-0that	0
sm-0that	0
sf-0that	0
this woot I wel: si	1
I woot it wel: sm	1
that I woot: sf	1
for aught I w. w.: si	1
for aught I w. w.: sm	2
God woot: si-0that	14
God thow woost: si-0that	1
God woot: si-that	4
si-if	1
si-wh	1
God woot: sm-0that	10
sm-that	1
sm-wh	1

10. Ambiguity in modality

God woot: sf-0that	1
sf-wh	1
God it woot: si	3
sm	1
c. conjunction	
and	8
but	10
for	11
e. modality in proposition	
indicative	62
wol	6
wolde	2
shal	0
sholde	0
may	3
myghte	1
moot	1
moste	0
coude	0
owe	0
oghte	0
f. rhyme	
rhyme word	2
non-rhyme word	76
g. speakers	
narrator	I woot /God woot 2 /12
character	
Troilus	13/11
Criseyde	10/5
Pandarus	13/11
Diomede	1/0

N.B.: w.w.=*woot wel*, wh=*wh-interrogative*

Let us look at *gesse* and *witen*. *Gesse* is used as a modal (51 times) nearly three times as frequently as it is as a full verb (19 times). Distinguishing between modality and performative is a matter of emphasis. There are very few examples of the conjunction *that* after the verb (3 times). 'I gesse' is used only three times sentence-initially. Most examples are located sentence-medially (5 times) and sentence-finally (12 times). The same is true of 'as I gesse.' It is used only twice sentence-initially. Most instances are found sentence-medially (16 times) and sentence-finally (13 times). Most uses (47 times) are in a rhyming position (4 times in a non-rhyme position). On the other hand, with regard to *woot*, contrary to *gesse*, its modal use is only half (78 times) of its use as a full verb (136 times). The conjunction *that* is occasionally found after the verb (I woot: 8 times; God woot: 4 times). Most are located sentence-initially (I woot: si=27 times, sm=5 times, sf=1 time; God woot: si=21 times, sm=12 times, sf=2 times). As mentioned in Section 10.4.4.1, hardly any examples are found in a rhyming position. In *Troilus and Criseyde* remarks by the narrator containing *woot* have this word almost entirely preceded by *God* (11 times); 'I woot' occurs only twice, while the characters use both 'I woot' (37 times), a subjective type and 'God woot' (27 times), an objective type.[133] Since *woot* can at times retain its full verb sense, it should be noted that the speaker can use it in this way when necessary.

'I woot wel' in (38) is used sentence-medially. If we regard it as parenthetical and articulate it with a rising intonation, we would construe it as having a modal function 'as far as I know' by which the truth value of the proposition is undetermined. However, if we regard it as a politeness marker, it would be understood as having an illocutionary force. On the other hand, if we make a pause after *gilteles*, and understand it as constituting a participial construction, the clause containing 'I woot wel' would be understood as the main clause. Then we can assume the original meaning of *woot*, and consequently that Criseyde recognizes the proposition 'gilteles ... I yow leve' with an objective stance 'I know well.' Incidentally Donaldson (1975) has no commas both before and after 'I woot wel.' The interpretation of the phrase is left to the reader, the second prism.

(47) And gilteles I woot wel I yow leve—

In this way there seems to arise ambiguity between the original meaning of *woot* and its modal meaning, or between the modal meaning and the performative meaning.

10.4.4.3.
> [3] (If [2b] is chosen) the following questions are worth asking regarding the modalising function of the phrase.
> [3]a What type of modal lexical verb is 'I woot wel'? (a comparative view)
> i. objective
> ii. subjective
> [3]b How evaluative is the proposition to which the modal is attached?
> [3]c Whether the proposition is modalised through modal auxiliary/adverb?

Let us consider [3a], why Chaucer chose to make Criseyde say 'I woot wel' and not other verbs. 'I woot wel' is more subjective than 'God woot' (although the expression 'God knows' was to a certain extent formulaic), but it is more objective than 'I gesse.' 'I woot wel' is located just in between subjective and objective observations, and as such determines the degree of certainty of the proposition.

As for [3b], Brinton (1996: 218-23) points out that the proposition is subject to the speaker's evaluation, and observes eight types of it as in (48).

> (48) Kinds of proposition in terms of evaluation
> First .... Comparative and superlative forms are common in such utterances ... as well as <u>evaluative terms</u> .... Second, they occur with statements of more general opinion or truth .... Third, they occur with statements of expected consequences or results of actions .... Fourth, they may occur with stated expectations concerning the actions or reactions of others .... Fifth, they are attached to statements expressing the possible, presumed, or required

---

133 Brinton (1996: 255-6) regards 'I woot' as subjectively epistemic and 'God woot' as objectively epistemic.

causes of events (or their lack of causes) .... Sixth, they may occur with deductions from evidence or judgements based on appearances .... Seventh, they are used when a belief or feeling is attributed to another .... Finally, they are used emphatically when promising or asserting. (Underlines are mine.)

In Brinton's scheme *gilteles*, an evaluative adjective, would be classified under the first type 'evaluative terms.' Criseyde assumes that assessment of her *un/trouthe* (phenomenon of the double prism structure) is not self-evident, but involves the speaker's judgement. The reader, the second prism, feels that she chose 'I woot wel' as a middle way between the objectivity of 'God woot' and the subjectivity of 'I gesse.' Let us turn to [3c]. The indicative form of *leve* is used in (38). No modal devices such as *may* or *shal* are added which further complicate her psychological presentation. As we can see in (43), (44) and (45), it is rare for the verbs in the proposition to collocate with modal auxiliaries.

10.4.4.4.
[4] (If the proposition is evaluative) what kinds of criteria does the speaker apply?
 a local scope: The speaker emphasises the truth of the proposition (the agreement between the speaker and the hearer is assumed)
 b global scope: The speaker expects that the hearer contradicts him or her (the disagreement between the speaker and the hearer is assumed)

Modal lexical verbs presuppose the speaker's judgement for which he or she is expected to have criteria. They are, according to Oh (2000), divided into two types: those having local scope and those having global scope. Local scope indicates that the speaker emphasises the proposition in total agreement with the hearer, while global scope indicates that the speaker expresses his or her opinion expecting the hearer's contradiction.[134] The tail rhyme romance, *Amis and Amiloun*, for example, begins with the following reference to the characters in the story and where they lived. This is a typical example of local scope.

(49) In Lumbardy, *y vnderstond*,
 Whilom bifel in þat lond,
 In romance as we reede,
 Two barouns hend wonyd in lond   *Amis and Amiloun* 25-8

 In þat tyme, *y vnderstond*,
 A duk wonyd in þat lond,
 Prys in toun and toure;   *Amis and Amiloun* 61-3

The modal lexical verb, 'I understand,' is used. If the audience rejects this introduction with strong scepticism on the above 'who' and 'where,' the story would not develop properly. By contrast, 'I woot wel' as examined here is more subtle, open also to global scope, which allows for contradiction of the content of the proposition not only on the part of the addresser but also of the implied readership.

---

134 As mentioned in Section 10.3, Oh (2000) distinguishes between 'local scope' and 'global scope' regarding modal adverbs. I have applied this to modal lexical verbs.

10.4.4.5.
[5] (Besides degrees of certainty of the proposition) whether the proposition *per se* is taken as polysemous?
   a. the word *leve*
   b. the syntax regarding *gilteles*

We are induced further to explore the meaning of the proposition itself to which the speaker's modality is attached? Let us examine the polysemy of the proposition, that is, the polysemy of the word *leve* and the syntax regarding *gilteles* belonging to the category of ambiguity III: Ambiguity in linguistic domains. The point is who is 'guiltless': Criseyde or Troilus? Let us look at this example in a much wider context, as shown in (50). We refer to Criseyde's thoughts and reactions on the right margin. She, feeling sympathetic with Troilus and keeping some distance from him, or blaming herself, or attempting self-justification, finally ascribes herself to sliding Fortune.[135]

(50) Criseyde's monologue after betraying Troilus
But trewely, the storie telleth us,	[The narrator's attitude (trewely ...)]
Ther made nevere womman moore wo	[No woman making greater sorrow than she]
Than she, whan that she falsed Troilus.	
She seyde, "Allas, for now is clene ago	
My name of trouthe in love, for everemo!	[Criseyde's complaint:
For I have falsed oon the gentileste	Loss of her honour by betraying Troilus]
That evere was, and oon the worthieste!	

---

135 *MED* has the following treatment of the word *gilteles*.
  1. Adj. (a) guiltless, sinless; blameless, inculpable; – of persons, things, actions
  2. As adv. [?adj. in early examples]: (a) without guilt, undeservedly, unjustly; (b) in a guiltless manner, innocently.
  A quoted example of 2.(b):
  And somme murthes to maken as munstrals cunne,
  And gete gold with here gle *giltles*, I trowe.
  (*Piers the Plowman*, C. Passus I. 33-4; A. Prol. 34 'synneles')

  MED 2 relates the word *gilteles* to the object of the sentence (18 examples) except for PPl. Prologue.34. This is because the verbs refer to immoral acts such as murder/slaughter and the victim is an innocent one.
    Chaucer's syntax of *gilteles* is in the same vein. In the case of the sentences containing both the subject and the object, three examples of *gilteles* are related to the subject (all the three objects refer to abstract things: CYT VIII (G) 1005, LGW 1982, Anel 301) and eight examples of *gilteles* are related to the object (KnT I (A) 1314, MLT II (B1) 674, WBP III (D) 385, FranT V (F) 1318, PardT VI (C) 491, Tr 2.328, LGW 2092, MercB 17). We quote three examples of the latter type below.

a.	And seyde, "If that ye don us bothe dyen	
	Thus *gilteles*, than have ye fisshed fayre!	Tr 2.327-8
b.	A voys was herd in general audience,	
	And seyde, "Thou hast desclaundred, *giltelees*,	
	The doghter of hooly chirche in heigh presence;	MLT II (B1) 673-5
c.	Right at his owene table he yaf his heeste	
	To sleen the Baptist John, ful *giltelees*.	PardT VI (C) 490-1

10. Ambiguity in modality

"Allas, of me, unto the worldes ende,
Shal neyther ben ywriten nor ysonge
No good word, for thise bokes wol me shende.
O, rolled shal I ben on many a tonge!
Thorughout the world my belle shal be ronge!
And wommen moost wol haten me of alle. [Women will hate me the most]
Allas, that swich a cas me sholde falle!

"Thei wol seyn, in as muche as in me is,   [I have dishonoured women
I have hem don deshonour, weylaway!   (though I was not the first)]
Al be I nat the first that dide amys,
What helpeth that to don my blame awey?
But syn I se ther is no bettre way,   [Too late to regret my deed]
And that to late is now for me to rewe,
To Diomede algate I wol be trewe.   [I will be true to Diomede]

"But, Troilus, syn I no bettre may,
And syn that thus departen ye and I,   [No other way than to depart from Troilus]
Yet prey I God, so yeve yow right good day,
As for the gentileste, trewely,
That evere I say, to serven feythfully,   [Hoping Troilus will be true to her
And best kan ay his lady honour kepe."   and keep her honour]
And with that word she brast anon to wepe.   [She burst into tears]

(→cleansing of her sin → her self-recovery→regaining her position as a courtly lady)

"And certes yow ne haten shal I nevere;   [I will not hate you]
And frendes love, that shal ye han of me,   [You shall have my friendship]
And my good word, al sholde I lyven evere.
And trewely I wolde sory be   [I will be sorry if you are in adversity]
For to seen yow in adversitee;
And gilteles, I woot wel, I yow leve.   [Without guilt... I know/think ...]
But al shal passe; and thus take I my *leve*." [Recognition that time must move on]
                                                                Tr 5.1051-85

First we deal with the lexical ambiguity of *leve* in (51).

(51) The lexical meaning (abbreviated lex) of *leve*
    lex-1. leve=<leave, depart from > [*OED* s.v. leave v1. 7. To go away from. 1225—]
    lex-2. leve=<believe, trust> [*OED* s.v. leve v2. 2. Trans. a. To believe, give credence to (a person) 971-1570]

These two senses are homonymously derived, which are well attested in Chaucer. (Cf. The rich rhyme scheme favours the semantic distinctiveness of the pair. If this is applied here (leve (verb)–leve (noun)), we are encouraged to support the sense of 'believe.') They allow the syntactic ambiguity to occur, as shown below.

(52) The syntax (abbreviated syn) regarding *gilteles*
    syn-1. *gilteles* is related to *yow*
    syn-2. *gilteles* is related to *I*
    syn-3. *gilteles* is related to *yow* and *I*

The combination between the lexis, syntax, and modality (degrees of grammaticalisation) is shown in (53).

(53) The combination between the lexis, syntax and modality

Types of Interpretation	Lexis	Syntax	Modality
I	leave/depart (lex-1)	I leave <u>you who are guiltless</u> (syn-1=yow)	as far as I know (subjective) / I know well (objective)
II	leave/depart (lex-1)	<u>I who am guiltless</u> leave you (syn-2=I)	as far as I know (subj) / I know well (obj)
III	leave/depart (lex-1)	<u>I who am guiltless</u> leave <u>you who are guiltless.</u> (syn-3=yow/I)	as far as I know (subj) / I know well (obj)
IV	believe (lex-2)	I believe <u>you guiltless</u> (syn-1=yow)	as far as I know (subj) / I know well (obj)?

Notes: *The abbreiviations 'subj' and 'obj' stand for 'subjective' and 'objective' respectively. The modal 'I woot wel' (as far as I know) under IV is considered to function as a harmonic or supportive phrase for the speaker, Criseyde's belief (I believe ...). The juxtaposition of the objective 'I woot wel' (I know well) and her belief seems to occur rarely if ever.*

We can summarise types of interpretations in a tree diagram as in (54).

(54) The diagram of types of interpretation

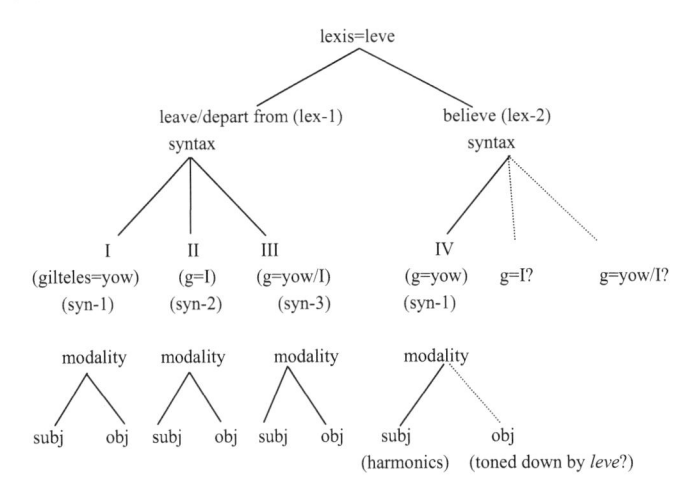

```
                          lexis=leve
                         /          \
          leave/depart from (lex-1)   believe (lex-2)
                syntax                    syntax
              / |  \                    / ⋮ ⋮
            I  II  III                IV  g=I?  g=yow/I?
    (gilteles=yow) (g=I) (g=yow/I)  (g=yow)
       (syn-1)   (syn-2) (syn-3)    (syn-1)
       modality  modality modality  modality
        / \      / \      / \       /     ⋮
      subj obj subj obj subj obj  subj    obj
                                (harmonics) (toned down by leve?)
```

N.B.: The letter 'g' is an abbreviation of 'gilteles.' 'The question mark '?' indicates that the interpretation in question is contextually implausible. The dotted lines show the implausibility of the interpretations.

10. Ambiguity in modality 181

The meaning 'depart from' itself is open to the triple relationships between *gilteles* and the pronouns. In accordance with the ideal required of a medieval courtly lady, the interpretation (53I) where *gilteles* works as a free adjunct related to Troilus seems the most likely, perhaps with further interpretation excluded. She sincerely regrets and feels great sorrow about 'leaving Troilus who is guiltless.' However, when we find that she achieves her self-recovery after reflecting on her sin and cleansing it by weeping, there remains something unsatisfactory about this interpretation. Here the interpretation (53II) comes to the reader's attention. Some readers might think that Criseyde saying 'I am guiltless after betraying Troilus' is too bold for the medieval times and quite unworthy of the traditional image of a courtly heroine. However, it should be noticed that her betrayal is not so much attributed to her positive attitude as to being a result of external pressures on her such as her sojourn in the Greek camp and the importunate attentions of Diomede. It is not too much to say that she is also a victim. (Cf. Cox's feminism interpretation of Criseyde as a victim (1998: 47-8).) Further, the interpretation (53III) attracts our attention. This interpretation is not determined by either (53I) or (53II), but embraces both. At the surface level it is in accordance with the medieval ideal of a courtly heroine, who regrets her sin and admits that 'Troilus is guiltless' (especially relevant to the reading of *leve*='depart from'). But at a deeper level, she implies 'I am guiltless too, since I am driven by the vicissitudes of Fortune.' Here Criseyde is at once able to avoid destroying her ideal heroine image and to offer self-justification as well as making a confident assertion about her own situation. This shows the multi-layered structure of her character. In this interpretation 'But al shal passe' (Tr 5.1085) means 'It is not that any human being is to be blamed, but that they can encounter something beyond their power, in other words, they are obliged to accept the fluctuations of Fortune as they are.'

The meaning 'believe' is, on the other hand, more noticeable in that Criseyde is as it were answering an unasked question. We do not have to ask about Troilus's innocence. Assuming that she has recovered herself and stands in a superior position to that of Troilus, however, we can understand how she can refer to him with some aloofness.[136] In this sense the interpretation (53IV) is only relevant.

As we have seen above, Criseyde does not say the above propositions as self-evident, but with modal colourings attached to them, subjectively 'as far as I know' or objectively 'I know well.' Let us here consider the interaction between the propositional content and 'I woot wel.' If we assume *leve* to mean 'depart from,' the syntax of *gilteles* and the pronoun becomes very complex: *gilteles=yow, I, yow/ I*. There 'I woot wel' can be subjective (rising intonation) or objective (falling intonation). A falling intonation would suggest the heavy tone of Criseyde's realisation. On the other hand, if we take *leve* to mean 'believe,' the syntax of *gilteles* and the pronoun will be restricted to *gilteles=yow*. There 'I woot wel' seems to function as 'harmonics' in that it is semantically similar to and therefore tends to overlap with *leve*. It is likely to be used subjectively with a slight rising intonation. (See the discussion of Nakao (2006b).)

---

136 Cf. OED s.v. leave 1: To allow to remain in a specified condition (1205-). If this sense is applicative here, the meaning will be "I allow you to be guiltless." This is also suggestive of Criseyde's standing in a superior position to that of Troilus.

The language above or the expression of the double prism structure induces the reader, the second prism, to produce multiple interpretations. The critics, lexicographers, editors, and translators are varied in interpretations. However, they are silent about the degrees of certainty due to 'I woot wel' although they might have chosen one of them.

(55) The combination between the lexis, syntax and modality

Types of Interpretation	Lexis	Syntax	Modality
I	leave/depart (lex-1)	I leave you who are guiltless (syn-1=yow)	as far as I know (subjective) I know well (objective)
I	<Examples> Tatlock and Mackaye (orig. 1912): and I know well I leave thee without the guilt of thine. Miyata (1979): machigattakoto wo nasatta wakedemonai noni anata wo omisuteru nodatte koto wa yokuwakatte imasu keredo (=I know well I depart from you, who are guiltless) Karita (1949): nanno togamo nai noni watakushi ga anatasama wo sutetakoto mo yoku shitte orimasu (=I know well I depart from you, who are guiltless)		
II	leave/depart (lex-1)	I who am guiltless leave you (syn-2=I)	as far as I know (subj) I know well (obj)
II	<Example> Wetherbee (1984)		
III	leave/depart (lex-1)	I who am guiltless leave you who are guiltless. (syn-3=yow/I)	as far as I know (subj) I know well (obj)
III	<Example> Nakao's added interpretation		
IV	believe (lex-2)	I believe you guiltless (syn-1=yow)	as far as I know (subj) I know well (obj)?
IV	<Examples> Stanley-Wrench (1965): Free from all blame, all guilt are you, I know. (No reference to Criseyde's 'departing from') Coghill (1971): And you are guiltless, as I well believe. Windeatt (1998): and I believe you to be guiltless. Similarly, Fisher (1989), Wetherbee (1984), and Benson (1993).		

N.B.: *Regarding the interpretation 'IV,' the modal 'I woot wel' (as far as I know) is considered to function as a harmonic phrase for Criseyde's belief (I believe ...).*

In view of all this, an increase in ambiguity is inevitable here. There are differences in the interpretation of *leve* (leave or believe) and 'I woot wel' (objective, parenthetical (subjective), harmonics). Indeed, every reader agrees that Troilus (*yow*) is guiltless. But the reader, the second prism's interpretations can further be divided into 'Troilus is guiltless,' 'I am guiltless' and 'though Troilus is guiltless, I am guiltless, too.' Thus we have a rich source of ambiguity. It is hardly possible to say which interpretation is right, and which not.

Now can Criseyde say all the meanings so economically in one line? How about the author, the first prism? Does the reader, the second prism, expand the scope of its interpretation developing from the intention of the author? In my opinion, it is inconceivable that the lexical ambiguity of *leve* is caused by the speaker Criseyde herself. The different lexical sense induces the different syntactic meaning. The same difficulty is perhaps applied to the author. It is not certain to what extent he is conscious of this ambiguity. The concurrent processing of these two senses would be too much for one speaker. This ambiguity may be due to the second prism. On the other hand, the syntactic ambiguity surrounding *gilteles* (when *leve* means 'depart from') is considered to be caused by the second's prism's inference about the heroine's feelings or 'slydynge of corage.'

The semantic development of 'I woot wel' (41[2]), the degrees of modal force (41[3]), the scope of the criteria (41[4]) and the polysemy of the proposition (41[5]) are closely related to one another. This suggests that the ambiguity regarding 'I woot wel' (Category II:Ambiguity in interpersonal domains ((3) in Section 3.2) arises in conjunction with the ambiguity in characterisation of Criseyde (Category I: Ambiguity in textual domains) and with the ambiguity in the word and syntax of the proposition (Category III: Ambiguity in linguistic domains).[137]

10.5. Final remarks

In Part III, we have described how ambiguity in interpersonal domains is likely to arise under the double prism structure. In Chapter 9, dealing with ambiguity due to the speaker's intention, we have made clear the processes whereby the characters are likely to choose expressions of wide application to refer to their reprehensible actions, i.e. expressions which can be understood literally or with indirect meaning, according to the reader, the second prism. In Chapter 10, dealing with ambiguity due to modality, we have found that the instability of the events in the story involves the speaker's judgement or inference, and that modality is attached to his or her propositional contents, and that how to assess their veracity of such content is left to the reader. We have pointed out, too, that modal ambiguity is closely related to texual domains and linguistic domains.

In Chapters 9 and 10 we have dealt with ambiguity due to the speaker's intention and mental attitude to the content of the utterance. Next and finally we will examine ambiguity in the content of the utterance, or linguistic domains. In Part IV we will describe how ambiguity is likely to occur with regard to syntax (Chapter 11), words (Chapter 12), and voice (Chapter 13) under the double prism structure.

---

[137] In relation to how far a modal force is extended to, we have also taken discourse ambiguity into account: the scope of modality (Tr 4.1667-80), the identification of the proforms (Tr 2.232-8), and the reconstruction of elliptical elements (Tr 3.588-90). Further rhetorical ambiguity is worthy of note: overstatement (Tr 2.680-6) and understatement (cf. But *sikerly* she hadde a fair forheed; / It was almoost a spanne brood, *I trowe;* / For, *hardily,* she was nat undergrowe. / Ful fetys was hir cloke, *as I was war*. CT GP I (A) 154-7 'Prioress').

Part IV: Ambiguity in linguistic domains

11. Ambiguity in syntax

11.1. Introductory remarks: the double prism structure and syntax

As mentioned before, *Troilus and Criseyde* reflects Chaucer's increasing interest in human condition. His insight into human psychology is deepened and his language changes accordingly. There arise layers of meaning in a linguistic expression, to which different readers apply different interpretation. When words are combined to form a phrase or sentence, the whole acquires a meaning which transcends that of its individual parts. How they are combined or to what extent they are united are often open to complex semantic questions. This chapter describes the rise of syntactic ambiguity through the double prism structure.

We examine syntactic ambiguity with a focus on Criseyde's shifting affections (including language and descriptions by the other characters and the narrator). This is one of the focal points, which draws the reader's attention. To what extent is the state of her mind made clear? How far is it reflected in the syntax? How does the reader reconstruct her psychology and understand its syntax? To borrow Jakobson (1960)'s words, how the contiguity between words gets loosened and gives rise to ambiguity is our concern.

Before analysing syntactic ambiguities, let us look at the syntactic features of Middle English. Blake (1977: 67) points out a comparatively flexible relation between words to allow for the reader's participation in understanding them, and his or her alternation in it.

(1) ... each reader would be forced to make the necessary connections between the parts of the sentence himself. Naturally different readers could reach different results. The effect of the modern editor's approach is on the contrary to imply that there is only one possible meaning and his pronunciation strives to make that meaning obvious to his readers.

In the transition from oral culture to printing culture, that is, manuscript culture (a literary work written to be read aloud), sentence structure is not rigidly grammatical but rhetorical on many occasions. Subsequently the logic of the sentence is weakened. The semantic delivery of an utterance is not necessarily due to the logical relation of sentence elements but to oral sytnax (the word relation of a sentence is likely to be implicit owing to elliptical syntax), to phonetic features such as rhythm and pause (words are easily movable from their normal positions by separation or displacement), or to rhetorical techniques such as repetition, parallelism, or contrasts. The fact that grammatical punctuation was not developed in medieval manuscripts is probably due to this. Furthermore, it is possible that the syntax of the original texts (Latin, French, etc.) affected the syntax of English when translated or adapted. The syntactic fluidity of Middle English is reflected in the variation of the word order of the manuscripts or in that of the editors' punctuation.[138]

---

138 Regarding the textual variation of the four modern editions of *Troilus and Criseyde*, see Jimura, et al. (1999).

This syntactic tendency is seen in Chaucer. It made it easy for Chaucer to select his favourable patterns according to metrics (iambic pentameter) or rhyme royal. Usually it does not destroy meanings. However, on some occasions it seems to be indicative of the narrator's or the characters' conflicting states of mind.

In what follows we examine the phrase *as she that* used repeatedly in the characterisation of Criseyde, and other syntactic examples.

11.2. The phrase *as she that*[139]

11.2.1. The meaning of the *as she that*-phrase

Owing to its apparent simplicity, the ME phrase *as he/she that* has attracted little attention except for (Nakao 1993, 1995, 2004; Yager 1994). Nakao (1993) was reinterpreted in Nakao (2004) according to the double prism structure with some comparative notes to Yager (1994). This section is based on the discussion in Nakao (2004).

Nakao (1995) discussed the semantic possibility of the phrase, and arrived at the following conclusion. The phrase *as he/she that*, as Prins (1952: 59) pointed out, is a calque on the French *com cil/cele qui*.[140] The calque, stabilized in the form of a phrase, tends to be taken in an idiomatic sense rather than in a word-by-word literal sense. However, it should be noted that the *as he/she that*-phrase can be interpreted in a less idiomatic way. The phrase can thus be understood either as a portion of the total calque phrase in a causal sense 'as/since' or according to the ordinary native sense of the phrasal structure 'like one who.' Further, there seems to arise an intermediary sense 'in the role/capacity of one who, as is proper for one who.' As a result, we can infer that an English comparative sense and an intermediary 'role' sense are added to a causal sense due to the calque on French.

---

139 Nakao (1995) examined the phrase 'as she that' from a historical point of view, and Nakao (1993) pointed out that the phrase was repeatedly used for Criseyde, and that it was open to ambiguity brought about by her adaptability. Yager (1994) also examined the ambiguity of this phrase. I refer to it in the present discussion where my interpretation differs from hers.

140 See for example Prins (1952: 59), Mustanoja (1960: 199), Kerkhof (1982: 278), and Kivimaa (1996a: 88, 102; 1996b: 15). Chaucer translates 'con cele qui' into 'as she that' as below.

N'el n'auoit sa robe chiere
En maint leu l'auoit desciree,
Con cele qui mout fu iree.   *Le Roman de la Rose* 316-8

And for to rent in many place
Hir clothis, and for to tere hir swire,
As she that was fulfilled of ire.   *The Romaunt of the Rose* 324-6

Similarly see *Le Roman de la Rose* 3030 / *The Romaunt of the Rose* 3256 and Macaulay (1899): 25413, 27942, 28248, 28883, 28900, etc. Cf. Latin: *quippe qui, ut qui, utpote qui*.

Typical examples of each sense are given in (2).

(2) sense 1: 'like one who'
"Thow farest ek by me, thow Pandarus,
As he that, whan a wight is wo bygon,
He cometh to hym a paas and seith right thus:
'Thynk nat on smert, and thow shalt fele non.'   Tr 4.463-6

sense 2: 'in the role of one who'
Quen he had made his orisun,
Vnder þis tre he sett him dun,
He thoghte a-pon ful mani thing,
Als he þat was suilk a lauerding
A temple thoght he ma to dright,   *Cursor Mundi* C 8263-7

quen he had made his orisoun
vnder þis tree he sette him doun.
he þo3t on mony selcouþ þing.
as fallis to a grete lording.
A temple make þorou goddis mi3t.   *Cursor Mundi* F 8263-7

sense 3: 'as/since ...' (causal sense)
for he hath late translated the Epystlys of Tulle, and the
Boke of Dyodorus Syculus and diverse other werkes oute of
Latyn into Englysshe, not in rude and olde langage but in
polysshed and ornate termes craftely, *as he that hath redde*
Vyrgyle, Ovyde, Tullye and all the other noble poetes and
oratours to me unknowen.
        Caxton's Own Prose [prologue to his translation of *Eneydos*], p. 80.

11.2.2. The function of the *as she that*-phrase

The phrase was extended in its occurrence between early ME and late ME.[141] In late ME or in the times of Chaucer we find that the phrase *as he/she that* is capable of bearing the above three senses.[142] There are two ways of treating the potential ambiguity of the phrase: one is to reduce or avoid it and the other is to let it remain or leave its interpretation to the audience. As is usual with polysemic words, the former way is more probable. The latter way seems to be taken on very rare occasions if ever. As is well known, Gower frequently uses the phrase in *Confessio Amantis* (we find 207 occur-

---

141 In the Early Modern English, we can see the phrase in Bourchier's translation of Froissart's Chronicle in sense (2c). However, this is exceptional. In Spenser's *Faerie Quene*, we can see the phrase only in the form of 'as one that ...' (Book 1, ci, s4, 6; Book 1, cix, s24, 4-5) and there its meaning is restricted to (2a).

142 The degrees of the unity of a phrase and its subsequent semantic extension can be reexamined as part of gramaticalisation. See Hopper and Traugott (1993: 2, 45-6). The semantic difference depends on whether the words of a phrase still retain their lexical senses (source) or whether they are interpreted as an inseparable unit resulting in a metaphorical transfer (target). Cf. This applies also to the question of a phrase or a compound noun. For instance. 'goode-wyf' in the ShipT can be taken analytically in the sense of 'good wife' or as a compound meaning just 'wife.' If we assume the former meaning, it is likely to develop an ironical tone.

rences including those found in variant texts). And there he seems to use it in the former way. It is taken in sense 3 (e.g. vii 4915, 4921); in sense 2 (i 369; ii 1076); and in sense 1 (i 1620-1; ii 1017).[143] In his work we can hardly find examples illustrative of the way in which the phrase is intended to carry multiple senses simultaneously.

Chaucer' use of the phrase is more or less the same as Gower's. His use of the phrase *as she that* in *Troilus and Criseyde*, however, deserves special notice. Some examples of this phrase are assumed to be produced in the latter way. In accordance with Chaucer's characterisation of Criseyde, the full potential of the phrase seems to be brought into play. Thus this chapter is devoted to examining his use of the *as she that*-phrase in *Troilus and Criseyde*, particularly its ambiguous status. Before we enter into the discussion of the use of the phrase in this work, it is worth while to show how often Chaucer uses it in his works. See the frequency in (3).

(3) The frequency of the *as she that*-phrase and its equivalents

Antecedents (Total: 68)	he	she	they	I	ye	d.p	c.n.
Rom	1	3	0	0	0	0	1
BD	0	0	0	0	0	0	0
HF	1	0	1	0	0	0	0
Anel	0	0	0	0	0	0	0
PF	1	1	0	0	0	0	0
Tr	19	11	1	0	0	0	1
LGW	1	4	0	0	0	0	0
CT	8	1	3	0	0	1	4
SHP	0	0	0	0	0	0	0
Bo	1	0	3	0	0	0	1
Astr	0	0	0	0	0	0	0

N.B.: d.p.=demonstrative pronouns; c.n.=common nouns

As shown in the above Table, *Troilus and Criseyde* abounds with the phrase. Most of the examples in it, particularly those applied to Troilus (Tr 1.797-8; Tr 4.948, Tr 4.1692; Tr 5.1660-5, Tr 5.1803-4), Pandarus (Tr 4.824), Sarpedoun (Tr 5.435-6), and Diomede (R 5.89-90, Tr 5.106, Tr 5.795), are more or less limited in sense since they emphasise, rather than question/weaken, the referents' typical qualities. To give a few examples relating to Troilus suffices. The example in (4), used to describe his 'desires to care fore nothing' (Benson 1987: 484), is definitely used in sense 1.

(4) But [thow] list as he that lest of nothyng recche.
What womman koude loven swich a wrecche?

Tr 1.797-8 ([thow] is my supplement.)

A comparative sense (sense 1) of the phrase is not necessarily used to show the exact state of the referents' qualities with the implication that Criseyde is 'like one who ....'

---

143 Yager (1994) refers only to Gower's use of this phrase. She does not examine its semantic features.

The question of how sense 1 is actually operative is clarified only by taking into account our total view of those referents. As to Troilus, there seems to be little or no evidence in the context on which to question how his nature is affected by love[144]. The example in (5) is most probably limited to sense 3.

(5) Ful sodeynly his herte gan to colde,
    As he that on the coler fond withinne
    A broch that he Criseyde yaf that morwe
    That she from Troie moste nedes twynne,
    In remembraunce of hym and of his sorwe.
    And she hym leyde ayeyn hire feith to borwe
    To kepe it ay! But now ful wel he wiste,
    His lady nas no lenger on to triste.   Tr 5.1659-66

On the other hand, some examples seem to remain problematical. Chaucer's use of the phrase *as she that* for Criseyde is such a case, and our particular attention is concentrated on this.

11.2.3. Ambiguity in the *as she that*-phrase and characterisation of Criseyde

The *as she that*-phrase appears in *Troilus and Criseyde* eleven times, every instance of which refers to Criseyde. Chaucer uses the *as she that*-phrase very seldom elsewhere in his works. In *The Canterbury Tales* there are courtly ladies such as Emelye, Constance, and Dorigen, but he never uses the phrase in connection with them. He applies only once to the goddess Luciana in the FranT (CT V (F) 1053). We may safely say that the frequency of this phrase is unusually high in the case of Criseyde. Actually eight examples (Tr 1.96; Tr 3.1227; Tr 5.18, Tr 5.25-6, Tr 5.177-9, Tr 5.709-11, Tr 5.953-4, Tr 5.1413) are found in those parts where Chaucer deviates from and expands *Il Filostrato* (Fil) while three (Tr. 4.673-7 [Fil 4.79.5], Tr. 4.704-5 [Fil 4.83.4.], Tr. 4.898 [Fil 4.104.2.]) are more or less close to the original.

There seems to be a general tendency in Chaucer's use of the phrase for Criseyde. It tends to occur at crucial and transitional moments in the story where she is exposed to some psychological pressure, in other words, where her nature and sensitivity as a courtly romance heroine are put to the test. In the 'ascending scenes' Books 1 to 3 where the relationship between Troilus and Criseyde becomes increasingly strengthened and reaches a climax, the phrase is seldom seen: once in Book 1 (Tr 1.96), and once in Book 3 (Tr 3.1227). It increases in number in the 'descending scenes' where the relationship between Troilus and Criseyde becomes increasingly unstable and eventually collapses because she betrays him: three times in Book 4 (Tr 4.673-8, Tr 4.704-5, Tr 4.897-8), and six times in Book 5 (Tr 5.18, Tr 5.25-6, Tr 5.177-9, Tr 5.709-11, Tr 5.953-4, Tr 5.1413).

The narrator uses the phrase to highlight her sensitivity and vulnerability when she was in dire straits: knowing her father's treachery against Troy (Tr 1.96) and being

---

[144] The verbs contained in the phrase tend to be aspectually 'stative' (or 'typical' in the case of dynamic verbs). This semantic feature contributes to describing the characters' attributes (for instance the idealised features of Criseyde as a courtly lady).

parted from her lover Troilus (Tr 5.18). He also uses it to reconfirm her apparent fidelity to Troilus when her future betrayal of him is coming close: after the parliamentary decision upon the exchange of her and Antenor has been made (Tr 4.673-8) and she is in the Greek camp separated from Troilus (Tr 5.177-9).

Each time the phrase is used, the audience must determine what it actually means/implies. It depends on our attitude towards the heroine. In adapting *Il Filostrato*, Chaucer delves into Criseyde's internal history—especially her *pitee* (e.g. Tr 5.824)—while he follows the basic outline of her external history, that is, her betrayal of Troilus. This enables the poet to have a new or sympathetic view of Criseyde. His sympathetic view of the so-called betrayer seems to have been taken as more unexpected and therefore more creative and imaginative, since betrayal was strongly condemned as a vice in medieval Europe as in other times and places. Thus the narrator can be at once a sympathetic and detached viewer of Criseyde. As a result, a number of linguistic tensions are brought out. The phrase *as she that* is in the same vein.

We can simplify the problem of evaluating this phrase by asking the two opposing questions. Is the audience, the second prism, encouraged to sympathise with and believe in Criseyde? If so, he or she will take the phrase as having a causal 'sense 3' or being indicative of the proper role 'sense 2.' Or is the audience encouraged to keep some distance/detachment from and be sceptical about Criseyde? If so, he or she will emphasise the non-factual implication which a simile may carry 'sense 1.' Criseyde can thus be evaluated on a scale between the two opposing points of view. The first instance of the phrase is found when she is distressed because Calkas, her father, has betrayed Troy. Chaucer, departing from *Il Filostrato*, identifies with her and pinpoints her sensitivities in this plight.

(6) For of hire lif she was ful sore in drede,
     As she that nyste what was best to rede;   Tr 1.95-6

It is fitting for a romance heroine to be affected thus. The scribes seem to have been unsure as to how to interpret this first instance in *Troilus and Criseyde*. According to Windeatt (1990: 91), the scribal variants are given in (7).

(7) H4, Ph, H2 <independent clause>
        H4, Ph Ne in al þis world she nyste what to rede
        H2   Ne in al þis world she nyst not what to rede
     A, H3 <conjunctive clause>
        A   As she nat nyste what was best to rede
        H3   As she nyste what was best to do
     Cx, Th (early editors) <coordinate construction>
             And wyst neuer what best was to rede

The other extant manuscripts adopt the phrase *as she that*.[145] Caxton uses the phrase himself (Blake 1973: 80), but here (if we can assume that he came across it in his exemplars—a lost manuscript of the β (Retc) tradition), he seems to have rephrased it, probably in order to avoid its Gallic flavour.[146] The H4, Ph, H2, A, H3 scribes were

---

[145] From the speech level point of view, this phrase is formal rather than colloquial. It is used in the literary texts translated from OF sources, such as devotional texts and legal documents. For details of this, see Nakao (1995).

[146] See Vinaver [rev. Field] (1988: 973).

explicit in describing Criseyde's embarrassment. And so were the modern translators, as shown in (8).

(8) Tatlock and MacKaye (1912): ... not knowing what to do
     Coghill (1971): ... not knowing where to go or whom to heed
     Stanley-Wrench (1965): ... without one friend to whom to moan
     Windeatt (1998): ... not knowing what was the best advice

Incidentally, no scribal variant 'Like...' can be traced here. This variant is generally rare, and all I have is Caxton's translation of the *com cil qui* to the *like as he that* (see Mossé (1952: 228)). The very critical reader may say that the phrase is potential evidence of Criseyde's future betrayal. However, at this stage of the story the anti-romantic context for her is only implied (mostly by our foreknowledge). It may be too hasty to regard this phrase as an abortive simile.

From a metrical point of view, the *as she that*-phrase attracts our notice in that it comprises an iambic weak-strong-weak pattern. It is probably because of this that most instances begin the line. However, we should also note that that phrase is not obligatorily chosen for a weak syllable, as is evidenced in the scribe A: As she nat nyste what was best to rede. We will deal with the metrical aspects of the phrase further in Chapter 13.[147]

Elsewhere in *Troilus and Criseyde* the *as she that*-phrase has no significant scribal variants except for *As she that/As ye that* (Tr 5.1413). This may suggest that the phrase is Chaucer's own, not scribal.

In Book 2 we find no instances of *as she that*. In Book 3 we find one. Criseyde and her company stay overnight in Pandarus's house. Troilus comes into her bed chamber. She asks why he has come. Knowing that this is because of his jealousy, she makes a long disquisition on the subject. The narrator justifies her action, as seen in (9).

(9) Criseyde, al quyt from every drede and tene,
     As she that juste cause hadde hym to triste,
     Made hym swych feste it joye was to sene,
     Whan she his trouthe and clene entente wiste;   Tr 3.1226-9

In the phrase we can examine her caution and level-headedness as two of the qualities befitting a courtly lady. *As she that* is one line after rephrased by the factual statement 'When ....' However, some critical listener may go back to her statement 'Ne hadde I er now, my swete herte deere, / Ben yolde ywys, I were now nought heere!' (Tr 3.210-1). Noting that she has already justified her trust in him, he or she may be bold enough to ask why the above is said as if it were for the first time.

The remaining instances of the phrase are all found in Books 4 and 5. In these Books, the question of what Criseyde is expected to be and what she really is are more poignantly counterbalanced. We are thus more actively encouraged to question the meaning of the phrase. Is the phrase really evocative of those feelings and motives typical of the courtly heroine? In the Trojan parliament it is determined that Criseyde 'Ygraunted was in chaunge of Antenore' (Tr 4.665). The news comes to Criseyde, but

---

147 Yager (1994) does not analyse this phrase in terms of scribal variation nor with regard to the effects of voice.

she does not dare to ask whether it is true or not. Here the phrase is used again.

(10) But shortly, lest thise tales sothe were,
    She dorst at no wight asken it, for fere.

> *As she that hadde hire herte and al hire mynde*
> *On Troilus iset so wonder faste*
> *That al this world ne myghte hire love unbynde,*
> *Ne Troilus out of hire herte caste,*
> *She wol ben his, while that hire lif may laste.*
> And thus she brenneth both in love and drede,
> So that she nyste what was best to reede.   Tr 4.671-9

As Windeatt (1990: 389) points out, Chaucer's use of binding imagery demonstrated in lines Tr 4.673-6 elaborates Boccaccio's brief depiction of Criseida—her desire for Troilo is kindled—, and adds her loyalty until death. The narrator, sympathetic towards Criseyde, appears to take on her feelings as if they were his own. As a result, he gets the phrase inflated a great deal. In the eyes of Criseyde and of those who love her, the meaning of the line is clear. The phrase is taken in sense 3. However, a sceptical reader may be encouraged to search for hints of her future betrayal. This is not impossible particularly for the sort of woman who is susceptible to and able to accept varying circumstances. The sympathetic narrator seems to have failed a little in his intended expression because he did not pay enough attention to the semantic range of the phrase.

It is not certain whether the other two examples of the phrase show only the narrator's sympathy/sentimentality or imply his criticism. A group of women come to Criseyde to comfort her, but what they do turns out to be a mere representation of vanity. They do not know what she is really sad.

(11) Swich vanyte ne kan don hire non ese,
    As she that al this mene while brende
    Of other passioun than that they wende,   Tr 4.703-5[148]

Pandarus gives Criseyde a message from Troilus about how to remedy their misfortunes. She says, as seen in (12).

(12) "Gret is my wo," quod she, and sighte soore
    As she that feleth dedly sharp distresse;   Tr 4.897-8

Now let us turn to the examples in Book 5. As mentioned earlier, the narrator uses the phrase as many as six times there. We find the first instance when Criseyde departs from Troy. She is escorted to the Greek camp by Diomede.

(13) Ful redy was at prime Diomede,
    Criseyde unto the Grekis oost to lede,
    For sorwe of which she felt hire herte blede,
    As she that nyste what was best to reede.   Tr 5.15-8

---

148 Chaucer's 'Swich vanyte ne kan don hire non ese, / *As she that* al this mene while brende / Of other passioun than they wende' (Tr 4.703-5) corresponds to Boccaccio's '*Come a colei che sentia nella mente / Tutt'* altra passion che non vedeano' (*Il Filostrato* 4.83.4-5). There are eleven similar examples of the phrase in *Il Filostrato* which were not adopted by Chaucer: (1.15.6, 1.20.7, 2.35.5, 2.48.5, 2.102.7-8, 2.130.8, 3.30.5, 4.137.7, 5.41.1, 5.49.2, 6.11.1).

We find the second instance just after this. In the same situation we see Troilus attending on her.

(14) This Troilus, withouten reed or loore,
As man that hath his joies ek forlore,
Was waytyng on his lady evere more
*As she that was the sothfast crop and more
Of al his lust or joies heretofore.*   Tr 5.22-6

The first instance is exactly what we have seen in Book 1. But this time, her self-composure and balanced view soon become obvious (Tr 5.193-4), and what is stated in the phrase seems to be open to doubt. The second instance is uttered through Troilus's perspective. To him (not necessarily to others) this utterance works as a factual statement. Compare this with the instance in (15) which is used in his letter to Criseyde.

(15) And fareth wel, goodly, faire, fresshe may,
As she that lif or deth may me comande!   Tr 5.1412-3

Let us move to the third example. The context is this: it is decided that Criseyde should be sent to the Greek camp in exchange for Trojan prisoners; she is escorted by Diomede to the Greek camp; on the way, he is bold enough to offer his service of love to her. The narrator draws our attention to her response to his offer, using the phrase in (16).

(16) Criseyde unto that purpos lite answerde,
*As she that was with sorwe oppressed so
That, in effect, she naught his tales herde*
But here and ther, now here a word or two. Tr 5.176-9

She evinces a deep sadness and dismay typical of the romance heroine parted from her lover. This is an added part by Chaucer to *Il Filostrato*, and according to Windeatt (1990: 455), it is contrasted with Benoît, where Briseide welcomed Diomede and listened attentively. So, sympathetic towards Criseyde's situation, Chaucer seems to have expanded/transformed his source texts. And yet the narrator's description of her reactions to Diomede in the next stanza invites us to think that the sympathetic reading does not tell the whole story.

(17) *But natheles* she thonketh Diomede
Of al his travaile *and* his goode cheere,
And that hym list his frendshipe hire to bede;
And she accepteth it in good manere,
And wol do fayn that is hym lief and dere,
And tristen hym she wolde, *and* wel she myghte,
As seyde she; and from hire hors sh'alighte.   Tr 5.183-9

The adversative conjunction 'But natheles' (Tr 5.183) is so sudden, and seems to break up the narrative coherence.[149] How do we understand the point that her moods and attitude can shift so swiftly? In this stanza the narrator elaborates on how she thanks Diomede for his offer. The coordinate constructions by a marked repetition of *and* suggest how smoothly and easily she expresses her thanks to him. We may question her hearing little of Diomede's speech. A reader sympathetic towards Criseyde may state

---

149   This question of coherence was examined in terms of conjunction in Chapter 8.

that her expression of gratitude merely shows the politeness required by the courtly ideal. A cynical reader, however, may disagree with this and comment that this could be encouraging Diomede to persist in his amorous advances for her. Here the stanza as a whole is ambiguous.[150] This stanza is, it seems to me, intended to cast doubt on the veracity of one point of view. From a sympathetic point of view, the *as she that*-phrase can be taken in sense 2 'as is expected of/proper for one who is so oppressed' or in sense 3 'since she was so oppressed.' From a critical point of view, it can be taken in sense 1 'like one who is oppressed,' and to what extent Criseyde is oppressed by her sadness presents a problem of interpretation. The choice may be left to the reader. Donaldson's (1970: 74) statement that 'one does not know whether to read the indicative or the subjunctive' is worth attention, but the semantic difference there is not derived from the implication of simile but from the polysemy from a cognitive perspective.[151]

Let us go to the fourth instance. Criseyde realises the impossibility of coming back to Troy, although she yearns for it.

(18) Ful pale ywoxen was hire brighte face,
    Hire lymes lene, *as she that al the day*
    Stood, whan she dorste, and loked on the place
    Ther she was born, and ther she dwelt hadde ay; Tr 5.708-11

Away from Diomede's tenacious wooing of her, she seems to be genuinely in great sorrow for Troilus. The audience may be encouraged to agree on the narrator's sympathetic view of her. However, the place is functional as a metonymy of the container and the contained, which implies Troilus (other examples of metonymy: Tr 5.956-7, Tr 5.1006-8). Criseyde is distant from Troilus both physically and psychologically. Here we cannot completely reject the possibility of sense 1.

Finally let us turn to the second offer of Diomede's love service to her. He speaks so well that she allows him to speak with her, ironically enough, on the eleventh day of her departure from Troy (she has promised to Troilus to come back to Troy not later than the tenth day). Before her reply to Diomede's offer, the narrator inserts the *as she that*-phrase, and again, developing from *Il Filostrato*, highlights the ineradicable firmness of Criseyde's devotion to Troilus.

(19) And thus to hym she seyde, as ye may here,
    As she that hadde hire herte on Troilus
    So faste that ther may it non arace;   Tr 5.952-4

And the narrator seems to have not been completely satisfied with the phrase, and he deliberately paraphrases it into the following.

(20) And *strangely* she spak, and seyde thus: Tr 5.955

---

150 This example was dealt with in Chapter 9 as an example of the speaker's intention causing ambiguity.
151 Yager (1994) disregards Donaldson's comment (1970: 71):
    All but the very simplest uses of *as* to express equivalence cause a distancing between the things compared: 'He spoke as one who had suffered' is not as direct or unambiguous a statement as 'One could tell from his speech that he had suffered.'

According to *OED*, 'strangely' means 'In an unfriendly or unfavourable manner; with cold or distant bearing' (Tr 5.955 is adduced here as the earliest instance). At first she spoke "distantly" to Diomede, but it should be noted that she behaved in the same way towards Troy as shown in her actual speech (Tr 5.956-1008). There she is found fluctuating between Troy (Troilus) and Greece (Diomede), as can be seen from the following passage.

(21) a. "That Grekis ben of heigh condicioun
I woot ek wel; *but certeyn, men shal fynde
As worthi folk withinne Troie town,
As konnyng, and as parfit, and as kynde,
As ben bitwixen Orkades and Inde;
And that ye koude wel yowre lady serve,
I trowe ek wel, hire thank for to deserve.* Tr 5.967-73

b. Herafter, whan ye wonnen han the town,
Peraventure so it happen may
That *whan I se that nevere yit I say
Than wol I werke that I nevere wroughte!* Tr 5.990-3

c. If that I sholde of any Grek han routhe,
It sholde be youreselven, by my trouthe!
I say nat therfore that I wol yow love,
N'y say nat nay; but in conclusioun,
I mene wel, by God that sit above!" Tr 5.1000-4

Note her repeated use of the coordinate construction *and* in Tr 5.972 and *but* in Tr 5.968 to refer both to Greece and Troy. Also noteworthy are the equivocal conditional clause in Tr 5.990-3 and Tr 5.1000-1 and the neutral mode of expression in Tr 5.1002-4. A sympathetic reader, emphasising how Criseyde stands by Troilus in such a predicament, is encouraged to give the phrase sense 2 'as is proper for a courtly romance heroine' or to take it in sense 3 'since she had set her heart on Troilus so fast.' These meanings in this phrasal form have a respectable overtone. On the other hand, a reader disposed to be critical of Criseyde and to give credence to her predisposition towards Diomede, is encouraged to give the phrase sense 1 'like one who ....' Barney, the editor of *Troilus and Criseyde* in Benson (1987: 1026), confirming Kerkhof (1982: 278), restricts the meaning of the phrase to the causal sense. Therefore he seems to be sympathetic towards Criseyde. On the other hand, Donaldson (1970: 78), who understands the phrase as a simile, states: 'the opposite of what it purports to be saying—of turning its own sense inside out. Criseyde spoke like a woman who loved Troilus, but she was most imperfectly like a woman who loved him, as her speech shows.' Thus he tends towards the critical camp. The disagreement in interpretation between Barney and Donaldson suggests that the phrase itself is functional in a dual way. Furthermore, modern translators do not agree about the interpretation of the phrase, as shown in (22).

(22) Tatlock and MacKaye (1912): With her heart so fast set on Troilus ...
Stanley-Wrench (1965): She, who had set her heart on Troilus ...
Coghill (1971): Like one whose heart was set on Troilus ...
Windeatt (1998): like one who had ever heart set so firmly on Troilus ...

To derive the meaning of the phrase only from the meter seems to be a little too simplistic because semantic or stylistic considerations are treated as insignificant.

Yager (1994: 157) says 'the ambiguous phrase seems to me to be a syntactic correlative to the thematic ambiguity of the *Troilus*.' From our point of view, we regard this as an instance of the fusion of the syntactic category and the macro-structural one (theme). Since Yager has not established the category of ambiguity, her awareness of this fusion is only partially applied. Furthermore, Yager (1994: 165) points out that the interpretation will vary from reader to reader, but that multiple interpretations are also possible. This shows the workings of the second prism and the way in which interpretations can be varied whether within one reader or between readers. Of course she does not argue it under the double prism structure.

Thus the meaning of the phrase is more or less left to the reader. His or her interpretation depends on the processes whereby Criseyde becomes eventually unfaithful to Troilus. What view the reader takes of her determines his or her interpretation of the phrase. Consequently, the second prism is strongly activated. Varieties of readers such as editors, critics, and translators lead to different interpretations. Compared with synonymous utterances (like ..., who ..., -ing (participial construction) ..., as/since ..., etc.), the phrase can only represent both the factual and non-factual implications. Chaucer, the first prism behind the narrator, must have been aware of the full potential of the phrase. Actually it is by his exploitation of its potential ambiguity that he managed to hold in balance his opposing attitudes towards Criseyde.

11.3. Other examples of syntactic ambiguity

The double prism structure is also found to be working in other aspects of syntax. When Criseyde's shifting affections are the phenomenon to be described, the first prism to describe it, or either the narrator or the characters seem to make it equivocal by choosing fluid syntactic structures. We analyse some examples in which the second prism readers are likely to be divided in their interpretation.

The context of (23) is this. Troilus falls in love with Criseyde. He cannot confess his love to her. He is in great stress. Pandarus notices this, and acts as a bridge between Troilus and Criseyde. Pandarus visits her, and before describing his intentions seeks to assure himself that his intercessions will be well received. However, his words seem to be deliberately ambiguous. This quotation has already been mentioned in our discussion of cohesion in (2) in Chapter 8. We will reexamine it from a syntactic point of view.

(23) "For, nece, by the goddesse Mynerve,
And Jupiter, that maketh the thondre rynge,
And by the blisful Venus that I serve,
Ye ben the womman in this world lyvynge—
Withouten paramours, to my wyttynge—
That I best love, and lothest am to greve;
And that ye weten wel youreself, I leve."   Tr 2.232-8

Where to put the pauses in relation to 'Withouten paramours' presents a problem. When we put a pause before the phrase 'Withouten ...' (Tr 2.236) it is separate from the immediately preceding participial clause 'lyvynge ...' (Tr 2.235) and more closely related to the clause that follows. Pandarus refers to the social relation between uncle and niece, and intends the meaning 'You are the woman that I love best ... except for lovers/by way of love.'[152] This interpretation is the most plausible. The prepositional phrase 'in this world lyvynge' is emphatically used in collocating with the superlative 'best... lothest.' On the other hand, if we do not make a pause before the phrase 'Withouten paramours,' and reads it in enjambement, we might assume a new syntactic structure like 'the womman ... lyvynge / Withouten paramours.'[153] Furthermore, if we put a pause both before and after the phrase 'Withouten parmours,' the relation between the phrase and its modifying clause will be controlled with the rise of subtle suspension. Ross (1972: 154) regards this ambiguity as a 'complicated piece of multiple significance worthy of Shakespeare's poetry at its most mature and complex.' The editors' punctuations of this part are shown in (24).

(24) The editor's punctuation

	after lyvynge	after paramours	after wyttynge
Baugh	,	,	,
Donaldson	—	,	—
Fisher	—	zero punctuation	—
Howard	—	—	—
Pollard et al.	,	,	,
Robinson	,	,	,
Root	,	,	,
Skeat	,	,	,
Windeatt	—	zero punctuation	—

Donaldson, Fisher, Howard, and Windeatt make a dash both before and after the phrase 'Withouten...' and make a pause explicitly. This suggests the editor's tension in regarding the syntactic relation of the phrase. However, no editors have 'the womman ...lyvynge / Withouten parmours' with no pause in between *lyvynge* and *Withouten*. They might have regarded this interpretation as too much against social norm. Whatever punctuation they adopt, it is the editors'. Pandarus's metalinguistic or epistemic comment on the proposition in question—'to my wyttynge' and 'that ye weten wel youreself, I leve' (see Chapter 10) seems to hint at the double semantic structure which hides the deviant syntactic meaning behind the normative syntactic meaning. For the existence/non-existence of a pause before and after the phrase 'Withouten paramours' and the semantic change due to this, see the discussion of ambiguity in voice in Chapter 13.

---

152 See Roscow's (1981: 19-21) 'displacement.'
153 *OED* s.v. without: †5. In addition to c1205-1535; †6. except c1000-c1320; 7.a. (a) With absence of c1200-.

The love between Troilus and Criseyde begins and develops in Book 2 and is consummated in Book 3. Meanwhile, the exchange of Criseyde for the prisoners is decided by the Parliament. Thereby their love is put in jeopardy in Book 4. We have looked at (25) from the point of view of speech presentation in (6) in Chapter 7 and from the point of view of modality in (26) in Chapter 10. Troilus proposes running away with her. But she suggests going to the Greek camp and coming back to Troy within ten days. Here the narrator draws the reader's attention to the sincerity in her speech. We now reexamine it from a syntactic angle.

(25) And *treweliche*, as writen wel I fynde
 That al this thyng was seyd of good entente,
 And that hire herte trewe was and kynde
 Towardes hym, *and* spak right as she mente,
 And that she starf for wo neigh whan she wente,
 And was in purpos evere to be trewe:
 Thus writen they that of hire werkes knewe.   Tr 4.1415-21

The narrator accumulates pieces of evidence regarding her sincerity by repeating the coordinate conjunction *and* (Tr 4.1417, Tr 4.1418, Tr 4.1419, Tr 4.1420). When a sentence is constructed in this way, the logical relationships between its parts become blurred. The point is the gradual weakening, particularly in acoustic image, of the relatedness between the modal adverb *treweliche* and its modifying proposition. When the syntactic relation is strongly maintained, the proposition 'hire herte trewe was and kynde / ... trewe ' (Tr 4.1417-20) appears to be within the scope of the narrator's judgement, while when the relation is weakened, the proposition is likely to indicate his assertion of truth. This is as if he were reconstructing Criseyde's logic of justification—at first hesitation, and finally conviction. The syntactic ambiguity as regards the above relation is due to which interpretation the second prism readers give weight to, the narrator's judgement or her own conviction.

Immediately before she is sent to the Greek camp, Criseyde confesses to Troilus how she is determined to accept his love. She accumulates reasons for justifying her determination as seen in (26).

(26) "For *trusteth wel* that youre estat roial,
 Ne veyn delit, *nor* only worthinesse
 Of yow in werre *or* torney marcial,
 Ne pompe, array, nobleye, *or* ek richesse
 Ne made me to rewe on youre destresse,
 But moral vertu, grounded upon trouthe—
 That was the cause I first hadde on yow routhe!

 "*Eke* gentil herte and manhod that ye hadde,
 And that ye hadde, as me thoughte, in despit
 Every thyng that souned into badde,
 As rudenesse and poeplissh appetit,
 And that youre resoun bridlede youre delit,
 This made, aboven every creature,
 That I was youre, and shal while I may dure.   Tr 4.1667-80

'For trusteth wel that ...' (Tr 4.1667) is an epistemic expression with a modal lexical verb *trust* (see Section 10.4). The proposition followed by 'trusteth wel that' indicating that she showed her pity to Troilus not because of his appearance but because of his 'moral vertu' (Tr 4.1672) is presented with the speaker's judgement. However, her repetition of the coordinating conjunctions *ne*, *nor*, *or*, and *and* gradually reduces the epistemic function of the clause 'trusteth wel that' and thus much reinforces the impression that the above proposition is a fact. How far the epistemic force is extended is due to the reader. In this way we find instances of ambiguity due to the degrees of acoustic images to be retained by the reader, the second prism in (25) and (26). (Concerning the validity of her words 'moral vertu' (Tr 4.1672), see ambiguity derived from causality in Section 8.3.)

Immediately before Criseyde yields to Diomede, Chaucer expands *Il Filostrato* and finds himself in the ambivalent situation in which he praises her as an ideal courtly lady and at the same time inherits the basic plot of the original which contains her betrayal. The last part of her character description is seen in (27).

(27) She sobre was, ek symple, and wys withal,
    The best ynorisshed ek that myghte be,
    And goodly of hire speche in general,
    Charitable, estatlich, lusty, fre;
    Ne nevere mo ne lakked hire pite;
    Tendre-herted, slydynge of corage;
    But trewely, I kan nat telle hire age.   Tr 5.820-6

'Tendre-herted' (Tr 5.825) and 'slydynge of corage' (Tr 5.825) are juxtaposed without any linking conjunction. The syntactic relation between them is undetermined. The reader, the second prism, assuming the first prism author's standpoint, is likely to produce a multiple relational structure as seen in (28).[154]

(28)

tendre-herted	relation	slydynge of corage
a. soft-hearted	<therefore>	heart is sensitive to motion
b. soft-hearted	<that is>	heart is sensitive to motion
c. warm-hearted	<but>	inconstant
d. feeble-hearted	<therefore>	inconstant
e. feeble-hearted	<that is>	inconstant

Interpretations (28a) and (28b) reflect the most restrained attitude towards her betrayal, and (28d) and (28e) the most unrestrained. On the other hand, interpretation (28c) is

---

154 The semantic range of the words *tendre-herted, slydynge,* and *corage* is roughly as follows.
    tendre-herted (*MED*): 6. (a) Sorrowful, heartfelt; piteous, painful, touching; (b) easily moved; of the heart: compassionate, sympathetic.
    Cf. *tender* (*MED*): [OF] 2. (a) Physically sensitive, esp. to pain; susceptible to injury, vulnerable; (b) easily injured, fragile; soft.
    slydynge (Davis, et al. 1979): [OE] changeable, unstable, inconstant, slippery, flowing, gliding.
    corage (Davis, et al. 1979): [OF] heart, spirit, disposition; nature; soul; courage; desire; inclination, intention.

half way between the restrained and unrestrained attitudes towards it. The *corage* in (28c), (28d), and (28e) is metonymically evocative of feelings contained in her heart, especially sexual desires (cf. Davis et al. (1979) s.v. *corage*: heart, spirit, disposition; nature; soul; courage, fighting spirit; <u>desire</u>; <u>inclination</u>, intention, attention).

Incidentally, we find the adversative conjunction *mais* in the corresponding description on Benoît, as can be seen in (29), which is close in wording to (28c).

(29) Mout fu amee e mout amot,
    Mais sis corages li chanjot;   (Benoît: *Roman de Troie* 'Les Portraits' 5285-6)

Example (30) comes after the above holistic description when the narrative develops again. Diomede visits her in her father's tent on the very day when she promised Troilus she would return to Troy. The narrator says she welcomes him.

(30) But for to tellen forth of Diomede:
    It fel that after, on the tenthe day
    Syn that Criseyde out of the citee yede,
    This Diomede, as fressh as braunche in May,
    Com to the tente ther as Calkas lay,
    And feyned hym with Calkas han to doone;
    But what he mente, I shal yow tellen soone.

    Criseyde, at shorte wordes for to telle,
    Welcomed hym *and down hym by hire sette*—
    And he was ethe ynough to maken dwelle!
    And after this, withouten longe lette,
    The spices and the wyn men forth hem fette;
    And forth they speke of this and that yfeere,
    As frendes don, of which som shal ye heere.   Tr 5.841-54

Lets us examine the use of *sette* (Tr 5.849). This example was dealt with from the point of view of discourse structure (cohesion: ellipsis) in (10) in Chapter 8. We reexamine this in terms of syntax. According to how we determine the agent/the patient regarding *sette*, we produce a different relational structure. In coordinate constructions we can omit the agent of the second verb if it is the same as that of the first verb. In Middle English, however, we can omit the agent of the second verb although it is different from that of the first verb provided that it carries old information. Accordingly we can interpret the elliptical subject as indicating either of the agents Criseyde and Diomede.[155] If we take Criseyde as the agent, it reflects her positive attitude to set him down beside her. Or this can be regarded as a mere verbalisation of her gesture inviting him to sit down. If so, her action is regarded as within the scope of her politeness and therefore as a purely formal act. This is related to the ambiguity of the speaker's intention in Chapter 9. On the other hand, it is also possible that we can regard the agent as Diomede in relation to *hym* in 'Welcomed hym' (Tr 5.849). There *hym* in 'hym ... sette' (Tr 5.849) is a reflexive pronoun *himself*. If this is right, it shows a nature derived from *sodeyn* Diomede whereby he is quickly responsive to her welcome, which controls her positive attitude. Incidentally, the examples of the verb *sette* in *Troilus and Criseyde*, as seen in (31), occur with a reflexive pronoun regardless of the ellipsis or non-ellipsis of the agent.

---

155   Regarding this kind of ellipsis of the subject, see Roscow (1981: 85-91).

(31)

	accusative	reflexive
non-ellipsis of agent	2	7
ellipsis of agent	1?	7 + 1? (1? = Tr 5.848)[156]

In *Il Filostrato* and Beauvau's French translation of it which it is possible that Chaucer used, Diomede's action is described from his point of view, which is shown in (32). There Diomede's positive attitude is emphasised. The possibility that Criseyde is the agent in seating him is remote.

(32) Prima di lei; e postosi a sedere,
    Di lungi assai si fece al suo volere.   *Il Filostrato* 6.11.7-8
    (... and after taking a seat he came gradually to his desires.)

    et premièrement se assist asuprès d'elle   Beauvau: Pratt (1956: 532) p. 262[157]

In terms of the intertexuality discussed in Chapter 5, it is highly plausible that this gave Chaucer an inspiration.

Windeatt (1990) understands the agent as 'she,' and Roscow (1981: 89) says that 'she' is more likely. On the other hand, Karps (1930: 135) chooses 'he.' The editors or scholars constituting the second prism reader are divided in interpretation, thus leading to ambiguity. If the first prism author intends a single reading, we may wonder why he did not express himself unequivocally.

We can find similar ambiguities in Chaucer's other works such as BD 192-9, KnT I (A) 1628-46, and CYT VIII (G) 1317-26 (see Roscow 1981), and in the works of other medieval poets such as *Sir Gawain and the Green Knight*, as can be seen in (33).

(33) Al studied þat þer stod *and stalked hym nerre*
    Wyth al þe wonder of þe worlde what he worch schulde.
                    Sir Gawain and the Green Knight 237-8
    [All who were standing stared and cautiously approached him;
    All stared him who was standing there, and [he] walked himself nearer.]

After receiving Criseyde's welcome, Diomede draws her attention to the destiny of Troy and puts much psychological pressure upon her. Then he makes his advances. He gets a promise from her to meet her on the eleventh day. He takes her glove, and leaves her. The clause 'Hire glove he took (Tr 5.1003)' implies that she accepted his wish, as shown in the ambiguity of the speaker's intention in Section 9.4. In (34) Criseyde tries to justify her quick decision.

(34) The brighte Venus folwede and ay taughte
    The wey ther brode Phebus down alighte;
    And Cynthea hire char-hors overrraughte
    To whirle out of the Leoun, if she myghte;

---

[156] Cf. And with that word *she doun on bench hym sette.*   Tr 2.91
    By Troilus adown right *he hym sette.*   Tr 3.700
    Yif thow me wit my lettre to devyse."
    And *sette hym down,* and wrot right in this wyse: Tr 2.1063-4
[157] Windeatt (1990: 491): Pratt compares Bv's Diomede who, however, sits himself down beside her.

And Signifer his candels sheweth brighte
Whan that Criseyde unto hire bedde wente
Inwith hire fadres faire brighte tente,

Retornyng in hire soule ay up and down
The wordes of this sodeyn Diomede,
His grete estat, and perel of the town,
And that she was allone and hadde nede
Of frendes help; and thus bygan to *brede*
The cause whi, the sothe for to telle,
That she took fully purpos for to dwelle.   Tr 5.1016-29

After Diomede departs from her, she takes into account his words and her circumstances, and decides to stay in the Greek camp. Let us examine the syntax of the participial contruction 'Retornyng ...' (Tr 5.1023). The participle *Retornyng* is established semantically when it is connected with its main clause with '-ing' as a relator. From a reader's point of view, this is a question of how to construct the contiguous relationship between the participle and its main clause. 'Retornyng ...' is related to 'Criseyde unto hire bedde wente' (Tr 5.1021) in the preceding stanza. The new sentence begins with 'and thus bygan to brede ...' (Tr 5.1027). On the other hand, the fact that the new stanza begins with 'Retornyng ...' is worth attention. In rhyme royal, according to Masui (1964: 226), the final couplet lines of the stanza generally show the conclusive part of the content expressed in it. The enjambement from stanza to stanza seldom happens. From this point of view, 'Retornyng ...' is likely to be related to 'thus bygan to brede' (Tr 5.1027) in the following sentence. However, as Pearsall (1986) says, because this participical construction is followed by the coordinate conjunction *and* as in 'and thus bygan to brede ....' (no textual variation), such a syntactic relation is improbable. As a result, this participial clause is held in balance as regards its syntax. According to how the reader, the second prism, analyses it, there is likely to be a syntactic ambiguity, as is the case of 'Tendre-herted, slydynge of corage' (Tr 5.825). If the syntactic relation is made clear, Criseyde's involvment in the decision-making is that much clearer, and if not, it is that much obscure. (The punctuation by the various editors after *tente* (Tr 5.1022) is as follows: Skeat and Warrington adopts a period, Baugh, Benson, Fisher, Robinson a comma, and Donaldson a semicolon.)

If the relation between 'Retornyg ...' (Tr 5.1023) and 'bygan to brede' (Tr 5.1027) is reinforced, we are likely to be under an illusion that *brede* is a transitive verb (*MED* s.v. brede 7: Of deisre, malice, grief, hardship, strife, sin, etc. (a) to engender, induce). If this is right, she is regarded as an agent who is making a cause to stay in the Greek camp. However, the verb *brede* is followed by 'The cause ...' (Tr 5.1028). It is reinterpreted as an intransitive verb (*MED* s.v. brede 7. (b) to arise, develop, grow), and there her cause to stay in the Greek camp is understood as if arising naturally. There arises an illusionary syntactic ambiguity on the part of the reader, the second prism, (The psychological syntax here is interactive with the ambiguity due to the free indirect speech as shown in (8) in Section 7.2.)

Criseyde at last yields to Diomede. The narrator says that no one was in a greater sorrow than when she betrayed Troilus. This description is followed by her monologue (Tr 5.1054-85). In her argument here she is attached to and detached from Troilus, and gradually makes a self-recoverry and self-persuasion. In (50) in Section 10.4, we looked at the propositional ambiguity in relation to the modal verb. Through the double prism structure we described the rise of the syntactic ambiguity due to the relation of 'gilteles' and 'I/yow' in 'And gilteles, I woot wel, I yow leve.' (Tr 5.1084).

When Criseyde does not return from the Greek camp in the due time, Troilus becomes anxious and sceptic about her return, and has such a dream as shown in (35). This example has already been dealt with as part of metatextual variation ((25) in Section 4.7.4).

(35) And by this bor, faste in his armes folde,
    Lay, *kyssyng ay,* his lady bryght, Criseyde.   Tr 5.1240-1

In his dream Troilus sees Criseyde and a boar embracing with each other. The participial construction 'kyssyng' (Tr 5.1241) implies a problem. Who kisses whom is likely to involve the reader in an illusionary syntax since this action is reciprocal. According to his or her assumption of the agent/patient as regards the kissing action, the degrees of Criseyde's positive attitude towards it is determined.

Apart from the phrase *as she that*, we have described some instances of syntactic ambiguity with special regard to Criseyde's shifting affections.

11.4. Final remarks

We have described the rise of syntactic ambiguity through the double prism structure. As for the phenomenon of the first prism's observation, we have focused on Criseyde's shifting affections, which is the central and most sensitive point of this work. The narrator and the characters reflect their conflicting psychologies in their syntax. Through this syntax the reader, the second prism, is attached to and detached from her, and is encouraged to produce alternative interpretations. The reader's view of her character determines his or her way of analysing the syntax, and his or her way of analysing the syntax in turn determines his or her view of Criseyde's character.

In Chapter 12 we will focus on words. Let us examine through the double prism structure how the polysemy of a word contributes to the semantic complication of a sentence and thus to the rise of ambiguity.

12. Ambiguity in words

12.1. Introductory remarks: the double prism structure and words

Words are generally poets' favourite expressions in that they can easily condense thoughts and feelings in them. This is applied to Chaucer. This chapter examines the choice of words which Chaucer puts into the mouths of his characters, especially at times of mental conflict. Through the double prism structure we examine the semantic complexities of selected vocabulary and the meanings the reader, the second prism, creates for himself or herself.

In this connection we have focused on the following three aspects.

(1) a. The semantic relationship between words
 b. Polysemy
 c. The semantic relationship between language and reality

(1a) relates to paradigmatic word choice or selection from the lexical system. Aitchison (1992: 85) conceives of this system as a mental lexicon, or a lexical network in the possession of the speaker and the hearer. She regards it as 'word-web' (semantic network) and deals with related concepts such as 'coordination' (semantic field), 'subordination' (hyponymy), 'collocation,' 'synonymy,' and a 'network of similar-sounding words.'[158] But this 'word-web' involves the speaker/hearer's way of experience. We examine what Chaucer chooses and what he does not from among similar or related words. We will do so by comparing positive evidence and negative evidence.[159]

(1b) relates to the meaning of an individual word as this affects the speaker's choice. The lexical definition of a word and the actual use of it are not identical. The former is concerned with *langue* and the latter with *parole* according to the well known Saussurean definitions of these terms. In the actual use of it, the meaning is not 'present' but 'born' involving the speaker-hearer interaction and the information of the situation it is used in.[160] The definition of a word refers to the meaning of it established in Chaucer's times. But that definition is always influenced by pragmatic information leading to its modification and remodification. According to the semantic content of words, we have the phenomena of homonymy and polysemy, but these are to certain extent based on subjective judgement and etymology. The individual speaker, who may or may not be familiar with word-origins, may regard a given lexical item as

---

158 Leech (1969) illustrates the interaction of words due to their 'chiming' effects. The semantic overlapping here is concerned with words and voice, which will be dealt with in Chapter 13 as one type of ambiguity triggered by sounds.
159 See Bakhtin's (1998) 'dialogical imagination.' If we choose a word (from a paradigmatic list of words), it means that we do not choose other words. The chosen word and the unchosen words are likely to be cognised and interactive with each other.
160 Fukaya and Tanaka (1996) is a study of meaning which pays ample attention to the speaker's actual use of language. What they call 'imizuke' (signification of the language according to the context) does not focus on the fixed meaning of the language expression but on the meaning to be created through the experience of the speaker and the hearer and the situation they are involved in.

one word or many. An example of this is the ModE word *range*. A glance at the dictionary shows that this is a word of broad semantic scope covering widely distract concepts and objects as illustrated in compounds, phrases and contexts such as the following: kitchen range, rifle range, Home on the Range, we have a large range of goods (synonym: selection), this car has a range (=maximum distance without refuelling) of 200 miles, mountain range, etc. Then of course there is the verb *range*. Are we to regard these various nouns with their often apparently unrelated meanings as one word with differing meanings (polysemy) or as many words which just happen to sound the same (homonymy)? The dictionaries tell us that they all have a common etymology, but does that affect the way we use them? Should it? We are all aware that *scent, sent* and *cent* are different words, and would be even if we were illiterate, but with a word such as *range*, speaker attitudes are inevitably more subtle. There is sometimes overlap between homonymy and polysemy: where the meaning between apparent homonyms can be seen to be sufficiently close, then homonymy can be said to be acting temporarily as polysemy.

The semantic relationship between words and reality (their referents) in (1c) is not direct. The thought and cognition of the first and second prisms intervene. Here we are concerned with to what extent words are applicable to the description of reality, in other words, with the question of the fuzzy edge as regards the 'prototype' and the 'periphery' of the actual word use according to Aitchison (1992). In Chaucer words of abstract reference are especially worth noticing. The meaning of words is determined not merely by lexical definition but by taking into consideration the narrative context as a whole or information from many sources. In what follows we examine (1a-c) viewed through the double prism structure. We focus on words relating to Criseyde's infidelity (a most noteworthy phenomenon) as listed in (2) below.

(2) a. Ambiguity of *slydynge* and related words:
 paradigmatic choice, sense relation in these words, interaction between these words and their surrounding structure
 b. Ambiguity of *sely*:
 paradigmatic choice, lexical relation, sense relation in this word
 c. Ambiguity of *weldy*:
 interaction between its linguistic meaning and pragmatic meaning
 d. Ambiguity of *pite*:
 interaction between its pragmatic meanings
 e. Ambiguity of *frend/shipe* and *gentil/esse*:
 the fuzzy edge arising from the relationship between these words and the world they denote

12.2. Ambiguity of *slydynge* and related words

12.2.1. Words and Context

It may be taken axiomatic that the meaning of a word is determined not only by its referential contents but also by the context in which it is used. A word is given life when it is located in a phrase, clause, sentence, and text as a whole. On some occasions its meaning is strongly influenced and modified by social and cultural elements beyond the text boundary. The category of ambiguity in Chapter 3 was set up considering multiple contexts surrounding the expression concerned. The semantic scope of *slydynge* and related words is modified by the contexts and deepens its semantic condensation. There we focus on the speaker's psychological background running through various contexts, the discussion of which by scholars has so far not matched their importance. The psychological background is bipartite in that it consists of a positive (unrestricted) and a negative (restricted) attitude towards the object of observation. The 'positive' and 'negative' aspects represent two poles between which degrees of attitude may be observed. These psychological tendencies are closely related to the author, the first prism's intention in the characterisation in *Troilus and Criseyde* and determine both the choice of words and the structure in which they are embedded.

12.2.2. Criseyde's shifting affections and their expression

The word *slydynge* (Tr 5.825) expressive of Criseyde's shifting affections is regarded as a crux of Criseydan criticism, which has been discussed by many scholars. Previous studies have concentrated on the interpretation of the word itself, but here we attempt to consider such a paradigmatic question as the relation between the author's attitude and his word choice, and the meaning behind it, with a full investigation into related words.

Criseyde's unstable heart is a shared knowledge between the poet and the audience as regards the plot of the poem. It has been traditional in *Troilus* studies to consider the sources and Chaucer's departure from them; and scholars have concentrated their attention on how Criseyde's inconstancy has been expressed against that background. Considering the multiple values of medieval *trouthe* (faithful relation between a feudal lord and his vassals, man and wife, a man and a woman in courtly love), the breaching of such trust and how to put it into words must have been a sensitive issue for a medieval poet and his audience alike. Chaucer employs a whole semantic field of terms of infidelity to cope with this uncomfortable aspect of his source material. In this semantic field, what are the positive and negative terms he employs in referring to Criseyde's infidelity? The series of words contained here may be regarded as constituting part of the poet's 'Wertwelt' according to Héraucourt (1939). According to Aitchison (1992), they belong to 'coordination,' which is considered to constitute a semantic field in the mental lexicon of the poet and the audience. The boundary of the related words as regards her inconstancy is considered to be delineated by this psychologically shifting pendulum.

In relation to *slydynge*, we have chosen words expressing Crisyede's shifting affections, mutability, unfaithfulness, separation and forsaking. Appendix A indicates *slydynge* and related words. The abbreviated letters, N, T, C, D, and M stand for Narrator, Troilus, Criseyde, Diomede, and Monologue respectively. The arrow—> indicates 'speaks to.' It constitutes a paradigmatic list of words expressing Criseyde's inconstancy. To begin with, we focus on *sylydynge*.

12.2.3. Definition of *slide/slydynge*

The *OED* defines *slide* as in (3) below.

(3) The definition of *slide*
   1. a. To pass from one place or point to another with a smooth and continuous movement, esp. through the air or water or along a surface. a950–
   2. Of streams, etc.: To glide, flow. Now *rare*. 1390–
   3. Of reptiles, etc.: To glide, crawl. a1300–
   4. a. To move, go, proceed unperceived, quietly, or stealthily; to steal, creep, slink, or slip away, into or out of a place, etc. 1382-
   5. a. To pass away, pass by, so as to disappear, be forgotten or neglected, etc. Now *rare*. c1250- (Chaucer Tr 5.769. The third cit.) b. With *let* (or *allow*). In later use freq., to let (something) take its course. (Chaucer ClT IV (E) 82. Earliest cit.) c. Of time: To pass, slip away, go by, imperceptibly or without being profitably employed. (Chaucer Tr 5.351. Earliest cit.)
   6.†a. To fall asleep, etc. *obs*. c1330–1513
   7.a. To move, pass, make way, etc., in an easy or unobtrusive manner. (Chaucer Bo.3.p.12.190. Earliest cit.)
   8. a. To slip; to lose one's foothold. a1225–
   9. *fig* To lapse morally; to commit some fault; to err or go wrong. a1000–

In ME *slide* has nine senses according to the manner of sliding, the subject in question and by metaphorical extension. Chaucer takes advantage of these widely ranging semantic properties.[161] Four examples of *slide* in his translation of Boethius's *De Consolatione Philosophiae* correspond to Boethius's original as seen in (4). Meun's equivalents are listed by the side. This is the lexical information obtained through the intertextuality in Section 4.2.[162]

(4)

Chaucer		Boethius	Meun
Bo 3.p.12.190	slideth	dilabatur	escolorge
Bo 4.p.6.347	slideth	relabatur	rechiet
Bo 5.p.2.29	slyden	dilabuntur	descendent
Bo 5.p.3.36	slideth	relabi	rechiet

Boethius uses two words *dilabatur* (resolve) and *relabatur* (slide back) and Meun uses three words *descendent* (descend), *escolorge* (flow) and *rechiet* (lapse again). Chaucer condenses these ideas in one word *slide*. This word is thus of wide semantic scope. It should be noted that this word is not unequivocally pejorative, but—being polysemic—it is an ambiguous and neutral word.

---

161 Entities Chaucer uses *slide* in relation to are: my sorwes (BD 567), hir sorwe (FranT V (F) 924), all othere cures (ClT IV (E) 82), The dredful joye (PF 3), swiche folies (FranT V (F) 1002), The tyme (Tr 5.352), the devyne substaunce (Bo 3.p12.189), the soules of men (Bo 5.p2.26), this necessite (Bo 5.p3.36), that science (i.e. alchemy) (CYT VIII (G) 680), wight (Bo 4.p6.345), bothe Troilus and Troie town (Tr 5.768).

162 For the Latin text of Boethius, we used Tester (1918) and for Meun's translation of it, we used Dedeck-Héry and Venceslas (1952).

Next, let us consider *syldynge*. The *OED* gives three senses in ME.

(5) The definition of *sliding*
   1. *fig.* a. That slides or slips away; transitory; unstable, inconstant; passing. a900- (Chaucer quoted: Bo 1.m.5.34, CYT VIII (G) 732) †b. Of persons: Slippery, unreliable; apt to fall or transgress. *Obs.* c1435-
   2. Slippery; steeply sloping. *rare.* c1325-1616
   3.a. That moves by sliding or slipping; flowing, gliding, etc. c1374- (Chaucer quoted: Bo 5.m.1.17)

In (6) we have listed the five examples in Chaucer, which include the quotation of them, where appropriate, in the *OED*, Davis et al.'s (1974) definitions, the Latin originals of Boethius, and the French equivalents of Meun.

(6)

Chaucer	OED	Davis	Boethius	Meun
slydynge fortune (Bo 1.m.5.34)	1	inconstant	lubrica	escoulouriable
slidynge and desceyvynge hope (Bo 4.m.2.14)		inconstant	lubrica	escouloriable et decevable
the slidynge water (Bo 5.m.1.17-8)	3	flowing gliding	lapsi	escoulorjant
slydynge of corage (Tr 5.825)		changeable unstable		
That slidynge science (CYT VIII (G) 732)	1	slippery		

N.B.: *The numbers in OED correspond to those in (5) above.*

Meun adds *decevable*, which is absent in the original, to *escouloriable*. He might have thought that *escouloriable* alone would be unclear. Chaucer follows Meun, which might be an indication that he thought *slydynge* alone was open to ambiguity.[163]

With *slydynge,* as with *slide*, the semantic scope ranges from the literal/etymological to the figurative. When Chaucer, the first prism, expresses Criseyde's infidelity by means of *slide* and *slydynge*, the psychology behind his presentation seems to be this. In Book 5, where Diomede makes his appearance, he has to describe her betrayal as actual rather than foreseen as he has so far done. Since he has praised her qualities as a courtly lady, it must have been a burden on him to destroy this ideal image. However, if he sympathises with both Troilus and Criseyde, the story would proceed on separate and parallel lines. For the sake of consistency he needs to distance himself from her at some point, and to recast the plot. It is precisely at this critical moment of transition that he uses the potentially judgemental *slide*. The narrator's words in (7) appear to reflect the true voice of Chaucer the poet allowing for once his mask to slip.

---

163 Cf. Masui (1977: 133): When we consult the *OED* for the word *sliding*, we find that the editors do not quote the example here. This may be a result of their sensitive consideration. The poet leaves the implication of this word to the context of the situation.

(7) For bothe Troilus and Troie town
Shal knotteles thorughout hire herte *slide;* Tr 5.768-9

The *OED* quotes this example in the sense of (8), as we saw in (3) above.

(8) *OED* 5: To pass away, pass by, so as to disappear, be forgotten or neglected, etc.

Here the editor clearly wishes to stress the flavour of this word by glossing it with 'forgotten or neglected.' The same is true of the editors of *MED* who quote the example under s.v. slide 2.(b) to pass away; disappear, depart. Chaucer, however, does not suggest that Criseyde forgot or neglected Troilus. Rather he emphasises her anxiety for Troilus or her regret that she had betrayed him.[164] *Slide* here retains the etymological sense 'shift,' but further specification of it is left to the reader, the second prism. It may be said that Chaucer takes advantage of the semantic range of this word, or indeed that it was precisely the breadth of this range that induced him to choose it. At the most crucial turning point of the story he begins to write about Criseyde's inconstancy with equivocation.

If we compare the corresponding passage in *Il Filostrato*, it is obvious that Chaucer adopts a more restrained attitude. Boccaccio is clear in his criticism of Diomede and Criseyde:[165] for him Diomede is the 'novello amadore,' the intruder (Fil 6.8.2) while Criseyde is the faithless female, as we can see in (9).

(9) E'n breve spazio ne cacciò di fuore
Troilo e Troia, ed ogni altro pensiero
Che 'n lei fosse di lui o falso o vero.   *Il Filostrato* 6.8.6-8
(In a brief space he drave forth from it Troilus and Troy and every other
thought which she had of him, or false or true.)[166]

56 lines later *slide* finds an echo in 'slydynge of corage.' The center of description is shifted from the event to the character of Criseyde. *Slydynge* is used in a series of expressions to describe her immediately before she yields to Diomede. There with the holistic image of Criseyde in between, we have first that of Diomede, and finally that of Troilus. This description itself interrupts the narrative development which may reflect Chaucer's hesitation to immediately go into description of Criseyde's betrayal. There is a big difference between this and its equivalent in *Il Filostrato* (6.11 develops directly into 6.12) where her betrayal is described at once, without insertion. (In the macro-structure of Chapter 6 we have dealt with this part as regards the interaction of situations. See (17).) The description of Criseyde is made both externally (Tr 5.806-19) and internally (Tr 5.820-6). In the former her feminine beauty is praised, and in the latter especially her kindness. This kindness is gradually highlighted as shown in (10).

---

164 Chaucer emphasises Criseyde's feelings of pity towards Diomede (Tr 5.1044-50).
165 Windeatt (1990: 487):
Fil's active imagery of D driving Troiolo and Troy forth from Criseida's thoughts (8/6) is replaced by Ch's more passive image of Troilus and Troy slipping through C's heart like a knotless string.
166 While Boccaccio also describes Diomede as her 'new lover' (Fil 5.14.8, Fil 7.31.8, Fil 7.49.8, Fil 7.56.3, Fil 7.58.1, Fil 8.6.1), Chaucer is reticent about giving such a description of Diomede.

(10) She sobre was, ek symple, and wys withal,
    The best ynorisshed ek that myghte be,
    And goodly of hire speche in general,
    Charitable, estatlich, lusty, fre;
    Ne nevere mo ne lakked hire pite;
    Tendre-herted, *slydynge* of corage;
    But trewely, I kan nat telle hire age.   Tr 5.820-6

Her character traits 'Charitable, ... fre, ... pite' are given attention, and *Tendre-herted* is placed next to 'slydynge of corage' without any conjunction.[167] Her abundant love and pity seen here are worthy of a courtly lady. But they imply a dangerous feature which may destroy her image if taken to excess (see the analysis of *pite* in Section 12.5). It is obvious that Chaucer makes a subversive use of *pite* and *tendre-herted* as he does with the Prioress in the General Prologue to *The Canterbury Tales* and with May in *The Merchant's Tale*.[168] Since she cannot be unkind to Diomede as she cannot be to Troilus, *pite* and *tendre-herted* are likely to be double-edged, and *slydynge* is therefore an inevitable consequence. The term *slydynge* can imply both adverse criticism and praise depending on how one views variations in her mental make-up.[169] This is why her character is "ambiguous" or "ambivalent." The final evaluation here is left to the reader. Incidentally, the *MED* applies the sense s.v. sliden 1.(c) *fig*, 'untrustworthy, delusive' to Bo.1.m.5.37 'slydynge Fortune,' whereas it does sense 1.(d) *fig*, 'unstable, irresolute' to Tr 5.825. Past studies have tended to pass either critical or laudatory judgement on her *slydynge* nature. Chaucer, the first prism, appears to intend neither such judgement. He cannot depart from the traditional plot, but at the same time identifies with his heroine and so chooses to express himself in a way which is open to alternative interpretations.[170]

---

167 As for the suppression of the relation between the two phrases, see Section 11.3.
168 Regarding Prioress and May, see CT I (A) 143-50 and IV (E) 1982-97. Burnley (1979: 148) points out that 'although ... the balance between reason and emotion ... is generally maintained, yet in the fourteenth century, excesses of pietism are exceedingly common.'
169 I have pointed out that *slydynge* indicates the attribute of Fortune in *Boece* 1.m.5.34. Since this attribute is latent in Criseyde's character, it deepens ambiguity in her character as to whether her betrayal is due to her character itself or to the external workings of Fortune.
170 Regarding the relation between the two phrases, Smith (1949: 5) stresses the positive side: 'It (i.e. Criseyde's heart) may have changed from sympathy and tenderness, rather than from fickleness and instability, for note that 'slydynge of corage' follows immediately 'tendre-herted.' On the other hand, Donaldson (1970: 59, 77) emphasises the negative aspect and regards the phrase 'sylydynge of corage' immediately after the phrase 'tendre-herted' as showing an 'anticlimax.' Elliott (1974: 325) can go as far as to say 'a particularly slippery kind of inconstancy.' Burnley (1981: 95) points out that *slydynge* in the ME texts and its equivalents *lubrica* and *escoulorjant* respectively in Boehius's original and in Meun's translation of it are used with immoral implication, and regards the above 'slydynge of corage' as being in the same vein. Compared with these views of *slydynge*, Masui's (1977:148) view is worthy of note: 'her unstable nature—in this the evaluative distinction of good and bad is not included.' Shigeo's (1982: 77) also merits attention, suggesting: 'her shifting nature here shows her nature adjusting itself to changing situations or her flexibility by which to accept all and let them go. My interpretation of *slydynge* basically accords with those of Masui and Shigeo. For a critical history of 'slydynge of corage,' see Kaminsky (1980: 154-5).

From the above we can see that *slydynge* is part of the vocabulary whereby the narrator, or perhaps Chaucer the poet, exercises restraint in his description of Criseyde's faithlessness.[171] His attitude induces him to choose an equivocal word, which in turn causes the reader, the second prism, further to interpret.

12.2.4. Words associated psychologically with *slydynge*

Let us first look at *knotteles* and *unkynde* as having affinities with *slide* and *slydynge* when seen as words which express the restrained attitude of the speaker, the first prism, to Criseyde's misbehaviour. (*Pite* will be dealt with in Section 12.5.) *Knotteles* is collocated with *slide* in (7) with an effect of semantic chiming.[172] For the sake of convenience we repeat those lines here.

(11) For bothe Troilus and Troie town
    Shal *knotteles* thorughout hire herte slide;   Tr 5.768-9

Both the *OED* and *MED* have articles on this *knotteles*. Their respective definitions are given in (12) below.

(12) *OED*: Without a knot, free from knots; unknotted. quasi-adv.=like a thread without knots, smoothly; without check or hindrance (earliest citation).

MED: adj. Of a thread: without a knot; used *fig.* (unique citation).

Chaucer condenses the literal sense and the metaphorical one of *knotteles* as he did with *slide*. His equivocation regarding Criseyde's infidelity seems to have resulted in his coinage. There is a great discrepancy in strength between *knotteles* and *trecherie* and *chaunge*.

The word *unkynde* is used by the narrator to foreshadow Criseyde's betrayal at the beginning of Book 4, that is, in the scene where Troilus and Criseyde's love is on the wane. See (13). (In (6) in Chapter 9 we dealt with this quotation in terms of the narrator's intention.)

(13) For how Criseyde Troilus forsook—
    Or at the leeste, how that she was *unkynde*—
    Moot hennesforth ben matere of my book,   Tr 4.15-7

Muscatine (1957) points out, quoting this passage, that ambiguity arises when the narrator comments on the central actions in the story.[173] Significant here is the semantic range of *unkynde* itself in this comment. The word *unkynde* is of course polysemous in ME. The *MED* lists the following meanings for *kinde*.

---

171 Cf. 'Mais sis corages li chanjot' (Benoît: *Le Roman de Troie*: 5286); 'animi constantiam non seruasset' (Guido: *Historia Destructionis Troiae* Book III). Chaucer seeks to limit a negative evaluation of his heroine by using the word *slydynge*. For other comparative notes of sources, see Root (1952: 544), Gray (1979: 191-3), and Windeatt (1990: 491).
172 Masui (1977: 146-7) comments on the metaphorical and blurring effect of the word *knotteles*.
173 Muscatine (1957: 155):
    The dramatic action and the editorial comment together produce a kind of controlled ambiguity that is increasingly apparent as the poem progresses.

(14) 1. natural, normal, healthful, innate, proper, inborn
    2. native, inherent, genuine, uncontaminated, pure
    3. legitimate, akin, hereditary
    4. dutiful, moral, customary
    5. benevolent, pleasant
    6. generous, constant, true, brave, wellborn

This word is negated by the prefix *un-*. Like *kinde* the negative form has a wide semantic range which gives it ample scope for ambiguity.[174] It therefore suits Chaucer's intention at this point to blur the fact of Criseyde's infidelity.[175] Incidentally, *unkynde* appears in an extended part of Boccaccio's original. The examples in (15) give further instances of the use of this word to denote Criseyde's breach of promise.

(15) a. And seyde hire, "Certes, if ye be *unkynde*,
       And but ye come at day set into Troye,
       Ne shal I nevere have hele, honour, ne joye.   Tr 4.1440-2

    b. He ne eet, ne dronk, ne slep, ne word seyde,
       Ymagynyng ay that she was *unkynde*,
       For which wel neigh he wex out of his mynde.   Tr 5.1440-2

In these lines Troilus does not hint at infidelity. The following instance of 'nat ... kynde' in (16) is in the same vein.

(16) That Troilus wel understod that she
     Nas nought so kynde as that hire oughte be.   Tr 5.1642-3

From the paradigmatic list of similar words such as 'not kynde—unkynde—cruel'[176] and 'not trewe—untrewe—false,' the author, the first prism, seems to have chosen appropriate words according to whether he takes a judgemental or a restrained view of Criseyde's fickle heart. When his mode of expression is retrained, the reader, the second prism, is involved in its ambiguous readings.

---

174 The negation of *kynde* is not polarised in the same way as the negation of *man* automatically produces *woman*, but gradational with several stages between the two poles, not, therefore, automatically suggesting 'a cruel person nonchalant of betrayal.' See Jespersen (1917: 85) and Aitchison (1992: 85).

175 Burnley (1992) points out that the ambiguity of *kynde* was problematical with medieval lawyers and that they tried to reduce it by resort to the shared sense of repeated similar words. Although Kanno (1998) states that the word *unkynde* turns out to mean 'untrewe,' it should be noted that Chaucer did not choose the word *untrewe* (a more definitive word to reveal the idea of 'untrue'). In *Troilus and Criseyde*, as manifested in 'For may no man fordon the lawe of kynde.' (Tr 1.238) or 'Perauncer thynkestow: though it be so, / That Kynde wolde don hire to bygynne / To have a manere routhe upon my woo, / Seyth Daunger, 'ay, thow shalt me nevere wynne!' (Tr 2.1373-6), this word is concerned with deep-rooted human emotion and therefore used in widely ranging senses such as human affection, sympathy, love, and faithfulness.

176 Since the expression 'nought kynde' is a combination of two words, it is likely to be weaker in negative straightforwardness than the word *unkynde* where the prefix *un-* and the stem *kynde* are combined into one word.

12.2.5. Words expressing harsher criticism of Criseyde's inconstancy

When the author wishes to express adverse criticism of Criseyde's infidelity, he uses words such as *false, betrayed, tresoun, variaunce, forsook*, etc., which are quite the opposite in effect of the vocabulary discussed in Sections 12.2.3 and 12.2.4. Generally *untrewe* is more explicit than *unkynde, false* is more than *untrewe, betray/tresoun* are more than *false* and are a long way removed from the relatively mild *slydynge*. The words *chaunge* and *variaunce* are also more direct in their judgemental potential.

When Chaucer abandons his equivocation and uses straightforward vocabulary upbraiding his heroine for her behaviour, he variously speaks through the narrator, Troilus, Criseyde, or Pandarus. The quotations in (17) give examples of this.

(17) a. In which ye may the double sorwes here
     Of Troilus in lovynge of Criseyde,
     And how that she *forsook* hym er she deyde.   Tr 1.54-6 [Narrator]

  b. For I have *falsed* oon the gentileste
     That evere was, and oon the worthieste!   Tr 5.1056-7 [Criseyde]

  c. "My lady bryght, Criseyde, hath me *bytrayed*,
     In whom I trusted most of ony wight   Tr 5.1247-8 [Troilus]

  d. And of this broche, he tolde hym word and ende,
     Compleynyng of hire hertes *variaunce*,   Tr 5.1669-70 [Narrator]

  e. "Thorugh which I se that clene out of youre mynde
     Ye han me *cast* – and I ne kan nor may,   Tr 5.1695-6 [Troilus]

  f. "If I dide aught that myghte liken the,
     It is me lief; and of this *tresoun* now,
     God woot that it a sorwe is unto me!   Tr 5.1737-9 [Pandarus]

The word *forsook* is rich in implication of betrayal, the abandonment of *trouthe* which would have overtones of treason or even apostasy in a medieval feudal/Christian society. See the effect of metonymy (inclusion) in such a way that her betraying of Troilus is associated with her deserting the ideal of feudalism or even God. (Cf. *MED* s.v. forsaken 1.)

If one compares Chaucer and Boccaccio, however, the latter is more judgemental of his heroine in that he blames her for two dictions, whereas Chaucer lets her off one of them.

(18) a. Del tutto veggio che m' hai discacciato
     Del petto tuo,...   *Il Filostrato* 8.15.1-2 [Troilo]
     (I see that thou hast driven me quite of thy breast ...)

  b. Tu m' hai cacciato a torto della mente,
     Laddov' io dimorar sempre credea,
     E nel mio luogo hai posto falsamente
     Diomede;...   *Il Filostrato* 8.16.1-4 [Troilo]
     (Thou hast wrongfully driven me forth from thy mind, wherein I thought to dwell forever and in my place thou hast falsely Diomede.)

c. "Thorugh which I se that clene out of youre mynde
   Ye han me cast... Tr 5.1695-6 [Troilus]

Chaucer's lines correspond only to (18a) in Boccaccio. (18b) is not reproduced and therefore Troilus is seen as milder in his criticism of her than Troilo.

A further contrast with (18) is provided by the fact that although Chaucer put in an additional description of her betrayal, it did not increase his negative evaluation of her. Criseyde confesses openly and honestly that she has betrayed Troilus. The depth of her regret can be seen from the fact that the object of 'I have falsed' (Tr 5.1056-7) is not simply the name Troilus, but epithets conveying the highest praise of the man she has wronged: *oon the gentileste ... oon the worthieste* (Tr 5.1056-7), which shows her recognition of his unchangeable personality. This is also emphasised by the narrator, as can be seen in (19) below.

(19) a. But trewely, the storie telleth us,
       Ther made nevere womman moore wo
       Than she, whan that she falsed Troilus.   Tr 5.1051-3

   b. For she so sory was for hire untrouthe,   Tr 5.1098

These insertions indicate Criseyde's betrayal explicity, but at the same time reveal her recognition of regret and thus underline her sincerity.

12.2.6. The semantic field of words denoting change, shifting, etc.: a paradigmatic list of vocabulary used to refer to Criseyde's inconstancy together with vocabulary not used

The words listed below express change, instability, unfaithfulness, deception, separation, desertion, lustfulness, etc. We have arranged them in the order of application from wide to restricted, and examined how they collocate with vocabulary relating to fortune, unfaithful individuals, etc. in Bo, LGW, and Henryson's *The Testamnent of Cresseid* (hereinafter referred to as Henryson).[177]

Appendix B gives the results of our investigation. The mark "+" shows that we have at least one example, and a blank shows that we have no examples. The words marked by slashes indicate variant forms, and the round brackets indicate that the words inside them are not found in Chaucer. From Appendix B we find that words are roughly divided into the four categories seen in (20) below.

(20) a. Words applied to Criseyde and other entities (*slydynge, passe, chaunge, untrewe, false,* etc.)
   b. Words applied not to Criseyde, but to other entities (*unstable, mutable, flitte, brotel, transitorie, unconstant, unstedefast, unfeithful, deceivable, trecherie, traitour, unclene, lecherous,* etc.)
   c. Words applied only to Criseyde (*knotteles, holde...in honde*)
   d. Words applied not to the entities in the works above (*tikel, unsad*)

---

[177] In *Boece* the mutability of human nature and the divine immovability are highlighted. In *The Legend of Good Women* man's treachery is contrasted with the goodness of woman. In Henryson the focus is placed upon Cresseid after she has betrayed Troilus, and there how she, repeatedly punished for it, comes to recognise and regret her sin. Regarding Henryson, I used Fox (1981).

Here are some examples of (20b). The word *brotel* (=fragile, changeable, fickle) and its derivatives are used to show the world's changeableness in Tr, men's betrayal (men in general and Demophone in particular) in LGW, and Cresseid's unfatihfulness in Henryson. The word *unstable* (=unsteady, fickle, variable) is used to denote the world's joy in Tr, Fortune in Bo, and Cresseid's unfaithfulness along with *brotel* in Henryson. The words *flitte* (=transfer, deviate, change) and *flittinge* (=changeable, transitory) are used to denote the instability of this world (kingdom) in Tr, and of Fortune and people in this world in Bo. The words *unconstant* (=inconstant), *fikill* (=false, treacherous, deceptive), and *lecherous* (=lascivious, sensual) are used to denote Cresseid's attributes in Henryson. The words *deceive* (=deceive) and *deceivable* (=deceitful, fraudulent, deceptive) are used to denote Fortune's deception in Tr and Bo, and *deceivable* hope in Bo. The word *traitour* (=traitor) is used to denote the attributes of men, that is, Calkas, Antenor in Tr, and of men, that is, Eneas, Jason, Theseus, Tereus, in LGW, and of Fortune in Tr.

Criseyde shares qualities with the entities to which this vocabulary is applied, and adjectives such as *fals* are indeed used to refer to her and them. But she differs greatly from these other entities: this vocabulary is of a fairly narrow application and implies unequivocally harsh criticism, which accounts for the fact that Chaucer, the first prism, does not apply it to her infidelity.[178] Instead, the reader, the second prism, is thus presented with milder vocabulary of wide application. In this way ambiguity is likely to be the result.

12.2.7. Words expressing Criseyde's inconstancy and their environments

We now examine the environments of the words listed in Appendix A. We look at collocations between nouns and adjectives and see whether the adjectives are attributive[179] or predicative in use, and whether the sentences they appear in are in the form of assertions or not. Adjectives tend to indicate the user's judgement and therefore they appear typically in character portrayal. When praising Criseyde, Chaucer often uses *goodly* and *bright* in the attributive position, as seen in (21).

(21)

	goodly	brighte
attributive use	9 (2)	14 (1)
predicative use	2	2

N.B.: *The round brackets (inlcuded numbers) indicate the absolute use of adjectives.*

---

[178] Burnley (1979: 94) states that 'there is no mention of her (i.e. Criseyde's) moral stability: she is never called *sad, stedefast, or stable.*' It should be noted further that those words explicitly expressive of her betrayal tend to be avoided. (Cf. *unstedefastnesse* LGW G 526.)

[179] As for the attributive use of adjectives, I applied Roscow's (1981: 29-33) 'attributive adjective' (premodifier, postmodifier and absolute use). Those nouns collocating with adjectives include Criseyde herself, her emotions, her actions, her characters, etc.

12. Ambiguity in words

These attributive adjectives are used to praise Criseyde and highlight the stable side of her character,[180] whereas adjectives conveying criticism of her are used predicatively. Of the five examples of *slydynge*, the predicative use is only applied to Criseyde. The situation with *fals* is exactly the same, and there are contrasts with the other works mentioned in Section 12.2.6. Shakespeare is added in the following table.

(22)

	Criseyde	Other characters in Tr	Men in LGW	Cresseid in Henryson	Cressida in Shakespeare
attributive use	0	11	17 (1)	3	6 (3)
predicative use	6	6	6	0	3

As can be seen, the attributive use is generally more frequent except in the case of Chaucer's Criseyde, and this is surely noteworthy. Henryson and Shakespeare used the term almost as a fixed epithet, a classification for their heroine, and indeed she has become a symbol of faithlessness ever since, as shown in (23).

(23) O *fals Cresseid* and trewe knicht Troylus!
                                          Henryson *The Testament of Cresseid* 545
   O Cressid! O *false Cressid*! *false, false, false*!
                                          Shakespeare *Troilus and Cressida* 5.2.178 [181]

The same is true of Boccaccio. As we can see in (24), he uses adjectives attributively (attributo, epiteto) for Criseyde's betrayal.

(24) a. Lascimal tor del mondo il più dolente
     Corpo che viva: lasciami, morendo,
     Contenta far la nostra *fraudolente*
     Donna ...   *Il Filostrato* 7.35.1-4

    (Let me take away from the world the most sorrowful body alive; let me
    in my death give contentment to our deceitful lady)

  b. Cotal fin' ebbe la speranza vana
     Di Troilo in *Criseida villana*.   *Il Filostrato* 8.28.7-8

    (Such was the end of the vain hopes of Troilus in base Cressida.)
    (Cf. il tuo falso spergiuro (thy trecherous lying) *Il Filostrato* 8.13.3.)

---

180   attributive use:
     And fareth wel, *goodly, faire, fresshe may*,
     As she that lif or deth may me comande!   Tr 5.1412-3

     Now maistow sen thiself, if that the liste,
     How trewe is now thi nece, *bright Criseyde*!   Tr 5.1711-2

    predicative use:
     "O mercy, God," thoughte he, "wher hastow woned,
     That art *feyr and goodly* to devise?"   Tr 1.276-7

     Hire hewe, whilom *bright*, that tho was pale,
     Bar witnesse of hire wo and hire constreynte;   Tr 4.740-1
181   The repeated 'false, false, false' is regarded as absolute in use.

We may contrast this with Chaucer's words below.

(25) Swych fyn hath *false worldes brotelnesse*! Tr 5.1832

(24b) is described of Criseida herself, but (25) refers to the world as a whole. In terms of hyponymy, Chaucer's attributive use seems to be possible because of his replacement of Criseyde by a superordinate word (world). There is a big discrepancy between the first prisms, Chaucer and Boccaccio, as regards their attitude towards Criseyde's inconstancy.

Chaucer highlights a classificatory feature of men's betrayal as in (26).

(26) a. In makyng of a glorious legende
Of goode wymmen, maydenes and wyves,
That weren trewe in lovyng al hire lyves;
And telle of *false men* that hem bytraien,   LGW Prol. F. 483-6

b. Or as a welle that were botomles,
Ryght so can *false Jason* have no pes.   LGW 1584-5

c. But thus *this false lovere* (i.e. Theseus) can begyle
His trewe love (i.e. Adriane), the devel quyte hym his while!   LGW 2226-7

The fact that Chaucer only uses *fals* predicatively when referring to Criseyde suggests that her infidelity is a temporary lapse and not an intrinsic part of her character. Cf. 'false Poliphete' (Tr 2.1467) and 'for wommen that bitraised be / Thorugh false folk' (Tr 5.1780-1). The author, the first prism's restrained attitude towards her infidelity is central to the rise of ambiguity.

Next, let us examine assertive/non-assertive forms. Assertive forms are affirmative declarative sentences in a finite clause. Non-assertive forms are the following: 1) negative sentences, 2) interrogative sentences, 3) conditional sentences, 4) concessive sentences, 5) subordinating clauses following modal lexical verbs such as *wene* and *deme*, 6) verb phrases with modal auxiliaries denoting obligation or conjecture, and 7) down-toners (modal adverbs, comments for defending Criseyde's inconstancy). While assertive forms are indicative of her shifting heart explicitly, non-assertive forms are indicative that the author, the first prism, hesitates to show it, questions it, guesses about it, assumes it, and even negates it.[182] We have applied the above criteria 1) to 7) to those words indicative of Criseyde's shifting heart (Appendix A). The result is the table below.

---

182 Cf. Donaldson (1972: 42):
... for Chaucer truth was never simple, always so qualified that the only way to express it satisfactorily was to mix statements of fact with many contradictory truths. In a way, the image of his poetry is that of the false report and the true one which unite inseparably to get out of the House of Rumour into history.

(27)

Books	1	2	3	4	5	Total
Assertive forms	1	0	0	2	7	10
Non-assertive forms	0	5	8	19	17	49
1) negative sentence	0	4	5	3	2	14
2) interrogative sentence	0	1	1	0	2	4
3) conditional sentence	0	0	1	8	1	10
4) concessive sentence	0	0	1	2	1	4
5) modal lexical verb	0	0	0	0	3	3
6) modal auxiliary	0	0	0	4	5	9
7) down-toner	0	0	0	2	3	5

The words which clearly indicate betrayal such as *forsook*, *falsen*, 'torne ... out of my thoughte,' etc. are mostly in non-assertive forms. This tendency is maintained even after Criseyde has betrayed Troilus or Troilus has discovered the fact (Tr 5.1051-3, Tr 5.1086-8, Tr 5.1682-3, Tr 5.1678-80, etc.). All the six examples of predicative use of *fals* for Criseyde appear in non-assertive forms. On the other hand, five examples of the predicative use of *fals* in *LGW* appear in assertive forms while one appears in a non-assertive form. We give two examples each from Tr and LGW in (28).

(28) a. And Attropos my thred of lif tobreste
   If I be fals! Now trowe me if yow leste!   Tr 4.1546-7

   b. How darstow seyn that fals thy lady ys
   For any drem, right for thyn owene drede?   Tr 5.1279-80
   (Smilarly, Tr 3.802-4, Tr 4.615-6, Tr 4.1534-7, Tr 5.697-8)

   c. Whi sufferest thow that Tereus was bore
   That is in love so fals and so forswore,   LGW 2234-5 [Tereus]

   d. For fals in love was he, ryght as his syre.
   The devil sette here soules bothe afyre!   LGW 2492-3 [Demophon]
   (Smilarly, LGW 2446-7, 2555-6, 2570-1)

Chaucer does not ignore the fact of Criseyde's betrayal, but he is reticent about expressing it assertively. This reticent stance encourages the reader, the second prism, to put his or her own interpretation on the text, which leads us to ambiguity in its evaluation. (The discussions of Sections 12.2.6 and 12.2.7 are based on Nakao (2011a).)

12.2.8. Final remarks

We have paid attention to Criseyde's infidelity (phenomenon), a crux of Criseydan criticism, and investigated the expression of it with regard to *slydynge* and related terms. We have focused on the author, the first prism's attitude, judgemental or restrained, towards her inconstancy. We have understood that such widely applied and ambiguous words as *slydynge* and *unkynde* lead to equivocation. Those words making her betrayal explicit and devaluing her social-moral standing tend to be avoided. The collocation between *fals* and its nouns is only applied predicatively in the case of Criseyde, whereas in LGW it is applied attributively to men, thus suggesting a permanent and intrinsic feature of their nature. Such words as *forsook* of narrow semantic application tend to be used in non-assertive structures. In this way Criseyde in *Troilus and Criseyde* is different from Cressida in Chaucer's original *Il Filostrato* and Cresseid in Henryson's sequel, *The Testament of Cresseid*.

While Chaucer follows the traditional plot of Criseyde's betrayal (which implies criticism of the heroine), he makes much of the internal process leading to her act of betrayal and thus tends to mitigate it. The judgemental and the forgiving attitudes are reconciled, as we have seen in line Tr 5.1832 quoted in (25) above. By this reconciliation, the second prism readers are encouraged to choose which attitude they prefer, and thus to differ in interpretation. This is likely to give rise to ambiguity.

12.3. Ambiguity in *sely*

According to the *OED*, the semantic history of *sely* is as follows. The sense 'happy/fortunate' which can be observed up to the late 15th century (OE—1483) is also the meaning we find in OE *saelig* and OHG *salig*. This is productive of another sense 'spiritually blessed' (OE—1400) which relates to salvation, redemption, and eternal life. So the word refers to both worldly and spiritual bliss. The spiritual sense naturally gives rise to the related meanings 'pious, good, holy' (attested early 13th to early 17th century), and alongside this, from the late 13th century we find the associated sense 'innocence, harmless.' 'Innocence and harmlessness,' however, can—and clearly were assumed to—derive from another source—'simple-mindedness.' Indeed the English word *simple* itself—of neutral reference—now also means 'imbecillic.' Thus must have arisen the senses 'pitiable, helpless' (also found from the late 13th to the early 17th century). In the same period, and lasting till the mid-17th century, we find the meaning 'insignificant, feeble'; and the modern senses of *silly* are attested from 1529 onwards. In London English of the late 14th century the sense 'happy' is already in decline while that of 'foolish' is already in the ascendant. Chaucer's *sely* has all the above senses, and is therefore pregnant with ambivalence: 'pious, blessed, and happy' appear at one end of the scale and 'pitiable, feeble, and foolish' at the other, with 'innocent' in between. These senses must have been impinged on each other in the mental lexicon of late 14th century users of the language.

We have made a componential analysis of *sely* and related words. This is given in tabular form at (29) below. Meanings "a" to "j" are given in the Note below the table. In the table itself a plus sign indicates that the meaning in question exists for a particular word; a minus sign indicates that it does not.

As can be seen, *sely* has a wider semantic range than those of the other words. Here the choice of this word itself deserves particular attention.

Chaucer uses *sely* 43 times in all, and its frequency increases as his writing progresses. He does not use it at all in the early works. There are 10 examples in his middle period (Mars: 2, Tr: 8), and the use continues to increase as time goes on (LGW: 8, CT: 25). It is found that Chaucer grew to be more active in the use of this word. In fact, the highest incidence is in MilT, WBP, and SumT in CT.[183] Although the seman-

---

183 For a complex use of *sely* in MilT, see Cooper (1980). For a general survey of *sely* in Chaucer, see Nakao (1988a), and for the ambivalent use of this word, see Nakao (1988b). Knapp (1999)

tic content of this word is not particularly complex in *Troilus and Criseyde,* nevertheless the nature of its later complexity is adumbrated here.

(29)

	a	b	c	d	e	f	g	h	i	j
sely	+	+	+	+	+	+	+	+	−	−
innocent	−	−	−	+	−	−	−	+	−	−
blisful	+	+	−	−	−	−	−	−	−	−
holy	−	−	+	−	−	−	−	−	−	−
pitous	−	−	+	−	+	+	−	−	−	−
feble	−	−	−	−	−	−	+	+	−	−
nyce	−	−	−	−	−	−	−	+	+	−
fool	−	−	−	−	−	−	−	+	−	+

N.B.: a: happy; b: spiritually blessed; c: holy, good, pious; d: innocent, harmless; e: pitiable, helpless; f: full of pity; g: insignificant, feeble; h: simple, foolish; i: scrupulous; j: senseless, lecherous

When we look at the nouns which *sely* qualifies, we find the following contexts: Troilus's agony of love for Criseyde (*sely* Troilus Tr 1.871, Tr 2.683, Tr 5.529); his invocation of death as a release from the pangs of love ('sely is that deth' Tr 4.503), his reference to Trojans as contrasted with Greeks (*sely* Troians Tr 4.1490), his description of love affairs ('a sely fewe pointes' Tr 1.338); the narrator's reference to Criseyde's unstable love situation ('the sely larke' Tr 3.1191), and his reference to the image of Criseyde betraying Troilus ('this sely woman' Tr 5.1093).[184] We can detect the central meaning of the *sely* used in each context, but since its senses strongly overlap with each other, we have the impression that some senses are emphasised and others would remain as residues.

The narrator's use of *sely* focuses on Troilus as a servant of a courtly lover. This word clusters around the predicaments he encounters in his development of love for Criseyde. In (30) he is persuaded by Pandarus to confess who he has fallen in love with.

(30) Tho gan the veyne of Troilus to blede,
For he was hit, and wax al reed for shame.
"A ha!" quod Pandare; "Here bygynneth game."

And with that word he gan hym for to shake,
And seyde, "Thef, thow shalt hyre name telle."
But tho gan *sely* Troilus for to quake
As though men sholde han led hym into helle,
And seyde, "Allas, of al my wo the welle,
Thanne is my swete fo called Criseyde!"
And wel neigh with the word for feere he deide.   Tr 1.866-75

---

discusses Chaucer's use of *sely* but with no reference to its ambiguity.
184 Criseyde uses the word *selynesse* to show the mutability of this world (Tr 3.813, Tr 3.825, Tr 3.831). According to Windeatt (1990), we find that the manuscript variants of *sely* are: Tr 1.338 sely]Gg om., Tr 3.1191 sely]lytel R, Tr 4.503 sely]happy Cx.

Criseyde, seeing Troilus returning to Troy in triumph, is likely to look upon him with favour. In (31) the narrator says that Venus too is on his side and wishes to free him from sorrow.

(31) And also blisful Venus, wel arrayed,
Sat in hire seventhe hous of hevene tho,
Disposed wel, and with aspectes payed,
To helpe *sely* Troilus of his woo.
And soth to seyne, she nas not al a foo
To Troilus in his nativitee;
God woot that wel the sonner spedde he.   Tr 2.680-6

In (32) Troilus and Pandarus go to look at the empty house of Criseyde, who is now in the Greek camp.

(32) For syn we yet may have namore feste,
So lat us sen hire paleys atte leeste."

And therwithal, his meyne for to blende,
A cause he fond in towne for to go,
And to Criseydes hous they gonnen wende.
But Lord, this *sely* Troilus was wo!
Hym thoughte his sorwful herte braste a-two.
For whan he saugh hire dores spered alle,
Wel neigh for sorwe adoun he gan to falle.   Tr 5.524-32

Focus is placed on the sorrow Troilus experiences before getting Criseyde's love and in losing her love. The *wo/o* (Tr 1.873, Tr 2.683, Tr 5.529) situated close to and interactive with *sely* describes the state of his heart. In this word is condensed his innocence, his sincere love, and his wounded and sensitive emotions stemming from his unrequited love. The senses of *sely* 'helpless,' and 'pitiable' are primary, but the secondary meanings 'innocent' and 'feeble' are clearly discernible. All those meanings interact at this point.

Furthermore from an intertextual point of view, the framework of the character Troilus's genuine love and his later suffering for it in *Troilus and Criseyde* is analogous to the suffering of the saints of Christian legend, martyred for their devotion to God, but receiving their reward in heaven. Since courtly love is quasi-religious in nature, the connection with hagiography is clear. The use of *sely* applied to saints can be seen in the following quotations.

(33) a. Þer ha heuen up / hare honden to heouene; / & swa somet readliche, / þurh *seli* martirdom, / ferden, wid murðe, / icrunet, to Criste, / o þe þreottude dei / of Nouembres moned. *Life of Saint Katherine*, 1407-14
(There they lifted up their hands to heaven; and so together readily, through blessed martyrdom, went, with joy, crowned to Christ, on the thirteenth day of the month of November.)

b. Mayden euer vurst and late
Of heueneriche *sely* ȝate   17 *Aue Maris Stella* 3-4

c. And wiss me waies þare,
þare santes has þair *seli* sete;   29 *An Orison to the Trinity* 45-6

> d. I Come vram an vncouþe londe as a *sely* pylegrym, þet
> ferr habbe i-souȝt   36 *How christ shall Come* 8 [185]

When applying this word to the world of sinners which is fluctuating and mendacious, Chaucer seems to be aware that devotion has both positive values 'innocent' and 'good,' and negative ones 'defencelss' and 'gullible.' The negative senses are clearly illustrated in the case of the cuckolded John in *The Miller's Tale* ('This sely carpenter' MilT I (A) 3601 and 3614). Incidentally, Benson (1987: 1287) takes this word in the sense of 'hapless' or 'wretched' in Tr 1.871, and takes it in the sense of 'happy' in Tr 2.683. In the latter interpretation the narrator emphasises his good fortune that he was born to be helped by Venus rather than his pang on the way to getting his love.

In (34) dismayed at the parliamentary decision to exchange Criseyde for the prisoners, Troilus expresses his wish to die.

(34) "Nay, God wot, nought worth is al thi red,
   For which, for what that evere may byfalle,
   Withouten wordes mo, I wol be ded.
   O deth, that endere art of sorwes alle,
   Com now, syn I so ofte after the calle;
   For *sely* is that deth, soth for to seyne,
   That, ofte ycleped, cometh and endeth peyne.

   "Wel wot I, whil my lyf was in quyete,
   Er thow me slowe, I wolde have yeven hire;
   But now thi comynge is to me so swete
   That in this world I nothing so desire.   Tr 4.498-508

Troilus's desire for death as a blissful release can be compared to Christian martyrdom. In this secular world, however, this choice of death cannot be guaranteed. In (35), if Criseyde goes to the Greek camp, she will receive the service of noble knights, and contrast this favourably with Trojan boorishness.

(35) "Ye shal ek seen so many a lusty knyght
   Among the Grekis, ful of worthynesse,
   And ech of hem with herte, wit, and myght
   To plesen yow don al his bisynesse,
   That ye shul dullen of the rudenesse
   Of us *sely* Troians, but if routhe
   Remorde yow, or vertu of youre trouthe.   Tr 4.1485-91

From this description of the Greeks and the collocation of *sely* with *rudenesse*, it is obvious that the word means 'simple' and 'foolish.' However, these qualities are not reprehensible; rather they stem from goodness or at worst gullibility. Whatever the meaning may be, that is only one aspect of the whole semantic scope of the word.

(36) "In nouncerteyn ben alle youre observaunces,
   But it a *sely* fewe pointes be;
   Ne no thing asketh so gret attendaunces
   As doth youre lay, and that knowe alle ye;
   But that is nat the worste, as mote I the!

---

185   The examples of *sely* (33 b, c, d) are quoted from Brown (1952).

> But, tolde I yow the worste point, I leve,
> Al seyde I soth, ye wolden at me greve.   Tr 1.337-43

In the quotation we are told that the rules of love are uncertain except for a few 'trivial' points. Secular love is essentially relative since it is dependent on unstable human relationships. Ironically, this becomes true of Troilus himself later. Benson (1987) translates *sely* in this context as 'insignificant.' However, Troilus's choice of this word itself deserves notice. Since it is used in his discussion of love, it is possible that the contemporary hearer/reader perceived echoes of the other still extant senses—'happy,' 'innocent,' 'defenceless,' and 'trivial.'

The final two examples relate to Criseyde. In (37) Troilus and Criseyde have a chance to meet clandestinely through the mediation of Pandarus, and consummate their love.

(37) He hire in armes faste to hym hente.
And Pandarus with a ful good entente
Leyde hym to slepe, and seyde, "If ye be wise,
Swouneth nought now, lest more folk arise!"

What myghte or may the *sely* larke seye,
Whan that the sperhauk hath it in his foot?
I kan namore; but of thise ilke tweye—
To whom this tale sucre be or soot—
Though that I tarie a yer, somtyme I moot,
After myn auctour, tellen hire gladnesse,   Tr 3.1187-96

The narrator compares Criseyde in Troilus's arms to a lark held by a hawk in its talons. (Cf. 'To flee as the **Lark** does the sparhawk' Whiting (1967: L84).) Through the adjective *sely* Chaucer emphasises her defencelessness. However, we find here that Troilus is also terrified and disconcerted in the presence of Criseyde, or both of them may be put off by the close proximity of the ladies-in-waiting who are very close to their bedchamber. The collocation between *sely* and *larke* itself is open to alternative interpretations.

The most subtle example (38) describes the holistic image of Criseyde, who yields to Diomede and so betrays her former lover. This appears at the ending of the story where assuming the anger of the audience, the narrator tries to defend her.

(38) Ne me ne list this *sely* womman chyde
Forther than the storye wol devyse.
Hire name, allas, is publysshed so wide
That for hire gilt it oughte ynough suffise.
And if I myghte excuse hire any wise,
For she so sory was for hire untrouthe,
Iwis, I wolde excuse hire yet for routhe.   Tr 5.1093-9

In the ordinary way *sely* is more suitable as an epithet for one betrayed, not the betrayer. From this lexical point of view, the narrator treats both Troilus and Criseyde as betrayed. She appears to be presented as the victim of Fortune or society (as the instigator of war) or of the male sex in general, here in the persons of Troilus, Pandarus and Diomede. She survives many social trials and yet is induced to deviate from stereotyped images of courtly love and social morals. The second prism readers sympathetic to Criseyde are likely to regard the fact that the author, the first prism, treats her predilection positively as an indication of her human, if all-too human, nature. Such readers will take *sely* to carry the senses 'innocent,' 'good,' 'hapless,' and 'pitiable.' On the other hand, the critical second prism readers are likely to concentrate on the fact of her treachery rather than the motivation for it, and take this word negatively in the sense of 'foolish.' Indeed, even modern editors and translators vary in their interpretation of this word.

(39) a. Donaldson (1975), Warrington (1975): 'poor'; Howard (1976): 'hapless'; Fisher (1989) 'foolish'
b. Tatlock and MacKay (1912): 'unhappy'; Stanley-Wrench (1963): 'foolish'; Coghill (1971): 'hapless'; Windeatt (1998): 'poor'; Karita (1948): 'awaremu beki' (pitiable); Miyata (1979): 'aware na' (poor)

The word *sely* often denotes a multiplicity of feelings and motivations evoked by the amatory activities of the characters. Conventional morality would condemn their 'silliness,' while a liberal outlook would underline their intrinsic humanity. Hence a series of paradoxes arise. The characters described as *sely* reveal a complexity of personality traits of which the interpretation will vary according to the frame of mind of the second prism readers.

12.4. Ambiguity in *weldy*

The word *weldy* (Tr 2.636) is dealt with in terms of the metatext ((5) in Chapter 4) and speech presentation ((1) in Chapter 7). In this section we reexamine a paradigmatic problem of the choice of *weldy* and the meaning behind it taking into account other levels of ambiguity.

The word *weldy* appears at an important turning point in the story, i.e. where Chaucer departs from his original *Il Filostrato* to describe Troilus's triumphal return to Troy. Boccaccio merely has Troilus passing beneath the upper window, whereas Chaucer introduces a battle topos typical of romance. While in *Il Filostrato* we have a description of Criseyde catching sight of Troilus from the upper storey of her house and experiencing love at first sight, her emotion in Chaucer's version is more restrained.

(40) So lik a man of armes and a knyght
 He was to seen, fulfilled of heigh prowesse,
 For bothe he hadde a body and a myght
 To don that thing, as wel as hardynesse;
 And ek to seen hym in his gere hym dresse,
 So fressh, so yong, so *weldy* semed he,
 It was an heven upon hym for to see.   Tr 2.631-7

Observing the manly figure of Troilus in his victorious progress past her house, she reacts in precisely the way demanded of a courtly heroine. She is not precipitate in her amorous response. As can be seen in *The Romaunt of the Rose*, for example, she is at first defensive and cautious as the sense of *daunger* in her prompts. Gradually, however, as she receives proof of the man's true love and fidelity, she begins to acquiesce. *Pitee* and *Gentilesse* operate strongly within her, and finally she accepts his love. The love she gives in return, fired in the crucible of courtly idealism, is thus immovable. And so her worth as a courtly lady passes the test.

From the above quotation (40), we wish to look first at lines Tr 2.633-4 'For bothe he hadde a body and a myght / To don that thing.' We have already dealt with this from the point of view of ambiguity in cohesion (see (5) in Chapter 8). Critics disagree on how to determine the reference of *that thing*. Brewer and Brewer (1969) relate them to the action expected of an ideal knight in a romance, and notes 'presumably meaning deeds of arms.' Since Troilus is seen as 'So lik a man of armes and a knyght' in the immediately preceding lines, this interpretation may be seen to have credibility. (Cf. *OED* s.v. thing 4: 'That which is done or to be done; a doing, act, deed, transaction. c1000-.') Donaldson (1970), however, takes *thing* to have the sense 7c. given by *OED*: 'Used indefinitely to denote something which the speaker is not able or does not choose to particularize,' and thus regards the phrase as meaning 'performing a sexual act.' He admits no other interpretation. Which of these two widely different interpretations one favours depends of course on one's view of how Criseyde as a woman looks upon masculine attractiveness—i.e. as evidence of suitability for prowess in battle or in bed.

Incidentally, Criseyde seems to be sensitive to the sexual innuendo of *ryng* and *ruby*: 'Wel in the ryng than is the ruby set. / There were nevere two so wel ymet, / Whan ye ben his al hool as he is youre;' (Tr 2.585-7) 46 lines earlier. If this is the case, the sexual side of her nature does not emerge for the first time in the above quotation, but has been underlying for some time, constituting a layer of the contexts behind the phrase. If Criseyde sees Troilus for the first time and responds sexually to him, she deviates greatly from the moral obligations placed on her as a courtly lady, such as taking due note of the incompatibility between *daunger* and *pitee*, and the need for circumlocution.

Troilus is riding fully armed along the street. His freshness and youth are apparent to the Trojans and Criseyde among them. It is at this point that Chaucer uses *weldy* as one of the words describing the conquering hero. This word is subject to scribal variations. We have listed them in (6) in Chapter 4, but will repeat them below.

(41) weldy] worþi GgH3H5JRCx (Cx=Caxton's edition 1483)

The earliest α manuscripts and the intermediary γ manuscripts have *weldy*, while the latest β manuscripts (Gg, H3, H5, J, R) have *worþy*. Furthermore the early edition Cx based on the β manuscripts has *worþy*. In view of the general tendency of scribes 'to change special expressions to plain ones,' *weldy* must be seen as more 'special' than *worþy*. In terms of frequency, *worþy* is overwhelmingly more common than *weldy* in Chaucer: 184 occurrences as opposed to one (see Benson 1993). In addition, there is one occurrence each of *unweldy* and *unwelde*. Among modern editions only Root has *worþy*. These two words are likely to be associated with each other since they are similar in sounds ([w], [þ]/[d], [i]) and are both of two syllables and semantically close in that *weldy* means 'strong, vigorous' and *worþy* 'deserving a man of arms' or 'valiant.' As mentioned in Chapter 4, we would opt for *weldy*.

The *OED* gives examples of the verb 'wield' from OE, but takes the adjective 'wieldy' in Chaucer as the earliest instance.

(42)   *OED* s.v. wieldy 1. Capable of easily 'wielding' one's body or limbs, or a weapon, etc.; vigorous, active, agile, nimble. *Obs.* exc. *dial.* Tr 2.636 (earliest citatation) -1677

    Cf. *OED* s.v. unwieldy: †1. Of persons, the body, etc.: Lacking strength; weak, impotent; feeble, infirm. 1386 Chaucer MancP IX (H) 55 (earliest citation)-1659 [found in the Hengwrt manuscript]

The same is true of the *MED*, which takes this as the earliest instance in the sense '(a) Of a person: vigorous, agile.' As for modern editors, they take it in the sense 'vigorous' or 'active' except for Donaldson (1970). Troilus's wielding his limbs and arms is expected from a knight. This is plausible from Brewer and Brewer (1969)'s interpretation of 'to doon that thing' mentioned above. On the other hand, Donaldson (1979: 9) perceives a sexual implication here as he has done with 'to doon that thing': Troilus is a man who easily deals with women. However, this meaning is not textually explicit but restricted to this context and the perception of this particular woman, not of people in general. The departure of her viewpoint from the narrator's is hinted at in the verb *semed* (Tr 2.636) and the emotional utterance of 'It was an heven ...' (It was ecstatic [for her] to see ...) (Tr 2.637). The quotation above can be taken as an instance of free indirect speech, as seen in Chapter 7. Incidentally, although Donaldson suggests the sexual implication of *weldy*, he does not illustrate it with examples. On this point Hanna III (1971) refers to the sexual implication of the alliterative phrase 'welden a woman' in *The Awntyrs off Arthure at the Terne Wathelyn.* (43) gives an example of this.

(43)   Ho was þe worþiest wight þat eny welde wolde;
      Here gide was glorious and gay, of a gressegrene. 365-6
      (Ho=a lady lufsom of lote ledand a kniȝt 345)

This describes a sexually attractive woman leading a knight to Arthur. (44) is Hanna III's note of it.

(44)   In alliterative poetry the phrase *welden a woman* has a very specific sense not recognized by O.E.D., 'to have sexual knowledge of a woman.'

His note gives an instance of the interaction of sound and meaning, or what Leech (1969) calls 'chiming' to be discussed in Chapter 13. By means of the alliteration [w], *welde* and *worþiest wight* are encouraged to be semantically linked together.

In (45a—m) we have examples of *welde* having sexual implications. In addition to the alliterative archetype 'welde a woman' (j, m), we have variants such as 'welcum to welde' (d), 'wylle and welde' (d, e), 'wicked to welde' (h), and 'welde ... wolde' (i). Even in rhyming verses, we also have alliterative phrases such as 'welde ... wille' (b, c) and 'In wedlocke to welde' (g). Furthermore, 'þou schalt hir weld' (a) and 'welde hire at mi wille' (b) in rhyming verses have a pronoun *hir* with no alliteration, but since the pronouns indicate a woman, they are suggestive of the archetype 'welde a woman.' This also applies to 'welde his love at wille' (c).

(45)   a. Y wot þou louest par amour
        Ygerne þat swete flour, ...
        Y schal þe lese out of þi sorwe?'
        'Merlin' quaþ þo þe king
        'Help me now in þis þing
        And þou schalt haue whatow wilt ȝerne—

Do me to haue swete Ygerne.'...
'Now' quaþ Merlin 'þi pais þou held
And ar day *þou schalt hir weld*.*'

                              *Glos. *weld,* v. have at one's (sexual) will
                              (*Of Arthour and of Merlin* 2479-92 [Auchinleck MS])

b. I wolde it miht so befalle,
   That I al one scholde hem alle
   Supplante, and *welde hire at mi wille.*
                              (Gower *Confessio Amantis* ii 2409-11)

c. Bot he schop thanne a wonder wyle,
   How that he scholde hem best beguile,
   So that he mihte duelle stille
   At home and *welde his love at wille*:
                              (Gower *Confessio Amantis* iv 1825-8)

d. He sayde, 'ȝe ar *welcum to welde* as yow lykez
   þat here is; al is yowre awen, to haue at yowre *wylle*
   and welde.'
                              (*Sir Gawain and the Green Knight* 835-7)

e. ȝif ȝe luf not þat lyf þat ȝe lye nexte,
   Bifore alle þe wyȝez in þe world wounded in hert,
   Bot if ȝe haf a lemman, a leuer, þat yow lykez better, ...
   þe knyȝt sayde, 'Be sayn Jon,'
   And smeþely con he smyle,
   'In fayth I *welde* riȝt non,
   Ne non wil *welde* þe quile.'
                              (*Sir Gawain and the Green Knight* 1780-91)

f. Hir sone stode and hir byhelde:
   'Wele were him þat myght *þe welde!*'
                              (*Sir Eglamour of Artois* 1090-1 [Lincoln])

g. I truste hym so well, withouten drede,
   That he would neuer do that dede
   But yf he myght that lady wynne
   In wedlocke to welde, withouten synne;
                              (*The Squire of Low Degree* 367-70)

h. Wyues wille were ded wo,
   ȝef he is *wicked forte welde*;
   þat burst shal bete for hem bo,
                              (*The Harley Lyrics:* 2. 'The Three Foes of Man' 34-6)

i. Mosti ryden by Rybbesdale,
   wilde wymmen forte wale,
   ant *welde whuch ich wolde,*
   founde were þe feyrest on
   þat euer wes mad of blod ant bon,
   in boure best wiþ bolde.
                              (*The Harley Lyrics* 7. 'The Fair Maid of Ribblesdale' 1-6)

j. Than suld I waill ane full weill our all the wyd realme
   That suld my *womanheid weild* the lang winter nicht;
   And quhen I gottin had ane grome, ganest of uther,
   ȝaiþ and ȝing, in the ȝok ane ȝeir for to drawe,
           (Dunbar *The Tretis of the Tua Mariit Wemen and the Wedo* 76-9)

k. All the soueranis by assent assignet me hir,   (Hesione)
   ffor to wirke with *my wille*, & *weld as myn owne*;   (Telamon)
           (*The 'Best Hystoriale' of the Destruction of Troy* 1880-1)

l. And me, þat am mete & of more power
   þen hym þat þou hade and held for þi lorde,   (Helen)
   Wyuly to weld; & I the wed shall,
           (*The 'Best Hystoriale' of the Destruction of Troy* 3357-9)

m. "I wold yonder worthy weddit me hade,   (Medea)
   Bothe to burde & to bede blessid were I:
   So comly, so cleane to clippe vpon nightes,
   So hardy, so hynd in hall for to se,
   So luffly, so lykyng with lapping in armys;
   Well were that *woman might weld hym* for euer."   (Jason)
           (*The 'Best Hystoriale' of the Destruction of Troy* 472-7)

Of Arthure and Of Merlin is contained in the Auchinleck manuscript compiled around 1330. Example (45a) is worth attention since it is possible that Chaucer read this manuscript and that the expression is similar to the archetype above both in the form and the content. Merlin hears Uter's wish, and promises him to help him to deal with another man's wife as he wishes. This adulterous love results in the birth of Arthure. Furthermore Chaucer might have accessed the examples of *Confessio Amanits* (45b, c) and have been aware of the implications of the phrase. If our assumption of the intertexture regarding *welde* is right, it is not unnatural that the linguistic meaning of *welde* and its sexual implication overlap and thus are likely to produce ambiguity.

12.5. Ambiguity in *pite*

12.5.1. Pragmatic implications of *pite*

Words reflecting medieval ethical values such as *courtesie*, *gentil*, *kynde* and *grace* are comparatively stable when applied to people adherent to social/moral ideals, and yet when applied to people of realistic human status, are not necessarily clear as to their contextual values. Those values are subject to argument and relative. Chaucer's use of *pite* is a case in point. This section is devoted to examining his use of *pite* and semantically related terms (*routhe*, *mercy*, *misericorde*, *tendre*) with special reference to their pragmatic implications. Our particular attention is paid to *pite* descriptive of Criseyde's character.

Pite in ME has a multiple significance: a tender quality intrinsic to humanity, a moral as well as social virtue (a quality of a kind nature proper to a 'gentil man') and further a religious overtone, the tenderness and mercy of the Virgin Mary and even of God. The definition of *pite* in the *OED* is in (46).

(46) pity sb. [OF *pite* ad. L. *pietas*]
  †1. The quality of being pitiful; the disposition to mercy or compassion. *Obs.* a1225-1613
  2.a. A feeling or emotion of tenderness aroused by the suffering. c1290-
  3.a. transf. A ground or cause for pity, a regretable fact or circumstance. c1369-
  †4.a. A condition calling for pity. a1400-50-1622-77
  †5. Grief for one's own wrong-doing. 1483-1591
  6.a. Piety. 1340-1483

Chaucer is assumed to have been sensitive to this significance.[186] It has so far been examined by many scholars: Héraucourt (1939) regards *pite* as an important component of the medieval value system; Mathew (1948) and Mathew (1968) take up *pite* in relation to the knightly/chivalric virtue; Masui (1977) points out Chaucer's increasing interest in the heroine's tender or even vulnerable state of heart; Gray (1979) throws light on the pathos in Chaucer; Windeatt (1992) considers *pite* as building up one of the themes in Tr.

It should be noted, however, that Burnley (1979: 114, 170) is more sensitive to the perceptive processes regarding *pite,* as shown in (47).

(47) In Chaucer's world, too hard a heart is reprehensible. Simply for the process of perception to operate, a certain tenderness is required in the heart, *ymaginacioun,* or *celle fantastik.* But beyond the physiological processes of perception, the degree of hardness or tenderness of the heart becomes problematic, subject to argument, and relative. (114)

  In the *gentil* man, then, we have the spectacle of a moral ideal insecurely founded and perpetually poised on the edge of chaos. The tyrant and the churl, the saint, the philosopher and the just king were all in their own ways static and invariable symbols of moral good or evil according to the estimation of one ethical system or another, but the *gentil* man was a dynamic symbol poised between the tyrant and the philosopher, and as much closer to human nature as it was ordinarily experienced. (170)

In his view, excessive sentimentality and piety were widespread in the fourteenth century as evidenced by the love of pathos in literature (romance, lyrics, religious devotional writings), the courtly idealism—*gentilesse,* affective ethics, religious mysticism, etc.

Here, *pite* is not an absolute value, but likely to be regarded positively or negatively according to whether its emotion is in accord with reason. On this point, Gower says, as shown in (48).

(48) Bot *Pite*, hou so that it wende,
  Maketh the god merciable,
  If ther be cause resonable
  Why that a king schal be *pitous.*
  Bot elles, if he be doubtous

---

186 The situations in which *pite* is involved are classified roughly into the following pairs: i. God / Mary—human (e.g. ParsT); ii. king—people (e.g. KnT, Gower *Confessio Amantis* vii.); iii. judge—criminals (e.g. Rotuli Parliamentorum); iv. courtly lady—knight in a great pang for his love of her (e.g. Tr); v. parent—child (e.g. MLT, PhyT); vi. friend—friend (e.g. Tr); vii. audience/reader—hero/heroine going through varieties of predicaments in the story. Here the left hand element of the pair shows a grantor of pity and its right hand element shows a receiver of it.

> To slen in cause of rihtwisnesse,
> It mai be said no *Pitousnesse*,
> Bot it 'is Pusillamite,
> Which every Prince scholde flee.
> For if *Pite* mesure excede,
> Kinghode may noght wel procede
> To do justice upon the riht: *Confessio Amantis* vii 3520-31

The ambivalent features of *pite* go in parallel with the relative features of the macrostructure (theme, characterisation, plot) in Tr, which is demonstrated in Chapter 6. This relativity induces the first and second prisms to operate with a rise of pragmatic ambiguity.

Pite and its similar words are shown in (49).

(49) a. Frequency of *pite* and its similar words

	CT	BD	HF	Anel	PF	Bo	LGW	SHP	Ast	Rom	Tr
pite	52	5	5	0	0	8	17	24	0	20/2	13
pitous	33	2	0	1	0	1	2	2	0	8/3	12
pitously	23	1	0	1	0	1	4	2	0	2/1	20
routhe	19	5	5	5	1	0	15	0	0	1/1	30
routheles	1	0	0	1	0	0	0	0	0	0/0	1
rewe	16	0	1	3	0	0	4	3	0	4/0	23
reweful	2	0	0	0	0	0	0	0	0	0/0	0
rewefully	0	0	0	0	0	0	0	0	0	0/0	3
mercy	74	6	2	0	1	0	9	24	0	9/0	31
merciful	1	0	0	0	0	0	0	0	0	1/0	0
merciable	4	0	0	0	0	0	4	2	0	0/0	0
misericorde	13	0	0	0	0	1	0	2	0	1/0	1
compassioun	9	0	0	0	0	1	4	2	0	0/0	3
tendre	22	0	0	0	0	1	2	1	1	8/4	5
tendrely	11	0	0	1	0	0	6	1	0	3/1	6
tendrenesse	1	0	0	0	0	0	1	0	0	0/0	1

N.B.:   *The numbers to the right of the slash in Rom are from Fragment A only.*

232 Part IV: Ambiguity in linguistic domains

(49) b. Frequency of *pite* and its similar words in CT

	GP	KnT	MilT	RvT	CkT	MLT	WBT	FrT	SumT	ClT	MerT
pite	0	8	0	0	0	6	0	0	1	2	4
pitous	1	6	0	0	0	4	0	0	0	6	0
pitously	0	5	0	0	0	4	1	1	0	1	1
routhe	0	3	0	1	0	4	0	0	0	2	1
routheles	0	0	0	0	0	1	0	0	0	0	0
rewe	0	4	3	0	0	2	0	0	0	1	2
reweful	0	1	0	0	0	1	0	0	0	0	0
rewefully	0	0	0	0	0	0	0	0	0	0	0
mercy	0	12	1	0	0	5	2	0	1	1	3
merciful	0	0	0	0	0	1	0	0	0	0	0
merciable	0	0	0	0	0	0	0	0	0	0	0
misericorde	0	0	0	0	0	0	0	0	1	0	0
compassioun	0	2	0	0	0	1	0	0	0	0	0
tendre	2	1	0	0	0	1	0	0	0	6	7
tendrely	0	2	0	0	0	1	0	0	1	5	0
tendrenesse	0	0	0	0	0	1	0	0	0	0	0

	SqT	FranT	PhyT	PardT	ShipT	PrT	Thop	Mel	MkT	NPT	SNT
pite	1	5	3	1	0	1	0	5	2	0	2
pitous	3	2	2	2	0	1	1	0	2	1	1
pitously	4	2	0	2	0	1	0	0	1	0	0
routhe	1	5	1	0	1	0	0	0	0	0	0
routheles	0	0	0	0	0	0	0	0	0	0	0
rewe	0	1	0	0	0	0	0	0	0	1	0
reweful	0	0	0	0	0	0	0	0	0	0	0
rewefully	0	0	0	0	0	0	0	0	0	0	0
mercy	0	2	1	0	1	3	0	12	0	1	2
merciful	0	0	0	0	0	0	0	0	0	0	0
merciable	0	1	0	0	0	1	0	2	0	0	0
misericorde	0	0	0	0	0	0	0	1	0	0	0
compassioun	2	2	0	0	0	0	0	0	1	0	0
tendre	0	0	0	1	0	1	0	0	0	0	0
tendrely	1	0	0	0	0	0	0	0	0	0	0
tendrenesse	0	0	0	0	0	0	0	0	0	0	0

12. Ambiguity in words

	CYT	MancT	ParsT
pite	1	0	10
pitous	0	0	1
pitously	0	0	0
routhe	0	0	0
routheles	0	0	0
rewe	2	0	0
reweful	0	0	0
rewefully	0	0	0
mercy	2	0	25
merciful	0	0	0
merciable	0	0	0
misericorde	0	0	11
compassioun	0	0	1
tendre	0	1	2
tendrely	0	1	0
tendrenesse	0	0	0

What is to be noted in (50) below is that instances of *pite* are presented not simply by the narrator but through the characters or more specifically their subjective points of view. Those characters are often forced to cope with fluctuating situations. As is discussed below, *pite* tends to be used in contexts where jusfititfcation is being offered for the potentially reprehensible actions of the characters. The abbreviations are as follows: B=Book Number, N=Narrator, T=Troilus, C=Criseyde, P=Pandarus, D=Diomede, H=Helen, Ca=Calkas.

(50) Frequency of *pite* and its similar words in Tr according to characters

	pitee, piete					pitous, piteous					pitously/ich				
B	1	2	3	4	5	1	2	3	4	5	1	2	3	4	5
N	1	1	0	4	1	2	0	2	3	2	0	2	0	6	7
T	1	0	0	0	0	1	0	0	1	1	0	0	0	0	2
C	0	1	1	1	1	0	0	0	0	0	0	0	0	1	0
P	1	0	0	0	0	0	0	0	0	0	0	1	0	0	0
D	0	0	0	0	0	0	0	0	0	0	0	0	0	0	1
H	0	0	0	0	0	0	0	0	0	0	0	0	0	0	0
Ca	0	0	0	0	0	0	0	0	0	0	0	0	0	0	0

	mercy					misericorde					comapssioun				
B	1	2	3	4	5	1	2	3	4	5	1	2	3	4	5
N	1	1	0	0	4	0	0	0	0	0	2	0	0	0	0
T	2	0	6	2	1	0	0	0	0	0	0	0	1	0	0
C	0	3	1	4	0	0	0	1	0	0	0	0	0	0	0
P	1	1	0	2	0	0	0	0	0	0	0	0	0	0	0
D	0	0	0	0	2	0	0	0	0	0	0	0	0	0	0
H	0	0	0	0	0	0	0	0	0	0	0	0	0	0	0
Ca	0	0	0	0	0	0	0	0	0	0	0	0	0	0	0

	routhe					routheles					rewe				
B	1	2	3	4	5	1	2	3	4	5	1	2	3	4	5
N	1	3	0	0	3	0	0	0	0	0	0	1	1	2	3
T	0	1	1	3	2	0	0	0	0	0	2	0	1	3	1
C	0	2	0	3	1	0	0	0	0	0	0	1	1	2	2
P	1	7	2	0	0	0	1	0	0	0	0	0	0	0	0
D	0	0	0	0	0	0	0	0	0	0	0	0	0	0	0
H	0	0	0	0	0	0	0	0	0	0	0	1	0	0	0
Ca	0	0	0	0	0	0	0	0	0	0	0	0	0	2	0

	rewefully					tendre					tendrely				
B	1	2	3	4	5	1	2	3	4	5	1	2	3	4	5
N	0	0	1	1	1	0	0	0	0	2	1	0	0	3	2
T	0	0	0	0	0	0	0	0	0	0	0	0	0	0	0
C	0	0	0	0	0	0	0	0	1	0	0	0	0	0	0
P	0	0	0	0	0	0	1	1	0	0	0	0	0	0	0
D	0	0	0	0	0	0	0	0	0	0	0	0	0	0	0
H	0	0	0	0	0	0	0	0	0	0	0	0	0	0	0
Ca	0	0	0	0	0	0	0	0	0	0	0	0	0	0	0

	tendrenesse				
B	1	2	3	4	5
N	0	0	0	0	0
T	0	0	0	0	1
C	0	0	0	0	0
P	0	0	0	0	0
D	0	0	0	0	0
H	0	0	0	0	0
Ca	0	0	0	0	0

In *Troilus and Criseyde*, even the narrator's point of view is not omnipresent; owing to his involvement with the suffering lovers, more often than not it tends towards the subjective.

The 'degree of hardness or tenderness of the heart' becomes problematic, and easily subject to the varying assessments of the characters', the narrator's, and perhaps more importantly the second prism readers' varying assessments. Previous scholarship has not addressed on this problem.

12.5.2. Criseyde's *pite*: internal history of her betrayal

Troilus and Criseyde is basically adapted from Boccaccio's *Il Filostrato*. As with this original, one of the focal points in Chaucer's work, perhaps the most significant one, is Criseyde's betrayal of Troilus. However, it should be noted that Chaucer reinterprets what he has inherited and develops it a great deal.

Chaucer transforms Boccaccio's sensually oriented Criseida into a medieval heorine by placing emphasis on courtly idealism, her tender circumspection, her *gentilesse*, her moral analysis in her own decision-making, her courtly manner, etc. In so doing, he brings her *pite* to our special notice.

It is true that Boccaccio refers to Criseida's *pieta/pietosa*, but the concept of *pite* is much intensified by Chaucer, as shown in (51).

(51) Corresponding terms in Tr and the Fil and Chaucer's extension of the concept of *pite*
[Tr corresponds to the Fil]

Fil	Tr
pio (1.5.6.)	pyte (1.23), compassioun (1.50)
pietoso (1.6.4.)	*pitous (1.111)
mercè (1.12.8)	mercy (1.112)
pietoso (1.13.1.)	pitous (1.113)
pietà (1.43.6.)	*rewe (1.460)
pietade (2.4.1.)	routhe (1.582)
mercede (2.92.2)	*routhe (2.1007)
pietosa (2.104.1)	pitousli gan *mercy for to crye (2.1076)
pietà (4.28.1)	for piete of herte (4.246)
pietosa allegrezza (4.80.6)	pitous ioie (4.683)
pietà (4.109.3)	tendrely (4.950)
pietà (6.16.2)	mercy (5.888)

[Tr develops from the Fil]
pitee: *1.522, *899; *2.655; 3.1033 (piete); 4.368, 847; *5.824, 1598 (pietee), etc.
pitous: 4.1499; 5.555, etc.
pitously: 4.1174, 1438; 5.216, 522, 1346, *1424, 1584, etc.
mercy: *3.1282, *1356; 4.1149, 1231, *1500, 1604; *5.168, 591, *1011, 1861, 1867, 1868, etc.
misericorde: *3.1177
compassioun: 1.467; 3.403
routhe: *2.349, *664, *1280, *1371, *1375; 3.895, 1511; *4.1476, *1490, *1673; *5.1000, 1099, *1587, etc.
rewe: 4.104, 738, 1176, 1531, *1671; 5.560, 707, etc.

N.B.: *The examples marked with an asterisk are used in reference to Criseyde.*

It is not too much to say that the first prism poet endeavours to regard what one might call external fact—Criseyde's betrayal—as an internal(ised) and therefore reinterpretable subject—her *pite*. In terms of a paradigmatic set of words indicative of 'betrayal,' he seems to have succeeded in avoiding such explicit words as *unconstant, unstedefast, deceivable, trecherie, newfongilnes,* and *lecherous*. In this semantic field, *pite* is taken as one of the most equivocal words, easily given a positive value. For further details of this, see (10) in Section 12.2.3. As discussed later, her betrayal is not dealt with as an instance of betrayal, but reinterpreted as an internal process leading to it, or a question of the workings of *pite*.

12.5.3. Ambiguity in Criseyde's *pite*

In the story it should be noted that Criseyde's *pite* comes to our attention at crucial moments in the story: when she is likely to shift her feelings, encouraged by Pandarus to sympathise with Troilus pining for her love; when she and Troilus cosummate their love; [at the denoument of the story] when she yields to Diomede, while still having Troilus in her thoughts; when she responds to Troilus, after betraying him.

Troilus, who at first scorned love, is punished by the god of love, and falls in with her at first sight. He suffers greatly from the consequent pangs, and when Pandarus discovers that Criseyde is the object of Troilus's affections, he approves. She is possessed of many virtues, and it therefore follows that *pite* must be among them, as can be seen from (52) below.

(52) "And also thynk, and therwith glade the,
That sith thy lady vertuous is al,
So foloweth it that there is som *pitee*
Amonges alle thise other in general;
And forthi se that thow, in special,
Requere naught that is ayeyns hyre name;
For vertue streccheth naught hymself to shame. Tr 1.897-903

Incidentally, the corresponding part of *Il Filostrato* is given in (53).

(53) Solo una cosa alquanto a te molesta
Ha mia cugina in sè oltre alle dette,
Che ella è più che altra donna onesta,
E più d' amore ha le cose dispette: *Il Filostrato* 2.23.1-4
("Only one trait, somewhat troublesome to thee, hath my cousin
beyond those mentioned, that she is more virtuous than other
ladies, and holdeth matters of love more in contempt.)

Pandaro suggests that Criseida in her widowhood has returned to a kind of virginity and therefore guards her honour ("virtue"). Pandarus, on the other hand, refers to a quite different kind of "virtues," the good human qualities of which Criseyde possess many. Among these qualities *pite*, ultimately leading to surrender, must surely be found.

Pite, Chaucer's addition to the Fil, accords with the courtly idealism found in Rom, and also with moral/Christian doctrines.[187] In Chaucer the word *pite* is present

---

187 Cf. The poet goes through the allegorical conflict between *Pite* and *Daungere* to approach the

especially in documentary literature such as Bo, Mel and ParsT. (See the frequency of this word in (49).) In a semi-religious courtly context as here, it seems no wonder that the secular sense 'pity' and the religious sense 'piety' should be intermingled. To encourage Troilus to get her love, Pandarus seems to have been aware of and exploited the positive side of *pite* in the courtly/religious register.[188]

However, there seems to arise a subtle ambiguity here, which while never destroying the integrity of the above valuation of *pite*, hints at other perspectives and registers. Taking full account of the latter half of his speech (Tr 1.901-3) as Gordon (1970) suggests, we are encouraged to view the above *pite* from a pragmatic and non-courtly perspective. In the view of Pandarus, Criseyde is assumed to be virtuous if her susceptibility to *pite* does not cause a 'shame' (scandal), and not if it does. Here, his assumption of virtue seems to imply criticism. There seems to arise ambiguity according to how the second prism readers evaluate it.

The mixture of the courtly and pragmatic perspectives is also present in his later use of *pite*. In order to persuade Criseyde to be sympathetic towards Troilus, he states as in (54).

(54) "Wo worth the faire gemme vertulees!
 Wo worth that herbe also that dooth no boote!
 Wo worth that beaute that is *routheles*!
 Wo worth that wight that tret ech vndir foote!

 Rose.
 And while I was in this torment,
 Were come of grace, by God sent,
 Fraunchise, and with hir *Pite*.
 Fulfild the bothen of bounte,
 They go to *Daunger* anoon-right
 To further me with all her myght,   Rom 3499-504

188 Davies (1963): *Medieval English Lyrics*
 Why have ye no *reuthe* on my child?
 Have *reuthe* on me, ful of murning.
 Taket down on Rode my derworthy child,
 Or prek me on Rode with my derling.   44 Mary suffers with her son 1-4

 Jesu, I pray thee forsake nat me,
 Thogh I of sin gilty be:
 For that thef that henge thee by,
 Redily thou yaf him thy *mercy*.

 Jesu, that art so corteisly,
 Make me bold on thee to cry:
 For wel I wot, without drede,
 Thy *mercy* is more than my misdede.   45 A devout prayer of the Passion 133-40

 Francis (1987), *The Book of Vices and Virtues,* The degrees of mercy 191:
 For alle we beþ membres of on body, þat is to seie þe holi chirche, bi grace, and þat on membre haþ kyndeliche *rewþe* on þat oþer. After, we ben alle bouȝt be on prys, þat is bi þe precious blod of Ihesu Crist þat he schedde on þe crosse for to bien vs from þe deþ wiþ-wouten ende. Whan Goddes sone þat was so *pitous* and so *merciable* aȝens vs, wel schulde haue *pite* and *rewþe* eche of vs oþer, and helpe and socoure eche of vs oþer.

> And ye, that ben of beaute crop and roote,
> If therwithal in yow ther be *no routhe*,
> Than is it harm ye lyuen, by my trouthe!   Tr 2.344-50

These four lines have the effect of a set of aphorisms. As is typical of Pandarus, his reference to *routheles* is made in moralistic/generalised terms. And yet from a pragmatic point of view, what he expresses as universal truths are then particularised as threatening devices with a view to forcing her to accept Troilus. Note that the above aphorisms are juxtaposed with the specific statement in the second person *ye/yow*. Furthermore, he repeats his reference to his own and Troilus's possible death due to her lack of mercy (Tr 2.320, Tr 2.322, Tr 2.323, Tr 2.327, Tr 2.335, Tr 2.338, Tr 2.351) and to her cruelty (Tr 2.337, Tr 2.385, Tr 2.399).

In (55), where Pandarus gives Troilus instructions on how to achieve his love, he combines the two recommended strategies even more boldly.

(55) And god toforn, yet shal I shape it so,
 That thow shalt come into a certeyn *place*,
 There as thow mayst thiself hire preye of *grace*.

 "And certeynly – I noot if thow it woost,
 But tho that ben expert in loue it seye—
 It is oon of the thynges forthereth most,
 A man to han a layser forto preye,
 And siker place his wo forto bywreye;
 For in good herte it mot *som routhe* impresse,[189]
 To here and see the giltlees in distresse.

 "Peraunter thynkestow: though it be so,
 That Kynde wolde don hire to bygynne
 To haue *a manere routhe* upon my woo,
 Seyth Daunger, 'nay, thow shalt me neuere wynne!'
 So reulith hire hir hertes gost withinne,
 That though she bende, yeet she stant on roote;
 What in effect is this unto my boote?   Tr 2.1363-79

We have here a representative instance of the words with which *pite*—here represented by *routhe*—is related in terms of synonymy (*grace, Kynde*), antonymy (*Daunger*), and hyponymy (*herte, impresse*), and thus tends to collocate. In this semantic field, *routhe* is most probably given a positive value. However, it is also true that it can bear a pragmatic sense. Among others, the following rhyme-pair is conspicuous in its effect: the courtly and semi-religious *grace* and the pragmatically oriented *place* (a safe 'place' for his coming union with Criseyde) are semantically as well as phonetically linked, and thus the suggestion of their fusion is strengthened. For a narrowing/localised implication of 'grace,' see Wetherbee (1984: 77-8). In this context, more or less

---

189 The word *routhe* (< ON *hrygg* 'sorrow,' 'penitence') is defined, according to the *OED*, as follows: pitifulness 1175-; remorse 1200-; sorrow 1205-; †matter of occasion of sorrow or repent 1200-1626. This word is seldom used in religious expository writings as shown in (49) in Chapter 12. It seems to be endowed with secular implications. It should be noted that this word and its derivatives are used in a courtly love context and that they are frequently used in *Troilus and Criseyde*.

the same is true of her *routhe*. We can find a near counterpart in the MerT. In (56) May, taking on the lovesick Damyan, her husband Januarie's squire falling in love with her, decides to accept him. See also (2) in Chapter 5 above.

(56) But sooth is this, how that this fresshe May
 Hath take swich impression that day
 Of *pitee* of this sike Damyan ...
 Lo, *pitee* renneth soone in gentil herte!
  Heere may ye se how excellent franchise
 In wommen is, whan they hem narwe avyse.
 Som tyrant is, as ther be many oon
 That hath an herte as hard as any stoon,
 Which wolde han lat hym sterven in the *place*
 Wel rather than han graunted hym hire *grace*, ...
  This gentil May, fulfilled of *pitee*,
 Right of hire hand a lettre made she,
 In which she graunteth hym hire verray *grace*.
 Ther lakketh noght oonly but day and *place*
 Wher that she myghte unto his lust suffise, MerT IV (E) 1977-99

The chiming of rhyme words (*place-grace* 1991-2, 1997-8), synonymy (*gentil, franchise*), antonymy (*tyrant, hard, crueel, pryde*), hyponymy (*herte*), and collocation (*impression...Of pitee*) are instanced here, which are similar to those of Pandarus. Comparing various texts by Chaucer, we can see all the more readily that *pite* as used by Pandarus does not have its general meaning but a specialised one which suits his particular purpose.

Now let us look at how Criseyde uses *pite*. Her response to the sight of Troilus riding triumphantly into town can be seen from the passages below.

(57) Criseÿda gan al his chere aspien,
 And leet it so softe in hire herte synke,
 That to hireself she seyde, "who yaf me drynke?"

 For of hire owen thought she wex al reed,
 Remembryng hire right thus, "Lo this is he
 Which that myn uncle swerith he moot be deed,
 But I on hym have *mercy and pitee*." [190]
 And with that thought, for pure ashamed, she
 Gan in hire hed to pulle, and that as faste,
 While he and al the peple forby paste,

 And gan to caste and rollen up and down
 Withinne hire thought his excellent prowesse,
 And his estat, and also his renown,
 His wit, his shap, and ek his gentilesse;

---

[190] The word *mercy* (< F *merci*, L *mercedem* 'reward') is religiously defined as sympathy shown to those persons involved in situations preventing them from requesting *pite* for themselves, or to those persons atoning for their sins. Here in the courtly context the senses of 'reward' or 'permission' come to the fore. The phrase 'have merci/pite on' is regarded as calqued on French. This seems to be effective for producing such a formalistic tone as if obeying to the French courtly culture. Cf. Troilus shows his thanks to Criseyde with the word *mercy*: 'Heere may men seen that *mercy* passeth right' (Tr 3.1282).

> But moost hire favour was, for his distresse
> Was al for hire, and thoughte it was a *routhe*
> To sleen swich oon, if that he mente trouthe.
>
> Now myghte som envious jangle thus:
> "This was a sodeyn love; how myght it be
> That she so lightly loved Troilus
> Right for the firste syghte, ye, parde?"
> Now whoso seith so, mote he nevere ythe!
> For every thing a gynnyng hath it nede
> Er al be wrought, withowten any drede.
>
> For I sey nought that she so sodeynly
> Yaf hym hire love, but that she gan enclyne
> To like hym first, and I have told yow whi;
> And after that his manhod and his pyne
> Made love withinne hire for to myne,
> For which by proces and by good servyse
> He gat hire love, and in no sodeyn wyse.   Tr 2.649-79

The corresponding part of *Il Filostrato* is given below.

(58) E sì subitamente presa fue,
    Che sopra ogni altro bene lui disia,   *Il Filostrato* 2.83.5-6
    (And so suddenly was she captivated that she desired him above every other good)

Faced with the impetuous concupiscence of Boccaccio's Criseida, Chaucer seeks to reinterpret this aspect; indeed he tones it down by courtly means to such an extent that his own heroine appears slow to change her affections. He throws light on her moralised analysis, tender circumspection, and courtly manner. Since pity (*mercy and pite* Tr 2.654, *routhe* Tr 2.969) is seen here to precede love, it would seem that Criseyde's *pite* serves as a deterrent to her falling in love with Troilus straight away, in the manner of her Boccaccion model.

However, it seems that the context of her *pite* is not completely limited to the courtly perspective. When the reader is careful and a little sceptical of her affective response to Troilus, he or she is likely to be sensitive to parts of the passage which hint at a non-courtly and earthier side to her response.

First, how should we interpret the phrase 'who yaf me drynke?' (Tr 2.651), an aside which Criseyde utters, immediately after Troilus's manly appearance has made its impression on her? There is a disagreement between editors/critics as to how to interpret the phrase. Barney (Benson 1987: 1033), while conscious of its metaphorical implication, tends to favour the literal sense 'any intoxicating beverage.' As a result, he seems to stress that the movement of her affections towards Troilus has only just begun, if at all. This interpretation accords with the above mentioned courtly context. On the other hand, Gordon (1970: 81), more sceptical of her response, stresses not unreasonably a metaphorical sense of the phrase, and takes it as a possible indication of her instantaneous love for him, a good counterpart of which is found, for instance, in the Prologue to WBT ('a manere love-drynke' III (D) 754). If she is right, Criseyde's reference to *pite*, which follows love rather than precedes it, is likely to be a justification for her over-anxious ardour.

Second, more or less the same is true of the next line 'of hire owen thought she wex al reed' (Tr 2.652). Apart from the author, Criseyde alone knows the contents of her mind. The redness of her cheeks of course indicates a sense of shame, though it is not clear precisely what thoughts have provoked this. (Cf. 'And of his owene thought he wax al reed.' ShipT VII 111.) According to which view (Benson/Gordon) we emphasise, the meaning of the above line will be different.

Thirdly, the narrator sheds light on the state of her heart, immediately before she is moved to pity Troilus:

(59) But moost hire favour, was for his distresse
    Was al for hire, and thoughte it was a *routhe*
    To sleen swich oon, if that he mente trouthe.   Tr 2.663-5

In the opinion of the narrator, perhaps at this point implying some criticism of her, she does not place so much emphasis on her rational thoughts towards Troilus as on her emotions towards him.

Thus, it is left to the second prism readers to decide whether *pite*, with its literal force, is endowed with a positive value or taken as a synonym or a euphemism for sensual love.

This ambiguity is reinforced by the discourse ambiguity running through the two stanzas that follow (Tr 2.666-79). With reference to the narrator's parenthetical remark on her 'not sodeyn' love, Brewer and Brewer (1969: 112), sympathetic towards Criseyde, state that it is 'not apparently ironical.' On the other hand, Donaldson (1970: 66) and Gordon (1970: 81-2)—more sceptical and critical readers of her response—stress its ironical effect. Which of the two we choose depends on our attitude to the character of Criseyde as a whole.

Let us look at another instance of Criseyde's use of *pite*. Her *pite* comes to our notice immediately before she and Troilus consummate their love. On the night in question, Toilus is taken to her bedroom where he begs forgiveness for any offence his words may have caused. As can be seen, she employs the word *misericorde* when bestowing her pardon.

(60) And seyde, "allas, upon my sorwes sike
    Have *mercy*, swete herte myn, Criseyde!
    And if that in tho wordes that I seyde
    Be any wrong, I wol no more trespace.
    Doth what yow list, I am al in youre grace."

    And she answerde, "of gilt *misericorde*!
    That is to seyn, that I foryeve al this;   Tr 3.1172-8

Burnley (1979: 107) says: '*Misericorde* is entirely limited, but for a single occurrence, to the religious situation: devotional texts or the speech of ecclesiastics....' *Misericorde* [< OF *misericorde*, L *misericordia*] is used with its stress on the guilt of the penitent. As shown in (49) above, this word is almost entirely limited to ParsT in Chaucer. (Parson gives a full account of *misericorde* as a virtue to remedy avarice X (I) 805, 806, 807, 809, etc.) The only exception is the above example. This is unique to Chaucer, and he may have introduced it to underline the semi-religious aspects of the courtly world he has created.

However, we must remember that some eighty lines before we have been told that as an intermediary between Troilus and Criseyde, Pandarus provides considerable physical assistance in getting the relationship under way: he goes so far as to undress Troilus and put him into her bed (Tr 3.1097-9). We have thus been given overtly sexual context in which we are prompted to question the validity of her *misericorde*. This bedroom scene is reminiscent of the fabliau in its sensuality (MilT, RvT, MerT).[191] The word *misericorde*, when applied to the courtly love context, assumes an ethical/religious status, and yet in realistic terms seems to work as a linguistic veil with which she can justify and promote her morally reprehensible act of love.

Troilus and Criseyde do not remain stable in their love for long. In Books 4 and 5, the so-called descending scenes, we find that the love between them is imperilled owing to the Trojan parliamentary determination that she should go to the Greek camp in exchange for Trojan prisoners. In these Books, the question of what Criseyde is expected to be as a courtly heroine and what she really is will be more poignantly counterbalanced. We are encouraged to question the validity of her *pite* further.

The narrator's references to *pite* are most frequent in these Books, as shown in (50). His use of this word is markedly objective (*OED* s.v. pity 3, 4), and there the second prism readers are encouraged to be involved with and sympathetic towards the lovers who are suffering because of their imminent separation. The pathos in the story is greatly intensified. A few examples illustrate this.

(61) He (i.e. Pandarus) stood this woful Troilus byforn,
    And on his *pitous* face he gan byholden.   Tr 4.360-1

    And to Pandare, his owene brother deere,
    "For love of god," ful *pitously* he sayde,   Tr 5.521-2

    Ful *rewfully* she loked upon Troie,
    Biheld the toures heigh and ek the halles;   Tr 5.729-30

Our primary concern, however, is with the subjective sense of this word (*OED* s.v. pity 2), by which the narrator describes her *pite*. In Book 5, where Diomede makes his appearance, the poet comes at last to the point when he has to bring about Criseyde's betrayal of Troilus, which he has foretold to the audience (Tr 1.56). So long as he conforms to the inherited basic plot and is sympathetic towards both Criseyde and Troilus, the story is likely to develop inconsistencies and fail to make progress. It is assumed that the poet has been looking for the very moment when he can detach from her, and thus restructure the plot. At this transitional moment, perhaps the most significant one in the story, he throws her *pite* into bold relief.

---

191 Cf. Green (1979: 121, 122):
    ... courtly poets were not simply preoccupied with a romantic idealisation of love, but were also aware of elements of make believe in that ideal ...; in the crucial bedroom scenes of the third fitt the English romance *Sir Gawain* is moving through, or disturbingly close to, fabliau country.
    Fewster (1987: 142) is in the same vein: 'some ambivalence by evoking a fabliauesque reductivism.' See ambiguity due to intertextuality in Chapter 5.

The context is this. Immediately before Criseyde yields to Diomede, the narrator—here perhaps Chaucer the poet—interpolates the Gestalt-descriptions of the three main characters: first Diomede, who is on hand and so in a position to ensnare her; last Troilus, who is nearly made to release his hold on her; in between, Criseyde, as if she were in a state of tension between the two. The interpolation here, an addition of Chaucer's to *Il Filostrato*, seems to indicate his sympathy with Criseyde, since it helps to delay her yielding to Diomede. By contrast, Boccaccio embarks directly upon Criseida's betrayal of Troilo (6.11.2).

The description of Criseyde consists of two parts: one is of her beauty and feminine appearance (*effictio*) and the other of her internal properties, centering upon her tender heart (*notatio*). It is notable that the tender heart is described *in crescendo* as shown in (62).

(62) She sobre was, ek symple, and wys withal,
　　The best ynorisshed ek that myghte be,
　　And goodly of hire speche in general,
　　Charitable, estatlich, lusty, fre;
　　Ne nevere mo ne lakked hire *pite*;
　　Tendre-herted, slydynge of corage;
　　But trewely, I kan nat telle hire age.　　　　Tr 5.820-6

The narrator pays attention first to her abundant generosity (*charitable, fre*), next, to her abundant sympathy (*pite, tendre-herted*), and lastly to her unstable affections (*slydynge of corage*). These qualities are central to a courtly romance heroine, except of course the last 'slydynge ....' We have pointed out in the example (10) above that the *pite* here works in a double-edged way: it can be both a virtue and a deadly vice. If Criseyde is too tender-hearted and receptive, she is in danger of destroying the essence of her courtly personality. Because of the excessive *pite*, we might say, she disregarded *mesure* (Gower *Confessio Amantis* vii 309), as shown in LGW with Dido (1237, 1255, 1257), in CT with the Prioresse (I (A) 142-5, 150) and on a more extensive scale, with May in the MerT (IV (E) 1977-89).[192]

Furthermore, medieval women, occupying in general an unstable position, are assumed to be much affected when exposed to external forces as she is, and in order to withstand these forces, to be required to be capable of adjusting or rather accommodating their emotions towards them. From the feminine perspective, the gentle pliancy of women is not so much a moral weakness as possible wisdom. If this is right, the first prism poet here seems to have gone beyond a medieval stereotyped view of a woman—a woman remaining faithful at all times and in all places. This perspective must have been new in the time of Chaucer, and therefore have been understood as the more creative and imaginative.[193]

Criseyde's *pite*, which has so far been bestowed upon Troilus, is bestowed upon Diomede when she encounters him. In responding to his advances she says:

192　Cf. Lydgate, Troy Book II 4760-2 (this part corresponds to Tr 5.824-5):
　　And, as seiþ Guydo, in love *variable*—
　　Of *tendre herte* and *vnste[d]fastnes*
　　He hire accuseth, and *newfongilnes*.
193　Cf. Saito (1993: 367).

(63) If that I sholde of any Grek han *routhe*,
It sholde be youreselven, by my trouthe!   Tr 5.1000-1

She realises that Diomede is suffering love's pangs on her account and so cannot refuse him. This *pite* can of course act as a precursor to the fulfilment of love. With regard to the rhyme pair—*trouthe/routhe*, Elliott (1974: 113) says: 'This is no mere mechanical convenience ... for the two concepts had close psychological association for Chaucer.' By her *routhe* for Diomede, however, she breaks her *trouthe* to Troilus. We have a similar instance in 5.1586-7. In general terms, every time she copes with external forces, whether Troilus's suffering for her love or that of Diomede, she seems to be seriously sympathetic and receptive. Not in spite of this but because of it, she turns out in the long run to be inconsistent and *slydynge* of heart.

After describing Criseyde's betrayal of Troilus, it seems that Chaucer feels the need to reconfirm his stance towards her, as shown in (64).

(64) Ne me list this sely womman chyde
Forther than the storye wol devyse.
Hire name, allas, is publysshed so wide
That for hire gilt it oughte ynough suffise.
And if I myghte excuse hire any wise,
For she so sory was for hire untrouthe,
Iwis, I wolde excuse hire yet for *routhe*.   Tr 5.1093-9

Since she has been widely disparaged for her deed, and feels sorry for it, he states that he will excuse her *for routhe*. Here, the narrator's sympathetic view and his traditional view of her are equally balanced. The phrase *for routhe* seems to imply a reciprocal sense: the narrator appreciates her 'remorse,' and therefore would excuse her out of his pity for her. Thus ambiguity is likely to arise in the word *routhe*.

The tension between the above two views is continued, perhaps in a more intensified way. Receiving a first letter from Troilus asking her to come back to Troy, she writes back to him with pity or *pitously* (if its subjective sense (*OED* s.v. piteous 2) is allowed here) according to the narrator, as shown in (65).

(65) Ful *pitously* she wroot ayeyn and seyde,
That also sone as that she myghte, ywys,
She wolde come, and mende al that was mys.   Tr 5.1424-6

And yet we find that the following stanza (Tr 5.1429-35) emphasises the point that Troilus found it 'but botmeles bihestes' (Tr 5.1431). Here there is likely to be an objective sense (*OED* s.v. piteous 1) regarding *pitously*, where we can assume the narrator's sympathy with Criseyde in writing back to Troilus. The adverb *pitously* of Tr 5.1584 seems to show the narrator's sympathy with Troilus writing to Criseyde.

When she responds to a second letter from Troilus, the narrator draws the attention of the audience once again to her *pite*, as in (66)

(66) To hire he wroot yet ofte tyme al newe
Ful pitously—he lefte it nought for slouthe—
Bisechyng hire that sithen he was trewe,
That she wol come ayeyn and holde hire trouthe.
For which Criseyde upon a day, for *routhe*—

> I take it so—touchyng al this matere,
> Wrot hym ayeyn, and seyde as ye may here: Tr 5.1583-9

It should be noted, however, that he immediately blurs the assertive force of his statement by a qualifying interpolation "I take it so." Agreeing with the point of view of the sympathetic 'I,' the audience, the second prism, is likely to believe in her *routhe,* and yet when sceptical and critical of the view of the 'I,' he or she is likely to give another, possibly the opposing, interpretation to her *pite.*[194] The value of her *routhe* is thus ambiguous. (For details of Chaucer's subjective use of *pite*, see Nakao (1994).)

12.5.4. Final remarks

While inheriting the basic plot—Criseyde's betrayal of Troilus—from *Il Filostrato*, the poet, the first prism, deals with it sympathetically, so much so that he reinterprets it as a complex functioning of her *pite*. Betrayal has always been the object of moral and social disgust. In medieval times a religious dimension was added to this. This reinterpretation is assumed to be the more creative and imaginative. In so doing, he intensifies her *pite*, and thus departs a great deal from *Il Filostrato*. Criseyde's *pite* comes to our notice whenever she is tender-hearted to and shifts her affections towards her beloved. The *pite* there is subjectively orientated to the extent that it admits of the reader, the second prism's dual point of view: they can be sympathetic and detached observers of her at the same time. Depending on the emphasis, her *pite* is susceptible to ambiguous (positive/negative) implication.

12.6. Ambiguity in *frend/shipe* and *gentil/esse*

12.6.1. Introductory remarks

The idea that 'the wordes mote be cosyn to the dede,' as seen in CT GP I (A) 742, MancT IX (H) 210, or Bo 3.p.12.206-7, continues to be Chaucer's concern. This reminds us of the philosophical dispute as to which is better, realism or nominalism. The former assumes the exact agreement between language and the world, and the latter assumes an arbitrary relation between them. As we have mentioned, Chaucer moves between the sacred and the secular, and therefore it is difficult to choose only one of them. In *Troilus and Criseyde* the narrator analyses and describes human complex feelings. We should note that it is hardly possible to adhere to realism when we regard the language dealing with characters' self-justifications, plots and lies in the story and that 'wordes' and 'dedes' are not straightforwardly correspondent to each other. Chau-

---

[194] The Monk in the General Prologue belies the ideal image of monks. Chaucer, hearing his opinion, agrees with him. His addition of 'I seyde' here seems to have an effect nearly equivalent to that of a modal lexical verb in that it suggests his point of view.
> Ne that a monk, whan he is recchelees,
> Is likned til a fissh that is waterlees—
> This is to seyn, a monk out of his cloystre.
> But thilke text heeld he nat worth an oystre;
> And *I seyde* his opinion was good.   CT GP I (A) 179-83

cer seems to have recognised far before modern semantics and pragmatics that 'wordes' and 'dedes' are only indirectly correspondent to each other through human subjectivity and to have been able to describe it.

In this section we examine those cases in which the phenomenon and its expression of the double prism structure are related through the speaker's subjectivity, and where the validity of the relation is subject to scepticism. In other words, we examine what Aitchison (1992) describes as 'fuzzy edge.' Talking the concept 'bird' as an example, a typical bird has two wings, two legs, a beak, can fly, chirp, and lay eggs. A sparrow corresponds to this central type, but a chicken does not in that it cannot fly properly; much less a penguin in that it cannot fly at all. From this point of view we may say that a sparrow is a 'prototype' of a bird whereas a chicken and a penguin may be ascribed to the 'fuzzy edge.' It is no wonder that there is likely to arise variation in the reader, the second prism's interpretation. This problem is different from that of the polysemy of a word regarding which of its senses is primary or secondary, as discussed in Sections 12.2—12.5.

We deal here with the words *frend/shipe* and *gentil/esse*. The word *frend/shipe* is not usually applied to the love between a man and a woman (see (67.1a)). But when it is applied to such a love, how does the reader respond to it? The word *gentil/esse* is usually applied to social and moral values (see (77.1a, 2a, 3a) below). However, when applied to the love between a man and a woman, again how does the reader respond to it? Here we have a problem of 'fuzzy edge,' which is likely to lead to ambiguity as discussed below.

12.6.2. Examination

12.6.2.1. The case of *frend/shipe*

'Friendship' is an important virtue indicative of human strong bond in medieval times, as typically shown between the heroes Amis and Amiloun, each of who fulfils his promise to the other beyond the call of moral duty. In fact in *Troilus and Criseyde frend/shipe* is found in various social relationships such as those between Troilus and Pandarus, Pandarus and Criseyde, Troilus and his brother Deiphebus, Criseyde and Troilus, and Criseyde and Diomede. The *OED* defines *frend* as in (67).

(67) 1.a. 'One joined to another in mutual benevolence and intimacy' (J). Not ordinarily applied to lovers or relatives (but cf. senses 3, 4). a1000–
    2. Used loosely in various ways: e.g. applied to a mere acquaintance, or to a stranger, as a mark of goodwill or kindly condescension on the part of the speaker. c1290–
    3. A kinsman or near relation. c1200–
    4. A lover or paramour, of either sex. 1490–
    5. a. One who wishes (another, a cause, etc.) well; a sympathiser, favourer. c1205–
    6. a. As opposed to enemy in various senses: One who is on good terms with another, not hostile or at variance. a1000–

Sense 1a in the list above is seen in Troilus's spiritual development stemming from his knowledge of love as can be seen in (68) below. *Frend/shipe* is an important knightly virtue together with nobility and generosity.

(68) For he bicom the *frendlieste* wight,
　　The gentilest, and ek the mooste fre,
　　The thriftiest, and oon the beste knyght
　　That in his tyme was or myghte be;　　　　Tr 1.1079-82

However, when *frend/shipe* is applied to the male-female relationship between Troilus and Criseyde or between Diomede and Criseyde, individual feelings are made more prominent than socially determined values. As the *OED* 1a says, this word is not usually applied to 'lovers.' It appears in a conflicting context in that while the love between them is problematic according to the criteria of social acceptance, it has to be described in such a way as to preserve Criseyde's social reputation. Here the word *frendshipe* is pushed to the fuzzy edge regarding its application, which gives rise to a subtle incongruity between the word and the deed.

When Pandarus tells Criseyde Trolus's love for her, and asks her to accept it, he knows well that she cannot help rejecting it since such an acceptance would contravene the code of courtly behaviour expected of a lady. Here he adroitly uses 'friendly cheere' and 'love of frendshipe' as compromise expressions. He says that the 'noble gentil knyght' only desires 'youre frendly cheere,' as shown in (69).

(69) "Allas, he which that is my lord so deere,
　　That trewe man, that noble gentil knyght,
　　That naught desireth but *youre frendly cheere*,
　　I se hym dyen, ther he goth upryght,
　　And hasteth hym with al his fulle myght
　　For to ben slayn, if his fortune assente.　　　Tr 2.330-5

The contact of Troilus and Criseyde does not go beyond being visual.[195] But Pandarus seems to know that this friendship will develop into love afterwards. In *Troilus and Criseyde* we have 'love of frendshipe' five times (Tr 2.371, Tr 2.379, Tr 2.962, Tr 3.1591, Tr 5.1080). In the first three examples, Pandarus implies the future development of the love between Troilus and Criseyde. The fourth is used by the narrator to show the friendship between Troilus and Pandarus. In the fifth instance, Criseyde, who did not keep her promise to Troilus, expresses the hope that friendship between them will be permanent. In (70) Pandarus says that though Troilus comes to Criseyde, people will regard the visit as an indication of 'love of frendshipe.'

(70) Men wolde wondren sen hym come or goon.
　　Ther-ayeins answere I thus anoon,
　　That every wight, but he be fool of kynde,
　　Wol deme it *love of frendshipe* in his mynde.　　　Tr 2.368-71

The *MED* takes 'love of frendshipe' in the sense of 'friendly affection, Platonic love' (1b), and quotes the example of Tr 2.371. Pandarus seems to intend this meaning so that Criseyde can accede to his request without anxiety. However, the reader, the second prism, is likely to assume at a deeper level that Pandarus has an insight into the later development of their friendship into their love. In (71), too, Pandarus stresses the

---

195　The word *cheere* could have functioned more psychologically than physically in the sense of 'attitude' *(MED* 6.(a) Kindness, friendliness, sympathy, hospitality). If this is right, we may regard Pandarus as more actively involved in the relationship between Troilus and Criseyde.

point that this 'love of frendshipe' prevails through the town.

(71) And ek therto, he shal come here so selde,
What fors were it though al the town byhelde?

"*Swych love of frendes* regneth al this town;
And wre yow in that mantel evere moo,   Tr 2.377-80

Pandarus's imperative 'wre yow in that mantel evere moo' (Tr 2.380) immediately after 'swych love of frendes' suggests the intention behind his use of the word. This is uttered from a pragmatic rather than moral point of view. This point of view is applied retroactively to 'swych love of frendes,' whose applicability is reduced to 'fuzzy edge.' Pandarus said that he won 'hire love of frendshipe' to Troilus, which is in (72).

(72) "For thus ferforth I have thi werk bigonne,
Fro day to day, til this day by the morwe
Hire love of frendshipe have I to the wonne,
And therto hath she leyd hire feyth to borwe.   Tr 2.960-3

This phrase is collocated with *wonne* as if it were treated as a trophy of a war. Gaylord (1968-9: 255) states that '"Love of frendshipe," within Pandarus's practice, is part of the game of love; it is a means of achieving an intimacy which can be further exploited. Its tactical advantage lies in the general connotations outside of the garden of romance ....' and notes its strategic implication. In Troilus and Criseyde *love* is used to refer not only to sexual love (*amor/ous*) but religious love (*charite*), which is rich in implication (see the thematic ambiguity in Chapter 6). Pandarus employs the potential ambiguity of abstract words for his tactical advantage, which gives rise to the question of 'fuzzy edge.'

Criseyde yields to Diomede, but seeks to justify herself by her expressions of remorse and sorrow as we have seen in (49) in Chapter 10 above, the last part of which is reproduced below. As can be seen, she claims that she will not hate him, but that he will have 'frendes love' from her for ever more as if she replaced her standpoint for his.

(73) "And certes yow ne haten shal I nevere;
And *frendes love*, that shal ye han of me,
And my good word, al sholde I lyven evere.   Tr 5.1079-81

After betraying Troilus, Criseyde manages to save her face by putting herself in a position of condescension and behaving kindly to him. In her letter to Troilus quoted in (74) Criseyde asks him to speak well of her since he can believe in her.

(74) But in effect I pray yow, as I may,
Of youre good word and of *youre frendship* ay;
For trewely, while that my lif may dure,
As for a frend ye may in me assure.   Tr 5.1621-4

Her appeal to their friendship at the stage at which their love finishes ironically underlines the most negative phase in their relationship. The positive value of their friendship is greatly diminished.

Diomede vows to Criseyde to be her friend in (75), and offers his service of love to her immediately. And in (76) she thanks him for his friendship.

(75) "And by the cause I swor yow right, lo, now,
To ben youre *frend*, and helply, to my myght,

And for that more aquayntaunce ek of yow
Have ich had than another straunger wight,
So fro this forth, I pray yow, day and nyght,
Comaundeth me, how soore that me smerte,
To don al that may like unto youre herte;

"And that ye me wolde as youre brother trete,
And taketh naught *my frendshipe* in despit;   Tr 5.127-35

(76) But natheles she thonketh Diomede
Of al his travaile and his goode cheere,
And that hym list *his frendshipe* hire to bede;   Tr 5.183-5

Diomede's intention perceptible in his offer of friendship to her is to win her love with favorable words to her. His use of it is short of its prototype image. Gaylord (1968-9: 262) significantly notes that 'His progress from "frendshipe" to "love" is accomplished in a few lines, rather than over many months and through several books.' On the other hand, Criseyde's thanks for his friendship may be a stimulus for him to become more positive in seeking her love.[196]

As shown above, we have examined above the extent to which the 'worde *frend/shipe* mote be cosyn to the dede.' The relation between them was intended by the speakers to be functional prototypically. However, when the characters justify their actions which deviate from social ideals by means of this word, the validity of its use is likely to be taken by the reader, the second prism, with a pinch of salt, and he or she will assume uses on the fuzzy edge of its semantic scope. This leads to the rise of ambiguity.

12.6.2.2. The case of *gentil/esse*

The word *gentil/esse* is also worth attention in medieval literature in that it is part of the vocabulary of feudalism, courtly idealism and courtly love. The *OED* defines *gentil* as follows.

(77) 1.a. Of persons: Well-born, belonging to a family of position; originally used synonymously with *noble*, but afterwards distinguished from it, either as a wider term, or as designating a lower degree of rank. a1225-

2. a. Of birth, blood, family, etc.: Honourable, distinguished by descent or position, belonging to the class of 'gentlemen.' (Cf. 1.) a1300-

3. a. Of persons: Having the character appropriate to one of good birth; noble, generous, courteous. Freq. in the phrase *a gentle knight*. Now only *arch*. 1297-

The importance of *gentilesse* is repeatedly emphasised in Chaucer. A few examples are the old hag's curtain lecture to a young knight on *gentilesse* in WBT, one of the motifs the narrator highlights in MancT, and Chaucer's short poem on *Gentilesse*. In *Troilus and Criseyde* this word is used to show Troilus's *gentil* nature repeatedly impressing Criseyde, or her sympathy shown to him in a predicament. There seems to be no mismatch when it refers straightforwardly to Troilus's nobility and courtly idealism. However, when it refers to her acceptance of his love, it requires careful examination.

---

196   See the speaker's intention in Chapter 9.

She appears as a widow in mourning dress. According to the courtly love tradition, her adultery is guaranteed. However, as we have seen in Chapter 6, the first prism Chaucer seems to have moderated this indelicate aspect of courtly love to accommodate the moral requirements of contemporary society. Anticipating the response of the audience, he may have censored the words and actions of his characters.

The word *gentil/esse* is used to justify Pandarus's persuasion of Criseyde, her acceptance of Troilus as a lover and then as a sexual partner. Since Pandarus knows well that all this contravenes the social-moral code, he tries to bring it about by the use of a socially based series of justifications. Through this linguistic veil the use of *gentil/esse* is converted from the 'prototype' to the 'fuzzy edge.' The reader, the second prism, is likely to interpret this in varying ways: he or she may take the word *gentilesse* literally, seriously, or as being used in an unusual way. Here we can perceive visibly what Burnley (1979: 170) describes as the 'dynamic' character of a *gentil* man, or 'human nature' insecurely founded between 'tyrant' and 'philosopher.'

Pandarus uses his reference to *gentilesse* as a means to secure Criseyde's love for Troilus. When revealing his love to her, he does not fail to impress her with such virtues as Troilus's truth, nobility, and *gentil* nature.

(78) a. And ek his fresshe brother Troilus,
    The wise, worthi Ector the secounde,
    In whom that alle vertu list haboune,
    As alle trouthe and *alle gentilesse*,
    Wisdom, honour, fredom, and worthinesse."   Tr 2.157-61

b. "Allas, he which that is my lord so deere,
    That trewe man, that noble *gentil* knyght,
    That naught desireth but youre frendly cheere,
    I se hym dyen, ther he goth upryght,   Tr 2.330-3

(78a) praises Troilus as following in the footsteps of his heroic brother Hector. This is an important prelude to his revelation of Troilus's love for her. She concurs with this image. (78b) appears after he has told her of Troilus's love to her. He emphasises the fact that Troilus is abundant in ideal knightly virtues, and that deeply affected with the love for her, he faces death if it is unrequited. This shows him to be what Burnley (1979) calls a *gentil* man as opposed to a 'tyrant.'

Troilus's *gentilesse* is also noticed by Criseyde at important turning points in the story. As we have seen in (1) in Chapter 7 and (5) in Chapter 8, when seeing Troilus retruning to Troy in triumph, a series of his features come to her attention starting with the external features and proceeding to the internal, spiritual ones. In this series *gentilesse* is located at the final position (Tr 2.701-2, Tr 2.1265-8) as if it were an afterthought. Criseyde has a chance to meet Troilus at Deiphebus's house. Assuming that Troilus respects *trouthe* and *gentilesse*, she decides to accept his service of love, as seen below.

(79) "Myn honour sauf, I wol wel trewely,
    And in swich forme as he gan now devyse,
    Receyven hym fully to my servyse,

> "Bysechyng hym, for Goddes love, that he
> Wolde, in honour of trouthe and *gentilesse,*
> As I wel mene, ek menen wel to me,
> And myn honour with wit and bisynesse
> Ay kepe; and if I may don hym gladnesse,
> From hennesforth, iwys, I nyl nought feyne.   Tr 3.159-67

Since Troilus's ideal knightly virtues safeguard her honour, she can accept his love. However, it should be noted that this safeguard does not necessarily resolve the problem of morality involved here.

Here we have to note that Pandarus reveals to Troilus that he made Criseyde believe his *gentilesse*. He uses this word as a strategy to develop their love.

(80) "That is to seye, for the am I bicomen,
Bitwixen game and ernest, swich a meene
As maken wommen unto men to comen;
Al sey I nought, thow wost wel what I meene.
For the have I my nece, of vices cleene,
So fully maad *thi gentilesse* triste,
That al shal ben right as thiselven liste.   Tr 3.253-9

In the view of Pandarus *gentilesse* is made a *meene* to encourage Criseyde to accept Troilus, and thus degraded midway between 'game and ernest.' However, Troilus does not regard 'swich a meene' (Tr 3.254) as Pandarus does as *bauderye* (Tr 3.397), but states in the following way: 'And this that thow doost, calle it *gentilesse*, / Compassioun, and felawship, and trist' (Tr 3.402-3). As seen in Section 9.2, that is his judgement. The *bauderie* he rejected is in fact reality, and *gentilesse* is rather a fiction constructed by the philosophy of Troilus.

When Pandarus persuades Criseyde to accept Troilus in her bedchamber at his house, he resorts to the word *gentil*. In (81) he says that if she leaves Troilus in danger, she does no *bounte* nor *gentilesse*.

(81) "Now loke thanne, if ye that ben his love
Shul putte his lif al night in jupertie
For thyng of nought, now by that God above,
Naught oonly this delay comth of folie,
But of malice, if that I shal naught lie.
What! Platly, and ye suffre hym in destresse,
Ye neyther bounte don ne *gentilesse*."   Tr 3.876-82

Gaylord (1964: 30), referring to the events which must ensue behind closed doors, notes that that 'It must be obvious to everyone, both characters and audience, what kind of virtue will result from a midnight colloquy in a private room.' Furthermore, Pandarus refers to Troilus's tender-heartedness and thus exerts more pressure, by stating that he will commit suicide.

(82) "This is so *gentil* and so tendre of herte
That with his deth he wol his sorwes wreke;   Tr 3.904-5

Through Pandarus, the social-moral status of *gentil* seems to be transformed into a more superficial physical sense 'vulnerable,' another sense to be developed in the Early ModE. Criseyde is repeatedly pressed to accept Troilus's love and eventually agrees to leave everything to Pandarus. Whereupon he praises her wise and *gentil* heart.

(83) "That is wel seyd," quod he, "my nece deere.
　　Ther good thrift on *that wise gentil herte*!
　　But liggeth stille, and taketh hym right here—
　　It nedeth nought no ferther for hym sterte.　Tr 3.946-9

His moral judgement ('that wise gentil herte' (Tr 3.947)) and his strategic directions as to how she should comfort herself physically (Tr 3.948-9) are juxtaposed. There is a high probability that the reader sees these as morally contradictory. In that case ambiguity is bound to arise.

Criseyde is embarrassed by the sudden appearance of Troilus in her bedchamber (Tr 3.956-9). Pandarus immediately draws her attention to Troilus's *gentil* nature.

(84) And seyde, "Nece, se how this lord kan knele!
　　Now for youre trouthe, se *this gentil man*!"
　　And with that word he for a quysshen ran,
　　And seyde, "Kneleth now, while that yow leste;
　　There God youre hertes brynge soone at reste!"　Tr 3.962-6

Here again are juxtaposed the expression 'this gentil man' (Tr 3.963) indicative of Troilus's good character and strategic directions relating to physical action (Tr 3.964). The word *gentil* is driven away from its prototype to the fuzzy edge, and thus becomes semantically unstable in the reader, the second prism's view.

After hearing from Troilus the reason why he has come to Criseyde—of his *peyne* and *jalousie*—she excuses him because he has repressed it so well with *piete* and because of his *gentilesse* (Tr 3.1030-6). The narrator reinforces this a little later in the following way.

(85) ... for every wyght, I gesse,
　　That loveth wel, meneth but *gentilesse*.　Tr 3.1147-8

Gaylord (1964: 30), commenting on these two lines, remarks pertinently: 'representative of the controlled ambiguity that Book III displays.' Furthermore when Troilus and Criseyde consummate their love, the narrator stresses the point that she cherishes his *worthynesse* or *gentilesse* in her heart.

(86) Criseyde also, right in the same wyse,
　　Of Troilus gan in hire herte shette
　　His worthynesse, his lust, his dedes wise,
　　His gentilesse, and how she with hym mette,
　　Thonkyng Love he so wel hire bisette,　Tr 3.1548-52

Criseyde makes other references to his *gentilesse* at various points in the poem: when she reveals the reason why she showed her sympathy to Troilus, immediately before going to the Greek camp, and in her reply to his letter after yielding to Diomede. Her respective utterances are: 'Eke *gentil* herte and manhod that ye hadde' (Tr 4.1674) and 'O swerd of knyghthod, sours of *gentilesse*' (Tr 5.1591), 'But now no force, / I kan nat in yow gesse / But alle trouthe and *alle gentilesse*' (Tr 5.1616-7). Troilus is endowed with *gentilesse* as she says. This is exactly so from a courtly love perspective. However, in higher reiglious terms, it is subject to being made relative, as is manifested in 'The blynde lust, the which may nat laste' (Tr 5.1824). His love begins with the visual effect that she makes on him; it penetrates his heart and so like all lovers he becomes blind. Although he grows in psychological stature, he loses percipience and dies in that deprived condition.

Finally *gentil* is used by Diomede, when advancing to Criseyde, to refer to himself.

(87) And seyde, "I am, al be it yow no joie,
 As *gentil man* as any wight in Troie.

 "For if my fader Tideus," he seyde,
 "Ilyved hadde, ich hadde ben er this
 Of Calydoyne and Arge a kyng, Criseyde! Tr 5.930-4

Although Diomede stresses the purely aristorcratic sense of *gentil*, 'well-born,' and 'honourable' (*OED* s.v. gentle 1.a, 2.a), there are here overtones of its use to describe character, 'noble,' 'generous,' and 'courteous' (*OED* 3.a). If he implies the latter here, his use of the word becomes a means of achieving his purpose with an implication of 'fuzzy edge (cf. Tr 5.771-84), as we have seen in Pandarus, and so the term is degraded.

As discussed above, although the words *frend/shipe* and *gentil/esse* are used mostly in their prototypical sense, their contexts provide a chance for the reader, the second prism to push them to the 'fuzzy edge.' This is likely to lead to ambiguity.

12.7. Final remarks

We have described how words are likely to produce ambiguity through the double prism structure. When the characters—condoned by the narrator—perform socially and morally reprehensible acts, they tend to use the polysemy of lexical items as one way of equivocation. The reader, the second prism, will be sensitive to the speaker's dual attitudes and form a dual judgement of his or her meaning. We have examined the semantic networks of words, i.e. the problem of paradigmatic word-choice, the tention between the senses of a word, between the sense of a word and its implication, and between the implications of a word, and the problem of 'prototype' and 'fuzzy edge' via-à-vis the application of a word to its referents in the real world. When senses of a word are contextually induced to overlap and increase their semantic unity, the interaction between the first and second prisms are likely to be activated and ambiguity is the consequence. This lexical ambiguity is reinforced in cooperation with intertexuality (see Chapter 5), macro-textual structure (see Chapter 6), discourse structure (see Chapter 8), speech act (see Chapter 9), and syntax (see Chapter 11).

In Chapter 13 we will focus on sounds as the smallest unit of language domains. They themselves have no meaning, but acquire such in connection with other textual constituents such as words, syntax, attitude and discourse. We will see how even in these minimal elements of a text ambiguity can arise.

13. Ambiguity in voice

13.1. Introductory remarks: the double prism structure and voice

Chaucer's literary discourse is characterised as 'narration' and basically transmitted to the audience through the narrator's voice. Responding to the narrator's articulation of sounds, that is, stress, pause, intonation, etc., they must have understood the meaning of the texts. We can naturally assume that the narrator observed their response, and therefore was attentive to and made the best use of it. However, the modern reader cannot easily be aware of the details of his performance. In particular those parts allowing both for different tunings and for their consequent different meanings are worthy of note. The question cannot be easily resolved as to whether Chaucer tuned his texts so as to remove ambiguity or allowed for variable tunings on them as an entertainer.

In this chapter we deal with the voice of some passages through the double prism structure, and describe how the reader/audience, the second prism, assumes it and how its interpretation is likely to vary according to his or her assumption. Since *Troilus and Criseyde* is a psychological poem, we find vivid representations of the psychologies of characters experiencing conflicts between their encounters with difficulties and their struggles to overcome them, and the narrator's empathetic feelings towards them. The various voices accompanying their language have a vital importance in that we can better understand its meaning.

13.2. Previous scholarship

Chaucer's sounds have been mainly investigated in terms of segmentals and metrics by such scholars as Ten Brink (1969), Southworth (1954), Robinson (1971), Sandved (1985), Fries (1985), etc. By contrast with segmentals, there is a tendency for suprasegmentals to have been avoided in investigation since their uncertainties cannot be easily resolved. Regarding metrical studies, particular attention has been paid to making clear how weak and strong syllables alternate in a line. An analytical approach to sounds to distinguish between sounds and meanings seems to have led to this tendency. A synthetic approach to sound with full consideration of sounds, syntax and meanings as found in such as Masui (1964), Gaylord (1976), Bowden (1987), and Barney (1993) merits attention. Bowden's *Chaucer Aloud* is especially significant. She examines how the same line in *The Canterbury Tales* allows for many different tunings and thus for many interpretations based on the evidence of recorded materials by eminent Chaucer scholars. This synthetic approach has not been adequately pursued in relation to *Troilus and Criseyde*. This chapter attempts to make good that deficiency.

13.3. Our approach: reconsideration from the viewpoint of the double prism structure

How does the author, the first prism, observe the phenomenon, and express it through the voices of the narrator and characters? And how does the reader, the second prism, assume them. Here we describe how the reader's multiple choices in this area will lead to multiple interpretations. As discussed in Section 6.3.1 above, it is of course impossible to determine what voice the poet used for his performance of his tale. The semantic gradability we are concerned with here is not produced by assuming a single ideal or fixed image of Chaucer's text, but by taking the role of the conductor of an orchestra or the producer of a play and transforming it into sounds.

The word 'voice' here is used to include those ways of producing sounds that Leech (1969: 95-6) calls 'chiming,' sound symbolism, and suprasegmental features such as pause, rhythm, and intonation. This voice is not restricted to a verse or a sentence. In Chapter 3 we mentioned that the rise of Chaucer's ambiguity is not restricted to a particular structural level of a text, but runs through its various levels. We have set up 'voice' as a level. However, this 'voice' itself has little meaning except for some onomatopoetic effects. Sounds are semantically functional only in conjunction with words, syntax, discourse or the speaker's attitude. We have divided ambiguity arising from sounds into three types, as in (1), according to the kinds of meaning.

(1)   a. Propositional meaning
       b. Informational meaning
       c. Interpersonal meaning

(1a) is the case in which the semantic range of a word or grammatical structure is affected by the adjustment of a stress, pause or intonation. This is concerned with syntactic ambiguity (discussed in Chapter 11) and lexical ambiguity (Chapter 12) (both belong to the category of ambiguity III). (1b) is the case in which the kinds of information (old/new information) are affected by the sound adjustment. This is concerned with ambiguity in information (see Chapter 8) (the category of ambiguity I). (1c) is the case in which the speaker's attitude towards the proposition concerned is affected by the adjustment. This is concerned with ambiguity in the speaker's intention (Chapter 9) and in his or her judgement (Chapter 10) (the category of ambiguity II). Voice ambiguity here is to be examined in terms of (1a, b, c). However, these three are likely to overlap with degrees of emphasis in one and the same piece of language. The more overlapping there is, the more abundant implications there will be.

In what follows we examine the meanings arising from (1a, b, c) and describe how each one of them or the overlapping of them contributes to polyphony.

13.4. Examination

Leech's (1969) 'chiming' works as a device to link different words together through similar sounds. We are reminded of the slogan 'I like Ike,' an example of what Jakobson (1960: 358) calls 'poetic function' ('The poetic function projects the principle of equivalence from the axis of selection into the axis of combination'). Here the three words are induced semantically to link together through the similarity of their sounds. The context of (2) is this. Trojans come to the temple on the festival of Palladion. Criseyde stands out among them as being the most beautiful.

(2) Among thise othere folk was *Criseyda*,
    In widewes habit blak; but natheles,
    Right as oure firste lettre is now an *A*,
    In beaute first so stood she, makeles.   Tr 1.169-72

A (Tr 1.171) rhymes with *Criseyda* (Tr 1.169). Through this rhyming effect these words are induced to overlap. Furthermore the *A* may extend extralinguistically to and alliterate with Anne of Bohemia, wife of Richard II. There is a possibility that King Richard and Queen Anne were in the audience when Chaucer read his poetry, as is suggested by the Frontispiece of the Corpus Christi College 61 MS.[197] The connection of words by similar sounds is dependent on the size of the hearer's memory or recallable stock of knowledge (cf. engram in Section 8.4).[198] Incidentally the word *makeles* (Tr 1.172) is effective for reinforcing the cohesion with Criseyda or Anne.[199] (1a) is primarily operative in this example, which induces the expansion of the semantic range of the words *(A/Criseyda/Anne)* with a subsequent rise of ambiguity.

The rhyme *Troie-joie* (including one *rejoie*) is repeatedly used (31 times in Tr). These words have no rhyming partners. The existence of the one leads one to expect the other. Since this rhyming runs across contrastive discourse contexts, we should note that the effect of engram is highlighted. As Masui (1964) pointed out, this rhyme is positively functional in the ascending scenes in which the couple's love develops, whereas in the descending scenes in which their love declines, it is likely to produce a subtle tension between positive and negative values to the extent that it reminds us of the ascending scenes. This chiming is doubly effective in that it gives rise to polyphony due not only to word associations but also to the rhyme pair associations realised through the contrastive scenes.

In the scenes where Troilus returns to Troy triumphantly, *Troie-joie* is positively used as in (3).

(3) And ay the peple cryde, "Here cometh oure *joye*,
    And, next his brother, holder up of *Troye*!"   Tr 2.643-4

---

[197] In the introduction of the Prioress in the GP to *The Canterbury Tales*, *A* is brought into focus: 'On which ther was first write a crowned *A*, / And after *Amor vincit omnia*' I (A)161-2.
[198] See 'the related arrangement of memory by the speaker' proposed by Fukaya and Tanaka (1995: 69-73).
[199] The word *makeles* is polysemous, which is, according to *MED*, defined as 'unequalled,' and 'without a mate.' Here its primary sense is 'unequalled' (*MED* quotes this word under this heading), but in view of Criseyde appearing as a widow (Tr 1.170) in the story, its secondary sense 'without a mate' cannot be rejected. Regarding this secondary sense, if we are allowed to suppose that the narrator uses it taking the whole narrative context into account, we can go so far as to say that it connotes her coping with changing situations and subsequently 'being without a partner and consequently without restraint upon her actions and apt to change.' This is not a lexically but a pragmatically based meaning. Cf. 'O ryng, fro which the ruby is out falle' (Tr 5.549).

When Criseyde is hesitating to accept Troilus's love, Antigone sings a hymn of love for her. Answering the question of who composed this poem, she exploits the rhyme pair *Troie-joie* in a positive context in the same way as in (3).

(4) "Madame, ywys, the goodlieste mayde
Of gret estat in al the town of *Troye*,
And let hire lif in moste honour and *joye*."   Tr 2.880-2

However, when the love between Troilus and Criseyde becomes hard to maintain, the rhyme pair is used in a negative context as shown in (5).

(5) Ful rewfully she loked upon *Troie*,
Biheld the toures heigh and ek the halles;
"Allas," quod she, "the plesance and the *joie*,   Tr 5.729-31

In the same way as in (5), the rhyme pair is used to bring into focus the fate of Troy in (6).

(6) Fortune, which that permutacioun
Of thynges hath, as it is hire comitted ...
Gan pulle awey the fetheres brighte of *Troie*
Fro day to day, til they ben bare of *joie*.   Tr 5.1541-7

Through this repeated use of the rhyme pair *Troie-joie*, we find the interaction of the two words as an example of propositional meaning (see (1a)), and the overlappings of the old and new information brought about by the rhyme-pair running through the different or even opposing contexts (see 1b)). In this way the rhyme pair is triggered to the reader, the second prism, and thus gives rise to complicated semantic associations leading to ambiguity.

The double effects of the rhyme-pair can be seen in *trouthe* (including *untrouthe*)-*routhe* (19 times). These words can have other rhyming partners, but in *Troilus and Criseyde*, they are most frequently rhymed with each other. The same is true of *sterve-serve* (13 times), and *place-grace* (18 times). Those rhyme-pairs are all used across the ascending and descending scenes.[200]

---

200   *Troilus and Criseyde* is written in a poetic scheme of rhyme royal (ababbcc). The rhyme pairs of the 'chiming' effects are mostly found in the cc couplet. (The underlined line numbers below show this.) Masui (1964: 226) finds a structure analogous to rhyme royal in the development of a Chinese *zekku*, which has the 'beginning, development, turning and conclusion.' He states: 'The seven-line stanza of the rime ababbcc which Chaucer employed in *Troilus and Criseyde*, the *Parliament of Fowls*, and others may pose an interesting problem in point of rime and line-structure. It has three parts, the *pedes* ab, ab and the *cauda* bcc. Roughly speaking, the first *pedes* (ab, ab) may serve for the beginning of a theme and its development, and the last *cauda* (bcc) for the turning (*or* surprise) (b) and the conclusion (cc) of the theme, thus forming a small unity within a single stanza. By so doing, stanza follows stanza with a circular and yet progressive movement of verse in accordance with the gradual and sustained development of a subject-matter. And the last two lines of the stanza often give us an effect of finality just as does the heroic verse. This effect of finality or summing up may certainly be achieved in part by the last rime cc. For that matter the structure of a seven-line stanza seems to resemble to some extent that of a Chinese *zekku* (quatrain) which has 'beginning, development, turning and conclusion.'
The rhyme pair of *Troye—joie* is used thirty one times in *Troilus and Criseyde* (underlined examples show that they appear in cc): Tr 1.1-4, Tr 1.118-9, Tr 1.608-9, Tr 2.139-40, Tr 2.643-4, Tr 2.748-9, Tr 2.881-2, Tr 3.356-7, Tr 3.790-1, Tr 3.874-5, Tr 3.1441-2, Tr 3.1450-52, Tr

Through alliteration and/or assonance or consonance, the interaction of words is induced with an increase in semantic chiming. When Troilus hesitates to confess his love to Criseyde, Pandarus points out to him the likely unfortunate consequences of his behaviour as seen in (7). The effects of alliteration and assonance/consonance of the line are noticeable.

(7) *Unknowe, unkist,* and *lost* that is *unsought.*   Tr 1.809

The initial sounds /un/ of the words (*Unknowe—unkist—unsought*), the medial consonant /k/ of the words (*Unknowe—unkist*), the final sounds /st/ of the words (*unkist—lost*), the final consonant sound /t/ of the words (*unkist—lost—unsought*), and the assonance /o/ and /ou/ of the words (*unknowe—lost—unsought*) contribute a great deal to the lexical and semantic interaction. Further, since the verbs are used all in passive voice, the cohesion between them is reinforced. This line is an exact reminder of Jakobson's (1960) 'I like Ike.' Here (1a) is mostly functional, so much so that the above four verbs interact with each other causing accidental polysemy. The line is thus abundant in implications.

We find in (8) a fully cooperative use of alliteration, rhyming, and assonance/consonance. This example is a part of (49) in Section 10.4 where we dealt with modal lexical verbs. As the reader can recall, the context is as follows: Criseyde, shamed of her betrayal of Troilus and anticipating severe criticism for it, expresses her profound mortification. As with (7), we find here a typical instance of the projection of 'the principle of equivalence from the axis of selection into the axis of combination.'

(8) "*Allas*, of me, unto the worldes ende,
     Shal neyther ben ywriten nor ysonge
     No good word, for thise bokes wol me shende.
     O, rolled *shal* I ben on many a tonge!
     Thorughout the world my belle *shal* be ronge!
     And wommen moost wol haten me of *alle*.
     Allas, that swich a cas me sholde *falle*!   Tr 5.1058-64

The sound /al/ in *Allas* (Tr 5.1058), the initial word of this stanza, is repeated, through *Shal* (Tr 5.1059, Tr 5.1061, Tr 5.1062) and *alle* (Tr 5.1063), to *Allas* (Tr 5.1264) of the final line, the same word with the initial word of the beginning line. The word *alle* (Tr 5.1063) alliterates with the next word *Allas* (Tr 5.1064) and rhymes with *falle* (Tr 5.1064). We find a similar example in /ol/ *rolled* (5.1061) and *sholde* (5.1064)). Fur-

---

3.1714-5, Tr 4.55-6, Tr 4.90-1, Tr 4.274-6, Tr 4.335-6, Tr 4.1306-7, Tr 4.1441-2, Tr 4.1630-1, Tr 5.27-8, Tr 5.118-9, Tr 5.393-5, Tr 5.426-7, Tr 5.608-9, Tr 5.615-6, Tr 5.729-31, Tr 5.779-81, Tr 5.930-1, Tr 5.1380-2, Tr 5.1546-7. For a semantic analysis of this rhyme pair, see Masui (1964: 270-1, 278-80): 'Thus, *Troy* is, by the principle of proximity, equated with *joy*.'

routhe—(un-)trouthe: Tr 1.582-4, Tr 1.769-70, Tr 2.349-50. Tr 2.489-50, Tr 2.664-5, Tr 2.1138-9, Tr 2.1280-1, Tr 2.1502-3, Tr 3.120-2, Tr 3.1511-2, Tr 4.1476-7, Tr 4.1490-1, Tr 4.1609-10, Tr 4.1672-3, Tr 5.1000-1, Tr 5.1098-9, Tr 5.1385-6, Tr 5.1586-7, Tr 5.1686-7.

serve —sterve: Tr 1.15-7, Tr 1.426-7, Tr 2.1150-2, Tr 3.153-4, Tr 3.389-90, Tr 3.713-4, Tr 3.1290-2, Tr 4.279-80, Tr 4.321-2, Tr 4.447-8, Tr 4.517-8, Tr 5.174-5, Tr 5.312-3.

grace—place: Tr 1.895-6, Tr 1.905-7, Tr 1.960-2, Tr 1.1063-4, Tr 2.30-2, Tr 2.1364-5, Tr 3.921-2, Tr 3.1269-71, Tr 3.1348-9, Tr 3.1455-6, Tr 3.1803-4, Tr 4.555-8, Tr 4.1684-5, Tr 5.169-71, Tr 5.580-1, Tr 5.940-3, Tr 5.956-7, Tr 5.1322-3.

ther, the sound /l/ (*Allas, rolled, falle*) is endowed with an effect of sound symbolism suggesting the flow—a good example of our argument above of Criseyde's bad reputation or her mortified emotion. In terms of (1a), Criseyde's sorrow at censure for her betrayal (*Allas*), her assumption of the world's criticism against it (*rolled, alle*), the inevitability of such criticism (*shal, falle*) are induced to overlap by the reader, the second prism, leading to ambiguity.[201] (9) has been dealt with in (2) in Section 8.2 where we addressed the matter of discourse and in (23) in Section 11.3 where we looked at syntax. Here we reexamine it from the point of view of voice.

(9) "For, nece, by the goddesse Mynerve,
And Jupiter, that maketh the thondre rynge,
And by the blisful Venus that I serve,
Ye ben the womman in this world lyvynge—
Withouten paramours, to my wyttynge—
That I best love, and lothest am to greve;
And that ye weten wel youreself, I leve." Tr 2.232-8

As mentioned before, different interpretations are likely to arise depending on where we assume a pause in relation to the phrase *Withouten paramours*. In terms of (1a), the grammatical relations in the sentence in question can vary. Pandarus confirms the trustful relation between them in that he loves her more than anyone but not as a lover (a pause before *Withouten paramours*). On the other hand, he may be suggesting that she lives without lovers (reducing a pause before *Withouten paramours*). This latter interpretation implies immorality on the part of Criseyde who is a widow mourning her husband. Furthermore, a pause both before and after the *withouten*-phrase produces a different effect—the above two relations are kept in tension. According to the different possibilities suggested above, not only the grammatical relations there but the images of the human relationships can vary. What is Pandarus's meaning? The interpersonal meaning (1c) is likely to be strongly affected. When the reader, the second prism, chooses to mix these alternatives, ambiguity is likely to arise.

We have already looked at (10) in (49) in Section 10.4.4.5 in view of modal lexical verb.

(10) "And certes yow ne haten shal I nevere;
And frendes love, that shal ye han of me,
And my good word, al sholde I lyven evere.
And trewely I wolde sory be

---

201 For other alliterative examples, see: 'Troie ... destroied' (Tr 1.68); 'Troye ... Destroyed' (Tr 1.76-8); 'Calkas ... calkulynge' (Tr 1.71); [Troilus and Troy are put in a metonymical relation] 'And Troilus to Troie homward he wente' (Tr 5.91), 'And forth I wol of Troilus yow telle. / To Troie is come this woful Troilus' (Tr 5.196-7), 'For bothe Troilus and Troie town / Shal knotteles throughout hire herte slide' (Tr 5.768-9). For similar examples of alliteration and assonance/consonance, Masui (1964) discusses the following series of words 'compleyne—peyne—twynne—tweyne' in *Troilus and Criseyde*: 'And ther I wol eternaly compleyne / My wo, and how that twynned be we tweyne' (Tr 4.475-6); 'Myn herte and ek the woful goost therinne / Byquethe I with youre spirit to compleyne / Eternally, for they shal nevere twynne; / For though in erthe ytwynned be we tweyne, / Yet in the feld of pite, out of peyne, 4.785-9; The soth is this: the twynnyng of us tweyne / Wol us disese and cruelich anoye / But hym byhoveth somtyme han a peyne' (Tr 4.1303-5).

> For to seen yow in adversitee;
> And *gilteles, I woot wel, I yow leve.*
> But al shal passe; and thus take I my leve."   Tr 5.1079-85

The adjective *gilteles* can, as shown in Chapters 10 and 11, be related to the pronoun *I* or *yow* or both of them. From the metrical point of view, *I* in 'I yow leve' is located in a stressed position and therefore chimes more with *gilteles*. This contributes to the grammatical meaning required by (1a). In terms of the information structure (1b), relatively more importance is given to *I* than to *yow*. Further, in terms of (1c), her attitude is involved in that the justification for her betrayal is brought into more focus than her regret for betraying guiltless Troilus. Chaucer appears to see Criseyde as the helpless victim of the plot he had inherited rather than as sinful by her own intention. It is not unnatural that she searches for possibilities to survive the predicament she faces.

However, this interpretation seems out of keeping with the medieval ideal of a courtly lady. Syntactically and semantically *gilteles* and *yow* belong more obviously together, especially since that interpretation would underline her remorse for her infidelity to the innocent Troilus, and thus demonstrate her adherence to that courtly ideal. This apparent confusion arising from the disharmony between the phonetic and syntacto-semantic aspects might well inspire the reader, the second prism, to look for a higher level of interpretation involving complex overlapping.

Furthermore, let us examine how 'I woot wel' is tuned. This has been dealt with in Chapter 10 with regard to its modal force. We also need to examine it in terms of voice. Let us assume that this is a first person parenthetical modal phrase with a slight pause before and after it and with a rising intonation. There the speaker's certainty about the proposition mentioned above is reduced. The punctuation by Benson (1987) invites this reading. On the other hand, let us assume that this phrase retains the original meaning 'know/recognize' (see Section 10.4.4.2) with no pause after it and with a falling intonation. Although it does not have a complementiser *that*, it can be regarded as the main clause of a complex sentence, indicating that the speaker is certain about the proposition. As mentioned in Section 10.4.4.2, Donaldson (1975) has no commas either before or after the phrase. The question as to how to intone this phrase is interpersonally determined (1c), involving Criseyde's judgement regarding the proposition and the reader, the second prism's image of her as a whole.

Similar examples are given in (11) and (12).

(11) Ne nevere mo ne lakked hire pite;
    Tendre-herted, slydynge of corage;
    But trewely, I kan nat telle hire age.   Tr 5.824-6

(12) And Signifer his candels sheweth brighte
    Whan that Criseyde unto hire bedde wente
    Inwith hire fadres faire brighte tente,

    Retornyng in hire soule ay up and down
    The wordes of this sodeyn Diomede,
    His grete estat, and perel of the town,
    And that she was allone and hadde nede
    Of frendes help; and thus bygan to brede
    The cause whi, the sothe for to telle,
    That she took fully purpos for to dwelle.   Tr 5.1020-9

(11) is the final part of the character portrayal of Criseyde inserted immediately before she yields to Diomede (see Section 12.2). If we make a pause after *Tendre-herted* with a slight rise of intonation, and then connect it with *slydynge of corage*, a concessive effect will be produced, with *tendre-herted* appearing in a positive light and *slydynge of corage* in a negative one. On the other hand, if we do not make any pause and read the two in one breath, there will be an equilibrium between the two and an indication that the narrator intends no comment on the positive or negative sides of the character of his heroine. Because of voice, there is a difference in interpretation regarding the grammatical relation of (1a) and the speaker's attitude of (1c). Furthermore, we are likely to ask which phrase he places more emphasis on. Does he utter the line in *decrescendo*? Or does he utter it *in crescendo*? Here the informational importance due to (1b) is affected. The determination of this importance affects his view of Criseyde due to (1c). When the reader, the second prism, can assume the manifold ways of observation by the speaker based on the phonetic content of the expression concerned, ambiguity is likely to occur.

(12) describes the state of Criseyde's psychology immediately before she accepts Diomede's advances in love ((34) in Section 11.3). Let us reexamine it in terms of voice. The participial construction 'Retornyng …' (Tr 5.1023) indicating how she chooses to decide to stay in the Greek camp is most naturally introduced with a pause, since it begins a new stanza, and should anticipate its main clause to come. However, as Pearsall (1986: 26) points out, it is followed not by the main clause but by 'and thus bygan to brede ….' (Tr 5.1027). As a consequence the participial construction is left detached from the anticipated main clause. Here we gain an insight into the state of Criseyde's mind as she tries to equivocate her responsibility for deceiving Troilus. There is another option open to the reader, the second prism, in the matter of voice. By the unusual device of running on the two stanzas without a pause he or she can connect the participial construction to the preceding predication 'Criseyde unto hire bedde wente …' (Tr 5.1021). Moreover, by assuming *brede* to be transitive with *cause* as its object, he or she can place responsibility for Criseyde's decision more clearly upon her, though the intransitive is more likely to be what Chaucer intended. There the subject of Criseyde who is 'Retornyng …' comes up to the surface. Where the pause is placed very much affects the grammar of this passage (1a) and the speaker's attitude (1c).

(13) focuses on the facial expressions of Diomede as he makes his advances to Criseyde.

(13) And with that word he gan to waxen red,
      And in his speche *a litel wight* he quok,
      And caste asyde *a litel wight* his hed,
      And stynte a while; and afterward he wok,
      And sobreliche on hire he threw his lok,
      And seyde, "I am, al be it yow no joie,
      As gentil man as any wight in Troie.   Tr 5.925-31

The phrase 'a litel wight' in Tr 5.926-7 may bear a different interpretation depending on whether the narrator articulates it in a level tone without any pause before or after it or in a rising tone with a pause before and after it. We have already been told that Diomede tries to 'fish her' and makes her his own (Tr 5.771-7). In view of the cunning which this elicits we may take a rising intonation as suggesting that his shaky voice is artificial and disingenuous. However, in view of his blushes we may take it that despite his earlier deliberate attempts to catch her he is charmed by her beauty and that his faltering voice is the genuine result of his discomposure. In this case we might expect a level intonation, suggesting that his usual cunning mask has been cast aside to reveal his true humanity. Thus the intonation at point indicates the narrator's view of Diomede (1c). (See the speaker's intention in Chapter 9.)

In (14) we find Criseyde's vow to be faithful to Troilus after hearing his sincere confession of love for her.

(14) "Now God, thow woost, in thought ne dede untrewe
    To Troilus was *nevere yet* Criseyde."   Tr 3.1053-4

In (15) Criseyde shows Diomede her true state of mind after hearing his advances to her.

(15) What I shal after don I kan nat seye;
    But trewelich, *as yet* me list *nat* pleye.   Tr 5.986-7

We have to note that the meaning of the sentence is affected by where the focus of negation marked by the primary stress is placed. In (14) is that stress given to *untrewe* meaning that Criseyde was never unfaithful to Troilus? Or is it given to the adverb *yet* with some scepticism meaning that she was not unfaithful but only up to now? From a metrical point of view, stress is given to both *untrewe* and *yet*. The voice here is related to (1a) regarding the grammar of negation, to (1b) regarding the information focus, and to (1c) regarding the view of Criseyde.

The same is true of (15). The meaning of the sentence varies according to whether the force of the negation applies to *pleye* or to *yet*. Metrically a stress is given to both *pleye* and *yet*. The former emphasises the point that the action itself is negated, but the latter suggests that the time for *pleye* has not come yet, thus intimating that she may yield in time (1a, b, c).

In (16) the narrator is describing Criseyde's response to the advances made by Diomede. Is this response part of her courtly training or an indication of her true instincts?

(16) But natheles she thonketh Diomede
    Of al his travaile and his goode cheere,
    And that hym list his frendshipe hire to bede;
    And she accepteth it in good manere,
    And *wol* do fayn that is hym lief and dere,
    And tristen hym she *wolde*, and wel she *myghte*,
    As seyde she; and from hire hors sh'alighte.   Tr 5.183-9

The modal auxiliaries *wol*, *wolde*, and *myghte* are metrically stressed. In terms of the information structure of (1b), Criseyde here makes her trust in Diomede explicit, and thus meets his expectation. She thus embarks on the road to deception, a breach of her *trouthe* to Troilus (1c). Of course, we may disregard such an interpretation if she intends this expression as a mere politeness marker as shown in (7) in Chapter 9 regarding its illocutionary force.

In the final line *seyde* bears the metrical stress. Does the narrator imply that she merely "said" so, but did not intend to fulfil her promise (1b), or that she responded very positively to Diomede beyond his expectations, indeed (1c)? The stress patterns of the expressions above combined with the speaker's attitude are likely to lead to ambiguity for the reader, the second prism.

We have already dealt with (17) in relation to its syntactic ambiguity. (See (19) in Section 11.2.3.)

(17) And thus to hym she seyde, as ye may here,

> *As she that* hadde hire herte on Troilus
> So faste that ther may it non arace;
> And strangely she spak, and seyde thus:
> "O Diomede, I love that ilke place
> Ther I was born; and Joves, for his grace,   Tr 5.952-7

In the phrase 'as she that ...' (Tr 5.953), *as* and *that* are metrically unstressed,[202] whereas *she* and its predicate verb are metrically stressed. If this metrical structure is activated by and combined with the grammatical structure (1a) and the information structure (1b), the phrase is likely to be treated as if it were an independent sentence as in '(As) she (that) hadde hire herte on Troilus ....' As shown in (6) in Section 11.2.3, we have such a scribal variant. This reinforces the factual interpretation of the phrase by contrast with the simile-based non-factual interpretation. This phrase underlines the image of Criseyde both as courtly lady and faithful lover. In terms of (1b), a reading which assumes that the phrase introduces an independent sentence merely makes it refer to old information about Criseyde. If, however, we assume a simile, then we have new or generic information ("one who ..."). The former reading ensures her qualification to be a courtly lady, while the latter weakens it by appearing to deny its factual existence. A combination of both interpretations seems to be the most creative one and the most satisfactory way out of this dilemma.

13.5. Final remarks

In this chapter we have looked at voice in its relation to the double prism structure and have shown how it can contribute to the occurrence of ambiguity. Sound itself is not semantic or informative: only when combined with words/syntax (1a), discourse/information structure (1b), and the speaker's attitude (1c), is it capable of producing meanings. We found that alternative interpretations of a given expression are induced through its 'chiming' effects or its manifold phonetic features (pause, stress, intonation, etc.), and that the combinations of (1a, b, c) reinforce the polyphony of the expression. This polyphony is a good impetus to ambiguity in the mind of the reader, the second prism.[203]

---

[202] As we have seen in Section 11.2, the phrase 'as she that' is repeated at important turning points for the characterization of Criseyde. The metrical patterns regarding this phrase is the same as (17) here.

[203] I have discussed the basic outlines of ambiguity arising from voice in Nakao (2000) and Nakao (2010b).

13. Ambiguity in voice

In Part IV, Chapters 11, 12, and 13, we have examined how ambiguity is likely to arise in linguistic domains as viewed from the double prism structure. In Chapter 11 we have looked at the phrase *as she that*, and shown how it can cause ambiguity depending on whether the reader, the second prism, takes it as a grammaticalised unit (causal meaning) or analytically (simile meaning). We have dealt with some other syntactical ambiguities in relation to her fluctuating emotions. In Chapter 12 we have focused on the paradigmatic question of words. We have examined what words Chaucer used to refer to Criseyde's unstable affections and what words he did not, and investigated how they were semantically and/or pragmatically distinguishable. The words which he did choose, such as *slydynge* or *pite*, were found to be frequently used in a way that created ambiguity for the reader, the second prism. In Chapter 13 dealing with voice, we described how a given verse allows for various ways of articulation providing the reader, the second prism, with chances of ambiguity.

In the last chapter (Chapter 14), we will make a brief summary of Chapters 1 to 13, and explain the structure of Chaucer's ambiguity obtainable from the above discussion.

Part V: Conclusion

14. Concluding remarks

14.1. Summary of this investigation

In this book we have examined the source of Chaucer's ambiguity with special reference to *Troilus and Criseyde*. We have identified various types of ambiguity and observed how they combine through the double prism structure we have proposed. There now follows a summary of our findings.

Part I was of three chapters. Chapter 1 set out the aim of the investigation which was to describe and explain the processes whereby ambiguity was likely to arise. In this connection it was necessary to emphasise certain important points. In Chaucerian texts having no Ur-texts, we have to consider not only the writer's point of view but also the reader's. When a gap in comprehension arises between the constituent elements of the text—between, for example, the principal and peripheral senses of a word—then ambiguity is bound to arise. It is necessary to note the processes of inference open to the reader, to observe the various levels in the text and to conduct one's investigation in such a way that it extends over all levels. We pointed out that previous studies of ambiguity in Chaucer based on these points have been inadequate.

In Chapter 2 we reviewed previous scholarship in the field, both theoretical and practical. We also suggested topics for future research. As to theoretical material, we found medieval rhetoric and allegory of limited use, but that modern work in the spheres of poetics (Jakobson, Bakhtin, etc.), semantics/pragmatics (Grice, Austin), and cognitive linguistics (Lakoff) was of more assistance in that it pointed the way to greater sensitivity to the subtle and sometimes hidden meanings of words. These writers take ample account not only of the speaker's point of view but the reader's, and thus of the interaction of the two. Their active use of the inferential processes, contiguity and similarity, contributing to the polysemantic understanding of an utterance, is one of their achievements. When dealing with Chaucer, we need to ensure that these inferential methods are applied not only to figures of speech but also to the reading process as a whole. However, these recent discoveries of poetics, semantics/pragmatics, and cognitive linguistics have little been applied to studies of his ambiguity. There have, on the other hand, been many practical studies of ambiguity in Chaucer, but no theoretical framework has been established and therefore a biased treatment has been the result. As we have shown, there has been no unified approach to this matter of ambiguity, nor has its mechanism been satisfactorily explained.

In Chapter 3 we proposed a methodology for describing the way in which ambiguity arises in Chaucer, i.e. the double prism structure as a framework for it. It consists of the following five elements: a phenomenon, the writer's view of it (the first prism), his way of giving expression to it, the reader's reconstruction of it through the expression (the second prism), and his or her interpretation. The reader is induced through the expression given to assume the speaker's view and to infer as best as he or she can the phenomenon originally observed (the first element). Naturally, when one interpretation is impossible, ambiguity occurs. We illustrated this framework using the example 'And gilteles, I woot wel, I yow leve' (Tr 5.1084). See also Section 1.2.3.

The phenomenon involves factors of the socio-cultural world in which the first and second prisms lived/live, and the two prisms are apt to be strongly affected by their interpersonal discourse contexts. The relationship between the first and second prisms is hierarchically structured: the character as a speaker and the character as a hearer inside the story, the narrator and the audience who read stage by stage parts of the story, and the author standing outside the story and integrating the work as a whole and the reader who can observe its development as a whole. We are encouraged to assume each of the viewpoints mentioned above and so proceed to an interpretation running across them.

Regarding the first prism, we paid particular attention to the observation of two overlapping extremes (the sacred and the secular, the serious and the playful, etc.) of medieval people, their allegorical way of thinking, and the way in which Chaucer understands his characters: as his understanding of them develops, so does his sympathy for them which leads to a clouding of his moral judgement. In our view the contemporary restrictions on freedom of speech probably led to his use of ambiguous expressions when discussing ticklish moral dilemmas. In his early works these mainly take the form of allegory or equivocation, but in his middle period, that of *Troilus and Criseyde*, a psychological dimension is added to his technique which produces works of a quality superior to that of the earlier ones. The second prism, which may loosely be termed as the recipient, ranges over a wide set of individuals—the contemporary courtly audience, fifteenth century scribes, early editors of the printed texts, modern editors and critics and the reader. The view-shifting 'I' is set up as integrator of these various readings. Sensitivity to the overlapping values of, say, the sacred and the secular as regards one phenomenon is central to the medieval way of thinking. We have already mentioned the need for the reader to act as a kind of switching device between the two stances.

We identified various categories of expression which cause ambiguity. We divided them, broadly speaking, into three groups depending on the nature of the context. Textual domains have the widest context, interpersonal domains are intermediate, and linguistic domains have the smallest. We then further divided them into subtypes, generating ten categories altogether. Textual domains constituting Part II include metatext (Chapter 4), intertextuality (Chapter 5), macro-textual structure (theme, characterization, plot) (Chapter 6), speech presentation (Chapter 7), and discourse structure (Chapter 8). Interpersonal domains of which Part III is composed include the speaker's intention (Chapter 9) and modality (Chapter 10). Linguistic domains belonging to Part IV include syntax (Chapter 11), word (Chapter 12), and voice (Chapter 13).

We have regarded the concept of ambiguity here as being defined through the double prism structure, and that the number and types of it as stipulated according to the category of ambiguity. We have decided the way of describing Chaucer's ambiguity in such a way that we go from textual domains to linguistic domains with the addition of cross-references when ambiguity crosses type/subtype-boundaries and so is deepened.

14. Concluding remarks

In Chapters 4 to 13, according to each type of expression, we have described how ambiguity is likely to arise through the double prism structure. In Chapter 4 we have focused on the psychology of scribes and modern editors as representing one of the second prism responses to Chaucer's text. They are readers challenging the author, the first prism, for the editorship of the text. Our examination has shown that variable textual evidence provided by scribes and modern editors regarding Criseyde's shifting affections is not the result of error but suggestive of the ambiguous state of his text. For instance, the variation between 'in hire armes' or 'in his armes' (Tr 5.1240—Troilus's dream of the boar) comes of course from the fact that an embrace is, or can be, mutual.

Chapter 5 examined the interaction of texts. Since medieval literary production features adaptation, intertextuality is inevitably involved. We discussed the intertexts assumed to be lying between *Troilus and Criseyde* and the second prism, the reader. We demonstrated that the meaning of the text is subject to change according to whether or not we assume the existence of an intertext behind it. Chaucer finished translating Boethius's *De Consolatione Philosophiae* into English immediately before commencing *Troilus and Criseyde*. The concept of love in *Troilus and Criseyde*, as it appears, for instance, in Tr 3.1744-71, may be thought of as universal or personal depending on whether the reader, the second prism, knows Boethius or not.

In Chapter 6 we examined the macro-structural elements of the text, that is, theme, characterisation, and plot. Although these three belong to the category of expression, the theme is related to the phenomenon the speaker tries to choose, the characterization is reflective of the first prism's view, and the plot is exactly relevant to the expression since it is shown syntagmatically on the text while the first two are paradigmatically oriented. These three are all open to dual interpretations through the second prism reader. Love can be sacred or secular—*agape*, *philia* or *eros*, or all at the same time. Within the narrator and the characters we find a merger of their ideal and their human aspects. In the plot the interaction of heterogeneous elements arises, e.g. the juxtaposition of courtly ideals and human self-interest.

In Chapter 7 we drew attention to the use of free indirect speech (Tr 3.918-24) in connection with Criseyde's immoral action. Because of this, it is difficult to distinguish between the objective narrative and Criseyde's subjective response to Troilus in a predicament. The reader, the second prism, has to make up his or her mind as to the proportion of each.

Chapter 8 examined the cohesion between proforms and their antecedents/ellipses and their reconstructions, the question of causality, and the relation between the word order of a sentence and its information structure (regarding the order of the speaker's recognition). In *Troilus and Criseyde* reprehensible acts are taken for granted between the persons concerned, and expressed economically by means of pronouns or ellipsis. We found there that the cohesion was not necessarily determined, and left to the reader, the second prism's inference, which led to ambiguity (Tr 2.484-97). Furthermore, depending on whether the word order implied the speaker's intention, we found that the meaning of the sentence could vary.

In Chapter 9 we focused on the illocutionary force or implicature of an utterance as against its literal meaning. We found that there were occasions on which characters were forced to temper their speech with some equivocation owing to the social and moral restrictions imposed upon them. As a means of dealing with the unspoken words of the first prism, the second prism is encouraged to take an active part in the interpretation of it. We examined whether the choice of a literal or an illocutionary meaning gave rise to ambiguity.

In Chapter 10 we looked at the speaker's mental attitude towards propositional content, and dealt with modal auxiliaries, modal adverbs, and modal lexical verbs. Because *Troilus and Criseyde* is psychologically profound, the use of modality and the generation of ambiguity through it are worth particular attention. The immoral acts perpetrated by the characters are not presented in black and white terms, but filtered through the judgement of the speakers and so ambivalently. Through this use of modality it often happens that the morally and ethically equivocal worlds of the characters are shown to the reader, the second prism, as presenting a very fine line between truth and falsehood. This is a fertile breeding ground for ambiguity, especially of the psychological type ('And treweliche, as writen wel I fynde / That al this thyng was seyd of good entente,' Tr 4.1415-6).

Chapter 11 was concerned with syntactic ambiguity. We found that this ambiguity was most obvious in descriptions of Criseyde's fluctuating states of mind. The speaker was found betraying his or her psychological conflict in his or her loose syntax, which allows for an ambiguous parsing of it on the part of the second prism readers ('And gilteles, I woot wel, I yow leve.' Tr 5.1084).

Chapter 12 described ambiguity arising from the sense relations of a word. We investigated word choice and its semantic features. We found that regarding Criseyde's shifting affections, the speakers were hesitant to make them explicit, and chose a word of multiple significance or high semantic condensation, such as *slydynge* (Tr 5.825) and *pite* (Tr 5.824), or a word of wide application such as *frendshipe* (Tr 2.962). These words activated the reader, the second prism's inference, leaving him or her in uncertainty regarding the choice of their central meaning or the validity of the correspondence between a word and the event it describes.

Chapter 13 focused on the semantic extension of an utterance via voice. Chaucer's narratives were primarily transmitted to the audience through sounds. Chiming, meter, stress, pause, intonation, etc. play an important role in the semantic production of an utterance. When one and the same utterance by the narrator/characters allows for manifold ways of articulation to the reader, the second prism, we found that it was semantically influential in three ways: the semantic range of a word or the syntax was likely to be affected (the category of ambiguity III in Chapter 3); the meaning of old and new information was likely to be altered (the category of ambiguity I): the interpersonally directed meaning, that is, the speaker's intention or his or her attitude regarding the propositional content, was likely to shift (the category of ambiguity II). Further, we found that the above three were functional in cooperation with one another ('Ye ben the womman in this world lyvynge— / Withouten paramours ...' (Tr 2.235-6)).

In Parts II to IV (Chapters 4 to 13) we described types of ambiguity and the interaction between one type and another type through the double prism structure. In this way we attempted to integrate methodology and interpretation as regards Chaucer's ambiguity, and to describe and explain how and why it is likely to arise.

14.2. The structure of Chaucer's ambiguity

Ambiguity in Chaucer is likely to arise in the following circumstances.

(1) Chaucer's ambiguity is likely to arise, when the phenomenon of the double prism structure is presented with diametrically opposed values such as the sacred and the secular or the real and the ideal, what Brewer (1974) calls Gothic art of 'juxtaposition' (see Chapter 2). The plot of *Troilus and Criseyde*, the rise and fall of their love, contains the seeds of psychological instability from the start. This instability is epitomised in Criseyde's own adaptability. Her inconstancy brought about by her *pite* exemplifies it particularly well. The reason why this love story has repeatedly been the subject of scholarly discussion is that it illustrates in condensed form the contrast between the behaviour expected of a courtly lady and the operation of her true human nature behind the scenes. Thus previous studies have dealt with this Gothic art of 'juxtaposition' again and again, but they have not addressed it as part of the structure of Chaucer's ambiguity. Here we have incorporated this into the double prism structure, i.e. the phenomenon observed by the author, the first prism or the characters he has created, or the phenomenon the reader, the second prism, infers from the words of the text and attempts to internalise for himself or herself.

(2) Chaucer's ambiguity is likely to arise when the author, the first prism, can see a phenomenon from various angles. The author, after all, occupies so to speak a vantage point, and when the actions of his characters contravene the social or moral code, he has the tendency to become involved with them, *engagé*, so to speak, and at the same time detached. Here we treated it as a function of the first prism of the double prism structure and discussed it in relation to other constituents (phenomenon, expression, the second prism). The author is usually hidden behind the text. We can only assume his existence through the words of the narrator or the characters. Those ambiguities apparently unintended by the first prism speaker were dealt with in relation to the second prism, and we described them as ambiguities allowed for by the text and permissible for the reader to assume.[204]

(3) Chaucer's ambiguity is likely to arise when expressions—a bridge between the first and second prisms—can have wide application. This happens particularly when characters are required to act against their social ideals, the author becomes involved in their psychological tension, and chooses the kind of expression which allows for different views and interpretations. Previous studies of Chaucer's ambiguity have shown bias when dealing with this aspect and have not treated it systematically. Here we set up the expression as a category of Chaucer's ambiguity, which enabled us not only to describe the features of am-

---

[204] The uncertainty stemming from how the speaker observes or views a phenomenon, in other words, the uncertainty due to the reader's inference, can be incorporated into the question of the reader, the second prism's recognition as viewed through the double prism structure.

biguity but also the interaction of types. Accordingly we occasionally dealt with the same example repeatedly and reexamined it from different angles. For example, 'And gilteles, I woot wel, I yow leve.' (Tr 5.1084) has been dealt with in terms of modality (the effect of the modal phrase 'I woot wel' attached to the proposition), in terms of syntax (whether *gilteles* is related to *I* or *yow*), and in terms of voice (the stress of the pronoun, the intonation regarding 'I woot wel'). The overlapping of various types produced various evidence enabling the development of the ambiguity of Criseydan images, illustrated Chaucer's tendency to view mankind tenderly and sympathetically, and showed us the intensive and generative features that give rise to his ambiguity.

(4) Chaucer's ambiguity is likely to arise when the reader, the second prism, in all its guises (the audience who listened to Chaucer's narration directly, scribes, modern editors, the view-shifting 'I') assumes the author's point of view, and develops his or her inference in different directions. As mentioned above, sympathetic with characters who are required to act against their social ideals, the author has a tendency to observe their actions from some distance, and leave the final judgement of them to the readers. It is not unnatural that since they have a different experiential background, they interpret them in a different way. Further, they can read into what the author has stated unconsciously or what he has not intended to state, where assimilating themselves to the first prism, they are involved in producing new ways of interpretation. Past studies have adopted either the idealistic approach which sought to follow the author's single intention or the path of the reader-response interpretation. In this book, using both of the first and second prisms, we have attempted to describe our supposition of the author's intention and to present an interpretation from the reader's point of view, and thus been able to point out the disagreement as well as the agreement between the two prisms. For example, we have concluded that ambiguity arising from the question whether *leve* means 'depart from' or 'believe' in 'And gilteles, I woot wel, I yow leve.' (Tr 5.1084) is created not so much by the first prism (Chaucer or the author behind Criseyde) as by the reader, the second prism. The vital cognitive devices for producing meaning, metonymy (contiguity) and metaphor (similarity) have so far been only inadequately examined in relation to ambiguity in Chaucer. In this study we have attempted to remedy that defect.[205]

(5) Chaucer's ambiguity is produced when a second prism reader alone can find various interpretations, or when several readers can. We are not content to rely

---

[205] Metonymy is a type of inference based on contiguity. The category of ambiguity shown in Section 3.2 is due to this inference. It brings about the interactions between the larger or containing types and the smaller or contained types of ambiguity and those between constitutive elements of each type such as one text and another, and one sense of a sentence (linguistic meaning) and another (its illocutionary force). Metaphor, on the other hand, is based on similarity. The semantic relation condensed in an expression as typically shown in the polysemy of a word (e.g. *slydynge*) is dependent on this inference. The strong interaction between these two inferences seems to have enabled the reader easily to participate in the interpretation of the text.

14. Concluding remarks

merely on lexicographers, modern editors or critics for the interpretation of such and such an expression. We have set up the double prism structure specifically as a framework to describe interpretations. In relation to this work, the readers' interpretations will obviously be most sharply divided over the matter of Criseyde's shifting emotions. Ambiguities arising from her character have often been discussed. However, how and why they actually occur have not thoroughly examined. Here we have described them through the double prism structure from the higher to the lower level and across the levels. In this we have sought to expand thoroughly on the previous treatments of the matter. Throughout our investigations we found that ambiguity in Chaucer goes beyond a mere rhetorical figure, and becomes key means of understanding the work as a whole. We concluded that what lies behind his ambiguity, connecting a local element with a global and vice versa and functioning as a powerful magnet, is the double prism structure, which is crucial to the whole poem. Chaucer's language is influenced by various contextual factors, and the meanings of the expressions he uses are likely to fluctuate accordingly. One example of this is 'slydynge of corage' (Tr 5.825) over the interpretation of which the readers are likely to be divided. An illustration of the double prism structure using the example of Tr 5.1054 (see (1) in Chapter 1) is given on the next page.

In this study we have attempted to clarify this structure of which the illustration is a summary in diagrammatic form.

The categories of ambiguity which I have mentioned as deriving from the double prism structure are by no means fixed. The framework and the types belonging to it will continue to be restructured by the reader as deficiencies emerge and the search for new developments becomes desirable. The examples adduced are not a definitive list; rather they were chosen from among many as suitable for my investigation. I plan a more elaborate discussion of this subject in due course and indeed an extension of my investigations beyond *Troilus and Criseyde* so that a comparison between the individual works may be made. In the fullness of time I also hope to do the same in relation to other poets of the period—Gower, Langland, and the *Gawain*-poet, to name but three. This study has merely paved the way.[206]

---

[206] With regard to studies of Chaucer's ambiguity, language as parole is more important than language as langue, since various factors are condensed in, and contributory to, the rise of ambiguity such as language, literature, culture and society. A language-as-langue approach to his ambiguity can describe it only to a limited extent. Our approach to it is an attempt to study the language viewed from a language-as-parole.

274   Part V: Conclusion

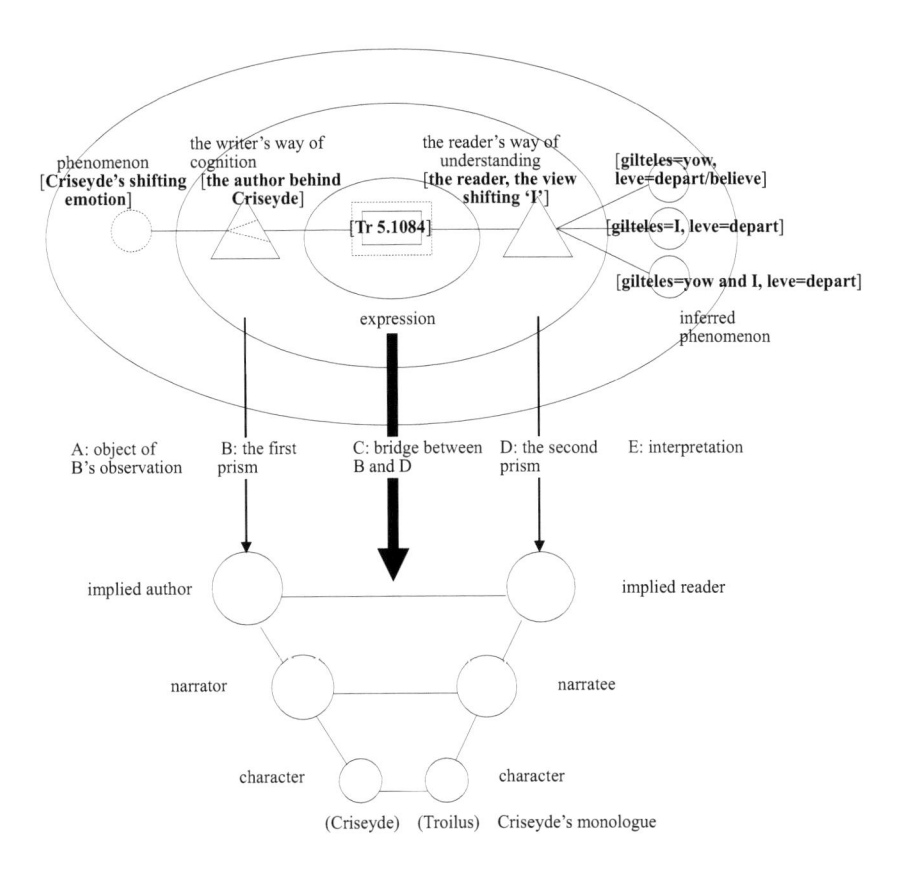

phenomenon | the writer's way of cognition | the reader's way of understanding | [gilteles=yow, leve=depart/believe]
[Criseyde's shifting emotion] | [the author behind Criseyde] | [the reader, the view shifting 'I'] | [gilteles=I, leve=depart]
[Tr 5.1084] | | | [gilteles=yow and I, leve=depart]

expression

inferred phenomenon

A: object of B's observation   B: the first prism   C: bridge between B and D   D: the second prism   E: interpretation

implied author — implied reader

narrator — narratee

character — character

(Criseyde) (Troilus)   Criseyde's monologue

Appendix A

Lines referring to Criseyde's shifting affections

(Abbreviations are as follows: T=Troilus, C=Criseyde, P=Pandarus, N=Narrator, M=Monologue. The arrow '→' stands for 'speaks to.')

Book lines	Words	Speaker-Hearer
1.56	And how that she forsook hym er she deyde.	N
2.477	"But that I nyl nat holden hym in honde,	C→P
2.666-7	Now myghte som envious jangle thus: "This was a sodeyn love; ...	N
2.667-8	" ... how myght it be That she so lightly loved Troilus	N
2.673-4	For I sey nought that she so sodeynly Yaf hym hire love, ...	N
2.678-9	For which by proces and by good servyse He gat hire love, and in no sodeyn wyse.	N
2.1222-4	... but holden hym in honde She nolde nought, ne make hireselven bonde In love; ...	N
3.269-70	For that man is unbore, I dar wel swere, That evere wiste that she dide amys.	P→T
3.783-4	That, but it were on hym along, ye nolde Hym nevere falsen while ye lyven sholde.	P→C
3.803-4	My deere herte wolde me nought holde So lightly fals! ...	C→P
3.806	"Horaste! Allas, and falsen Troilus?	C→P
3.983-4	Al thoughte she hire servant and hire knyght Ne sholde of right non untrouthe in hire gesse,	N
3.1049	And if that I be giltif, do me deye!	C→T
3.1053-4	"Now God, thow woost, in thought ne dede untrewe To Troilus was nevere yet Criseyde."	C→T
3.1499-50	"Ye ben so depe in-with myn herte grave, That, though I wolde it torne out of my thought,	C→T
4.15	For how Criseyde Troilus forsook—	N
4.16	Or at the leeste, how that she was unkynde—	N
4.615	And if she wilneth fro the for to passe,	P→T
4.616	Thanne is she fals; so love hire wel the lasse.	P→T
4.675-6	That al this world ne myghte hire love unbynde, Ne Troilus out of hire herte caste,	N
4.744-6	I, woful wrecche and infortuned wight, ... Moot goon and thus departen fro my knyght!	C (M)
4.754-5	Syn he that wont hire wo was for to lithe She moot forgoon; ...	N
4.773	That ilke day that I from yow departe,	C (M)
4.785-7	"Myn herte and ek the woful goost therinne Byquethe I with youre spirit to compleyne Eternaly, for they shal nevere twynne;	C (M)

4.788	For though in erthe ytwynned be we tweyne,	C (M)
4.860-1	Wol he han pleynte or teris er I wende? I have ynough, if he therafter sende!"	C→P
4.904	"Grevous to me, God woot, is for to twynne,	C→P
4.1118	Myn herte seyth, 'Certeyn, she shal nat wende.'	P→T
4.1270	But for the cause that we sholden twynne.	C→T
4.1303-4	"The soth is this: the twynnyng of us tweyne Wol us disese and cruelich anoye,	C→T
4.1436-7	But natheles, the wendyng of Criseyde, For al this world, may nat out of his mynde;	N
4.1440-2	... "Certes, if ye be unkynde, ... Ne shal I nevere have hele, honour, ne joye.	T→C
4.1494-5	Ne dredeles, in me ther may nat synke A good opynyoun, if that ye wende,	T→C
4.1534-7	"For thilke day that I for cherisynge ... Be fals to yow, my Troilus, my knyght,	C→T
4.1546-7	And Attropos my thred of lif tobreste If I be fals! ...	C→T
4.1551-2	That thilke day that ich untrewe be To Troilus, myn owene herte fre,	C (M)
4.1613-4	Ne, parde, lorn am I naught fro yow yit, Though that we ben a day or two atwynne.	C→T
4.1630-1	And by my thrift, my wendyng out of Troie Another day shal torne us alle to joie.	C→T
4.1635	That er that I departe fro yow here,	C→T
5.678-9	Fele I no wynd that sowneth so lik peyne; It seyth, 'Allas! Whi twynned be we tweyne?'"	T (M)
5.768-9	For bothe Troilus and Troie town Shal knotteles thoroughout hire herte slide;	N
5.824-5	Ne nevere mo ne lakked hire pite; Tendre-herted, slydynge of corage,	N
5.911-2	"What wol ye more, lufsom lady deere? Lat Troie and Troian fro youre herte pace!	D→C
5.1052-3	Ther made nevere womman moore wo Than she, whan that she falsed Troilus.	N
5.1056-7	For I have falsed oon the gentileste That evere was, and oon the worthieste!	C (M)
5.1067-8	Al be I nat the first that dide amys, What helpeth that to don my blame awey?	C (M)
5.1073-4	And syn that thus departen ye and I, Yet prey I God, so yeve yow right good day,	C (M)
5.1084	And gilteles, I woot wel, I yow leve.	C (M)
5.1086-8	But trewely, how longe it was bytwene That she forsok hym for this Diomede, Ther is non auctour telleth it, I wene.	N
5.1097-9	And if I myghte excuse hire any wise, For she so sory was for hire untrouthe, Iwis, I wolde excuse hire yet for routhe.	N
5.1247-8	My lady bryght, Criseyde, hath me bytrayed, In whom I trusted most of ony wight.	T (M)
5.1266-7	But who may bet bigile, yf hym lyste, Than he on whom men weneth best to triste?	T (M)
5.1279-80	How darstow seyn that fals thy lady ys For any drem, right for thyn owene drede?	P→T

Appendix A

5.1297-8	That if so is that she untrewe be, / I kan nat trowen that she wol write aycyn.	P→T
5.1440-1	He ne eet, ne dronk, ne slep, ne word seyde, / Ymagynyng ay that she was unkynde,	N
5.1445-8	He thought ... Joves of his purveyaunce / Hym shewed hadde in slep the signifiaunce / Of hire untrouthe and his disaventure,	N
5.1569-70	But natheles, though he gan hym dispaire, / And dradde ay that his lady was untrewe,	N
5.1634	Hym thoughte it lik a kalendes of chaunge.	N
5.1669-70	And of this broche, he tolde hym word and ende, / Compleynyng of hire hertes variaunce,	N
5.1679-80	That syn ye nolde in trouthe to me stonde, / That ye thus nolde han holden me in honde!	T (M)
5.1682-3	Allas, I nevere wolde han wend, er this, / That ye, Criseyde, koude han chaunged so;	T (M)
5.1684-6	Ne, but I hadde agilt and don amys, / So cruel wende I nought youre herte, ywis, / To sle me thus! ...	T (M)
5.1695-6	"Thorugh which I se that clene out of youre mynde / Ye han me cast—...	T (M)
5.1706-8	God," ... "that oughtest taken heede / To fortheren trouthe, and wronges to punyce, / Whi nyltow don a vengeaunce of this vice?	T (M)
5.1726-8	For sory of his frendes sorwe he is, / And shamed for his nece hath don amys,	N
5.1738-9	... of this tresoun now, / God woot that it a sorwe is unto me!	P→T
5.1774	That al be that Criseyde was untrewe,	N
5.1775	That for that gilt she be nat wroth with me.	N
5.1776	Ye may hire gilt in other bokes se;	N

277

Appendix B

Words indicative of instability—an overview by works (Tr, Bo, LGW, Henryson)

word/works	Tr				Bo		LGW	Henryson		
	Criseyde	Fortune	worldly joy	Calkas, Diomede, etc.	Fortune	worldly joy, creature, thing	Jason, Tereus, etc.	Cresseid	Venus	Fortune
slide slydynge	+				+	+				
moeve moevable moevablete					+	+				
fle			+		+	+	+			
passe	+				+	+	+			
unstable		+			+			+	+	
mutable mutabilite mutacyoun		+			+	+			+	
muable remuable		+	+			+				
flitte flitting			+		+	+				
gerful		+								
chaunge chaungeable	+			+	+	+	+	+	+	
vary variaunt variaunce	+					+			+	
brotel brotelenesse		+			+	+	+	+		
light/e	+					+	+			
transitorie			+		+	+				
temporal						+				
sodeyn sodeynly	+			+	+	+			+	
inconstance unconstant								+	+	
fikelnesse (fickill)								+		+
tikel tikelnesse										
(frivoll) (frivolous)								+		+
unkynde unkyndenesse	+	+					+			

Appendix B

word/works	Tr				Bo		LGW	Henryson		
	Criseyde	Fortune	worldly joy	Calkas, Diomede, etc.	Fortune	worldly joy, creature, thing	Jason, Tereus, etc.	Cresseid	Venus	Fortune
cruel cruelte	+	+			+		+			
feeble feeblesse						+				
frele freletee frelenesse						+				
infirme infirmete						+		+		
don/goon/fare amys	+			+		+				
vice	+					+	+			
gylt	+						+			
bigile agylten	+	+		+	+		+			
holden ... in honde	+									
untrewe	+			+			+	+		
unstedefast						+				
unsad unfaithful					+					
fals falsly falsen falsnesse	+		+	+	+	+	+	+	+	
deceit deceive deceivable		+	+	+	+					
dissimulen dissimuler								+		
feyn				+		+	+			
forsworn							+			
bitraye trayen	+				+					
bitrayse traysen				+			+			
tresoun	+			+			+			
trecherie				+	+					
traitour traitorye		+	+	+		+	+			
forgon	+					+				
cast/drive/ torne/throwe out of herte/mynde	+	+		+						
forsake	+				+					

Appendix B

word/works	Tr				Bo		LGW	Henryson		
	Criseyde	Fortune	worldly joy	Calkas, Diomede, etc.	Fortune	worldly joy, creature, thing	Jason, Tereus, etc.	Cresseid	Venus	Fortune
knotteles	+									
wende wendynge	+						+			
departe fro	+				+	+				
leve						+	+			
twynne atwynne	+					+	+			
lusty	+			+		+	+	+		
unclene						+		+		
lecherous lecherie						+		+		
wantown wantownesse								+		

N.B.: *(i) The words in ( ) do not appear in Chaucer.*

(ii) The words marked by slashes show variants of the same construction.

Bibliography

I. Texts and translation

Baugh, A. C. (ed.)
  1963 *Chaucer's Major Poetry*. Englewood, New Jersey: Prentice-Hall.
Benson, Larry D. (ed.)
  1987 *Riverside Chaucer. Third Edition Based on The Works of Geoffrey Chaucer Edited by F. N. Robinson*. Boston: Houghton Mifflin Company.
Bergen, H. (ed.)
  1906 *Lydgate's Troy Book*. EETS ES 97.
  1908 *Lydgate's Troy Book*. EETS ES 103.
  1910 *Lydgate's Troy Book*. EETS ES 106.
  1935 *Lydgate's Troy Book*. EETS ES 126.
Beadle, Richard and J. Griffiths (eds.)
  1983 *John's College, Cambridge, Manuscript L.1., A Variorum Edition of the Works of Geoffrey Chaucer*. Norman, Oklahoma: Pilgrim Books.
Blake, N. F. (ed.)
  1973 *Caxton's Own Prose*. London: Andre Deutsch.
  1980 *The Canterbury Tales Edited from the Hengwrt Manuscript*. London: Arnold.
Brewer, D. S. and L. E. Brewer (eds.)
  1969 *Troilus and Criseyde (abridged) Geoffrey Chaucer*. London: Routledge & Kegan Paul.
Brook, G. L. (ed.)
  1964 *The Harley Lyrics*. Manchester: Manchester University Press.
Brown, C. (ed.)
  1952 *Religious Lyrics of the Fourteenth Century*. (2nd edn. rev. G. V. Smithers). Oxford: Clarendon Press.
Coghill, Nevill (tr.)
  1971 *Geoffrey Chaucer Troilus and Criseyde*. London: Penguin.
Davies, R. T. (ed.)
  1963 *Medieval English Lyrics*. London: Faber and Faber.
Davis, Norman (ed.)
  1967 *Sir Gawain and the Green Knight*. (2nd edn.) Oxford: Clarendon Press.
Dedeck-Héry, V. L. and Louis Vencesals (eds.)
  1952 Boethius' *De Consolatione* by Jean de Meun. *Medieval Studies* XIX: 165-275.
Donaldson, E. T. (ed.)
  1975 *Chaucer's Poetry: An Anthology for the Modern Reader*. New York: The Ronald Press Company.
Einekel, Eugen (ed.)
  [1884] *The Life of Saint Katherine*. EETS OS 80. [Kraus Reprint Co. Millwood, N.Y.] 1978

Fisher, J. H. (ed.)
  1989 *The Complete Poetry and Prose of Geoffrey Chaucer.* 2nd edn. New York: Holt, Rinehart and Winston.
Fox, Denton (ed.)
  1981 *The Poems of Robert Henryson.* (Medieval and Tudor Series.) Oxford: at the Clarendon Press.
Francis, W. N. (ed.)
  1987 *The Book of Vices and Virtues: A Fourteenth Century Translation of the 'Somme le Roi' of Lorens D'Orleans.* Millwood, New York: Kraus Reprint.
French, W. H. and C. B. Hale (eds.)
  1930 *Middle English Metrical Romances.* New York: Russell & Russell.
Furnivall, F. J. (ed.)
  1982 *A Parallel Text Print of Chaucer's Troilus and Criseyde from the Campsall MS. of Mr. Bacon Frank, Copied for Henry V. When Prince of Wales, the Harleian MS. 2280 in the British Museum, and the Cambridge University Library MS. Gg.4.27.* London: The Chaucer Society, First Series, LXIII, LXIV.
Furnivall, F. J. and G. C. Macaulay (eds.)
  1894-1895 *Three More Parallel Texts of Chaucer's Troilus and Criseyde*, London: Published for the Chaucer Society. Kegan Paul, Trench, Trübner & Co. Limited.
Gallo, Ernest (tr.)
  1971 *Poetria Nova and Its Sources in Early Rhetorical Doctrine.* The Hague: Mouton.
Gollancz, I. (ed.)
  1892 & 1925
    Hoccleve's Works: The Minor Poems, EETS ES 61 & 73.
Griffin, N. E. and A. B. Myrick (eds. & trs.)
  1978 *The Filostrato of Giovanni Boccaccio.* New York: Octagon Books.
Hamilton, A. C. (ed.)
  1977 *Edmund Spenser: The Faerie Qveene.* London: Longman.
Hanna, Ralph III. (ed.)
  1971 *Awntyrs off Arthure at the Terne Wathelyn.* Manchester: Manchester University Press.
Howard, D. R. (ed.)
  1976 *Geoffrey Chaucer Troilus and Criseyde and Selected Short Poems.* New York: New American Library.
Karita, Motoshi (tr.)
  1949 *Koi no Toriko (Caught in Love).* Tokyo: Shingetsusha.
Kinsley, James (ed.)
  1979 *The Poems of William Dunbar.* Oxford: Clarendon Press.
Ker, William Paton (intro.)
  1967 *The Chronicle of Froissart translated out of French by sir John Bourchier Lord Berners annis 1523-25, Vol. 1.* New York: AMS Press, Inc.
Leach, MacEdward (ed.)
  1960 *Amis and Amiloun.* EETS OS 203.

Macaulay, G. C. (ed.)
  1900-1901 *The English Works of John Gower*, 2 Vols, EETS ES 81, 82.
  1899 *The Complete Works of John Gower: The French Works (Mirour de l'Omme)*. Oxford: Clarendon Press.
Macrae-Gibson, O. D. (ed.)
  1973 & 1979 *Of Arthour and Of Merlin*, 2 Vols. EETS 268 & 279.
Manly, J. M. and E. Rickert (eds.)
  1940 *The Text of the Canterbury Tales: Studied on the Basis of All Known Manuscripts*, 8 Vols. Chicago & London: The University of Chicago Press.
Miyata, Takeshi (tr.)
  1979 *Troirasu to Kuriseide (Troilus and Criseyde)*. Otemae Women's University Anglo-Norman Institute.
Morris, Richard (ed.)
  1874-1878 *Cursor Mundi*. EETS OS 57, 59, 62, 66, 68.
  1892-1893 *Cursor Mundi*. EETS OS 99, 101.
Panton, G. A. and D. Donaldson (eds.)
  1968 *The 'Best Hystoriale' of the Destruction of Troy*. EETS OS 39, 56.
Parkes, M. B. and Richard Beadle (intr.)
  1979 *Poetical Works Geoffrey Chaucer: A Facsimile of Cambridge University Library MS GG.4.27*. Cambridge: D.S. Brewer.
Parkes, M. B. and E. Salter (intr.)
  1978 *Troilus and Criseyde Geoffrey Chaucer: Facsimile of Corpus Christi College Cambridge MS 61*. Cambridge: D.S. Brewer.
Pollard, A. W. et al. (eds.)
  1898 *The Works of Geoffrey Chaucer*. (The Globe Edition) London: Macmillan.
Richardson, F. E. (ed.)
  1965 *Sir Eglamour of Artois*. EETS 256.
Robinson, R. N. (ed.)
  1957 *The Works of Geoffrey Chaucer*. London: Oxford University Press.
Root, R. K. (ed.)
  1952 *The Book of Troilus and Criseyde by Geoffrey Chaucer*. Princeton: Princeton University Press.
Rossetti, Wm. Michael (ed.)
  1873 *Chaucer's Troylus and Cryseyde* (from the Harl. MS. 3943). London: Published for the Chaucer Society.
Rotuli Parliamentorum ut et Petitiones et Placita in Parliamento, Tempore Edwardi R. I (ad Finem Reguni Edward IV). Parliament XXI Ric. II AD. 1397. 1783 & 1832. Record Commission—Misc. Publs. Vol. 3. London: H.M.S.O.
Sands, D. (ed.)
  1986 *Middle English Verse Romances*. Exeter: University of Exeter.
Schmidt, A. V. C. (ed.)
  1995 *William Langland The Vision of Piers Plowman: A Critical Edition of the B-Text Based on Trinity College Cambridge MS B.15.17*. J. M. Dent • London: Everyman.

Sinclair, John D. (ed.)
  1975 *The Divine Comedy of Dante Alighieri (1: Inferno, 2: Purgatorio, 3: Paradiso)*. Oxford, Oxford University Press.
Shoaf, R. A. (ed.)
  1989 *Geoffrey Chaucer Troilus and Criseyde*. East Lansing: Colleagues Press.
Skeat, W. W. (ed.)
  1898 *The Complete Works of Geoffrey Chaucer: Boethius and Troilus*. Oxford: Oxford University Press.
Stanley, E. G. (ed.)
  1960 *The Owl and the Nightingale*. London: Nelson.
Stanley-Wrench, Margaret (tr.)
  1965 *Troilus and Criseyde by Geoffrey Chaucer*. London: Centaur Press Ltd.
Stewart, H. F., E. K. Rand and S. J. Tester (eds. and trs.)
  1969 *Boethius: The Consolation of Philosophy*. The Loeb Classical Library. Cambridge, MA: Harvard University Press.
Sutherland, Ronald (ed.)
  1967 *The Romaunt of the Rose and Le Roman de la Rose: A Parallel-Text Edition*. Oxford: Basil Blackwell.
Tatlock, J. S. P. and P. MacKaye (tr.)
  1912 *The Modern Reader's Chaucer The Complete Works of Geoffrey Chaucer Now First Put into Modern English*. London: The Macmillan Company.
Vinaver, E. (ed.) [Revised by P. J. C. Field.]
  1987 *The Works of Sir Thomas Malory*, 2nd edn., 3 vols. Oxford: Clarendon Press.
Waker, Alice (ed.)
  1972 *Troilus and Cressida*. (The New Shakespeare) Cambridge: Cambridge University Press.
Warrington, J. (ed.)
  1975 *Geoffrey Chaucer Troilus and Criseyde*. London: J.M. Dent & Sons.
Willock, G. D. and A. Walker (eds.)
  1936 *The Arte of English Poesie by George Puttenham*. Cambridge: Cambridge University Press Library Edition.
Windeatt, B. A. (ed.)
  1990 *Geoffrey Chaucer Troilus & Criseyde: A New Edition of 'The Book of Troilus.'* London: Longman. [First publ. 1984.]
Windeatt, B. A. (tr.)
  1998 *Geoffrey Chaucer Troilus and Criseyde: A New Translation by Barry Windeatt (Oxford World Classics)*. Oxford: Oxford University Press.

II. Concordances and dictionaries

Benson, Larry D. (ed.)
   1993 *A Glossarial Concordance to The Riverside Chaucer*. New York and London: Garland Publishing, Inc.
Blake, Norman, David Burnley, Masatsugu Matsuo and Yoshiyuki Nakao (eds.)
   1994 *A New Concordance to 'The Canterbury Tales' Based on Blake's Text Edited from the Hengwrt Manuscript*. Okayama: University Education Press.
Davis, N. et al. (eds.)
   1979 *A Chaucer Glossary*. Oxford: Clarendon Press.
Godefroy, Frédéric (ed.)
   1965 *Lexique de L'Ancien Français*. Paris: Librairie Honoré Champion, Éditeur.
Jimura, Akiyuki, Yoshiyuki Nakao, and Masatsugu Matsuo (eds.)
   1988 *A Comprehensive List of Textual Comparison between Blake's and Robinson's Editions of The Canterbury Tales*. Okayama: University Education Press.
Jimura, Akiyuki, Yoshiyuki Nakao and Masatsugu Matsuo (eds.)
   1998 *A Comprehensive Textual Comparison of Troilus and Criseyde: Benson's, Robinson's, Root's, and Windeatt's Editions*. Okayama: University Education Press.
Kurath, H., S. M. Kuhn and R. E. Lewis (eds.)
   1952-2001 *Middle English Dictionary*. Ann Arbor: The University of Michigan Press.
Lewis, Charoton T. and Charles Short (eds.)
   1969 *A Latin Dictionary*. Oxford: Clarendon Press.
Matsuo, Masatsugu, Yoshiyuki Nakao, Shigeki Suzuki, and Takao Kuya (comps.)
   1986 *A PC-KWIC Concordance to the Works of Geoffrey Chaucer Based on Robinson (1957)*. Unpublished.
Oizumi, Akio (ed.)
   1988 *A Complete Concordance to the Works of Geoffrey Chaucer, Programmed by K. Miki*. Hildesheim: Olms-Weidmann.
Simpson, J. A. and E. S. C. Weiner (eds.)
   1989 *The Oxford English Dictionary*. 2nd edn. Oxford: Clarendon Press.
Tatlock, John S. P. and Arthur G. Kennedy (eds.)
   1963 *A Concordance to the Complete Works of Geoffrey Chaucer*. Washington (1927): The Carnegie Institution of Washington; Gloucester, Mass.: Peter Smith.
Whiting, B. J. (ed.)
   1967 *Proverbs, Sentences, and Proverbial Phrases from English Writings Mainly before 1500*. Cambridge, MA: The Belknap Press of Harvard University Press.

III. Books and articles

Aitchison, Jean
   1988 *Words in the Mind: An Introduction to the Mental Lexicon*. Oxford: Blackwell.

Ando, Sadao
   1976 *A Descriptive Syntax of Christopher Marlowe's Language*. Tokyo: University of Tokyo Press.

Ando, Sadao
   1986 *Eigo no Ronri • Nihongo no Ronri: Taishogakuteki Kenkyu* (*English Logic and Japanese Logic: A Contrastive Linguistic Study*). Tokyo: Taishukan.

Andretta, Helen Ruth
   1993 *Chaucer's Troilus and Criseyde: A Poet's Response to Ockhamism*. New York, Washington D. C., Baltimore: Peter Lang.

Austin, J. L.
   1962 *How to Do Things with Words*. (2nd edn. J. O. Urmson and Marina Sbisa, editors). Cambridge, Mass.: Harvard University Press.

Bakhtin, M. M.
   1998 *The Dialogic Imagination: Four Essays by M. M. Bakhtin*. (Holoquist Michael (ed.), Caryl Emerson and Michael Holoquist (trs.)) Austin: University of Texas Press.

Barney, S. A.
   1993 *Studies in Troilus: Chaucer's Text, Meter, and Diction*. East Lansing: Colleagues Press.

Barthes, R.
   1970 "Style and Its Image." In *Style: A Symposium*, S. Chatman (ed.). London and New York: Oxford University Press, 3-15.
   1977 *Image, Music, Text*. (Engl. Tr.) New York: Hill and Wang.

Baum, Paul F.
   1956 "Chaucer's Puns." *PMLA* 71: 225-46.
   1958 "Chaucer's Puns: A Supplemental List." *PMLA* 73: 167-70.

Beaugrande, Robert de and Wolfgang Dressler
   1981 *Introduction to Text Linguistics*. London and New York: Longman.

Bennett, H. S.
   1947 *Chaucer and the Fifteenth Century*. Oxford: Clarendon Press.

Benskin, Michael and Margaret Laing
   1981 "Translations and *Mischsprachen* in Middle English Manuscripts." In *So Meny People Longages and Tonges: Philological Essays in Scots Medieval English Presented to Angus McIntosh*, M. Benskin and M.L. Samuels (eds.). MEDP: Edinburgh, 55-77.

Blake, N. F.
   1977 *The English Language in Medieval Literature*. London: J. M. Dent & Sons Ltd.

Bowden, Betsy
 1987 *Chaucer Aloud: The Varieties of Textual Interpretation*. Philadelphia: University of Pennsylvania Press.
Brewer, D. S.
 1974 "Some Metonymic Relationships in Chaucer's Poetry." *POETICA* 1: 1-20.
 1986 "Chaucer's poetic style." In *The Cambridge Chaucer Companion*, Piero Boitani and Jill Mann (eds.). Cambridge: Cambridge University Press, 227-42.
Brinton, Laurel J.
 1996 *Pragmatic Markers in English: Grammaticalization and Discourse Functions*. Berlin · New York: Mouton de Gruyter.
Brink, Bernhard Ten
 1969 *The Language and Metre of Chaucer*. (Second edn., revised by Fredrich Kluge. Translated by M. Bentinck Smith.) New York: Greenwood Press, Publishers.
Brown, G. and G. Yule
 1983 *Discourse Analysis*. Cambridge: Cambridge University Press.
Brown, Peter (ed.)
 2000 *A Companion to Chaucer*. Oxford: Blackwell Publishers.
Burnley, J. D.
 1979 *Chaucer's Language and the Philosophers' Tradition*. Chaucer Studies ii. Cambridge: D. S. Brewer.
 1981 "Criseyde's Heart and the Weakness of Women: An Essay in Lexical Interpretation." *Studia Neophilologica* 54: 25-38.
 1983 *A Guide to Chaucer's Language*. London: Macmillan.
 1992 "Lexis and Semantics." In *The Cambridge History of the English Language. Vol II 1066-1476*, Norman F. Blake (ed.). Cambridge: Cambridge University Press, 409-99.
Bybee, J. et al.
 1992 *The Evolution of Grammar*. Chicago and London: The University of Chicago Press.
Chamberlin, John
 2000 *Medieval Arts Doctrines on Ambiguity and Their Place in Langland's Poetics*. Montreal & Kingston · London · Ithaca: McGill-Queen's University Press.
Chickering, H.
 1990 "Unpunctuating Chaucer." *The Chaucer Review* 25 (2): 97-109.
Clemen, Wolfgang
 1963 *Chaucer's Early Poetry*. London and New York: Methuen.
Coates, J.
 1983 *The Semantics of the Modal Auxiliaries*. London: Croom Helm.
Cooper, Goeffrey
 1980 "'Sely John' in the "Legende" of the *Miller's Tale*." *JEGP* 79: 1-12.
Cox, Catherine S.
 1998 *Gender and Language in Chaucer*. Gainesville: University Press of Florida.

Culler, J.
　1983　*On Deconstruction: Theory and Criticism after Structuralism*. London: Routledge and Kegan Paul.

Derrida, J.
　1976　*Of Grammatology*. Baltimore: Johns Hopkins Press.

Donaldson, E. T.
　1970　*Speaking of Chaucer*. University of London: The Athlone Press.
　1972　"Chaucer and the Elusion of Clarity." *Essays and Studies* 25: 23-44.
　1979　"Briseis, Briseida, Criseyde, Cresseid, Cressid: Progress of a Heroine." In *Chaucerian Problems and Perspectives: Essays Presented to Paul E. Beichner C. S. C.*, E. Vasta and Z. P. Thundy (eds.). Notre Dame: University of Notre Dame Press, 3-12.

Elliott, Ralph W. V.
　1974　*Chaucer's English*. London: Andre Deutsch.

Empson, W.
　1930　*Seven Types of Ambiguity*. Harmondsworth: Penguin Books.
　1967　*The Structure of Complex Words*. Ann Arbor. The University of Michigan Press.

Fewster, C.
　1987　*Traditionality and Genre in Middle English Romance*. Cambridge: Cambridge University Press.

Fludernik, L. D.
　1993　*The Fictions of Language and the Languages of Fiction: The Linguistic Representation of Speech and Consciousness*. London and New York: Routledge.

Frank, R. W.
　1972　*Chaucer and the Legend of Good Women*. Cambridge, MA: Harvard University Press.

Fridén, Georg
　1948　*Studies on the Tenses of the English Verb from Chaucer to Shakespeare with Special Reference to the Late Sixteenth Century*. The English Institute in the Universtiy of Uppsala.

Fries, Udo
　1985　*Einführung in die Sprache Chaucers: Phonologie, Metrik und Morphologie* (Anglistische Arbeitshefte 20). Tübingen: Max Niemeyer Verlag.

Fukaya, Masahiro and Shigenori Tanaka
　1996　*Kotoba no <Imidukeron>: Nichijogengo no Nama no Itonami* (*Ways of Significations of Word: Workings of Daily Language*). Tokyo: Kinokuniyashoten.

Gaylord, A. T.
　1964　"*Gentilesse* in Chaucer's *Troilus*." *Studies in Philology* 61: 19-34.
　1968-9　"Friendship in Chaucer's Troilus." *The Chaucer Review* 3 (4): 239-64.
　1976　"Scanning the Prosodists: An Essay in Metacriticism." *The Chaucer Review*, 11 (1): 22-82.

Gordon, I. L.
　1970　*The Double Sorrow of Troilus: A Study of Ambiguities in Troilus and Criseyde*. Oxford: Clarendon Press.

Goto, Masahiro
  1996 *Aimaibun no Shoso: Eigo no Honshitsu no Kenkyu (Aspects of Ambiguous Sentence: Investigations into the Essence of English)*. Tokyo: Soyoshuppan.
Gray, Bickford Charles
  1970 *The Influence of Rhetoric on Chaucer's Portraiture*. Ph.D diss. University of Penssylvania.
Gray, Douglas
  1979 "Chaucer and 'Pite'." In *J.R.R Tolkien, Scholar and Storyteller: Essays in Memoriam*, Mary Salu and Robert T. Farrell (eds.). Ithaca, N.Y., 173-20.
Green, P. H.
  1979 *Irony in the Medieval Romance*. Cambridge: Cambridge University Press.
Grice, H. P.
  1975 "Logic and Conversation." *Syntax and Semantics* 3: 41-58.
Halliday, M. A. K. and R. Hasan
  1976 *Cohesion in English*. London: Longman.
Halliday, M. A. K. (Rev. Christian M. I. M. Matthiessen)
  2004 *An Introduction to Functional Grammar*. London: Arnold.
Hanna III, Ralph
  1996 *Pursuing History: Middle English Manuscripts and their Texts*. Stanford, CA: Stanford University Press.
Héraucourt, W.
  1939 *Die Wertwelt Chaucers: Die Wertwelt einer Zeitwende*. Heiderburg: Carl Winter's Universitätsbuchhandlung.
Hiscoe, David Winthrop
  1983 *Equivocations of Kynde: The Medieval Tradition of Nature and Its Use in Chaucer's Troilus and Criseyde and Gower's Confessio Amantis*. U · M · I Dissertation Information Service.
Hopper, Paul J. and Elizabeth Closs Traugott
  1993 *Grammaticalization*. Cambridge: Cambridge University Press.
Howard, D. R.
  1987 *Chaucer and the Medieval World*. London: Weidenfeld and Nicolson.
Ito, Tadao
  1993 "The Mechanism of Ambiguity" (A paper read at a Symposium *Varieties of Ambiguity in Medieval English Romances*, the Ninth Congress of the Society for Medieval English Studies). [Unpublished]
Jakobson, Roman
  1960 "Closing Statement: Linguistics and Poetics." In *Style in Language*, T. A. Sebeok (ed.). Cambridge, Massachusetts: The M.I.T. Press, 350-7.
  1985 "Two Aspects of Language and Two Types of Aphasia Disturbance." *Language in Literature*. Cambridge, MA and London, England: The Beknap Press of Harvard University Press, 95-119.
Jespersen, Otto
  1917 "Negation in English and Other Languages." *Selected Writings of Otto Jespersen*. Tokyo: Senjo Publishing Co, 3-151. [1962; Orig. publ. 1917.]

Johnson, Mark
  1985 *The Body in the Mind: The Bodily Basis of Meaning, Imagination, and Reason*. Chicago and London: The University of Chicago Press.

Jordan, R. M.
  1985 *Chaucer's Poetics and the Modern Reader*. Berkeley, Los Angeles and London: University of California Press.

Kaminsky, Alice R.
  1980 *Chaucer's "Troilus and Criseyde" and the Critics*. Ohio: Ohio University Press.

Kanno, Masahiko
  1998 *Word and Deed: Studies in Chaucer's Words*. Tokyo: Eihôsha.

Kawasaki, Masatoshi
  1993 *Choosaabungaku no sekai: 'yugi' to 'topogurafi' (Chaucer's Literary World: 'Game' and Its Topography)*. Tokyo: Nanun-do.

Kerkhof, J.
  1982 *Studies in the Language of Geoffrey Chaucer*. Leiden: E. J. Brill/Leiden University Press.

Kittredge, G. L.
  1915 *Chaucer and His Poetry*. Cambridge, MA.: Harvard University Press.

Kivimaa, Kirsti
  1996a "*þe* and *þat* as Clause Connectives in Early Middle English with Especial Consideration of the Emergence of the Pleonastic *þat*." *Commentationes Humanarum Litterarum Societas Scientiarum Fennica* 39 (1).
  1996b "The Pleonastic *That* in Relative and Interrogative Constructions in Chaucer's Verse." *Commentationes Humanarum Litterarum Societas Scientiarum Fennica* 39 (3).

Knapp, Peggy A.
  1998 *Time-Bound Words: Semantic and Social Economies from Chaucer's England to Shakespeare's*. London: Macmillan.

Kökeritz, Helge
  1954 "Rhetorical Word-play in Chaucer." *PMLA* LXIX: 937-52.

Lakoff, G.
  1973 "Hedges: A Study in Meaning Criteria and the Logic of Fuzzy Concepts." *Journal of Philosophical Logic* 2 (4): 458 - 508.

Lakoff, G. and M. Johnson
  1980 *Metaphors We Live By*. Chicago and London: The University of Chicago Press.

Lakoff, G.
  1987 *Women, Fire, and Dangerous Things: What Categories Reveal about the Mind*. Chicago and London: The University of Chicago Press.

Leech, G.
  1969 *A Linguistic Guide to English Poetry*. London: Longman.
  1971 *Meaning and the English Verb*. London: Longman.
  1981 *Semantics*. London: Penguin Books.
  1983 *Principles of Pragmatics*. London: Longman.

Leech, G. and J. Coates
  1979 "Semantic Indeterminacy and the Modals." In *Studies in English Linguistics for Randolph Quirk*, S. Greenbaum, G. Leech and J. Svartvik (eds.). London and New York: Longman, 79-90.
Leech, G. and M. Short
  1981 *Style in Fiction*. London: Longman.
Levinson, S.
  1983 *Pragmatics*. Cambridge: Cambridge University Press.
Lewis, C. S.
  1932 "What Chaucer Really Did to *Il Filostrato*." *Essays and Studies* 17: 56-75.
  1936 *The Allegory of Love: A Study in Medieval Tradition*. London: Oxford University Press.
Lyons, John
  1977 *Semantics, Vol. 2*. London · New York · Melbourne: Cambridge University Press.
MacQueen, John
  1970 *Allegory*. London: Methuen & Co Ltd.
Malone, Kemp
  1951 *Chapters on Chaucer*. Westport, Connecticut: Greenwood Press.
Masui, Michio
  1954 *Eibunpo Shiriizu Sharu to Wiru*. (*English Grammar Series: Shall and Will*). Tokyo: Kenkyusha.
  1977 *Choosaa Kenkyu*. (*Studies in Chaucer*). Tokyo: Kenkyusha.
  1964 *The Structure of Chaucer's Rime Word: An Exploration into the Poetic Language of Chaucer*. Tokyo: Kenkyusha.
  1970 *Choosaa no Sekai*. (*Chaucer's World*). (Iwanamishinsho 966) Tokyo: Iwanamishoten.
Mathew, Gervase
  1948 "Ideals of Knighthood in Late-Fourteenth Century England." In *Studies in Medieval History Presented to Frederick Maurice Powicke*, R.W. Hunt, W. A. Pantin and R. W. Southern (eds.). Oxford: Clarendon, 354-62.
  1968 *The Court of Richard II*. London: John Murray.
Mehl, Dieter
  1974 "The Audience of Chaucer's *Troilus and Criseyde*." In *Chaucer and Middle English Studies: In Honour of Rossell Hope Robbins*, Beryl Rowland (ed). London: George Allen and Unwin LTD, 173-89.
Mitchell, B.
  1985 *Old English Syntax, Vol. II*. Oxford: Oxford University Press.
Mossé, Fernand
  1952 *A Handbook of Middle English*. Baltimore: The Johns Hopkins Press.
Muscatine, C.
  1957 *Chaucer and the French Tradition: A Study in Style and Meaning*. Berkeley, Los Angeles and London: University of California Press.
Mustanoja, Tauno F.
  1960 *A Middle English Syntax*. Helsinki: Société Néophilologique.

Nakano, Hirozo
1993 *Eigohojodoshi no Imiron (The Semantics of English Modal Auxliaries)*. Tokyo: Eichosha.

Nakao, Yoshiyuki
1988a "Chaucer no Aimaisei no Yoho: *Sely* no Baai" (Chaucer's Use of Ambiguity: The Case of *Sely*). In *Eibeigogakukenkyu: Matsmoto Hiroshi Sensei Taikankinen Ronbunshu (Studies in English and American Language and Literature: Essays in Honour of Professor Hiroshi Matsumoto)*, K. Kawai (ed.). Tokyo: Eihôsha, 401-7.

1988b "Chaucer's Ambiguity in *The Legend of Good Women*." *ERA (The English Research Association of Hiroshima). New Series* 6 (1): 14-49.

1993 "The Ambiguity of the Phrase *As She That* in Chaucer's *Troilus and Criseyde*." *Studies in Medieval English Language and Literature* (The Japan Society for Medieval English Studies) 8: 69-86.

1994 "The Affectivity of Criseyde's *pite*." *POETICA* (Shubun International) 41: 19-43.

1995 "A Semantic Note on the Middle English Phrase *As He/She That*." *NOWELE (North West European Language Evolution)* 25: 25-48.

1996 "Chaucer no *Moot/Moste* no Imiron: Bunpoka to Shukanka no Ichijirei Kenkyu" (The Semantics of Chaucer's *Moot/Moste*: A Case Study of Grammaticalization and Subjectification). Yamaguchidaigaku *Eigo to Eibeibungaku* (Yamaguchi University *English and English-American Literature*) 32: 69-122.

1997 "Social-Linguistic Tension as Evidenced by *Moot/Moste* in Chaucer's *Troilus and Criseyde*." In *Essays on English Literature and Language in Honour of Shun'ichi Noguchi*, Masahiko Kanno, Masahiko Agari, and G. K. Jemger (eds.). Tokyo: Eihôsha, 17-34.

1998 "Causality in Chaucer's *Troilus and Criseyde*: Semantic Tension between the Pragmatic and the Narrative Domains." In *A Love of Words: English Philological Studies in Honour of Akira Wada*, Masahiko Kanno, Gregory K. Jember, and Yoshiyuki Nakao (eds.). Tokyo: Eihôsha, 79-102.

1999 "Chaucer no *Moot/Moste* no Imiron: Gaitekiyoin no Mibunkasei" (The Semantics of Chaucer's *Moot/Moste*: The Inseparable State of External Causals). In *Gengokenkyu no Choryu: Yamamoto Kazuyuki Kyoju Taikankinen Ronbunshu (Current Issues of Linguistic Studies: A Festschrift in Honour of the Retirement of Professor Kazuyuki Yamamoto)*, Sachio Oba et al. (eds.). Tokyo: Kaitakusha, 231-46.

2000 "*Troilus and Criseyde* niokeru 'Koe' no Ambiguity" (Voice Ambiguity in *Troilus and Criseyde*). In *Kyokou to Shinjitsu: 14 Seiki Igirisubungaku Ronshu (Fiction and Truth: Essays of the English Literature of the Fourteenth Century)*, Hisao Tsuru (ed.). Tokyo: Kiriharashoten, 133-44.

2001a "Chaucer no *Troilus and Criseyde* no Gengo no Ambiguity no Shikumi: Dokusha kara mita Tekusuto Kouseiyosokan no Kankeisei no Doai no Kosatsu" (The Structure of Ambiguity in the Language of Chaucer's *Troilus and Criseyde*: A Study of the Degrees of Relatedness between Textual Constituents from the Reader's Point of View). In *Dokuso to Bouken: Kanno*

Masaiko Sensei Gotaikankinen Eigoeibugaku Ronshu (*Originality and Adventure: Essays of English Language and Literature in Honour of Professor Kanno Masahiko*), Yoshiyuki Nakao and Akiyuki Jimura (eds.). Tokyo: Eihôsha, 225-49.

2001b "Chaucer no Me no Shigaku: *semely ... to see* LGW 2074 no Ganni" (The Poetics of Chaucer's Eyes: Implications of *semely ... to see* LGW 2074). *The News of the Association of the History of English* 6: 17-20.

2002a "The Semantics of Chaucer's *Moot/Moste* and *Shal/Sholde*: Conditional Elements and Degrees of Their Quantifiability." In *English Corpus Linguistics in Japan*, Toshio Saito, Junsaku Nakamura, and Shunji Yamazaki, (eds.). Amsterdam-New York: Rodopi, 235-47.

2002b "Modality and Ambiguity in Chaucer's *trewely*: A Focus on *Troilus and Criseyde*." In *And gladly wolde he lerne and gladly teche Essays on Medieval English to Professor Matsuji Tajima on His Sixtieth Birthday*, Yoko Iyeiri and Margaret Connolly (eds.). Tokyo: Kaibunsha, 73-94.

2003 Chaucer no Aimaisei no Kozo: *Troilus and Criseyde* 3.12-5 'God loveth ...' wo Chushin ni" (The Structure of Chaucer's Ambiguity: A Focus on *Troilus and Criseyde* 3.12-5 'God loveth ...'). In "FUL OF HY SENTENCE" Eigo Goironshu (*FUL OF HY SENTENCE: Essays in English Lexical Studies*), Masahiko Kanno (ed.). Tokyo: Eihôsha, 21-33.

2004 *Chaucer no Aimaisei no Kozo* (*The Structure of Chaucer's Ambiguity*). Tokyo: Shohakusha.

2006a "The Interpretation of *Troilus and Criseyde* 3.587: 'syn I moste on yow triste.'" In *Textual and Contextual Studies in Medieval English: Towards the Reunion of Linguistics and Philology*. (Studies in English Medieval Language and Literature) (Edited by Jacek Fisiak 13), Michiko Ogura (ed.). Bern: Peter Lang, 51-71.

2006b "The Structure of Chaucer's Ambiguity with a Focus on *Troilus and Criseyde* 5.1084." *Studies in Medieval English Language and Literature* (The Japan Society for Medieval English Studies) 21: 55-63.

2010a "Chaucer's Ambiguity in Discourse: The Case of *Troilus and Criseyde*." In *Kotoba no Fuhen to Henyou* (Universals and Variation in Language) *Vol. 5*, Centre for Research on Language and Culture, Institute for the Development of Social Intelligence, Senshu University, 85-97.

2010b "Chaucer's Ambiguity in Voice." In *Aspects of the History of English Language and Literature: Selected Papers Read at SHELL 2009, Hiroshima*, Osamu Imahayashi, Yoshiyuki Nakao, and Mihciko Ogura (eds.). Internatiler Verlag der Wissenschaften: Peter Lang, 143-57.

2011a "Chaucer's Language: 'Subjectivisation' and 'Expanding Semantics.'" *Studies in Medieval English Language and Literature* (The Japan Society for Medieval English Studies) 25: 1-41.

2011b "Textual Variations in *Troilus and Criseyde* and the Rise of Ambiguity." In *From Beowulf to Caxton: Studies in Medieval Languages and Literature, Texts and Manuscripts*, Tomonori Matsushita, A.V.C. Schmidt and David Wallace (eds.). Bern: Peter Lang, 111-50.

Ogden, C. K. and I. A. Richards
  1960 *The Meaning of Meaning: A Study of the Influence of Language Upon Thought and of the Science of Symbolism*. London: Routledge & Kegan Paul, Ltd.
Oh, S.
  2000 "*Actually* and *in fact* in American English: a data-based analysis." *English Language and Linguistics* 4 (2): 243-68.
Ohe, Saburo
  1983 *Eibunkouzou no Bunseki: Komyunike-shon no Tachiba kara* (*Analysing the Structure of English: From a Communicative Point of View*). Tokyo: Yumishobo.
Ono, Shigeru
  1969 *Eigo Hojodoshi no Hattatsu* (*The Development of English Modal Auxiliaries*). Tokyo: Kenkyusha.
Palmer, F. R.
  1979 *Modality and the English Modals*. London: Longman.
Patterson, Lee
  1987 *Negotiating the Past: The Historical Understanding of Medieval Literature*. Wisconsin: The University of Wisconsin Press.
Pearsall, Derek
  1981 "The Gower Tradition." In *Gower's Confessio Amantis*, A. J. Minnis, (ed.). Cambridge: D. S. Brewer, 179-97.
  1986 "Criseyde's Choices." *Studies in the Age of Chaucer: Proceedings* 2: 17-29.
Prins, A. A.
  1952 *French Influence in English Phrasing*. Leiden: Universitaire Pers Leiden.
Quirk, Randolph et al.
  1985 *A Comprehensive Grammar of the English Language*. London: Longman.
Richards, I. A.
  1936 *The Philosophy of Rhetoric*. London and New York: Oxford University Press.
Robertson, D. W., Jr.
  1962 *A Preface to Chaucer: Studies in Medieval Perspectives*. Princeton, N.J.: Princeton University Press.
Robinson, I.
  1971 *Chaucer's Prosody: A Study of the Middle English Verse Tradition*. Cambridge: Cambridge University Press.
Root, R. K.
  1916 *The Textual Tradition of Chaucer's Troilus*. London: Published for the Chaucer Society. London: Kegan Paul, Trench, Trübner & Co., Ltd.
Roscow, G.
  1981 *Syntax and Style in Chaucer's Poetry*. Cambridge: D. S. Brewer, Roman and Littlefield.
Ross, T. W.
  1972 *Chaucer's Bawdy*. London: E. P. Dutton & Co. Inc.
Saito, Tomoko
  1993 "Chusei no Josei Criseyde" (A Medieval Woman Criseyde). In *Chuseieibungaku eno Junrei no Michi: Saito Isamu Kyoju Kanreki*

Kinenronbunshu (*A Piligrimage to Medeival English Literature: Essays in Honour of the Sixtieth Age of Professor Isamu Saito*), Hiroe Futamura, Kenichi Akishino and Hisato Ebi (eds.). Tokyo: Nanun-do, 355-69.

Saito, Isamu
  2000 *Chosa: Aimai/Akugi/Keiken* (*Chaucer: Ambiguity, Naughtiness, Devoutness*). Tokyo: Nanun-do.

Sandved, A. O.
  1985 *Introduction to Chaucerian English*. (Chaucer Studies xi). Cambridge: D.S. Brewer.

Sawada, Harumi
  1992 *Shiten to Shukansei: Nichieigo Jodoshi no Bunseki (Point of View and Subjectivity: An Analysis of Japanese and English Modal Auxiliaries)*. Tokyo: Hitsujishobo.

Schaar, Claes
  1967 *The Golden Mirror: Studies in Chaucer's Descriptive Technique and its Literary Background*. (Skrifter utgivna av Kungl. Humanistiska vetenskapssamfunder i Lund, 54.) Lund: Gleerup.

Sapir, E.
  1921 *Language: An Introduction to the Study of Speech*. New York and London: Harcourt, Brace & World, Inc.

Searle, J.
  1969 *Speech Acts: An Essay in the Philosophy of Language*. Cambridge: Cambridge University Press.

Shigeo, Hisashi
  1982 *Chusei Eibungaku Tenbyo* (*A Look at Medeival English Literature*). Tokyo: Gakusaisha (Enlarged edn. Shinkosha).

Smith, Manning
  1949 "Chaucer's Prioress and Criseyde." *Philological Papers* (West Virginia University) 6: 1-11.

Smith, Macklin
  1992 "*Sith* and *Syn* in Chaucer's *Troilus*." *The Chaucer Review* 26 (3): 266-82.

Southworth, J. G.
  1954 *Verses of Cadence: An Introduction to the Prosody of Chaucer and His Followers*. Oxford: Basil Blackwell.

Spearing, A. C.
  1976 *Chaucer: Troilus and Criseyde*. London: Edward Arnold.

Sperber, D. and D. Wilson
  1998 *Relevance: Communication and Cognition*. Oxford: Basil Blackwell.

Spitzer, Leo
  1962 *Linguistics and Literary History: Essays in Stylistics*. Princeton, New Jersey: Princeton University Press. (Rpt. New York: Russel & Russel.)

Su, Soon Peng
  1994 *Lexical Ambiguity in Poetry*. London and New York: Longman.

Sweetser, Eve
  1990 *From Etymology to Pragmatics*. Cambridge: Cambridge University Press.

Todorov, T.
  1983 *Mikhail Bakhtin: The Dialogical Principle.* (W. Godzich trans.) Minneapolis and London: University of Minnesota Press.
Toyama, Shigehiko
  1964 *Shujiteki Zanzo (Rhetorical Residues).* Tokyo: Misuzushobo.
Traugott, E. C.
  1989 "On the Rise of Epistemic Meanings in English: An Example of Subjectification in Semantic Change." *Language* 65: 31-55.
Ueno, Naozo
  1972 *Chosa no 'Toroirasu' Ron (Essays in Chaucer's Troilus).* Tokyo: Nanun-do.
Vasta, E. and S. P. Thundy (eds.)
  1979 *Chaucerican Problems and Perspectives.* Notre Dame and London: Notre Dame Press.
Visser, F. Th.
  1969 *An Historical Syntax of the English Language. Vol. 3.* Leiden: E. J. Brill.
Warner, Anthony R.
  1993 *English Auxiliaries: Structure and History* (Cambridge Studies in Linguistics 66). Cambridge: Cambridge University Press.
Wetherbee, W.
  1984 *Chaucer and the Poets: An Essay on Troilus and Criseyde.* Ithaca and London: Cornell University Press.
Whiting, B, J.
  1934 *Chaucer's Use of Proverbs.* New York: AMS Press.
Windeatt, B. A.
  1979 "The Scribes as Chaucer's Early Critics." *Studies in the Age of Chaucer* 1: 119-41.
  1992 *Oxford Guides to Chaucer: Troilus and Criseyde.* Oxford: Clarendon.
Yager, Susan
  1994 "'As she that': Syntactical Ambiguity in Chaucer's *Troilus and Criseyde*." *PQ* 73: 151-68.
Yamamoto, Tadao
  1940 *Buntairon: Hoho to Mondai (Stylistics: Methodology and Problems).* Tokyo: Kenbunkan.
Zeeman, Nicolette
  1999 "The Condition of *Kynde*." In *Medieval Literature and Inquiry: Essays in Honour of Derek Pearsall*, David Aers (ed.). Cambridge: D. S. Brewer, 1-30.

Index of terms

addressee 29, 35, 37, 43, 124
addresser 29, 35, 37, 43, 124, 178
adultery 70, 72, 77-78, 91, 250
Alisoun 70
allegory 27, 31, 40, 67, 69, 81, 267-268
alliteration 158, 227, 259-260
ambiguity 13-15, 21-25, 27-30, 32-33, 35-37, 39-45, 47-48, 52-55, 57, 64-65, 68, 70-71, 73, 75, 79, 81-84, 87-88, 90, 94-95, 97-98, 101-103, 105-109, 115, 117, 119, 121-123, 126, 128-129, 131, 135-137, 139, 142, 146-153, 155-156, 162-163, 165, 167-168, 170-172, 177, 179-180, 183-187, 194, 196-203, 205, 207, 209, 211-213, 216, 218-221, 225-226, 229, 231, 237, 241-242, 244, 246, 248-249, 252-253, 255-258, 260, 262, 264-265, 267-273
ambiguous 21, 35, 40-41, 43, 57, 63-64, 91, 93, 115-116, 118, 121, 139, 164-165, 188, 194, 196, 208, 211, 213, 219, 245, 268-270, 272-274
ambiguous sentences 41
ambivalence 220, 242
ambivalent 199, 211, 220, 231
Amis and Amiloun 124, 158, 178, 246
Amor vincit omnia 23, 257
amorous 71-72, 82, 86, 117, 128, 145, 194, 225
amphibologies 44, 64
anaphora 104
anaphoric 102, 104
and 97, 160, 193-199, 202
Anelida and Arcite 17
Anne of Bohemia 51, 257
Antenor 190, 216
anticlimax 56, 72, 128, 161, 211
Antony 166-167
architecture 32
Arcite 79, 140
α manuscript 56, 226
Arthour 228
ascending scenes 189, 257
as he/she that 186-187
as she that 25, 186-191, 194, 203, 264-265
assertive forms 218-219
asseveration 154
assonance 259-260
attributive use 216-218
auctorite 39
Aurelius 107

author 36-39, 41, 51, 55, 64-65, 67-68, 73, 81, 85, 87, 98, 106, 109, 126, 128, 135, 153-154, 165, 170, 184, 199, 201, 207, 213-214, 218-219, 225, 241, 256, 268-269, 271-272
authority 32, 41, 50, 73, 84, 88, 140, 143, 149
Awntyrs off Arthure at the Terne Wathelyn, The 231

bauderye 126, 251
Bayard 76-77
Benigne Love 82
'Best Hystoriale' of the Destruction of Troy, The 230
β manuscript 49-50, 53, 56-57, 120, 190, 226
blisse in hevene 73, 118
Blanche 90
Boece (Bo) 72, 118, 165, 211, 215
Book of the Duchess, The (BD) 17, 40, 51, 75, 132, 158, 172-173, 188, 201, 208, 231
brighte 98, 133, 194, 201-202, 216, 258, 261
Briseide 193
brotel 215-216
Brutus 166-167
bytrayed 214

Caesar 166-167
Calkas 80-81, 83, 159, 190, 200, 216, 233, 260
Cassandre 63, 126
Constance 189
Cresseid 87, 215-217, 220
Cressida 62, 217, 220
Criseida 62, 71, 80, 89, 165, 192, 210, 217-218, 235-236, 240, 243
Criseyde 22, 38-41, 43, 49, 52-57, 59-64, 67-73, 75-90, 93-98, 102-108, 110-112, 114-121, 125-135, 142-146, 148-153, 158-168, 170, 176-179, 181-186, 188-196, 198-203, 206-207, 209-226, 229, 233, 235-253, 257-265, 269-273
Canterbury Tales, The (CT) 13, 17, 23, 28, 40, 48, 51, 53-55, 57-58, 72, 78-79-80, 90, 94, 109, 119, 152, 155-156, 158, 189, 172-173, 183, 188-189, 211, 220, 231-232, 243, 245, 255, 257, 300
  Canon's Yeoman's Tale, The (CYT) 17, 157, 166, 178, 201, 208-209, 233
  Clerk's Tale, The (ClT) 17, 32, 59, 115, 208, 232
  Cook's Tale, The (CkT) 17, 232

Index of terms

Franklin's Tale, The (FranT) 17, 58-59, 107, 178, 189, 208, 232
Friar's Tale, The (FrT) 17, 58, 152, 232
General Prologue (GP) 13, 17, 115, 141, 155, 183, 232, 245, 257
Knight's Tale, The (KnT) 17, 19, 58-59, 140, 178, 201, 230, 232
Manciple's Tale, The (MancT) 17, 78, 233, 245, 249
Tale of Melibee, The (Mel) 18, 113, 156, 232, 237
Merchant's Tale, The (MerT) 18, 70, 77, 93, 115, 132, 211, 232, 239, 242-243
Miller's Tale, The (MilT) 18, 69-70, 79, 220, 223, 232, 242
Monk's Tale, The (MkT) 18, 232
Man of Law's Tale, The (MLT) 18, 54, 178, 230
Nun's Priest's Tale, The (NPT) 13, 18, 157, 166, 232
Pardoner's Tale, The (PardT) 18, 54, 141, 178, 232
Parson's Tale, The (ParsT) 18, 69, 73, 82, 95, 109, 113, 141, 230, 233, 237, 241
Physician's Tale, The (PhyT) 18, 230, 232
Prioress's Tale, The (PrT) 18, 232
Reeve's Tale, The (RvT) 18, 232, 242
Retraction (Ret, Retr) 18
Shipman's Tale, The (ShipT) 18, 141, 187, 232, 241
Second Nun's Tale, The (SNT) 18, 232
Squire's Tale, The (SqT) 18, 58, 95, 232
Summoner's Tale, The (SumT) 18, 142, 220, 232
Tale of Sir Thopas (Thop) 18, 53, 232
Wife of Bath's Tale, The (WBT) 18, 58-59, 240, 249
cataphoric 104
charite 73, 82, 248
Chaucers Wordes unto Adam, his Owne Scriveyn 48
chaunge 141, 191, 212, 214-215
chere 53, 77, 86, 96, 120, 239
chiming 33, 70, 119, 162, 205, 212, 227, 239, 256-259, 264
code 29, 37, 72, 78, 81, 84, 91, 149, 247, 250, 271
cohesion 25, 42, 67, 88, 95, 101-102, 108, 117, 119, 121, 196, 200, 226, 257, 259, 269
collation 50, 52
collocation 29, 32, 55, 57-59, 62, 166, 205, 219, 223-224, 239

com cil/cele qui 186, 191
commune profit 40, 75
communication 27, 29, 37-38, 44, 119-120, 123, 156
Complaint of Mars, The (Mars) 18, 87-88, 104, 220
complementizer 172
Confessio Amantis 48, 58, 144, 158, 166, 187, 228, 230-231, 243
conjunction 22, 40, 43, 50, 52, 56, 69-70, 73, 97, 101, 108-109, 111-113, 121, 127, 133-134, 139-141, 145, 147, 160, 166-167, 173-174, 176, 184, 193, 198-200, 202, 211, 256
Consolatione Philosophiae, De 31, 51, 67, 71-72, 208, 269
consonance 259-260
content disjunct 154
contiguity 23, 29, 31, 40, 75, 84, 89-90, 101, 108-109, 124, 185, 267, 272
control of ambiguity 44
convention 67
coordination 205, 207
cooperative principle 30, 101, 124, 126-128, 130-132, 134
corage 90, 135, 199-200, 211, 262
course of kynde 77
courtly idealism 52, 69-70, 73, 78-79, 81, 97-98, 115, 117, 226, 230, 235-236, 249
courtly language 68, 70-71, 73
courtly love 23, 37, 39-40, 67-68, 70, 72, 75, 76-78, 79, 81-82, 84, 91, 118, 129, 149, 207, 221-222, 225, 238, 242, 249-250, 252
counterfactual 155
Cp manuscript 47
cruel 213
Cupid 70-71, 82

Damyan 70, 77, 239
daunger 143, 225-226
decevable 209
definition of ambiguity 43
Deiphebus 246, 250
Demophone 149, 216
descending scenes 189, 242, 257-258
detachment 38-39, 170, 190
dialogical 29, 205
Diomede 39, 62, 78, 88-90, 97-98, 106-108, 118, 125-126, 128-129, 132-135, 151-153, 159, 162-168, 176, 180, 182, 188, 192-195, 199-202, 207, 209-211, 214, 224, 233, 236, 242-244, 246-249, 252-253, 261-264
direct speech 42, 93-95, 98, 143, 151

discourse 25, 29-30, 37-38, 42, 44-45, 61, 64, 99, 101, 103, 108, 117, 119, 121-122, 127, 141, 168, 184, 200, 241, 253, 255-257, 260, 264, 268
Divinia Comedia 85
Doctrina Christiana 27
Dorigen 107, 189
double-edged 211, 243
double entendre 39, 103
double prism structure 24, 29-31, 35-37, 39, 43, 45, 47, 52, 60, 64, 67, 73, 75, 87, 90, 93, 98-99, 101-102, 121, 123, 129, 132, 135, 137, 142, 152-153, 160, 167-170, 178, 183-186, 196, 203, 205-206, 246, 253, 255-256, 264-265, 267-271, 273
drynke 80-81, 120, 126-127, 133, 239-240

echoes 224
effictio 90, 243
ellipsis 61, 101-103, 106, 121, 131, 200-201, 269
Emelye 189
endophoric 104
Eneas 216
engram 21, 28, 84, 86, 117, 121, 257
enjambement 197, 202
epistemic sense 138-139, 146-152, 157
epistemology 117, 141, 149
evidential 153-154, 160-161, 163-164
exemplars 49-50, 190
exophoric 104-105
experience 32, 39, 41, 55, 73, 82, 87-88, 155, 205
external causals 138-145, 147, 150, 152
extralinguistic 141

fabliau 70, 73, 79, 140, 242
false 40, 134, 167, 210, 213-218
fame 40, 162
Faerie Quene 187
felicitous conditions 130
filler 127, 156-157, 170
first-person narrator 8, 38, 79
first prism 25, 29, 36-37, 39, 44, 47, 55, 60, 64-65, 67, 73, 79, 90, 98, 121, 128, 135, 142, 155, 165, 170, 184, 196, 199, 201, 203, 207, 209, 211-213, 216, 218-219, 225, 236, 243, 245, 250, 256, 267-272
Filostrato, Il 18, 31, 62, 67-68, 71-72-73, 80, 85, 89, 126-127, 159, 161-162, 165, 189-190, 192-193-194, 199, 201, 210, 214, 217, 220, 225, 235-236, 240, 243, 245, 284, 293

FIS (Free indrect speech) 19, 93, 98, 114-115, 120-121
flittinge 216
folde ... in armes 60-61, 63, 107, 203
for 70, 95, 109-115, 117, 160, 244
forsook 127-128, 212, 214, 219
franchise 239
freedom of speech 38-40, 95, 123, 142, 268
frend 206, 245-249, 253
frend/shipe 206, 245-247, 249, 253
fresshe 95, 193, 217, 239, 250
fuzzy 115, 206, 246-250, 252-253
fuzzy edge 206, 246-250, 252-253

game and ernest 78, 251
γ manuscript 53, 57, 120, 226
gentil/esse 206, 245-246, 249-250, 253
Gentilesse 225, 249
gilteles 22-23, 38-39, 164, 168, 170-171, 177-182, 184, 203, 261, 268, 270, 272
global scope 156-157, 160-161, 165, 167, 170, 178
Gothic art of 'juxtaposition' 32, 38-39, 271
goode 68, 82, 96-97, 114, 128, 151, 187, 193, 218, 249, 263
goodly 53, 77, 89, 96, 116, 120, 193, 199, 211, 216-217, 243
Gower Tradition, The 48
grace 54, 68-70, 82, 87, 96-97, 114-115, 229, 237-239, 241, 259, 264
grammaticalisation 155, 168, 170, 172, 180

hagiography 222
Harley Lyrics, The 228
harmonics 140, 149-150, 170, 172, 181-183
hedges 154
Hengwrt 53, 55, 57-59, 227
herte 40, 82-83, 88-89, 96-97, 107, 115-116, 125, 133-134, 146, 150, 152, 160, 162-163, 166, 189, 191-192, 194, 198, 210, 212, 222-223, 235, 238-239, 241, 243, 249, 251-252, 260, 264
hert (=hart)-huntynge 40
hert (=heart)-huntynge 40
hevene blisse 73, 75
holy bond of thynges 82
homonymy 205
honour 57, 63, 81, 83, 101, 105-107, 111-112, 114-115, 127, 131, 143-145, 164-165, 179-180, 213, 236, 250-251, 258
hool 104, 226
Horaste 145

House of Fame, The (HF) 17, 28, 40, 51, 74-75, 85, 158, 162, 167, 172-173, 188, 231
hyperbole 95, 110, 124, 126, 145
hyponymy 205, 218, 238-239

iambic pentameter 186
ID (Indirect Speech) 98
ideational 37, 108
illocutionary force 25, 42, 44-45, 123, 128-130, 135-136, 144, 167, 177, 263, 269, 272
implicature 30, 101, 123, 269
implied author/reader 35, 38, 51, 274
inchoative aspect 127
inference 22-23, 25, 27, 29-31, 36, 38, 40, 43, 47, 75, 93, 108-109, 114, 116, 121, 123-124, 126-127, 129, 131-132, 146, 150, 171-172, 184, 267, 269-272
information structure 42, 56, 95, 101-102, 108, 119, 121, 134, 261, 263-264, 269
innovation 67
I gesse 137, 167, 170, 173, 176-178, 252
I leve 102, 137, 167, 174, 196-197, 224, 260
I not 134, 163, 223
in crescendo 243, 262
in decrescendo 262
internal 40, 90, 93, 108-109, 111, 113, 115-117, 190, 220, 235-236, 243, 250
interpersonal 24-25, 37, 42, 45, 108, 122-123, 136, 140, 167, 184, 260, 268
intertexuality 201, 253
intonation 22, 42, 44, 137, 168, 177, 182, 255-256, 261-264, 270, 272
invention 154
involvement 28, 38-39, 98, 107, 111, 141, 144, 146, 153, 172, 235
I seyde 241, 245
I take it so 245
ironical ambiguity 31, 68, 80-81
irony 30, 68, 110, 124, 156, 166
It was an heven 52, 95, 104, 225, 227
I wene 135, 137, 164-165
I woot wel 22, 38-39, 42-45, 164, 168, 170-172, 177-178, 180-184, 203, 261, 268, 270, 272

Januarie 70, 77
Jason 216, 218, 229, 279-280-281
Jove 86-88
Julius Caesar 166
Juno 140

kissyng 62-63
knotteles 210, 212, 215, 260

kynde 31, 77, 89, 97, 160-161, 195, 198, 213, 229, 247
Kynde wyt 77

langue 205, 273
lawe of kynde, the 77, 117, 213
Legend of Good Women, The (LGW) 11, 17, 40, 51, 115, 149, 158, 172-173, 178, 188, 215-216-217-218-219-220, 231, 243, 279-280-281
lecherous 215-216, 221, 236
lechery 95
legend 37, 222
lexical cohesion 101, 104, 117
leve 22, 38-39, 112, 130, 132, 143-144, 164, 168, 170-172, 174, 177-184, 203, 261, 268, 270, 272
local scope 156-157, 165-167, 170, 178
locutionary force 123
lough 110, 118, 130, 143
love 71-73, 82, 248
Love 71-72, 75-77, 82
love of frendshipe 145, 247-248
lyrics 73, 230

macro-structure 73, 99
makeles 257
manuscript culture 185
marginalia 50
maxim of manner 124, 126-128, 131
maxim of quantity 101, 124, 127-131
maxim of quality 124, 127, 129, 131-132
maxim of relevance 124, 132
may/myghte 137, 147
May 70, 77, 132, 147, 149-150, 200, 211, 222, 239, 243
me 54-55
ME 54-55, 58-59, 64, 80-83, 87-88, 90, 103-104, 114, 116, 120, 124-127, 133, 137, 141, 147-149, 156-157, 160, 164-166, 171, 174, 180, 187, 193-194, 196, 198, 201, 213-215, 217, 219, 222-224, 227-229, 237-240, 244, 248-249, 251, 259-260, 263
Melibee 109, 156-157
MED 54, 62, 77, 110, 116, 134, 139, 146, 155, 179, 199, 202, 210-212, 214, 227, 247, 257
Medieval English Lyrics 237
mercy 104, 132, 217, 229-235, 237-241
metalanguage 25
metaphor 23, 25, 27, 30-31, 33, 36, 40, 89-90, 139, 272
metonymic principle 31, 139
metonymy 23, 25, 27, 30, 33, 75, 90, 133, 139,

Index of terms 303

194, 214, 272
micro-structure 73, 99
misericorde 229, 231-235, 241-242
mo 54-55
modality 25, 42, 45, 122, 136-137, 155, 161-162, 173-174, 176, 179-181, 183-184, 198, 268, 270, 272
modal adverb 25, 126, 137, 153-156, 164, 167-168, 178, 198, 218, 270
modal auxiliary 128, 170, 172, 177, 219
modal lexical verb 25, 42, 95, 129, 137, 167-168, 170, 172, 177-178, 199, 218-219, 245, 259-260, 270
moot/moste 137-139, 141-143, 145, 147, 152
moste 56-57, 86, 105, 111-113, 130-131, 138-139, 141-145, 150, 173, 175-176, 189, 258

narrative 31-32, 79, 84-85, 91, 93, 95, 97-98, 101, 110, 114-115, 153, 155-157, 161, 172, 193, 200, 206, 210, 257, 269
narrator 32, 38, 40, 54-56, 60, 64, 68, 71-72, 75-76, 79-81, 85-91, 93-95, 97-99, 106, 109-112, 114-117, 120-121, 124-129, 131-135, 143-145, 148, 153, 155, 159-167, 172, 174-177, 179, 185-186, 189-194, 196, 198, 200, 202-203, 209, 212, 214-215, 221-224, 227, 233, 235, 241-245, 247, 249, 252-253, 255-257, 262-264, 268-271
new information 102, 256, 258, 270
nature 78
natureelly 78
new information 102, 256, 258, 270
Nicholas 70
nominalism 245
non-factual 190, 196, 264
non-assertive forms 218-219
notatio 90, 243
novello amadore 210
NRA (Narrative Report of Action) 19, 93, 98

objective 22, 93-94, 97, 108, 112, 116, 121, 126, 139, 141-142, 144-145, 147, 149-150, 153, 155, 162, 170, 177, 181-183, 242, 244, 269
OE 111, 138, 154, 199, 220, 226
OED 43, 53, 57, 64, 69, 77, 104-105, 109-111, 116, 138-139, 146, 152-154, 156, 166, 180, 182, 195, 197, 208-210, 212, 220, 226-227, 229, 238, 242, 244, 246-247, 249, 253
OF 190, 199, 230, 241
Of Arthour and of Merlin 228
OHG 220

old information 200, 264
omniscient view 80, 90
ON 238
oral culture 185
oral transmission 117, 155
overstatement 184

Palamon 79, 140
palinode 87
Pandaro 236
Pandarus 52, 54-60, 68-69, 73, 77-78, 80-84, 87-88, 94, 96, 102-106, 110-112, 114-115, 117-120, 124-126, 129-132, 142-145, 149-150, 159, 166-167, 176, 187-188, 191-192, 196-197, 214, 221-222, 224, 233, 236-239, 242, 246-248, 250-253, 259-260
paradigmatic 29, 205-207, 213, 215, 225, 236, 253, 265
Parliament of Fowls, The (PF) 18, 51, 73, 75, 158, 172-173, 188, 208, 231, 258
parole 205, 273
paronomasia 27, 32, 36, 70, 160, 162
pathos 230, 242
perlocutionary force 123, 132
Philosophy 71-72, 84-85
Piers the Ploughman 77
pieta 235
pietosa 235
pite 69, 78, 84, 89, 103, 118, 143, 163, 199, 206, 211, 229-233, 235-245, 260-261, 265, 270-271
pitous 68-69, 96-97, 114, 145, 221, 230-233, 235, 237, 242
pitously 231-233, 235, 242, 244
philological cycle 28
place-grace 70, 239, 258
politeness 98, 107, 128, 131, 154, 156-157, 164, 167, 170, 172, 177, 194, 200, 263
polyphony 29, 256-257, 264
polysemy 25, 30, 32, 39, 42, 73, 95, 138-139, 162, 179, 184, 194, 203, 205, 246, 253, 259, 272
predicative use 216-217, 219
prive 68-70, 96-97, 114-115
privetee 70
proforms 104, 106, 184, 269
propositional contents 115, 136, 184
prototype 206, 246, 249-250, 252-253
proverb 53, 84, 118, 142
Prudence 156-157

reference 21, 31-33, 60-61, 71, 76, 88, 101-104,

107-109, 119, 126, 154, 164, 166, 168, 178, 183, 206, 220-221, 226, 229, 235, 238, 240-241, 250, 267
register 68, 237
reported speech 38, 42, 45, 68, 93
rhyme royal 56, 102, 119, 186, 202, 258
Richard II 51, 257
Roman de la Rose, Le 69, 186
Romaunt of the Rose, The (Rom) 18, 158, 172-173, 188, 231, 236-237
Roman de Troie 200, 212
root sense 138-139, 146, 148-151

sad 32, 162, 192, 216
Sarpedoun 188
Saturne 87, 140
second prism 25, 29-32, 36-37, 41-42, 44-45, 55, 60, 64, 67, 69, 73, 76, 79, 81-82, 87, 98-99, 101, 103, 106, 108-109, 119, 121, 123, 125-127, 132, 137, 142, 145-146, 148-150, 152-153, 155, 160-162, 164, 168, 170-171, 177-178, 183-184, 190, 196, 198-199, 201-203, 205-206, 210, 212-213, 216, 219-220, 225, 231, 235, 237, 241-242, 245-247, 249-250, 252-253, 255-256, 258, 260-262, 264-265, 267-272
self-controllability 148
sely 80, 127, 206, 220-225, 244
semantic network 25, 205, 253
semed 52, 77, 95, 104, 129, 225, 227
sentence-final 172, 174, 176
sentence-initial 166, 172, 174, 176
sentence-medial 172, 174, 176-177
sette hym 201
sexual innuendo 226
siker 68, 70, 96, 114-115, 238
similarity 23, 29, 31, 75, 89, 139, 257, 267, 272
Sir Eglamour of Artois 228
Sir Gawain and the Green Knight 58, 93, 144, 201, 228
shal/sholde 137, 139, 141, 147
shame 83-84, 221, 236-237, 241
simile 155, 190-191, 194-195, 264-265
sith 53, 55, 84, 96, 105, 110-111, 120, 131, 236
slide 118, 208-210, 212, 260
slydynge 63, 86, 89, 118, 163, 184, 199, 202, 206-212, 214-215, 217, 219, 243-244, 261-262, 265, 270, 272-273
slydynge of corage 86, 89, 118, 184, 199, 202, 209-211, 243, 261-262, 273
slydynge Fortune 118, 211
smyle 118, 228

speech act 25, 30, 93, 105, 108-109, 123, 130, 154, 253
speech presentation 25, 93-94, 98, 104, 121-122, 133, 198, 225, 268
stemma 49
sterve-serve 258
structural ambiguity 88, 90
style disjunct 154
substitution 101-102, 104, 121
sure 166-167
swearing 106, 154
syn 56, 59, 68, 70, 96, 105, 110-111, 114-115, 117, 131-132, 144, 149, 164, 180-181, 183, 222-223
syntagmatic 29, 101
synecdoche 29
synonymy 205, 238-239
syntagmatic 29, 101

tag 95, 114, 156-157, 164, 172
tail rhyme romance 177
tendre-herted 199, 211, 243, 262
tendre 199, 211, 229, 232-233, 243, 251, 262
Tereus 216, 219
Testament of Cresseid, The 87, 217, 220
that houre 104
that thing 52, 95, 104, 225-227
theme 22-23, 25, 27, 31, 39-42, 67, 73, 75, 78, 90, 102, 121, 196, 231, 258, 268-269
therof 55, 104-105, 110, 120, 131, 157
Theseus 216, 218
transitorie 215
trecherie 212, 215, 236
tresoun 214
Tretis of the Tua Mariit Wemen and the Wedo, The 229
trewe 48, 72, 97, 124, 151-152, 160-162, 167, 180, 198, 213, 217-218, 244, 247, 250
trewely 89, 103, 112, 135, 137, 153-160, 162-168, 179-180, 199, 211, 215, 243, 248, 250, 260-261
Troie-joie 119, 257-258
Troilo 71, 85, 165, 192, 210, 214-215, 217, 243
Troilus 21-22, 24, 31-33, 37, 39-42, 47-56, 58-61, 64-65, 67-73, 75-90, 93-98, 101-106, 108-121, 124-134, 137, 142-146, 148-155, 158-168, 171-172, 175-177, 179-180, 182-183, 185, 188-196, 198-203, 207-215, 217, 219-227, 233, 235-252, 255, 257-264, 267-271, 273
Troilus and Criseyde 21, 24, 31-33, 37, 39-42, 47-51, 56, 58, 67, 69, 72-73, 75-76, 78-79, 81-82, 84-87, 90, 93, 95, 97, 101-102, 108-110,

116, 118-119, 121, 130-131, 137, 142, 144-145, 149, 153-155, 158-159, 161, 167, 172, 175, 177, 185, 188-191, 195-196, 198, 200, 207, 209, 212-213, 220-222, 224, 235, 238, 242, 245-249, 252, 255, 258, 260, 267-271, 273
Troilus and Cressida 217
trouthe 88, 96, 112, 116, 125-126, 154, 159-161, 163, 178-179, 191, 195, 198, 207, 214, 223, 238, 240-241, 244, 250-252, 258-259, 263
Troy 22, 52, 54, 76-77, 80-83, 86, 94-95, 97-98, 104, 107, 118-120, 125-126, 129, 132, 134, 149-151, 165, 189-190, 192, 194-195, 198, 200-201, 210, 222, 225, 229, 243-244, 250, 257-260
Troy Book 243
tyrant 69, 230, 239, 250
types of ambiguity 25, 32, 43, 45, 68, 73, 267, 270, 272

unconstant 215-216, 236
understatement 184
unidirectionality 139
unkynde 127-128, 212-214, 219
unreliable narrator 109
unstable 47, 79, 85-87, 90, 118, 121, 170, 189, 199, 207, 209, 211, 215-216, 221, 224, 243, 252, 265
unstedefast 215, 236
untrewe 213-215, 263
untrouthe 153, 159, 170, 215, 224, 244, 258
Ur-text 21, 36, 45, 121, 267

vagueness 44
vantage-point 38
variaunce 214
Venus 40, 71, 75, 80-82, 86-88, 102, 127, 196, 201, 222-223, 260
view-shifting 'I' 268, 272
Virgin Mary 114, 229
virgule 59

weld/e/en 53, 227-229
weldy 52-53, 95, 104, 206, 225-227
withowten await 55-57, 105, 110-111, 120, 131
woot 53, 78, 80, 96, 106, 112-113, 127, 137, 167-168, 170-172, 175-178, 181-182, 184, 195, 214, 222, 272
wordes mote be cosyn to the dede, The 245
word-web 205
worthy 53-54, 75, 128, 166-167, 184, 197, 211, 229, 255
withouten paramours 102, 196-197, 260, 270
wol/wolde 147

Index of names

Aitchison, Jean 205-207, 213, 247, 288
Ando, Sadao 123, 139
Ando, Shinsuke 123, 139, 288
Andretta, Helen Ruth 288
Augustinus 27
Austin, J. L. 123-124, 132, 267, 288

Bakhtin, M. M. 29, 205, 267, 288, 298
Barney, S. A. 50, 54, 57-58, 61-62, 195, 241, 255, 288
Barthes, R. 29, 75, 288
Baugh, A. C. 18, 50, 57-58, 61, 197, 203, 283
Baum, Paul F. 32, 288
Beadle, Richard and J. Griffiths 52, 283, 285
Beaugrande, Robert de and Wolfgang Dressler 29, 67, 288
Beauvau 201
Bennett, H. S. 155, 157, 167, 288
Benoît 193, 200, 212
Benskin, Michael and Margaret Laing 48, 288
Benson, Larry D. 17-18, 22, 47, 50, 53-54, 57-58, 61, 77, 94, 182, 188, 195, 203, 223-224, 226, 241-242, 261, 283, 287
Bergen, H. 283
Blake, N. F. 15, 32, 53, 58-59, 124, 185, 190, 283, 287-289
Blake, Norman, David Burnley, Masatsugu Matsuo and Yoshiyuki Nakao 32, 64, 69, 211, 213, 216, 231, 242, 251
Boccaccio, G. 31, 67, 80, 131, 159, 165, 192, 210, 213-215, 217-218, 225, 236, 241, 244, 284
Boethius, M. S. 31, 51, 72, 84-85, 165, 208-209, 269, 283, 286
Bowden, Betsy 255, 289
Brewer, D. S. 31-32, 38-39, 102, 271, 283, 289
Brewer, D. S. and L. E. Brewer 226-227, 241, 283
Brink, Bernhard Ten 255, 289
Brook, G. L. 283
Brinton, Laurel J. 154-155, 167, 171, 176-177, 289
Brown, C. 29, 48, 69, 73, 223, 283, 289
Brown, G. and G. Yule 29, 289
Brown, Peter 48, 289
Burnley, J. D. 15, 32, 64, 69, 211, 213, 216, 231, 242, 251, 287, 289
Bybee, J. et al. 147, 289

Caxton, W. 16-17, 51, 187, 190-191, 226, 283, 295
Chamberlin, John 27, 289
Chaucer, G. 13-18, 21-24, 27-33, 36-41, 44-45, 47-51, 53-55, 57-59, 62-64, 67-69, 72, 75, 78-80, 82, 85-86, 89-90, 93-95, 98, 102, 105, 108-111, 115, 117, 119, 121-124, 127, 132, 137-139, 141-142, 145-147, 151, 153-159, 161-168, 171, 176, 178-179, 185-193, 196, 200, 202, 205-227, 230-231, 236-237, 240-242, 244-246, 250-251, 255-258, 261-262, 266-273, 281, 283-298
Chickering, H. 32, 60, 62, 289
Coates, J. 139, 142, 169, 289, 293
Coghill, Nevill 58, 63, 161, 182, 191, 196, 225, 283
Cooper, Goeffrey 221, 289
Culler, J. 29, 290

Dante, A 27, 85, 286
Davies, R. T. 238, 283
Davis, Norman 15, 283, 287
Davis, N. et al. 199-200, 209, 287
Dedeck-Héry, V. L. and Louis Venceslas 208, 283
Derrida, J. 29, 290
Donaldson, E. T. 18, 32, 50, 53-55, 57-58, 61-62, 105, 127-128, 132, 134, 155, 161, 176, 194-195, 197, 203, 211, 218, 225-227, 242, 261, 283, 285, 290

Elliott, Ralph W. V. 32, 155, 211, 245, 290
Empson, W. 21, 28-31, 35, 43-44, 290

Fewster, C. 69, 243, 290
Fisher, J. H. 18, 50, 58, 61, 182, 197, 203, 225, 284
Fludernik, L. D. 94, 290
Fox, Denton 215, 284
Francis, W. N. 238, 284
Frank, R. W. 32, 284, 290
French, W. H. and C. B. Hale 284
Fridén, Georg 148, 146, 290
Fries, Udo 255, 290
Furnivall, F. J. 284
Furnivall, F. J. and G. C. Macaulay 52, 284

Gallo, Ernest. 27, 284

Gawain-poet, the 273
Gaylord, A. T. 32, 96, 249-250, 252-253, 255, 290
Godefroy, Frédéric 287
Gollancz, I. 284
Gordon, I. L. 31, 68, 72, 80, 84, 96, 104, 126, 238, 241-242, 290
Goto, Masahiro 41-42, 44, 291
Gower, J. 48, 51, 158, 166, 18-188, 228, 231, 244, 273, 285, 291, 296
Gray, Bickford Charles 291
Gray, Douglas 212, 291
Green, P. H. 58, 69, 93, 144, 202, 228, 243, 283, 291
Grice, H. P. 29, 101, 123, 126-128, 267, 291
Griffin, N. E. and A. B. Myrick 62, 284

Halliday, M. A. K. 37, 291
Halliday, M. A. K. and R. Hasan 42, 101-102, 103, 104, 106, 108, 109, 117, 123, 291
Hamilton, A. C. 284
Hanna, Ralph III. 50, 53, 227, 284, 291
Henryson, R. 87, 215-217, 220, 279-281, 284
Héraucourt, W. 230, 291
Hiscoe, David Winthrop 77, 291
Hopper, Paul J. and Elizabeth Closs Traugott 187, 291
Howard, D. R. 18, 50, 54, 61-62, 79, 197, 225, 284, 291

Jakobson, Roman 29, 31, 33, 35, 75, 101, 185, 256, 259, 267, 291
Jimura, Akiyuki, Yoshiyuki Nakao and Masatsugu Matsuo 186, 287, 295
Jespersen, O. 213, 291
Johnson, Mark 28, 30, 292
Jordan, R. M. 32, 292

Kaminsky, Alice R. 211, 292
Kanno, Masahiko 15, 213, 292, 294-295
Karita, Motoji 58, 63, 149, 151, 182, 225, 284
Kawasaki, Masatoshi 32, 292
Ker, William Paton 284
Kerkhof, J. 109-110, 116, 137, 146, 155, 186, 195, 292
Kinsley, James 284
Kittredge, G. L. 137, 292
Kivimaa, Kirsti 186, 292
Knapp, Peggy A. 221, 292
Knight, S. 17, 40, 58, 79, 93, 132, 144, 202, 228, 283
Kökeritz, Helge 32, 292

Kurath, H., S. M. Kuhn and R. E. Lewis 287

Lakoff. G. 30, 154, 267, 292
Lakoff, G. and M. Johnson 28, 292
Langland, W. 48, 158, 166, 273, 285, 289
Leach, MacEdward 284
Leech, G. 120, 147, 154, 162, 205, 227, 256, 292-293
Leech, G. and J. Coates 142, 293
Leech, G. and M. Short 38, 93, 95, 98, 133, 293
Levinson, S. 29, 123, 293
Lewis, Charoton T. and Charles Short 287
Lewis, C. S. 67, 78, 293
Lydgate, John 119, 244, 283
Lyons, John 153, 293

Macaulay, G. C. 52, 186, 284-285
MacQueen, John 27, 293
Macrae-Gibson, O. D. 285
Malone, Kemp 155, 293
Manly, J. M. and E. Rickert 53, 285
Masui, Michio 15, 32-33, 75, 102, 119, 128, 148, 155, 203, 209, 211-212, 231, 255, 257-258, 259-260, 293
Mathew, Gervase 231, 293
Matsuo, Masatsugu, Yoshiyuki Nakao, Shigeki Suzuki and Takao Kuya 287
Meun, Jean de 208-209, 211, 283
Mitchell, B. 109, 116, 293
Miyata, Takeshi 58, 63, 149, 151, 182, 225, 285
Morris, Richard 285
Mossé, Fernand 191, 293
Muscatine, C. 32, 88, 212, 293
Mustanoja, Tauno F. 110, 186, 293

Nakao, Yoshiyuki 15-16, 33, 37, 43, 50, 59, 65, 71, 76, 108, 117, 140, 142, 145, 166-167, 181-182, 186, 190, 219, 221, 246, 265, 287, 294-295
Nakano, Hirozo 138-139, 294

Ogden, C. K. and I. A. Richards 21, 28, 37, 296
Oh, S. 156, 165, 177, 296
Oizumi, Akio 287
Ono, Shigeru 296

Palmer, F. R. 153, 296, 285
Panton, G. A. and D. Donaldson 285
Parkes, M. B. and Richard Beadle 285
Parkes, M. B. and E. Salter 51, 52, 285
Pearsall, Derek 32, 48, 59, 94, 97-98, 110, 162, 203, 262, 296, 298

Index of names

Pollard A. W. et al. 50, 56, 61-62, 197, 285
Prins, A. A. 186, 296

Quirk, Randolph et al. 154, 293, 296

Richards, I. A. 21, 28, 37, 296
Robertson, D. W. Jr. 31, 296
Robinson, I. 255, 296
Robinson, F. N. 18, 50, 54, 57-58, 61-62, 197, 203, 283, 285, 287, 296
Root, R. K. 19, 49-50, 53, 56-58, 61, 147, 197, 212, 226, 285, 287, 296
Roscow, G. 32, 106, 110, 197, 201-202, 216, 296
Ross, T. W. 32, 70, 104-105, 197, 296
Rossetti, Wm. Michael 52, 285

Saito, Isamu 32, 297
Saito, Tomoko 243, 296
Sands, D. 285
Sandved, A. O. 255, 297
Sapir, E. 23, 297
Sawada, Harumi 123, 297
Schaar, Claes 90, 297
Schmidt, A. V. C. 16, 285, 295
Searle, J. 123-124, 127, 130, 297
Shigeo, Hisashi 211, 297
Shoaf, R. A. 19, 50, 54, 58, 286
Simpson, J. A. and E. S. C. Weiner 287
Sinclair, John D. 286
Skeat, W. W. 19, 50, 54, 58, 61-62, 197, 203, 286
Smith, Manning 70, 211, 297
Smith, Macklin 110, 297
Southworth, J. G. 255, 297
Spearing, A. C. 32, 106, 297
Sperber, D. and D. Wilson 30, 37, 297
Spitzer, Leo 297

Stanley, E. G. 113, 286
Stanley-Wrench, Margaret 58, 63, 161, 182, 191, 196, 225, 286
Stewart, H. F., E. K. Rand and S. J. Tester 286
Sutherland, Ronald 286
Sweetser, Eve 108, 123, 139, 146, 156, 297

Tajima, Matsuji 15-16, 295
Tatlock, John S. P. and Arthur G. Kennedy 287
Tatlock, J. S. P. and P. MacKaye 58, 63, 161, 182, 191, 195, 225, 286
Thynne, William 51, 53
Todorov, T. 298
Toyama, Shigehiko 28, 67, 84, 117, 298
Traugott, E. C. 139, 147, 155, 171, 187, 291, 298

Ueno, Naozo 32, 72, 298

Vasta, E and S. P. Thundy 290, 298
Vinaver, E. 191, 286
Visser, F. Th. 110, 139, 146, 298

Waker, Alice 286
Warner, Anthony R. 153, 298
Warrington, J. 19, 50, 54, 61, 203, 225, 286
Wetherbee, W. 32, 182, 240, 298
Whiting, B. J. 119, 224, 287, 298
Willock, G. D. and A. Walker 63, 286
Windeatt, B. A. 19, 32, 49-50, 52, 54, 56-61, 63, 70, 85, 148, 160-162, 182, 190-193, 196-197, 202, 210, 212, 221, 225, 231, 286-287, 298

Yager, Susan 186, 188, 191, 194, 196, 298
Yamamoto, Tadao 16, 28, 294, 298

Zeeman, Nicolette 77, 298

Studies in English Medieval Language and Literature

Edited by Jacek Fisiak

Vol. 1 Dieter Kastovsky / Arthur Mettinger (eds.): Language Contact in the History of English. 2nd, revised edition. 2003.

Vol. 2 Studies in English Historical Linguistics and Philology. A Festschrift for Akio Oizumi. Edited by Jacek Fisiak. 2002.

Vol. 3 Liliana Sikorska: *In a Manner of Morall Playe*: Social Ideologies in English Moralities and Interludes (1350-1517). 2002.

Vol. 4 Peter J. Lucas / Angela M. Lucas (eds.): Middle English from Tongue to Text. Selected Papers from the Third International Conference on Middle English: Language and Text, held at Dublin, Ireland, 1-4 July 1999. 2002.

Vol. 5 Chaucer and the Challenges of Medievalism. Studies in Honor of H. A. Kelly. Edited by Donka Minkova and Theresa Tinkle. 2003.

Vol. 6 Hanna Rutkowska: Graphemics and Morphosyntax in the *Cely Letters* (1472-88). 2003.

Vol. 7 The *Ancrene Wisse*. A Four-Manuscript Parallel Text. Preface and Parts 1-4. Edited by Tadao Kubouchi and Keiko Ikegami with John Scahill, Shoko Ono, Harumi Tanabe, Yoshiko Ota, Ayako Kobayashi and Koichi Nakamura. 2003.

Vol. 8 Joanna Bugaj: Middle Scots Inflectional System in the South-west of Scotland. 2004.

Vol. 9 Rafal Boryslawski: The Old English Riddles and the Riddlic Elements of Old English Poetry. 2004.

Vol. 10 Nikolaus Ritt / Herbert Schendl (eds.): Rethinking Middle English. Linguistic and Literary Approaches. 2005.

Vol. 11 The *Ancrene Wisse*. A Four-Manuscript Parallel Text. Parts 5–8 with Wordlists. Edited by Tadao Kubouchi and Keiko Ikegami with John Scahill, Shoko Ono, Harumi Tanabe, Yoshiko Ota, Ayako Kobayashi, Koichi Nakamura. 2005.

Vol. 12 Text and Language in Medieval English Prose. A Festschrift for Tadao Kubouchi. Edited by Akio Oizumi, Jacek Fisiak and John Scahill. 2005.

Vol. 13 Michiko Ogura (ed.): Textual and Contextual Studies in Medieval English. Towards the Reunion of Linguistics and Philology. 2006.

Vol. 14 Keiko Hamaguchi: Non-European Women in Chaucer. A Postcolonial Study. 2006.

Vol. 15 Ursula Schaefer (ed.): The Beginnings of Standardization. Language and Culture in Fourteenth-Century England. 2006.

Vol. 16 Nikolaus Ritt / Herbert Schendl / Christiane Dalton-Puffer / Dieter Kastovsky (eds): Medieval English and its Heritage. Structure, Meaning and Mechanisms of Change. 2006.

Vol. 17 Matylda Włodarczyk: Pragmatic Aspects of Reported Speech. The Case of Early Modern English Courtroom Discourse. 2007.

Vol. 18 Hans Sauer / Renate Bauer (eds.): *Beowulf* and Beyond. 2007.

Vol. 19 Gabriella Mazzon (ed.): Studies in Middle English Forms and Meanings. 2007.

Vol. 20 Alexander Bergs / Janne Skaffari (eds.): The Language of the Peterborough Chronicle. 2007.

Vol. 21 Liliana Sikorska (ed.). With the assistance of Joanna Maciulewicz: Medievalisms. The Poetics of Literary Re-Reading. 2008.

Vol. 22 Masachiyo Amano / Michiko Ogura / Masayuki Ohkado (eds.): Historical Englishes in Varieties of Texts and Contexts. The Global COE Program, International Conference 2007. 2008.

Vol. 23 Ewa Ciszek: Word Derivation in Early Middle English. 2008.

Vol. 24 Andrzej M. Łęcki: Grammaticalisation Paths of *Have* in English. 2010.

Vol. 25 Osamu Imahayashi / Yoshiyuki Nakao / Michiko Ogura (eds.): Aspects of the History of English Language and Literature. Selected Papers Read at SHELL 2009, Hiroshima. 2010.

Vol. 26 Magdalena Bator: Obsolete Scandinavian Loanwords in English. 2010.

Vol. 27 Anna Cichosz: The Influence of Text Type on Word Order of Old Germanic Languages. A Corpus-Based Contrastive Study of Old English and Old High German. 2010.

Vol. 28 Jacek Fisiak / Magdalena Bator (eds.): Foreign Influences on Medieval English. 2011.

Vol. 29 Władysław Witalisz: The Trojan Mirror. Middle English Narratives of Troy as Books of Princely Advice. 2011.

Vol. 30 Luis Iglesias-Rábade: Semantic Erosion of Middle English Prepositions. 2011.

Vol. 31 Barbara Kowalik: Betwixt *engelaunde* and *englene londe*. Dialogic Poetics in Early English Religious Lyric. 2010.

Vol. 32 The Katherine Group. A Three-Manuscript Parallel Text. Seinte Katerine, Seinte Marherete, Seinte Iuliene, and Hali Meiðhad, with Wordlists. Edited by Shoko Ono and John Scahill with Keiko Ikegami, Tadao Kubouchi, Harumi Tanabe, Koichi Nakamura, Satoko Shimazaki and Koichi Kano. 2011.

Vol. 33 Jacob Thaisen / Hanna Rutkowska (eds.): Scribes, Printers, and the Accidentals of their Texts. 2011.

Vol. 34 Isabel Moskowich: Language Contact and Vocabulary Enrichment. Scandinavian Elements in Middle English. 2012.

Vol. 35 Joanna Esquibel / Anna Wojtyś (eds.): Explorations in the English Language: Middle Ages and Beyond. Festschrift for Professor Jerzy Wełna on the Occasion of his 70th Birthday. 2012.

Vol. 36 Yoshiyuki Nakao: The Structure of Chaucer´s Ambiguity. 2013.

www.peterlang.de